CINEMA
EXAMII

CINEMA EXAMINED

Selections from CINEMA JOURNAL

RICHARD DYER MacCANN
Editor, 1966–1976

and

JACK C. ELLIS
Editor, 1976–1981

E. P. DUTTON, INC.   NEW YORK

Published in the United States by E.P. Dutton, Inc., 2 Park Avenue, New York, N.Y.
10016

Library of Congress Catalog Card Number: 77-77937
ISBN: 0-525-47464-1

Published simultaneously in Canada by Clarke, Irwin & Company Limited, Toronto and
Vancouver

10 9 8 7 6 5 4 3 2 1

First Edition

Contents

Introduction

Is it a good thing to study the art of the film? This question seems to have been answered by the widespread growth of film courses in American colleges— over 4,000 of them according to a recent American Film Institute catalogue. Yet its implications are not easily resolved.

Some film viewers, like some novel readers, ask only for experiences: entertainment, enlightenment perhaps, intense moments of pleasure or revelation. They love the endless variety of movies and do not want to analyze them. Others insist on conscious intellectual response, ranging from judgments of aesthetic value to lengthy explications of all possible symbolic meanings. They accept first of all the Socratic proverb that the unexamined life is not worth living.

Students of today and tomorrow will continue to act on their belief that cinema, when examined, yields levels of meaning unknown to the artists who created the works. For those who hold a different view the future may look bleak. After reading a psychoanalytic interpretation of Leonardo da Vinci or F. W. Murnau, one may no longer be able to look at the pictures made by these men with an open and unfettered vision. Yet it is true that the works of art themselves will always be there to be looked at, with or without the deep-focus spectacles of linguistics, aesthetics, anthropology, semiotics, psychiatry, or Marxism. Another generation of critics may measure the works as they will—may even, instead of elaborating, simplify.

Cinema Journal has tried to follow a middle path between the buffs and the zealots, assuming that (1) there is work to be done in seeking to understand better the art of the film, (2) there is an increasing readership of well-informed students and teachers, (3) critical reviews of individual films can be largely left to other contemporary American magazines like *Film Comment* and *Film Quarterly,* and (4) the developing American tradition of scholarly writing about film ought to lodge somewhere between the elegant, lucid amateurism of *Sight and Sound* and the lengthy, doctrinaire theories of *Screen,* the two leading British film magazines.

Restless American film students are often unimpressed by prophets in their own country. For some the fascinating paradoxes of passionate Parisian philosophers offer a kind of secret language that will help them launch interesting or eccentric academic careers. Homegrown academic scholarship instead stresses caution, accuracy, and balance, along with actual footnoted research, support of assertions by examples, and direct references to shots on the screen. *Cinema Journal* in its first years was rather traditional, being wary of the winds of fashion. But it is a matter of special satisfaction to the editors that so many important contributions were made by younger members of the profession. Seven of the selections in this book were written when the authors were students.

The nearest thing to a policy statement or editorial manifesto was a brief announcement in the fall of 1968, which included the following:

> . . . We especially don't want to suggest that there is any secondhand substitute for alert and thoughtful screen-watching. We do hope to present—in a style that is at the same time serious, concise, interesting, and relaxed—some valuable contributions to the history and criticism of cinema.
>
> We plan to seek work of quality and authority, with or without footnotes. We welcome a variety of contributions from members and nonmembers—theoretical, historical, comparative, critical, controversial.
>
> The social implications of cinema are never far from our thoughts. We are also aware of the scientific aspects of film production and of audience analysis. But most of the time, we shall probably emphasize film as an art and the criticism of it as one of the humanities . . .
>
> Cinema is unlike any other field of study. Its source material is shadowy, unsteady, indescribable. We are searching for our best approach, our discipline. A journal is a familiar American way of doing it right out in the open with everyone watching.

The Society for Cinema Studies grew out of a series of meetings held at The Museum of Modern Art from 1957 to 1960. The purpose of those meetings was to draw together teachers in this new field in the manner of other academic organizations, to seek and to refine the concepts and approaches by which motion pictures could best be looked at in orderly—perhaps even scientific—ways. Corollary to this general purpose was the specific, practical assumption that only with the help of scholarly meetings and a journal could film teachers expect to impress college deans, presidents, and regents with the seriousness of film study: its growth and its ongoing promise of future significance for educated men and women. At one or more of these four meetings, the following universities and colleges were represented:

Alleghany College	New York University
Boston University	University of North Carolina
University of California	Northwestern University
City College of New York	University of Notre Dame
Columbia University	Ohio State University
Cornell University	Pennsylvania State University
Hunter College	University of Pittsburgh
University of Illinois	University of Southern California
Indiana University	Southern Illinois University
University of Iowa	Stephens College
Michigan State University	University of Wisconsin
University of Minnesota	

Professor Robert Gessner, undoubtedly the primary force in founding the society, liked to call himself the first professor of film in the United States (*Newsweek*, April 2, 1945). This may well have been true in terms of full-time film-study courses, as distinguished from the teaching of cinematography and film production. Certainly by the early 1950s there were others offering pioneer survey courses at Columbia, City College of New York, Cornell, Illinois, Purdue, Minnesota, and elsewhere. A number of dissertations on film subjects had been accepted in fields other than education. Meanwhile, the University of California at Los Angeles had begun its film program under theater arts in 1947, and the University of Southern California had been offering degrees in film production ever since 1932.

Research on the history and development of film study may someday establish the credits and the chronology more precisely, perhaps even documenting the evolution of cinema out of various other disciplines, as speech came out of English and English out of the classics. The growth and shaping of university departments and disciplines are not well-cultivated aspects of educational history.

At least it is certain, according to the minutes of the Second Conference on Motion Picture Education, held at The Museum of Modern Art, April 8 and 9, 1958, that a committee made up of Robert Gessner, Jack Ellis, Gerald Noxon (Boston University), and John Driscoll (then at Pennsylvania State) drafted a statement of purpose and a proposed constitution for a new academic society, adopted the following year.

The statement was written by Gessner and "estimated that 60 institutions of higher education offer 300 courses in motion pictures and television." There was a great need for developing those "academic criteria" that were thought to be well established in the fields of architecture, fine arts, drama, literature, and music. "By acquiring academic standards" the film teacher, now often "alone and isolated," could "end his second-class citizenship in university faculties."

One of the ways to promote the public's view of the new organization as a serious academic enterprise was to link it somehow with scientific methods. This was both a legacy of the German system of graduate studies and a direct result of Gessner's recent trip to Paris, where he had visited Gilbert Cohen-Séat and other self-styled "filmologists." He insisted therefore on the name, "Society of Cinematologists." The vote on this was a close one and much fought over—and it later kept a few people from joining—but thus it stayed until after Gessner's death. At a meeting in Los Angeles in 1969 the name was finally rejected, and a somewhat humbler Society for Cinema Studies began its second decade.

Meanwhile, in 1966, some basic questions had confronted the new officers: What direction of effort would be necessary for the society to stay alive and grow? Could the right kind of new members be found to build, from the wavering group of thirty or so, an organization that would be much more widely representative but still limited to working scholars? Could the *SOC Journal* become a more substantial publication? The questions, of course, were interdependent. A good journal would attract members. A larger membership would support a better journal.

The *Journal of the Society of Cinematologists* had been typewritten (double-spaced) on 8½- by 11-inch pages, multilithed, and bound together about once a year. Volumes 4 and 5, combined, covered 1964 and 1965. Each issue contained only papers given at annual meetings. Earlier editors were Gerald Noxon (1 and 2) Norman N. Holland (3), and William Sloan.

The new secretary of the SOC asked a question that had more far-reaching consequences than he realized at the time. Might it be possible to publish a printed magazine at the University of Kansas for about the same cost as these papers had been typewritten and multilithed in New York City? The answer, a few months later, was yes. Shortly afterward, Sloan resigned as editor to take charge of the new *Film Library Quarterly*. The president and council then appointed the secretary as editor.

There were two other decisions by the editor and the council. The new *Cinema Journal* would have to be published twice a year in order to be a copyrighted and mailable "periodical"; and the editors would have to select and reject manuscripts for the *Journal* to have professional standing.

Since that time, it is fair to say, the society has not looked back. Promising colleagues were sought out and encouraged to become members: anyone who taught courses or wrote articles or published books about film. By 1981 a membership of 312, plus 44 students, was reading and criticizing the *Journal*, mounting controversies at annual meetings, and generally behaving like its older and larger academic contemporaries.

At a moment of stock-taking, however brief, it is appropriate to pay tribute to certain early workers who responded to the challenge of film scholarship in the United States before there was group organization, university tenure, or government support. Harold Leonard, correspondent for *Sight and Sound* and at the end of his life a lecturer at the University of California at Los Angeles, was the editor of *The Film Index* (1941), still a basic reference work. Kenneth Macgowan—editor of *Theater Arts*, producer of films at 20th Century-Fox, head of UCLA's Department of Theater Arts, and founder of its motion picture division—was a pioneer also as one of the editors of the *Hollywood Quarterly* (1945–1951), the first serious American effort to draw on academic and industry people to examine periodically the moving image, its makers, and its effects. Siegfried Kracauer's path-breaking study of German films between the wars, *From Caligari to Hitler*, was published in 1947. Theodore Huff's biography, *Charlie Chaplin*, appeared in 1951, and he also wrote a number of analytical studies for The Museum of Modern Art and *Films in Review*. Lewis Jacobs (*The Rise of the American Film*, 1939), Arthur Knight (*The Liveliest Art*, 1957), Jay Leyda (*Kino*, 1960), and William Everson (*The Western*, 1962) have been able to make the transition to university teaching in recent years.

The publishing environment has changed radically since the 1950s. Beginning around 1963, the date of the first New York Film Festival, film books began to appear with the multiplying velocity of the flood sequence in Pare Lorentz's *The River*. The stream of new arrivals in bookstores has only been matched by the rapidity with which some of the most useful titles go out of print. Reference works alone have proliferated to a surprising degree, as may be seen by comparing two reports in *Cinema Journal*—Fall 1969 and Winter (special issue) 1974/75.

The magazine population has also increased. When *Cinema Journal* came on the scene in 1966, there were three leading American film magazines: *Film*

Quarterly, edited since 1958 by Ernest Callenbach and published by the University of California Press; *Film Culture*, founded in 1955 by Jonas Mekas and during much of its life a house organ for independent filmmakers in New York City; and *Film Comment*, founded in 1962, edited by Gordon Hitchens, and published by Clara Hoover. There was also *Films in Review*, which began monthly publication for the National Board of Review in 1950, edited by Henry Hart and offering important early attempts at filmographies and studies of directors and stars. There was *Cinema*, lavishly illustrated, published by Jack Martin Hanson in Beverly Hills from 1964 to about 1973, and *Film Heritage*, in the tradition of little literary magazines, edited from 1965 to 1977 (for most of that time at the University of Dayton) by F. Anthony Macklin. The quarterly *Journal* of the University Film Producers Association first appeared in 1949, and was edited successively by Lu Snyder, Sol Dworkin, John Mercer (1953–1956), and from 1956 by Robert Wagner at Ohio State University.

Today most of these magazines continue to make important contributions to the field. *Film Comment* has been edited since 1970 by Richard Corliss; his publisher since 1974 has been the Film Society of Lincoln Center in New York. In 1976 Timothy Lyons (Temple University, Philadelphia, later at the University of Houston and Southern Illinois University, Carbondale) was appointed editor of the *Journal* of the University Film Association, that organization having dropped the word *producers* from its title and its membership having moved increasingly toward sharing goals with the Society for Cinema Studies.

Since the advent of *Cinema Journal*, other magazines have appeared. The *Journal of Popular Film* (Bowling Green State University, Ohio) emerged from the *Journal of Popular Culture* as a separate quarterly in 1972, with Sam L. Grogg, Jr., Michael T. Marsden, and John G. Nachbar as editors. *Literature/Film Quarterly* was started in 1973 at Salisbury State College (Maryland) by Thomas L. Erskine, Gerald R. Barrett, and James M. Welsh.

Film students have been active in creating outlets for their interests. *Cinéaste*, begun by Gary Crowdus and other New York University students in 1967, has specialized in radical and political films. *The Velvet Light Trap* began with the help of University of Wisconsin students and the Wisconsin Arts Council in 1971. *Jump Cut* (1974, Chicago) has drawn on student and faculty talents at various midwestern campuses, especially Indiana. *Wide Angle* has been published quarterly by students and staff at Ohio University, Athens, since 1976, *Film Reader* annually at Northwestern, Evanston, since 1975.

In 1975 appeared the first issue of *American Film*, a monthly for the general reader, edited by Hollis Alpert for the American Film Institute and supported by a grant from the National Endowment for the Arts. In 1976 Ronald Gottesman (now at USC) and Michael Silverman (Brown University, Providence) initiated the *Quarterly Review of Film Studies* to do long book reviews, critical bibliographies, and issues devoted to special topics in theory and criticism.

The academic "criteria" and "standards" proposed at those early meetings at The Museum of Modern Art may be a long time coming. Most of today's film teachers would be reluctant to submit themselves to an accrediting agency, even if it were somehow staffed with bona fide film teachers. A special conference at the University of Southern California in August 1978 agreed provisionally to form a new organization of film/video departments. But the notion of accreditation was specifically rejected by the representatives of the invited institutions.

Cinema, so uncertain of its paternity, is still academically a wild card, difficult to classify. A large number of the Ph.D.s now teaching film earned the degree in some other discipline and have simply "studied up" on film subjects in their spare time. A specialist in comparative literature, for example, who feels that no one can properly approach film criticism without the very considerable bibliography with which he is acquainted, does not know what to make of a film program located in an art department. Professors of philosophy and aesthetics may also be interested in film: they are not well prepared to understand the professional and performance traditions of speech and drama departments, where most campus film courses are located. Sociologists, political scientists, and historians are interested in film as a reflection of society and as an influence on society, but documentary film courses are more likely to turn up in journalism departments. Then there are the humanities programs: whether focused on problems, works of art, or history, they may use a film every week and often the word *film* is part of the course title.

It may be that motion pictures, unlike English composition, will never come under the exclusive jurisdiction of a single similar department in every university. Multidepartmental committees have been set up at places like Pomona, Washington, Michigan, Purdue, Indiana, and Illinois. Even the older departments of cinema at USC and NYU—as well as the somewhat newer film subdivision of theater arts at UCLA and of speech or "communicative arts" at Iowa, Northwestern, Wisconsin, Boston, Temple, North Carolina, Houston, Southern Illinois, Texas, Stanford, and other universities—are inevitably looking at the field in a more interdisciplinary way. At the same time recent graduates with specialized Ph.D.s in film are beginning to raise questions about the kinds of knowledge and experience that may be essential for film study. Script analysis, critical studies, film theory, and film history may be undertaken by departments of English, comparative literature, philosophy, or history if professors without background in the creative process of filmmaking are willing to risk such offerings. But it seems likely that film study, especially in those places where it achieves independence, will maintain as its own unique contributions such courses as film writing, direction, and production. Such work is not easily handled by any of the established disciplines.

Cinema, like the mountain, is there, and students in increasing numbers are going to set about scaling its fascinating heights. Just as the universities are no longer limiting such student expeditions to a single department, so the Society for Cinema Studies has found itself accommodating a wide variety of methodologies and philosophies in its meetings and in *Cinema Journal*.

It was not easy to select the articles to be included in this book. The primary purpose was to pull together a collection of some scope and variety that would offer the most useful information to teachers and students already well informed about film subjects, a book they might turn to for uniquely specialized and challenging articles. At the same time the pieces reprinted here should offer fascinating reading to the ordinary film enthusiast who seeks new insights.

Our thanks to John Mercer (Southern Illinois University, Carbondale) for reading and commenting on this introduction.

Cinema Journal received a modest subsidy from the University of Kansas, Lawrence, and from the William Allen White Foundation from 1968 through 1970 and from the Department of Speech and Dramatic Art at the University of Iowa, Iowa City, from 1971 through 1973.

The following were presidents of the Society for Cinema Studies from 1960 through 1981: Robert Gessner, Gerald Noxon, Richard Griffith, Robert Steele, John Kuiper, George Amberg, Jack C. Ellis, Raymond Fielding, Donald Staples, Howard Suber, Timothy J. Lyons, Robert Sklar, John Fell.

A list of those who have assisted in the editing of *Cinema Journal* from 1967 through 1981, with their locations at the time of publication of this book, follows.

Associate editors: John L. Fell, San Francisco State University; Peter Harcourt, Carleton University, Ottawa; Virginia Wright Wexman, University of Illinois, Chicago Circle.

Advisory editors: Nick Browne, University of California, Los Angeles; William K. Everson, New York University; Raymond Fielding, University of Houston; Gorham Kindem, University of North Carolina, Chapel Hill; Arthur Knight, University of Southern California, Los Angeles; Gerald Mast, University of Chicago; Russell Merritt, University of Wisconsin, Madison; Andrew Sarris, Columbia University, New York; William Siska, University of Utah, Salt Lake City; Birgitta Steene, University of Washington, Seattle; Howard Suber, University of California, Los Angeles; Amos Vogel, University of Pennsylvania, Philadelphia.

Assistant editors: Robert C. Allen, University of North Carolina, Chapel Hill; Thomas E. Erffmeyer, Northwestern University, Evanston; Wes D. Gehring, Ball State University, Muncie; William Horrigan, Walker Art Center, Minneapolis; Timothy Lyons, Southern Illinois University, Carbondale; Linda Provinzano, Pacific Film Archives, Berkeley; Thomas G. Schatz, University of Texas, Austin; Kristin Thompson, University of Wisconsin, Madison.

Guest editors of special issues: John L. Fell, Film Music, 17, no. 2 (Spring 1978); Robert C. Allen and Douglas Gomery, Economic and Technological History, 18, no. 2 (Spring 1979); Virginia Wright Wexman, Film Acting, 20, no. 1 (Fall 1980).

JACK C. ELLIS
Editor, 1976–1981
Northwestern University
Evanston, Illinois

RICHARD DYER MacCANN
Editor, 1967–1976
University of Iowa
Iowa City, Iowa

AUTEUR STUDIES

CINEMA JOURNAL

Walter Korte: Marxism and Formalism in Visconti's Films

FALL 1971

VOLUME XI No. 1

John Schultheiss: The 'Eastern' Writer in Hollywood

SYMPOSIUM ON PUBLISHED SCRIPTS

The Chaplin World-View

Philip G. Rosen

The regard which the world once held for Charlie Chaplin's Little Tramp has not been equalled by any screen character of this century. But Charles Spencer Chaplin, the man who created and played that character so consummately, is not always remembered so fondly, especially in America. For his life was one which became as politically and socially controversial as a politician's, and his once friendly relationship with an adoring American public ended in a sharp, bitter separation in 1952.

Over the years, Chaplin's scattered public statements on political and social matters have offered an odd combination of left-wing and anarchist thoughts that seemed to anticipate some of the current New Left ideologies. His personal life included three sensationally unsuccessful marriages (before his lasting one with a young woman thirty-six years his junior) and one of the more spectacular paternity cases in recent American history. These factors, combined with Chaplin's increasingly bitter cinematic work, resulted in an American public opinion increasingly hostile to him.

This hostility became strongest, as one might expect, during that period when Senator Joseph McCarthy dominated the American political scene. In 1952 American Legion picketing and boycotts caused Chaplin's film, *Limelight*, which has no political content, to fail financially in this country. This was perhaps the most concrete public reaction to the various off-screen controversies in which Chaplin had been embroiled.

In the same year, Chaplin, who in forty-two years of residence and taxpaying in the United States had never bothered to become a citizen, sailed to Europe for his first visit since 1931. The U.S. Attorney General promptly announced that the comedian's re-entry into this country would be prevented pending an investigation into allegations that Chaplin was, for unspecific reasons, an undesirable alien. Chaplin regarded this act as the latest in a series of harassments and intrusions into his private life, and his case became a liberal *cause celebre*. He toured Europe in triumph, sent his wife (who was a citizen) back to the United States to obtain the contents of a safety-deposit box holding most of his assets, and purchased a home in

Vevey, Switzerland, where he still lives. The controversy was to continue for the rest of the decade, as Chaplin remained bitter and much of the mass media of America replied in kind.[1] By the next decade, however, the bitterness engendered by the nature of Chaplin's off-screen life had gradually dissipated.

Despite the controversy which has almost always surrounded him, Chaplin's conscious socio-political views have never been clear. It has been suggested by many[2] that this is because Chaplin never formulated a consistent or rigorous philosophy and world-view which he tried to use as the basis for his actions and opinions. Whatever the case, Theodore Huff's *Charlie Chaplin,* probably the best book on its subject in English, will soon be twenty years old. Chaplin has lived, worked, and written since Huff's book was published. Furthermore, some of the actor's close family and friends have also written of their experiences with him. In short, there is new material and it is time to review the evidence. Will it confirm Huff's opinion that Chaplin's socio-political philosophy was nothing more than a vague and unsystematized resistance to anything resembling regimentation?[3]

A purist might ask: Why bother? After all, Chaplin is a supreme creator in his chosen medium, and in the medium created a classic archetypical figure to deal with the world in which he lived. Should we not examine Chaplin's thought using only his chosen medium? Is this not a sufficient indicator of his beliefs, if indeed we must be interested in them?

The answer to this objection—and it is a legitimate one—is that any artist, but particularly a giant like Chaplin, becomes property of the scholars as soon as his artistry is generally acknowledged; he must expect to have every aspect of his life examined thoroughly. Such examination may help illuminate his art, although this is no sure thing. Perhaps this examination will help us understand the psychology of artists in general, a subject which has long been of widespread interest. At least one more good reason for such an examination is that it may help illuminate the culture from which the artist has risen and the interaction between art and culture (in an anthropological sense). Also, in Chaplin's case, the politically controversial nature of his life makes clear definition of his political views of interest to the historian.

The following is no attempt to discuss these broader implications of such an investigation of Chaplin's non-filmic expressions. It is an attempt to begin such a discussion by formulating something approaching the socio-political world-view held by Chaplin, using Chaplin's writings and first-hand

---

1. The mass magazines provide good examples of American hostility toward Chaplin during this decade. See the treatment of Chaplin in "Fist for Fist," *Time,* LXVII (May 7, 1956), 40; "Double Play: Chaplin to Robeson to Malenkov," *The Saturday Evening Post,* CCXXVII (Sept. 4, 1954), 10; James P. O'Donnell, "Charlie Chaplin's Stormy Exile," *The Saturday Evening Post,* CCXXX (March 8, 1958), 94-98, CCXXX (March 15, 1958), 44-45, 100-104, and CCXXX (March 22, 1958), 36, 107-110; and "Why Chaplin Paid Up," *Newsweek,* LIII (Jan. 12, 1959), 39.
2. See, for example, Peter Cotes and Thelma Niklaus, *The Little Fellow: The Life and Work of Charles Spencer Chaplin* (London, rev. 1952), p. 91; Walter Kerr, "The Lineage of Limelight," *Theatre Arts,* XXXVI (Nov., 1952), pp. 74-75; Paul Rotha, *Rotha on Film: A Selection of Writings about the Cinema* (London, 1958), pp. 80-81; and Edward Wagenknecht, *The Movies in the Age of Innocence* (Norman, 1952), p. 194.
3. Theodore Huff, *Charlie Chaplin* (New York, 1951), pp. 287-92.

accounts of others' experiences with him. What will emerge is a set of elements that constantly appear throughout Chaplin's life in his explications of his views, a series of *leitmotifs* in his thought.

The reason that a series of *leitmotifs* rather than a rigorous formulation of socio-political concepts emerges from examination of Chaplin's thought appears to be, as Huff and others contend, that Chaplin lacks a truly rigorous intellectual consistency necessary to such formulations. Chaplin himself has confirmed this. He concludes his autobiography by admitting:

> I have no design for living, no philosophy—whether sage or fool we all must struggle with life. I vacillate with inconsistencies. . . .[4]

As early as 1932, when he was just beginning the most politically controversial segment of his life, he mused in print:

> Many of us take a stand on principles and make resolutions, but they are colored by moods and desires. Time and circumstances change them.

He then approvingly quoted Whitman: "If I contradict myself, well, I contradict myself."[5]

DISTRUST OF INTELLECT

However, there may well have been a fairly consistent basis for this acceptance of inconsistency. Chaplin was something of a romantic, at least in his distrust of the intellect relative to the intuition. This orientation extended to all aspects of his life, including even his work. He once explained to Max Eastman that in conceiving his films he likes to start from a central idea that *feels* attractive, using his intellect only to discover what makes this specific idea feel attractive, and then exploit his discovery (rather than beginning with the intellect to construct an attractive idea on which to base his films.[6] As far as human knowledge is concerned, Chaplin in his old age consciously disparaged the intellect:

> That which can be imagined is as much an approximation of truth as that which can be proved by mathematics. One cannot always approach truth through reason. . . .
> My faith is in the unknown, in all that we do not understand by reason.[7]

"The intellect is not too great a thing," insists Chaplin,[8] and has used instead his intuition not only as a basis for masterpieces of filmic art, but also to guide his decisions within the real world.

4. *My Autobiography*, p. 535.
5. Charles Chaplin, "A Comedian Sees the World," *Woman's Home Companion*, LX (Dec., 1933), 36. Although written with assistance from Catherine Hunter, this article is generally believed to reflect Chaplin's thoughts; Huff uses it as a primary source. (See Huff's account of Chaplin's 1931 European trip in Huff, pp. 242-50).
6. Max Eastman, *Heroes I Have Known: Twelve Who Lived Great Lives* (New York, 1942), p. 176.
7. *My Autobiography*, p. 314.
8. Richard Merryman, "Ageless Master's Anatomy of Comedy," *Life*, LXII (March 10, 1967), p. 82.

4 / Auteur Studies

The Random House unabridged dictionary's first definition of intuition is "direct perception of truth, fact, etc., independent of any reasoning process; immediate apprehension." It is thus the immediate image of the real world forming a flash impression upon his psyche which would shape Chaplin's values and views of the world. And his first images of the world were filled with the hardship and poverty common among the lower classes in late Victorian London.

Virtually everyone who has attempted to analyze Chaplin's life has dwelt to some extent on the tremendous impact of this boyhood poverty on the consciousness of the grown man. The undeniable nostalgia and good feeling that creep into some of Chaplin's writing as he recalls his boyhood days[9] is probably due more to a man's remembrance of youth than a fondness for his earliest environment. The pitiless poverty which propelled him onto the stage at an early age also killed his father, drove his mother mad (and in the long run killed her too), broke up for long periods what family life he did have, and made a beggaring urchin out of him. Chaplin became quite bitter when he recalled W. Somerset Maugham's finding the key to his (Chaplin's) personality in a nostalgia for the slum life of his youth:

> This attitude of wanting to make poverty attractive for the other person is annoying. I have yet to know a poor man who has nostalgia for poverty or who finds freedom in it. Nor could Mr. Maugham convince any poor man that celebrity and extreme wealth mean constraint. I find no constraint in wealth—on the contrary I find much freedom in it. I do not think Maugham would ascribe such false notions to any character in his novels—even in the least of them. Such glibness as "the streets of southern London are the scene of frolic, gaiety and extravagant adventure" has a tinge of Marie Antoinette's airy persiflage.
>
> I found poverty neither attractive nor edifying. It taught me nothing but a distortion of values, an overrating of the virtues and graces of the rich and the so-called better classes.[10]

This attitude is not an isolated instance. One of the few constants in Chaplin's thought is a profound aversion to the phenomenon of poverty. Yet this aversion can take many forms. It has been recorded that in one breath he accused the poor of stupidity for accepting their lot without rebelling and in the next spoke with compassion of "the trap" of poverty.[11] From first-hand experience he can denounce as the worst of its effects the humility which poverty induces,[12] and yet take unashamed pride in the fact that he is a multimillionaire capitalist.[13] It seems safe to say that the fact that Chaplin is one of the select few in history who could do both of these things is an important clue to understanding the man.

---

9. For example, see Charles Chaplin, *My Trip Abroad* (New York, 1922), pp. 55-62, *passim* and *My Autobiography*, pp. 32-43 and *passim*. *My Trip Abroad* is another work written with assistance (from Monta Bell) but generally accepted as reflecting Chaplin's thoughts.

10. *My Autobiography*, pp. 291-92.

11. Robert Payne, *The Great God Pan: A Biography of the Tramp Played by Charlie Chaplin* (New York, 1952), p. 293.

12. Merryman, p. 82.

13. Charles Chaplin, Jr., with N. and M. Rau, *My Father, Charlie Chaplin* (New York, 1960), p. 183.

It is probably this acute awareness of and aversion to the effects of poverty which have influenced Chaplin to believe in a vague sort of determinism. This facet of his outlook puts great stress on economics. In his autobiography he recalls:

> A well-known lady novelist, hearing I was writing my autobiography, said: "I hope you have the courage to tell the truth." I thought she meant politically, but she was referring to my sex life. I suppose a dissertation on one's libido is expected in an autobiography, although I do not know why. To me it contributed little to the understanding or revealing of character. Unlike Freud, I do not believe sex is the most important element in the complexity of behavior. Cold, hunger and the shame of poverty are more likely to affect one's psychology.[14]

He seems to have become interested intellectually in economics around the time of the great depression. As Chaplin recalls, it was Upton Sinclair who set him to thinking of economic matters:

> We were driving to his house in Pasadena for lunch and he asked me in his soft-spoken way if I believed in the profit system. I said facetiously that it required an accountant to answer that. It was a disarming question, but instinctively I felt it went to the very root of the matter, and from that moment I became interested and saw politics not as history but as an economic problem.[15]

He came to have definite economic ideas, and during his European trip of 1931 he took to lecturing European notables such as Lloyd George, Ramsay MacDonald, and Albert Einstein on ways of ending the depression. His economic cures consisted of such actions as elimination of the gold standard, inflation, minimum wage laws, reduction of the hours of labor, and control of prices. He could support these measures glibly enough, although a bit simply. But all this was to be preceded by reduction of governmental power and influence, for he believed that "The world is suffering from too much government and the expense of it."[16] Apparently, the contradiction involved in implementing the sweeping series of measures he advocated with less government never crossed his mind. This may be a measure of the man's naiveté, but it can also be taken as an example of his ability to come to some good conclusions using little of the reasoning process to do so; it is instructive to remember that some of these measures were carried out during the Roosevelt administration by some of the best minds in government. His underestimation of the means necessary for sweeping economic reform is evidence that his economic views were the product of a shrewd intuition rather than the painstaking intellectual effort necessary to true economic understanding.

DETERMINISM OR INDIVIDUALISM?

Chaplin's vague determinism was not that of a simplistic Marxist, however, or at least it did not remain so. True, as recently as 1964 he still used

---

14. *My Autobiography*, p. 222.
15. *My Autobiography*, p. 380.
16. "A Comedian Sees the World," *Woman's Home Companion*, LX (Sept., 1933), p. 88. For Chaplin's statement of his economic cures as espoused on his European trip, see this account and the following article in October.

Marxist language, writing things like, "Poverty was not reduced by altruism or the philanthropy of governments, but by the forces of dialectic materialism."[17] Yet in the same section he writes of humanity *allowing* the individual to be cast into a matrix "of gigantic institutions that threaten from all sides, politically, scientifically and economically." He is distraught that "We have *permitted* these forces to envelop us with an utter disregard for the consequences."[18] The important thing here is the insistence on verbs which imply the freedom of man to thwart forces that exert deterministic pressure upon the course of his life. This leads to perhaps the most pervasive *leitmotif* in Chaplin's thought, the concept of escape from those forces exerting that deterministic pressure—that is, a fierce, egotistical individualism which asserted itself in his personality and became mingled with his thoughts on the nature of society and the individual's consequent relationship to it.

To one who has spent the most formative years of his life fighting his way up from the psychological and material restrictions of extreme poverty, it may be hard, once he has made good his escape, to accept an intellectual assertion that his life is still determined by the same forces in different guise. Chaplin, who never lived by strict intellectual formulations anyway, was to spend his life attempting to identify and resist those elements of his world which he believed overly deterministic toward the individual. ". . . I am what I am," he plaintively insists at one point in his autobiography, "an individual, unique and different, with a lineal history of ancestral promptings and urgings, a history of dreams, desires, and of special experiences, all of which I am the sum total."[19] Again and again during the course of his life he has insisted not only on this individuality, but also on his right to have it unimpeded by others.

This desire for independence seems to begin in Chaplin's mind from "an inflexible belief in the absolute rightness of his convictions," as one of his sons puts it.[20] This belief in himself appears to stem not only from his worldwide success, but also from a conviction that one *must* be sure of oneself to survive with integrity in a world such as this. One should not even depend on posterity for justification, he explained once when Clare Sheridan, the sculptress, caught him in a Whitmanesque mood:

> There must be no dreams of posterity—no desire for admiration—for these are not worth anything. You make something because it means something for you. You work because you have a superabundance of vital energy—not only can you make children, but you find you can express yourself in other ways. In the end it is all you—your work, yours the conception and the happiness, yours alone the satisfaction. Be brave enough to face the veil that hides the world, to lift it and see and know that within yourself is your world.[21]

17. *My Autobiography*, p. 509.
18. *My Autobiography*, pp. 508-09. Emphasis added.
19. *My Autobiography*, p. 292.
20. Michael Chaplin, *I Couldn't Smoke the Grass on My Father's Lawn* (New York, 1966), p. 96.
21. Clare Sheridan, *Naked Truth* (New York, 1928), p. 270.

This doctrine of self-confidence or self-belief is necessary to survival in an uncertain world. "You have to believe in yourself, that's the secret," he once told his eldest son:

> Even when I was in the orphanage, when I was roaming the streets trying to find enough to eat to keep alive, even then I thought of myself as the greatest actor in the world. I had to feel that exuberance that comes from utter confidence in yourself. Without it you go down to defeat.[22]

One thing that such a doctrine of self-importance demands is an absolute privacy, which by isolating one's self defends it against outside encroachment. Charles Chaplin, Jr., recalls that one of the most important rules in his father's household was to knock on closed doors:

> . . . I quickly discovered that opening a closed door without knocking could raise his hackles quicker than any other offense. Upstairs or downstairs, at home or at the studio, he could never bear to have anyone do it. And he would dress down not only his sons but his long-time associates, his closest friends and the servants for this infraction. That anger, at once so instantaneous and so desperate, could only have been bred in the humiliation of his childhood, when no closed doors of his were respected.[23]

Whether Charles, Jr., was correct or not as to the origin of his father's concern, this demand for privacy extended throughout his father's thought. No one should interfere with his individuality, not even friends: "To help a friend in need is easy, but to give him your time is not always opportune."[24] Chaplin recently summarized the role of friendship in his life:

> I've never been obsessed with friendship. In the first place I'm shy. In the next place I'm busy. People usually think I'm very sad, but I'm not sad. I am not a bit sad. Perhaps I've been sad in my youth for want of other companionship, but it was never suitable to me. It was either something I couldn't cope with or the other person couldn't cope with. So I've been alone. I've lived alone all my life I'd say—with the exception of this family and this last 20-odd years which have been wonderful.
> What has sustained me—the place where I have really existed—has been my work.[25]

That last sentence is the giveaway. His art—that is, his self-expression, the supreme evidence of his individuality—has substituted for friendship.

This insistence on privacy even to the point of denying anyone close friendship is probably somehow related to Chaplin's aversion to crowds, an aversion which can be quite inconvenient for a celebrity of Chaplin's magnitude. Whether the aversion to crowds came first and later the insistence on privacy or *vice versa* is a moot point. The few times recorded when he has seriously analyzed this aversion, however, Chaplin presents it as something more than a mere distaste for public life. For example, once Max Eastman admonished Chaplin for not appreciating the affection of a large

22. Charles Chaplin, Jr., p. 9.
23. Charles Chaplin, Jr., pp. 90-91.
24. *My Autobiography*, p. 291.
25. Merryman, p. 94.

crowd in New York, and Chaplin reacted by complaining of the crowd's
egotism in invading his privacy:

> "It isn't affection, it's egotism," he said. "None of those people cared a damn
> about me. If they did, they wouldn't embarrass me. They were thinking about
> themselves, feeling bigger because they had seen me and could go and brag about
> it."
>
> After he cooled down, he told me how differently the London crowds behaved.
> "When I went down to the East End to visit my old haunts," he said, "word
> got round, and a regular mob collected. But they always stayed as much as a
> hundred feet away, kind of hushed and whispering to each other. They never
> addressed me. They really made me feel that I was loved—but not these New
> Yorkers. I know them.[26]

There are hints that this fear of being in close proximity to crowds was
based on something more than just a simple desire for privacy. For example,
he once tried to rationalize his aversion to crowds:

> . . . my love for humanity was different than my love for the crowd. My love
> for humanity is a fundamental deep-seated instinct, but my love for the crowd
> depends upon my mood. At times they are inspiring, at other times frightening,
> for I instinctively sense that they are capable of either loving or lynching.[27]

If Chaplin would not surrender himself to friends or to the crowds that
supported him, he certainly would not lend himself to larger entities such as
nations or to the politicians who lead them. "Naturally," he writes,

> if the country in which I lived were to be invaded, like most of us, I believe I
> would be capable of an act of supreme sacrifice. But I am incapable of a fervent
> love of homeland, for it has only to turn Nazi and I would leave it without com-
> punction—and from what I have observed, the cells of Nazism, although dormant
> at the moment, can be activated very quickly in every country. Therefore, I do
> not wish to make any sacrifice for a political cause unless I personally believe in
> it. I am no martyr for nationalism—neither do I wish to die for a president, a
> prime minister or a dictator.[28]

With the exception of a very few politicians such as Churchill (whom he
knew personally and liked) and Franklin Roosevelt, Chaplin's attitude toward them can be summed up by his reaction to the great pianist Paderewski
becoming Prime Minister of Poland: ". . . I felt like Clemenceau, who said
to him [Paderewski] during a conference on the ill-fated Versailles treaty,
'How is it that a gifted artist like you should stoop so low as to become a
politician?' "[29]

UNLAWFULNESS, TRANQUILITY, SIMPLICITY

Despite his professed idealistic love for humanity, Chaplin is not even
sure if he can trust ideals. After all, patriotism is only a specific type of

26. Eastman, pp. 191-92.
27. "A Comedian Sees the World" (Dec., 1933), p. 23. The last sentence is particularly
striking in view of the events of the Forties and early Fifties.
28. *My Autobiography*, p. 387.
29. *My Autobiography*, p. 202.

idealism; other ideals can intrude on one's individuality as well as those of the state. "As for ideals," he is quoted as saying, "they are dangerous playthings and for the most part false."[30] He would not offer his body and soul for an ideal, whether that ideal is glory for the nation or an end to suppression of the working class. Max Eastman recalled Chaplin's attitude toward fighting for political and social ideals:

> Years ago, when we both thought—some of the time, at least—that a world revolution was coming, he remarked:
> "It's all right with me. I'm for the working class. But they needn't expect me on the barricades. I'm no hero—I've got too much imagination to be a hero. When the shooting starts, I'm going to take a loaf of bread and a can of sardines and beat it to the mountains."[31]

In fact, the only socio-political (as opposed to artistic) ideal which Chaplin seems to have actively, consistently, and consciously pursued throughout his turbulent life is that of personal independence—for himself. And as many critics noted of his famous tramp, it was an independence so extreme as to possess anarchic overtones. Chaplin has hinted that he at least partially understood the subversive nature of his perspective on and reaction to the social environment. When first observing Clare Sheridan's bust of him, he remarked, " 'It might be the head of a criminal, mightn't it?' and proceeded to elaborate a theory that criminals and artists are psychologically akin . . . 'both have a flame, a burning flame, of impulse, vision—a side-tracked mind and a deep sense of unlawfulness.' "[32]

Chaplin's "deep sense of unlawfulness" is more profound than that of a criminal, however; it is more the lawlessness of Rousseau and Thoreau than of Al Capone or even Robin Hood. His reactions to Bali during his 1931 world tour reveal much:

> Although I was in Bali only a few hours, it seemed I had always lived there.
> How easy [sic] man falls into his natural state. What does a career, civilization matter in this natural way of living? From these facile people one gleans the true meaning of life—to work and play—play being as important as work to man's existence. That's why they're happy. The whole time I was on the island I rarely saw a sad face.
>
> They may have no love as we understand it, yet they live happily compared to our western world that stands for all the virtues of love and romance with its moral insignia, "faith, hope and charity." Look into the faces of the masses in our large cities and you will see harrassed defeated souls and in the eyes of most of them weary despair. Yet in the eyes of the Balinese is tranquility.[33]

Thirty-three years later, he expressed virtually the same attitude in explaining why he did not miss the United States:

> . . . America has changed; so has New York. The gigantic scale of industrial institutions, of press, television and commercial advertising has completely divorced

---

30. Cotes and Niklaus, p. 132.
31. Eastman, pp. 183-84.
32. Sheridan, p. 271.
33. "A Comedian Sees the World," *Woman's Home Companion,* LXI (Jan., 1934), 22.

me from the American way of life. I want the other side of the coin, a simpler, personal sense of living—not the ostentatious avenues and towering buildings which are an ever-present reminder of big business and its ponderous achievements.[34]

Thus Chaplin's struggle to maintain personal independence and integrity, which began as a victory over the nineteenth century's industrial revolution, is ending as a defiant cry against the twentieth century's technological evolution. He insists that the ever-increasing complexities of this century are confusing and therefore anti-human:

I have faith that the people want simplicity. The world is so complicated—so many invasions into people's souls. . . . Complexity isn't truth. We get things so cluttered up, get so damn clever that it hides the simple truth in a situation. You have to watch every second.[35]

Chaplin's remedy for the situation in which humanity today finds itself is a return to the stress on intuition which one encounters throughout his thought. Harold Clurman has shrewdly pointed out:

Chaplin's politics—insofar as they exist at all—are chiefly "poetics." His approach to political affairs is intuitive, emotional, almost one might say a matter of aesthetics.[36]

Indeed, life as "a matter of aesthetics" is a good description of Chaplin's cure for what he thinks ails mankind. Again, this is no recent development on his part. In the wake of the red scare of 1920 he refused on essentially aesthetic grounds to deny an interest in Communism when asked by a reporter if he was a Bolshevik:

I am an artist. I am interested in life. Bolshevism is a new phase of life. I must be interested in it.[37]

Another example of this aesthetic analysis of social needs is his 1937 statement on censorship,[38] in which he did not deny the need for some sort of censorship, but only suggested that the social objectives of censorship might better be served if its basis were the questioned works' aesthetic merits rather than a standard of supposed good or evil based on current mores. He did not define the aesthetic basis on which to judge the fitness for the public of various films; probably he assumed that any sensitive person knows intuitively what it would be.

Chaplin has stated that ". . . the highest object in life is the pursuit of the beautiful,"[39] and in his autobiography his final complaint against the twentieth century is that it has ignored this end:

34. *My Autobiography*, p. 531.
35. Merryman, p. 86.
36. Harold Clurman, "Oona, Oxford, America and the Book," *Esquire*, LVIII (Nov., 1962), p. 182.
37. *My Trip Aboard*, p. 8.
38. This statement comprised the preface of a book by Gilbert Seldes. See Gilbert Seldes, *Movies for the Millions: An Account of Motion Pictures Principally in America* (London, 1937), pp. v-vi.
39. "A Comedian Sees the World," *Woman's Home Companion*, LXI (Jan., 1934), 86.

The accumulating complexities of modern life, the kinetic invasion of the twentieth century, find the individual hemmed in by gigantic institutions that threaten from all sides, politically, scientifically and economically. We are becoming the victims of soul-conditioning, of sanctions and permits.

This matrix into which we have allowed ourselves to be cast is due to a lack of cultural insight. We have gone blindly into ugliness and congestion and have lost our appreciation of the aesthetic.[40]

He goes on to make a statement of faith in art. The very cause of our troubles, the fact that man's "ingenuity has developed first and his soul afterwards," will in the end cause man to think or to destroy himself with the products of his ingenuity. "And under these circumstances, I believe that eventually his altruism will survive and his good-will toward mankind will triumph."[41] That is, man's soul will catch up with his ingenuity, his aesthetic sensibility will assert itself, and the overriding socio-political problems of our time will have been solved.

The analysis of Chaplin's thought thus ends on an appropriately platitudinous level, a level above which it seems Chaplin could rise only rarely in serious oral or written discussion. True, to list the *leitmotifs* found in Chaplin's socio-political thought is to touch occasionally upon some of the central questions bothering humanity. Such a list would include a conscious acceptance of his own inconsistency; reliance on intuition as opposed to rigorous use of reason; a strong aversion to economic deprivation; a vague determinism with some stress on economics; for defense against these determining forces, an individualistic outlook which possessed anarchic overtones not only in its distrust for the state and other forms of idealism, but also in its abhorrence of the complexity of modern, technology-dominated society; and finally a faith in aesthetic sensibility as a valid basis for social and political analysis and progress, and (relatedly) as a buffer between the individual and the deterministic forces of his environment.

But Chaplin rarely went much further than to list the problems as he saw them and occasionally to list the solutions. Because of his belief in the validity of intuition as an analytical base, he never bothered to make a rigorous formulation of the relations between the stated problems and his proposed solutions, which were only occasionally specific, anyway. To make such a rigorous formulation and to explicate his solutions to the point of real usefulness would have required, of course, an intense reliance on the reasoning faculty, the "ingenuity" which his intuition told him was to blame for the world's problems in the first place.

This is not to downgrade Chaplin's ability to inquire deeply and comment subtly upon his universe or, more particularly, upon his social environment. For depth and subtlety one need only see a few Chaplin films: critics are still searching for the superlatives to describe them. But Chaplin never demonstrated that intuition could serve outside his chosen medium as the same kind of solid foundation that it did in his art.

1969

40. *My Autobiography*, pp. 507, 509.
41. *My Autobiography*, pp. 509-10.

Marxism and Formalism in the Films of Luchino Visconti

Walter F. Korte, Jr.

The films of Luchino Visconti represent a study in polarities. The source of these polarities, and of the concomitant dialectical tension in the works, lies deep in the personal sensibilities of their creator. From *Ossessione* through *Death in Venice*, the pull between Visconti the Marxist and Visconti the aristocrat largely has determined the aesthetic cast of the films: the progressive element vying with the nostalgic, the formal-operatic element with the neorealist-naturalist. And it must be emphasized in discussing the genesis of any one of these films that Visconti's approach represents in each case a progression from a Marxist-progressive intent which is tempered by formalism before becoming a nostalgia firmly rooted in his aristocratic past.

There is, then, a contradiction in Visconti's work: he deals with pressing contemporary social problems and recreates historical problems in order to analyze them in terms of the Marxist canon, but he treats them in a manner which is fundamentally baroque in its emphasis on scenography, a direct extension of his parallel career in theatre, lyric and legitimate.

Part of the problem here is the whole matter of tradition. Visconti is one of the few directors who consciously develops his work from tradition. Where a Fellini or Antonioni sees or attempts to see from an angle apart from tradition, albeit a personal angle, Visconti is constantly immersed in traditions and is himself a part of them. The traditional approach extends to matters of cinematic form. Godard plays with the medium and many would argue that the inventive rhythms of his blocks of shadow and sound have created a new cinema. Visconti, on the other hand, does nothing really new in the formal use of film, with the exception of his use of color.

In Visconti's work one is struck by the primacy of formalism. In the majority of his films, the populist-progressive intent of the film-maker at the time of conception has been tempered and shaped, in the implementation, by the grand *mise-en-scène* of operaticism and the scenographic baroque. This even takes the form of changes in key characters from first scenario to final film: Antonio in *La Terra Trema*, Ciro in *Rocco and His Brothers*, Ussoni in *Senso*, Salina in *The Leopard*. In each case, the character is drained of much of the progressive function, becoming more an accompaniment to the *mise-en-scène*, rather than a determinant of it.

Before examining this process in any detail, we should focus on the film-maker's work in theatre, an area largely ignored by English and American criticism. The confusion between the "theatrical" and the "cinematic" in film still heavily burdens aesthetic judgment. While critical studies of such disparate directors as Eisenstein and Ophuls have suffered from this confusion, it is most obvious in evaluations of the work of Visconti, whose works variously have been ensnared in the classification of "social-realist" and the vilifications of decadent, operatic and "un-cinematic." The matter naturally is more complex than these labels would indicate. The personal drama of this director, one of the very few who works without compromising himself to current stylistic fashions, contains the contradiction stressed earlier. In his ideological position, in political ties, in his choice of subject matter, he views life according to Marxist principles; on the other hand, his artistic inspiration reveals an egocentric nature, anchored in his aristocratic past.

CONTRADICTIONS IN THE THEATRE

The psychological meeting point between ideology and passion lies in separation from bourgeois conventionalism and monotony which, with the exception of economic exploitation, Visconti despises above all else. He prefers the popular tradition of Italian melodrama and the *libretti* which have given substance to the lyric theatre. In his thirty years of film-making, Visconti has sought to shoot fundamentally *populist* films, tempered by the grand sentiments, gestures and *mise-en-scène* of operaticism and the scenographic baroque. Some would judge Visconti's career as a man of the theatre separately. But it would seem that his cinematic work and theatrical work move along similar lines, with frequent intersections.

In the period 1945-61, when the Italian theatre (lyric and legitimate) was struggling toward a renaissance, Visconti staged works which other directors were unwilling or unable to present. The "theatre of the bourgeois salon" constituted the prime target of this undertaking by Visconti and a few other artists. In contrasting Visconti's stagings with the bourgeois and naturalistic schools of theatre, the director's cinematic experience raises some interesting points. In the words of the actor Paolo Stoppa, one of Visconti's closest collaborators, the director (and a few other innovators) worked primarily in "two directions":

> One . . . carried him toward imitating the cinema, in the sense of carrying the method . . . of the cinema to the stage; the other, an opposing direction, [was] that of investigating pure theatrical convention. Visconti and E. Giannini hit on them simultaneously: on the one hand, precise *mise-en-scène* like *A Porte Chiuse, La Vita del Tobacco* or *Il Voto*, on the other, fantastic and almost surrealistic, like *Le Mariage de Figaro, As You Like it* or *Carosello Napoletano*. One might say, he went from cinematic naturalism (it was at the time Visconti shot *La Terra Trema*) to ballet.[1]

---

[1] Paolo Stoppa, at the Second Conference on the Relationship between Cinema and Theatre, XVII Venice Film Festival (1956).

Through "ballet" he sought to turn theatre to forms of movement to which
it was not accustomed. On the other hand:

> Through realistic detail, Visconti caught the public in an ambience so pre-
> cise that it was impossible to escape it. He created the illusion of participa-
> tion, with a richness of detail never before seen in the theatre.[2]

In addition, Visconti's staging imbued the spectacle with a unique impetus,
forcing particulars, objects and the significance of every scene forward to
the audience, seeking out the spectator with that which was the theatrical
equivalent of the close-up. Conventional theatrical rhythm was broken: the
duration of the spectacle was amplified. The visual element prevailed over
the purely dramatic element, in the conviction that a thing may be represented by *reflections* of the surroundings and that complementary images
may take the place of the central image. The word was separated from the
text and became a part of the vision and action, of pantomime, or of pauses
"in which objects stared at the public as bearers of symbolic significance, as
if shot by a camera."[3] Scenic space was, indeed, treated as a photograph.

Visconti further reacted against the trends of the time by carrying the
banner of Shakespearean theatre forward against those who held that drama
must repeat on the stage that which is read in newspapers or seen in modern
life. "I prefer to leave everything its own function," he explained, "so that
theatre does not imitate anything or anybody."[4] In short, Visconti embarked
on a road of experimentation and rediscovery of the "marvelous"—

> . . . of a world of marvels in which the theatre lost its way for a time and
> which we wish for it to rediscover, along with its destination—popular favor
> . . . In the panorama of spectacle, theatre has limits and differentiations
> which I have not discovered. Also, in the unique frame of the proscenium
> arch, let us leave all its possibilities of movement, color, light and magic
> intact. Not realism or neorealism, but fantasy, complete liberty of the spec-
> tacle. . . . Perhaps the age of Ibsen and Chekhov is over. . . . Today is
> certainly more the age of Shakespeare than of Chekhov.[5]

Cinematic experience and theatrical experience depart, then, from distant
and differing points, but their intermingling can be noted in Visconti's work
from 1945 onward. In his "marvelous" stage representations we notice meticulous reconstruction, an accumulation of filmic verisimilitude and sumptuous plastic material, while in his most neorealistic films, *Ossessione* and
La Terra Trema, the narrative material is permeated by the egocentric contemplation of form. Perhaps it is not surprising, then, that with the passing
of years, Visconti became converted to Chekhovian theatre, clarifying his
method of scenic preparation.

Many times I have been accused of violating theatrical texts. Perhaps this

[2] *Ibid.*
[3] *Ibid.*
[4] Visconti, interviewed in *Rinascita,* December 1948, p. 3.
[5] *Ibid.*

was true at the beginning of my career—now it is not, for I always accord the respect due to great theatre. . . . I do not believe that differences exist— true, notable differences—between theatrical direction and cinematic direction. The differences are practical, material—ways of working.[6]

Visconti goes on in this 1957 statement to say that in theatre "a drama of Chekhov, a comedy of Ibsen, a tragedy of Shakespeare is presented to the director in a form which is complete, untouchable," while a film script never commands such intimidating "respect" prior to realization.[7]

But it is not a question of a mutual gravitation of film and theatre; both experiences point towards a formal concern in Visconti's work—operaticism, melodrama, the scenographic baroque. Within this melodramatic-operatic form, the director effects groupings of apparently contradictory elements: "popular" material (in the semi-mythical sense that the term may have for a Marxist aristocrat), inflamed emotions and passions, a display of choreographic and scenographic fantasy, an intermingling of "choral" parts and hyperbolization of characters, contrast between "old" and "new."

The complex process by which the director's social and historical realism is tempered and shaped by formalism is most clearly revealed in two films: *La Terra Trema* (1947), a contemporary story dealing with the Italian "Southern question," and *The Leopard* (1963), a period piece set at the time of the Risorgimento.

FISHERMEN IN THE GRANDIOSE MANNER

[In *La Terra Trema*] he must balance two contrary forces: on the one hand, innate and refined decadence (his aesthetic, negative component), on the other, his programmatic (because sincere and conscious) socialism (his political, positive component).[8]

What exactly did Visconti hope to accomplish with *La Terra Trema?* The film may be characterized as a sort of watershed which exhausted the extant course of neorealism and opened new avenues of approach. Visconti's primary ambition was to carry the neorealist investigation to its limit: to express the greatest amount of truth, to push documentation to its furthest point, to show the nature of things without any non-realist excrescences. As if to impress this aim at the outset, the opening frame of the film reads:

The facts represented in this film occur in Italy, more specifically in Sicily, in the town of Acitrezza, which is found on the Ionian Sea a short distance from Catania.

A second purpose was fundamentally ideological: to construct, through the Sicilian village, a universal symbol of the harshness of the class struggle in

---

6 Visconti, interviewed in *Lo spettatore critico*, Vol. III, No. 1, January-February 1957, p. 3.

7 *Ibid.* The creation of a kind of *visual correlative* of the text as an interpretative instrument is described by some Italian critics as Visconti's most fertile theatrical innovation.

8 Fabio Carpio: *Cinema italiano del dopoguerra*, Schwarz, Milan, 1958, p. 37.

our time. (It should be borne in mind that Visconti was financed partially by the Italian Communist Party when he first went to Sicily.) In this connection, the opening frame continues:

> The story which this film relates is the same as that found for years in all those countries where men exploit other men.

The parable of Acitrezza was intended as a metaphor of the human condition. As Visconti himself has stated: "In *La Terra Trema* I was trying to express the whole dramatic theme as a direct outcome of an economic conflict."[9] A third, more formalist aim was to work with this "real" material in an ideological structure in order to create a form of archaic beauty, an orchestration of rituals in sight and sound.

The genesis of the film was complex. On the one hand, the director reflected on the text of Giovanni Verga's *I Malavoglia*, a classic novel of Sicilian life which provided part of the initial inspiration for Visconti's shift of interest to the South. In the director's words:

> To me, a Lombard reader, habituated through traditional custom to the clear rigor of Manzonian fantasy, the primitive and gigantic world of the Acitrezza fishermen and Marineo shepherds always appeared aroused in an imaginative and violent epic tone: to my Lombard eyes. . . . Verga's Sicily truly appeared as Ulysses' island, an island of adventures and fervent passions, situated immobile and proud against the billows of the Ionian Sea. So I thought about a film on *I Malavoglia*.[10]

On the other hand, he reflected on contemporary events on the backward island; the massacre of the peasants at Portella delle Ginestre and the political conspiracy of the Mafia, the struggle of the sulphur miners, the domineering triumph of the clergy. Acitrezza thereby became the locale where the remote past (feudal, immobile life) and the volatile future (the collective consciousness of the oppressed) could meet: so it was that "the earth trembles." *La Terra Trema* was to have been the title of a single epic film in three episodes, told in parallel.

The intermingling of the three episodes finds its ideological pivot in the motif of "the earth trembles." The narrative line, departing from the story of a family of oppressed fishermen, was to have shifted the problem to the miners and then to the peasants, developing it until it assumed the grand scope of a "chorus." The narrative was to examine the nucleus of an historical occurrence—the moment when the popular masses (confronted by the central bureaucracy, the forces of police and Mafia terrorism) moved powerful waves from below which bore witness to their new consciousness, their class intelligence, which moved them out of their centuries old resignation and hopeless misery and ended their isolation. Paying a heavy tribute of blood, they acquired awareness of their duties and power, thereby gain-

---

[9] Visconti, interviewed in *Films and Filming*, January 1961, p. 22.
[10] Visconti: "Tradizione e invenzione," in *Stile*, Vol. VIII, 1951, p. 3.

ing for the avant-garde movement the solid support and participation of all other workers.

Visconti here shows his adherence to Antonio Gramsci's solution to the southern problem, which envisaged an alliance between southern peasants and northern industrial workers to effect a radical restructuring of southern society. At that time, the earth would tremble beneath the feet of the parasites and their minions. Agreements would be created between peasants and apprentices, workers and peasants, the masses and the intellectuals. The Resistance would complete the circle by projecting the new man into the battle—the populist character with modern dignity and collective consciousness, modeled along Gramscian lines.

But at a certain point the director reneged on the scope of the project and limited himself to the first episode, "the episode of the sea," shifting the narrative to the story of a defeat. In this final version of *La Terra Trema*, the story is made to follow the basic outlines of the plot of *I Malavoglia*, without the Vergaesque *verismo* which had characterized so much of *Ossessione* five years earlier and which was to so influence *Rocco and His Brothers* (1960). In the film there are shifts, contextual and tonal, away from the novel's center of attention—from the *old* (the grandfather) to the *new* (the grandson), and from the *home* (as institution) to the *boat* (as economic symbol).

The overall narrative structure of the film is deceptively simple. To free himself and his family from the exploitation of the wholesalers, young Antonio ('Ntoni) Valastro sets up a small business of salted fish. The project is realized in spite of difficulties of every sort: economic sacrifices, the sale of many family possessions to buy barrels and salt and to supply a monetary base for the transportation of the barrels to the city, the scepticism of neighbors. When Antonio's small boat is wrecked off the gulf, in the ravages of a terrible storm, everything in his life collapses. But ultimately the young man succeeds in overcoming his discouragement, defies the wholesalers, returns to work and nourishes in his heart the idea that one day the others will recognize the justness of his attempt at independence.

After dropping his original idea, the director attempted to report the social antagonism within the confines of the marginal agglomeration of Acitrezza, and to show the new generation as opposed to the old, the grandson's avoiding spiritedly the grandfather's resignation. Humiliated and offended, the victim of fate, tormented by the envy and inertia of his compatriots, Antonio finds in misfortune a stubborn and bitter energy, perhaps the precursor of a not-far-distant success. It could be argued at length that the film's narrative structure corresponds to a classic dialectical triad: the *thesis* of the Valastros' deciding to go it alone; the *antithesis* of bad luck, discouragement and interior familial collapse; the *synthesis* of the surmounting of the prior condition in the new conscience and in the rigid determination with which the protagonist begins to live again.

Such a subject—summarized by Visconti as "the life of these people—their difficulties—their struggle which is almost always stopped by loss—their resignation"—is treated by the director in a fundamentally, but not purely, neorealist manner. The film was shot entirely on location; the crew lived in Acitrezza for nearly six months. Professional actors were eschewed—the fishermen played themselves, in their own dialect. The opening title frame of the film states:

All the actors in the film were selected from the town's inhabitants . . . they do not know any language other than Sicilian to express rebellion, sorrow, hope. The Italian language is not, in Sicily, the language of the poor.

No sound stages or obtrusive musical backgrounds were utilized; research was conducted with the aid of the area's inhabitants to excise every literary patina and rigidity in dialogue. All relevant elements are retained: the slowness of gestures, the lean polyphony of expressive emotions, the alternation of furious discouragement and hope.

Yet it is evident throughout the film that Visconti has imbued *La Terra Trema* with the myth of the grandiose landscape which enfolds the little man and his misfortunes. The rhythm of certain parts of the film is such that the characters' movements and gestures, even though "real," are intertwined with ritual—gestures of work and love, of suffering tenacity. One notices the way in which the work is constructed with a constant distance between narrator and material; the way that figures have of growing within a spatial profundity that balances the broadness of time; the necessity with which sounds take part in the story, alluding to the profundity from which they arise.

The first of these structural elements, the constant distance between film-maker (who speaks most of the narration in the film) and material, has been noted by Italian critics. In a 1949 assessment of the film, Renzo Renzi speaks of the "aloofness" of the director with regard to his narrative material, because of which the film develops "into a long, static contemplation of preordained events in which the author, even if against his will, does not participate."[11] So, either a substantial extraneity to the drama itself which, as Renzi points out, Visconti may have felt in spite of himself, or an overwhelming preoccupation with the formal-stylistical job of making the film, or perhaps both these factors, make *La Terra Trema* a monumental film which somehow falls short of its Marxist programmatic intent.

"Shabby Grandeur" Becomes Inflated, Gorgeous

The primacy of formalism is best illustrated in *The Leopard*, a film which, in the original print, contains a more "spectacular" construction than any other in the director's career. It is quite easy to see why Visconti was attracted to the novel. Tomasi di Lampedusa's novel has the characteristics of an autobiography, the projection of the author's present into the past, into his nineteenth-century ancestor Fabrizio, Prince of Salina, who is cut from

---

11 Renzo Renzi: "Mitologia e contemplazione in Visconti, Ford ed Eisenstein," in *Bianco e Nero*, Vol. X, No. 2, February 1949, p. 67.

the same mold. A number of motifs flow from the present into the past: dissatisfaction with the course of politics, a feeling of nostalgia, the bitter vision of the decay of the privileged class and contempt for the vulgarity of the new bourgeois order, a distrust of history and change, an "Islamic" indolence within a rational intellect, the metaphysics of a view without redemption.

Lampedusa's polemical flight from an unsatisfying present is represented in the form of the protagonist's lyrical and reflective soliloquy, rather than by giving his novel an epic narrative structure, full-blown and open-ended. The interior monologue, the primary form used by the protagonist/author to present his views, expresses three themes which interact with each other. *First,* the theme of delusion with life over the years, with the little that remains. *Second,* the theme of the desperation and solitude of the non-vulgar individual who refuses to join in society—isolated from his mediocre family, even from his favorite nephew; from the noble class with which he feels himself to have little in common; from the *nouveau riche* which disgusts him with its rapacious intrigues that kill good faith; from the Piedmontese who annex the South; from the withered and inept Bourbons. *Third,* the theme of death in the surrounding decrepitude, in the empty luxury of the noble palaces of the Bourbon monarchy in a divided Sicily.

In translating the novel to the screen, what were Visconti's intentions? To bring out into the light, with maximum impact, the contradictions of Italian Risorgimental history, the unsuccessful revolution, the choking effect of the conservatives, the annexation brought about according to the stipulation "if we want things to stay as they are, things will have to change." The director's position tends to coincide with the Prince's up to the point in which the pessimistic consideration of the political facts is delineated. But while Salina's pessimism regrets the fall of a class which, for all its immobility, was always a class, the director's pessimism tends to overburden itself with purpose, and in the place of regretting the feudal Bourbon class, aims to postulate a new one.

In its conception, Visconti's is a precise thrust of a critical-ideological nature on the plane of the democratic and Marxist historiography of Antonio Gramsci, the Italian communist theoretician. In its initial scripting, *The Leopard* was to show the distorted way in which the Piedmontese ruling class and its natural Sicilian allies carried the *new* forward by serving exclusively the false and depleting instruments of the *old*. Like Lampedusa, Visconti aimed to center his theme in the observations of the Prince. The director's usual separation between positive and negative characters occurs; the two aspects in this case are contained in the same protagonist and the same set of circumstances.

What of the outcome of the film? How can one explain the impression the film makes—visually, a sumptuous delight; dramatically, a loss of tension and incisiveness? Above all, one is struck by the contrast between a faithfulness to the letter of the novel and a narrative and pictorial expansion imposed upon the material of the plot. The film's structure is drawn up according to the patterns of epic narrative, with vast spaces, elegant compositions and the intersecting movements of masses and characters. But by constructing the story in this way, one loses the book's vital concentration on the protagonist, his soliloquy on life and death, the slow development of his reflections—that is to say, one loses *internal faithfulness* to the novel. Of course, such an internal correspondence was not an essential—as in all adaptations, the book's plot could have been a strict guide or merely an inspirational springboard. But Visconti did not *intend* to wander from the letter of the novel—he reaches the point of being materially faithful, but disarranges the narrative's internal balance. It is a case of his initial Marxist-progressive intent being subverted by a formal overindulgence.

The realism of the ambience (local and historical) and of the events is deficient. The director and his collaborators have stated that the novel's author idealized some events, rendering them rich and majestic with fantasy, when in reality they were not. But in the book's opening chapter one notes that the author always speaks of the "slightly shabby grandeur then customary in the Kingdom of the Two Sicilies," of the abusive aspect of grandeur, of dwellings that resemble catacombs—and the Prince's dining table is spoken of as being covered with a fine but *mended* lace cloth. The "majestic" distortion originates, it would seem, with the director.

This process of fantastic enlargement, the royal opulence of things that Lampedusa saw as *depleted* or *corrupt,* is found in the film in proportions vastly larger than those of the realistic strain. When Visconti wishes to expand the pictorial dimension by incorporating it in social contexts, the camera does not show us a decadent world, but rather exalts it by expressing regret for the passing of an era. This aristocratic Bourbon world lived, it is true, in monumental palaces, but it was a decadent world which fell into ruins. In the film it appears inflated in a gorgeous way, and the camera lingers over it. A veil falls on locations, events and progressive intentions, and Visconti greatly expands the novel's attention to detail, as if taking a meticulous inventory. His contemplation of the textures and colors of objects, of movements and symmetry, impoverishes the events, which, in some scenes, are only ornamental memoranda for *papier-maché* characters.

Visconti's direction, then, oscillates between enormous visual expansion and dramatic-thematic contraction. He greatly expands various visual "hints" in the text, while sometimes diminishing the text's significance by separating and flattening the interior reasoning of certain situations. Most of these reductions center around the Prince, who was to have been the key progressive character. The film lacks the fabric of reflection, that verbal "sounding-line" which describes, behind the action, the excellence of the character's dignity. This is very much related to the theme of death and solitude which appears during the ball at Ponteleone Palace, a key scene in both novel and film.

In the book the ball occupies one chapter, a few dense pages, with an interior moving line of *crescendo.* In the film, the visuals perpetually revolve around themselves—the sequence could last, one feels, another hour or be cut in half without changing anything. The scenographic baroque, in a word, emerges triumphant. The complex set of variations on the protagonist's interior monologue is not really present in the film. In this regard, the substitution of some narrative insertions (the execution of the deserters, the final symbol of *viaticum*), the frantic accumulation of details, the proliferation of objects, the tumult of *things* to give the impression of a world changing hands and of the slow decay of a class—all these things in the film are of limited usefulness. It is true that in the novel the point of view of the author and his character is somewhat conservative and anachronistic: history, progress and dialectics do not exist in the Marxist form which Visconti formulated in his initial plans. Yet Lampedusa conveys the situation of the protagonist with such virile passion that he communicates a sense of history to us; in other words, there emerges the history of an alternation of classes, of a political betrayal (the annexation). Visconti intended to involve directly the House of Salina in the process of transformation, but the proliferation of visual gratuities, especially in the ball sequence, prevented the implementation of the aim.

So, in considering the film, notwithstanding the historical and political additions, it must be admitted that its great power lies in its visual compositions. For example, the rooms of the palace are used, essentially, as a single set; the use of pillars, walls and doorways to block out or open up the scenes means that a single camera movement can have the syntactical effect of a series of cuts. In these moments, where Visconti's inspiration seems less bound by political pretenses and historical illustrations, the spectator encounters striking images in which one always has the petrification of objects and living forms. There are portraits of dead nature, characters framed like funereal monuments, certain sensations of opulent, immobile, decongested lighting: for example, the journey to the summer palace at Donnafugata across the sumptuous landscape; the picnic with its dazzling tablecloth, the composition of figures around the Prince, the harmonious disposition of objects, shadows and sounds; the shots of the girls at the ball and other details in this long sequence; the scene in which Don Fabrizio and his relatives are seated in the choir of the Donnafugata church during the Te Deum, dusty from the trip and rigid in their seats, giving, for a moment, the impression of funereal monuments under layers of dust; the colloquy with the Piedmontese emissary and the leave-taking at dawn with the people in the piazza.

Despite these visual glories, Visconti does not avoid certain miscalculations. Whenever the director has seen reality through eighteenth-century Neapolitan painting or pre-impressionist naturalism (as in the street battles at Palermo and in the political conversations between the Prince and Don Ciccio Tumeo), a slightly over-aesthetic veil of unreality is inserted between us and the screen. This is the overriding artistic problem of *The Leopard*.

The problematic center of all Visconti's work, the dialectical tension between Gramscian Marxism and formalism, is most explicitly expressed in this 1963 film. The sources of this conflict can be traced to the anomaly of

Visconti's position as both an aristocrat, living off a past heritage, and a Marxist, committed to a belief in a Socialist future. The structure of Visconti's films tends to be complex and sometimes equivocal, because of the ways in which the central conflict is expressed.

Nonetheless, it must be said that in the course of Visconti's film career he has maintained absolute fidelity to his own sources of inspiration and his chosen thematic material. Much can be made of his diversity as a director, the chameleon ability to follow a Di Lampedusa adaptation with one of Camus, and to intersperse *Sandra* and *The Damned* (films written originally for the screen), and to vary each time the angle from which his themes are approached, so that fresh stylistic insights are found constantly. Yet it is the unity of all his work which stands out: the manner in which he is able to go beyond his neorealist beginnings, mix prose and poetry, naturalism and operatic lyricism, while still remaining true to himself. Above all, he applies a wholly individual conception of the cinema's stylistic potentialities, running largely at variance with current fashion and practice.

1971

Alfred Hitchcock and the Ghost of Thomas Hobbes

Philip Dynia

1

In their sweeping, sometimes stimulating, but ultimately inadequate account of the interrelationship between politics and film, Furhammar and Isaksson offer this remark:

> It is just possible that Alfred Hitchcock is a political innocent who imagines that his films are not about politics. In the interviews he gives nowadays, it looks as if, like Ingmar Bergman, he carefully is avoiding any discussion of the subject.[1]

Immediately following are several pages of analysis of *Torn Curtain*, which the authors manage to explain away as still another instance of the propaganda films with which they are so intensely concerned. While only the most obtuse filmgoer would fail to see political themes in *Torn Curtain* (and Hitchcock's subsequent *Topaz*, not discussed by Furhammar and Isaksson because it appeared after their study was completed), the more sophisticated might certainly be forgiven for asking what *Frenzy* or *Marnie* or *The Birds* or *Psycho* (or half a dozen earlier films) have to do with politics?

Yet in a qualified sense Furhammar and Isaksson do have a point. And, to be perfectly fair, they themselves add the necessary qualification to the above quotation. For they continue:

> . . . during the period from *The Man Who Knew Too Much* (1934) to *Lifeboat* (1943), Hitchcock's films seemed to be greatly concerned with politics, even if the particular demands of the thriller pattern into which political situations were skillfully interwoven meant that a great deal remained obscure or only partially stated.[2]

---

[1] Leif Furhammar and Folke Isaksson, *Politics and Film* (Translated by Kersti French. New York: Praeger Publishers, 1971), p. 139.

[2] *Ibid.* Having thus rescued themselves, they manage, two sentences later, to raise again the hackles of those who may have reflected upon the implications of Hitchcock's political films by saying: "[Hitchcock] was also a fighting democrat, as he showed with particular clarity in *Foreign Correspondent* (1940)."

More recently, Raymond Durgnat attempted to disentangle the complex skein of Hitchcock's films, and he included some analysis of the political implications of the films to which Furhammar and Isaksson referred.[3] His study is quite as brilliant as anything he has done; but the great difficulty with a mind as fertile as Durgnat's is that every theme or overtone in a film suggests to him a veritable flood of allusions, cross-references, and intellectual or ideological antecedents. The product of this torrent-of-consciousness technique is a totality far greater than the sum of the individual films (which is certainly admirable); but those interested in singling out this supposedly obvious and yet elusive political element in Hitchcock's films must remain somewhat perplexed.

It is my own belief that this particular thread is well worth untangling and that one can indeed speak of a political dimension in certain Hitchcock films. However, it is necessary to examine not only the fairly overt political content,[4] but to enquire further whether Hitchcock is merely weaving political situations into the thriller pattern because of their strong dramatic and topical interest, or whether there are underlying political attitudes recurring in Hitchcock's work. In short, is Hitchcock the philosopher[5] also a political philosopher?

Bertolucci once suggested that we should not confuse political films with films about politics. A political film, I have argued elsewhere, is one which is largely the work of individuals (mostly writers, producers, and directors) with political awareness and convictions, contains a political message and attempts thereby to influence the audience's political attitudes, and is permeated formally and stylistically with an aesthetic derived from or influenced by political ideology.[6]

Given so stringent a definition, Alfred Hitchcock simply does not make political films. Yet quite obviously he has made films about politics (a very special kind of politics, as I will argue). Certain political activities are perfectly suited to the thriller genre in which Hitchcock's artistry thrives. These films refer, sometimes obliquely, to contemporary political events; in a few the political message becomes more overt. Indeed, public reaction to one of these particular messages so frightened that element in Hitchcock's personality concerned with the mass audience that for fifteen years he avoided political themes.

---

[3] Raymond Durgnat, *The Strange Case of Alfred Hitchcock* (Cambridge: The MIT Press, 1974).

[4] Which Furhammar and Isaksson quite correctly perceive, though they do not bother to explicate it beyond the above quotations.

[5] I refer here to the spate of studies of Hitchcock as a moralist. Durgnat develops this theme quite sensibly; also, cf. Robin Wood, *Hitchcock's Films* (2d ed.; London: Zwemmer-Tantivy, 1969) and Eric Rohmer and Claude Chabrol, *Hitchcock* (Paris: Editions Universitaires, 1957).

[6] See my forthcoming *Politics on Film.*

2

Hitchcock's peculiar blend of the thriller formula and political events first emerged with *The Man Who Knew Too Much* (1934). Intermixing gangs and spies and picaresque pursuits, it set a pattern to which Hitchcock returned frequently. A middle-class English couple become involved in a plot to assassinate a diplomat, and their young child is kidnaped and held hostage by the killers in order to assure the mother's silence about the assassination (planned to take place during a concert at Albert Hall). The mother's shout saves the diplomat's life, and the couple eventually discover the hiding place of the gang. There is a shoot-out with the police, and the mother herself (who earlier in the film was established as a crack shot) shoots the gunman who is threatening the child.

The precise political allegiance of the assassins is not known (though Hitchcock told Truffaut that the final shoot-out was based on the famous Sidney Street siege of 1910, directed against "some Russian anarchists . . .").[7] They are obviously European, and the political implication seems to be that a combination of continental political malignities (both Hitler and Mussolini were in power in 1934, and in England the General Strike had raised new fears of Bolshevik infiltration and disruption) are threatening to disturb the peace and order of Britain. Certainly the threat to a mere child drives the point home more intensely, and two years later (in *Sabotage*) a similarly endangered tyke is actually killed (to Hitchcock's everlasting artistic regret). Durgnat argues that the film "gropes" toward expressing a theme of "private involvement in apparently remote politics bringing civil anarchy in their train," but never quite finds it.[8] If there is a warning intended in the wife's cry, it is considerably muted; England chose to ignore the European threat.

Again in *The Thirty-Nine Steps* (1935) a rather ordinary chap (Canadian, not English), played by Robert Donat, becomes privy to the existence in England of a super-secret spy organization smuggling defense secrets out of the country on behalf of some European power. The spies kill a woman in Donat's apartment, and he is accused of the murder. He must expose the spies to clear himself, but when he accuses a respected country squire of being the mastermind of the gang, the authorities refuse to believe him. The chase and the efforts of the falsely accused Donat to clear himself are far more important than any political overtones; politics and espionage are only backdrops against which the drama can be played.

The following year, Hitchcock turned once more to the world of international espionage with *The Secret Agent,* based on several works of Somerset Maugham. Ashenden (John Gielgud) is an intelligence agent sent to Switzerland to kill a spy. He bungles, killing instead an innocent tourist; the real spy (Robert Young) dies accidentally in a train crash. The film was,

7 Francois Truffaut, *Hitchcock* (New York: Simon and Schuster, 1967), p. 60.
8 Durgnat, p. 125.

in Hitchcock's own words, an "adventure drama" in which the central figure had a purpose which was "distasteful" to him, making it difficult for
the audience to identify with him.[9] If there is any political commentary in
The Secret Agent, it may well be the transformation of "espionage as patriotic fun" into the realization that it is rather "sickmaking duty."[10] Certainly
Ashenden's reluctance to play his assigned role dovetailed nicely with
England's reticence in the face of Hitler's diplomatic challenges.

With *Sabotage* (1936), Hitchcock brings the threat of foreign politics
still closer to home. Verloc (Oscar Homolka) poses as the harmless manager of a small movie house living with his young wife (Sylvia Sidney).
Actually, he is a saboteur. Believing himself to be under surveillance by
the police, Verloc gives a time bomb (disguised as an ordinary package)
to John, his wife's young brother. He tells the little boy to carry it to the
other end of town, but the child is delayed, and he and the passengers on a
bus he is riding are incinerated when the bomb explodes. On learning the
truth, Sylvia Sidney stabs Verloc, but the murder escapes detection because an explosion destroys the evidence of her crime. Verloc's politics are
not clear—he may be a homegrown anarchist, or the agent of some foreign
power. The film seems today an uncanny portent of the terror that within
a few years would come during the blitz, but it is difficult to say what political conclusions audiences of the period drew from it.

After the interlude of *Young and Innocent*, Hitchcock returned to the
chaotic world of international espionage, and his references to contemporary political events were more explicit, as was his political message. *The
Lady Vanishes* (1938) is so often viewed (along with *The Thirty-Nine
Steps*) as the epitome of the Hitchcock thriller, and one of the jewels in
the crown of Hitchcock's "English period," that it is easy to overlook the
political content. The film was released about the time of the Munich crisis.
England's attentions were riveted on European politics and the question
whether intervention on behalf of Czechoslovakia or Poland might be
necessary, an action for which England was ill-prepared, psychologically
and militarily.

National complacency seems echoed in the reactions of a group of English tourists to the sudden threat presented at the end of the film. Tod-
hunter, representative perhaps of the appeasers, attempts to reason with
the authoritarian forces. His efforts are rewarded with a lethal bullet from
the enemy. The two "club bores,"[11] however, turn out, like the mother in
The Man Who Knew Too Much, to be expert marksmen who do not hesitate to apply their skills to several unfortunate militiamen of the mysterious
Ruritanian sovereignty which has been so foolish as to delay their efforts
to return to England in time for a championship cricket match. Again, if

9 Truffaut, p. 73.
10 Durgnat, p. 132.
11 *Ibid.*, p. 154.

this be propaganda, it is subtle. Durgnat says "its . . . force lies in the skill with which it equates a general atmosphere about dictatorships with urgent dangers to Britons, so tempting even diehard appeasers to start reading dictatorship as dangerous."[12] And if the superficially ideal Ashenden is incapable of performing the grubby tasks of espionage, that outwardly improbable embodiment of English virtues, Miss Froy (Dame May Whitty—possibly the unlikeliest espionage operative in screen history) now relishes the task.

By 1940, war had broken out in Europe, but Hitchcock had escaped to freedom and safety, if one can so characterize the tutelage of David O. Selznick. His first project was an un-Hitchcockian picture,[13] *Rebecca*. It was certainly unpolitical. However, in his next film, made the same year (1940), Hitchcock returned to a political context (possibly due to the influence of his producer, Walter Wanger, who "had always been interested in foreign politics"[14]).

Foreign Correspondent starred Joel McCrea as an American newspaperman. (Gary Cooper, Hitchcock's first choice, declined to become involved in a B picture.) Ignorant of European politics, Jonny Jones is assigned to go to Europe and assess the true political situation. In London he meets an elderly Dutch diplomat who is working for world peace (and who is privy to the secret clause of an important treaty). The Nazis assassinate a double and kidnap the real diplomat. Jones discovers that the diplomat is alive, and enlists Carol Fisher (Laraine Day) to help him. She and her father, an upper-class Englishman (Herbert Marshall), are the heads of an international pacifist organization. The father is actually a Nazi agent, and as war is declared he books passage on a plane to America. The plane is attacked and crashes into the ocean, and Fisher sacrifices himself, thus saving the young couple, who are reconciled and return to London. There, in the midst of the blitz, Jones warns America that the lights are going out in Europe and that America must become involved in the great struggle both as beacon and arsenal (such mixing of metaphors undoubtedly allowable under the stress of an apparently direct bombing of one's broadcast studio).[15]

Hitchcock commented that *Foreign Correspondent* was "in line with my earlier films, the old theme of the innocent bystander who becomes involved in an intrigue."[16] The fascination with political machinations was also very much in keeping with the thrillers of the English period. A key

---

12 *Ibid.*, p. 155.
13 Truffaut, p. 91.
14 *Ibid.*, p. 96. Also, cf. the discussion of Wanger in David M. White and Richard Averson, *The Celluloid Weapon* (Boston: Beacon Press, 1972).
15 David Zinman, perhaps tongue in cheek, quotes McCrea's speech as an example of the Hollywood tradition of "saving the best line for last." See his article in *The New York Times*, July 6, 1975, section D, p. 9.
16 Truffaut, p. 96.

difference lay in the overtness of the propaganda theme. The political message at the end is spoken directly to the audience; Hitchcock (with the aid of ringing bells and patriotic music) "set out to give American public opinion a nudge in favor of active intervention in the war against Hitler's Germany."[17]

For the usually circumspect Hitchcock, such a direct appeal was uncharacteristic, especially so, considering the still powerful forces of isolationism in America. But essentially the film is a thriller, and this last-minute propagandizing may have seemed as incongruous and disingenuous then as it certainly does today. Indeed, the "message" may have been more Wanger's than Hitchcock's, whose own political sentiments were probably akin to the simple faith of the Dutch statesman who relied upon "the little people who feed the birds."[18] Had Jones, in the grand propaganda film tradition, died at the end, the importance of his cause might have been driven home more forcefully. Instead he survived, albeit chastened and no longer politically naive. The rest of America had to experience Pearl Harbor before a similar transformation took place.

Once in the war, all of the nation's efforts were geared toward making America "the arsenal of democracy." And what greater and more insidious threat could one imagine than the enemy within? The year before, a group of Nazi agents actually *had* landed by submarine off the New Jersey coast (but were apprehended almost immediately by the ubiquitous FBI). And so, ever conscious of his audience's underlying fears, Hitchcock offered (after the quasi-Lubitschian interlude of *Mr. and Mrs. Smith* and the rather impersonal *Suspicion*) *Saboteur* (1942). Its hero (Robert Cummings) is a worker in an armaments factory. Falsely accused of sabotage, he flees. He wanders into a desert ranch where he encounters its grandfatherly owner (Otto Kruger) who is actually the leader of the Nazi sabotage ring. He escapes, and the remainder of the film is not greatly different from similar manhunts revolving around the theme of the pursuer pursued. In the course of the film, Hitchcock manages to place our hero in many disparate geographical locales, ending up in New York, featuring there the Brooklyn Navy Yard, a shoot-out in Radio City Music Hall, and mortal combat atop the Statue of Liberty, from which the Nazi saboteur eventually falls to his death.[19]

Saboteur is thus another amalgam of familiar Hitchcock themes utilized to illustrate to Americans the verity of the wartime maxim about slipped lips sinking ships. The political overtones are quite straightforward—the

17 Durgnat, p. 170.

18 Though there is certainly an implicit awareness that such faith is inadequate to the historical situation since the diplomat, shortly after reaffirming this creed, succumbs to torture (one of the elements which must have delighted Dr. Goebbels, who reputedly so admired *Foreign Correspondent*).

19 A mistake, Hitchcock felt, from the point of view of audience identification, and one which he corrected in *North by Northwest*.

enemy is the Nazi infiltrator and saboteur. And with the saboteur's plunge to his death, the hero's (and thus America's) grasp on Liberty seems reaffirmed.

Two years later, Hitchcock ended nearly a decade of concern with politics and propaganda. *Lifeboat* (1944) is a film so untypical of the standard Hollywood propaganda fare that it did quite poorly.[20] Critics were unkind to it; as Durgnat notes, aside from some comments on *Sabotage*, "it was the first Hitchcock film to arouse critical protests about its 'nastiness' . . ."[21]

The passengers of the lifeboat are a group of survivors from a ship torpedoed by a U-boat. They represent a cross-section of American society. The U-boat has also been sunk, and a German drags himself into the lifeboat. He is obviously the only one of the group skilled in navigation and soon takes command. His decisive actions are in marked contrast to the petty squabbling in which the others were engaged. Actually, he is no simple seaman but rather the captain of the U-boat and is steering the boat toward a German supply ship. Eventually the group discover the truth and brutally beat him to death. As they are approaching the German supply ship, an Allied gunboat appears on the horizon and sinks it. Another German survivor climbs into the boat and threatens them with a pistol; they disarm him, but instead of giving him a beating they agree to turn him over to the proper authorities.

Hitchcock is very explicit about the political intentions of the film (while simultaneously rejecting Truffaut's attempt to introduce a "shared guilt" theme). He says:

> We wanted to show that at that moment there were two world forces confronting each other, the democracies and the Nazis, and while the democracies were completely disorganized, all of the Germans were clearly headed in the same direction. So here was a statement telling the democracies to put their differences aside temporarily and to gather their forces to concentrate on the common enemy, whose strength was precisely derived from a spirit of unity and of determination.[22]

The representatives of democracy are pictured "as a pack of dogs," and it is not terribly surprising that "Dorothy Thompson gave the picture ten days to get out of town!"[23] What is striking is that Hitchcock, an eminently boxoffice and public-oriented film maker, would have thus challenged the propaganda banalities of the time. And more paradoxically, the unity Hitchcock was calling for seemed reasonably certain in 1944 (the United Nations was already planning for the postwar world); the squabbling of the sur-

---

20 Except for a successful run in New York; possibly, Hitchcock believes, because of fascination with the technical challenge of the film.

21 Durgnat, p. 90.

22 Truffaut, p. 113.

23 Again, Hitchcock's own words.

vivors in *Lifeboat* seemed more reminiscent of the democracies' response to Hitler at the time of Munich.

3

With the end of the war, Hitchcock (perhaps badly shaken by the critical responses to *Lifeboat*) avoided overt or even subtle political messages. While he may have been fascinated by the Cold War, it was not until the 1960s that he attempted to utilize such themes extensively.[24]

Notorious (1946) was concerned, presciently, with uranium and atomic secrets, but these elements were distinctly subordinate to the Cary Grant-Ingrid Bergman love affair and the suspense created by Bergman's role as a double agent.[25] In *North by Northwest* (1959), Hitchcock reshuffled elements from *The Thirty-Nine Steps* and *Saboteur*. Madison Avenue Executive Roger O. Thornhill (Cary Grant) is mistaken for a CIA agent (who doesn't really exist outside the mind of the intelligence bureaucracy) and pursued simultaneously by the (presumably Communist) spies *and* the police, who believe he has murdered a UN diplomat. The chase leads across the United States and ends in Rapid City, South Dakota, at the Mount Rushmore monument, the final action being played against the massive nostrils of the four American presidents there enshrined.

Durgnat sees in the film a comment on individual commitment vs. government authority,[26] but this particular political overtone must give way to the rather obvious Cold War belligerence and the conventional propagandistic contrasts between our side (which is admittedly rather callous at first to Thornhill's plight, though ultimately rescuing him) and their side. The enemy is led by the suavely sinister Van Damm (James Mason) who, in highly typical McCarthy-era Hollywood stereotype, is an intellectual and lover of the arts living in an ultra-modern, ultra-futuristic home.

It was not until *Torn Curtain* (1966) that Hitchcock again pursued some of the Cold War themes implicit in *North by Northwest*. Paul Newman plays (as he did in *The Prize*, a fascinating companion piece for *Torn Curtain*) an American nuclear physicist who pretends to defect to East Germany. Actually, Professor Armstrong hopes to make contact with the famous Professor Lindt, who has managed to solve an antiballistic missile formula. His plans are complicated when his fiancee (Julie Andrews) decides to follow him, and when later he has to kill, with great effort, Gromek, the East German security man assigned to guard him. Playing on

---

[24] See Karel Reisz's article, "Hollywood's Anti-Red Boomerang," *Sight and Sound*, vol. 22, no. 3 (1953).

[25] I have omitted any discussion of the remake of *The Man Who Knew Too Much*. Those who have seen the second version will understand why. In only two respects is it significantly different from the original: the scenes in the Albert Hall are far more interesting cinematically; and in the ending Doris Day manages to accomplish with her singing what Edna Best had to achieve with her shooting.

[26] Durgnat, pp. 306-308.

Lindt's egotism, Newman tricks him into revealing the secret formula, and he flees with his fiancee (suitably clad in a trenchcoat which must have been left over from *Foreign Correspondent* and which renders her about as inconspicuous as a Howard Johnson's in Red Square). Assisted by a secret anti-Communist group, and after a series of adventures, they eventually escape from East Germany.

Hitchcock makes no attempt in *Torn Curtain* to challenge the fairly prevalent view of Communist regimes as gloomy ("behind the Iron Curtain") as well as malignant. East Germany offers the perfect locale for such a theme.[27] Even color is used to enhance many of the propaganda points: Armstrong, dressed in light colors, is surrounded by the dark-suited representatives of the regime; skies and ruins seen through windows are shadowy and oppressive;[28] Gromek, the policeman-bodyguard, is a black-suited thug—the familiar Gestapo type of countless World War II films.

Finally, in 1969, Hitchcock offered a reprise on Cold War themes with *Topaz* (based on the Leon Uris novel). The film is set against the background of the 1963 Cuban missile crisis. It is a rather sprawling tale. A Soviet official defects and tells Western intelligence about Soviet missile activities in Cuba, and also that a Communist spy ring—code-named Topaz—has infiltrated the high NATO command. A French agent is enlisted to go to Cuba and confirm reports of the missile installations. Once in Cuba, he is reunited with a former love, Juanita de Cordoba, the widow of a national hero and the secret head of an anti-Castro resistance movement. Her lover, a high government official, murders her. The Frenchman returns to Paris, and the remainder of the film is devoted to the exposure of the Communists within NATO. They turn out to be senior government officials, and the highest of them, facing exposure and disgrace, commits suicide.

Hitchcock experimented with several endings to the film. In one, the French espionage agent and the Communist official fight a duel; in another, the Communist flees to the East; in the third, his suicide is implied.[29] But all three versions, including the now standard one (the third), contain another (anti) climax. On a Paris street an ordinary passerby looks over a newspaper headlining the denouement of the missile crisis. He drops the paper and walks away. "The bored indifference of the man in the street is contrasted with shots of all the Cold War's unknown warriors, who, like Juanita and the servants, have suffered in the continuous war of freedom against tyranny."[30]

---

[27] Other Eastern European countries would have been more difficult and would have required, according to Furhammar and Isaksson, "more subtle nuances of characterisation and setting" (p. 139).

[28] But red, as Furhammar and Isaksson point out, stands not for revolution, socialism or danger, but Freedom. *Ibid.*

[29] See the account in Durgnat, p. 379.

[30] *Ibid.*, pp. 379-80.

Topaz opens with a military parade in Red Square and a title which tells us that the defector, Kusenov, was bothered by his country's militarism and the Communist imperialism that it represented. Such a statement in 1969, with America's Vietnam depredations at their height, pretty well indicates, if not the level of Hitchcock's political sophistication, at least his total reluctance to question the ideological predispositions of the mass American audience. Throughout the film, the Communist agents are portrayed as violent, thus maintaining "the usual polarity between *our* side, whose resort to force is always minimal and reluctant, and the *other* side, whose violence is prompt, wanton, and callous."[31]

This necessarily superficial summary of those Hitchcock films which might legitimately be considered as somehow concerned with politics would indicate that Hitchcock's preferences in political themes were topical and conventional. He never seriously questioned the basic political assumptions and attitudes of the general audience as he perceived them. Political references and events, it could be said, served merely as a backdrop for Hitchcock's exercising his favored thriller formula. Thirty years of significant political changes produced only slight variations on Hitchcock's basic themes in the political films. It is possible that only in *Lifeboat* did Hitchcock come close to a rather personal political statement. But the criticism which that film elicited seemed to throw him back into a shell.[32]

Yet to stress only the predominance of the thriller formula is to do Hitchcock an injustice. Hitchcock, as Wood, Chabrol, Durgnat, and others argue quite persuasively, is not merely an entertainer. There are social, moral, and philosophical dimensions to his films, though these themes are always subordinated to a dramatic interest in the central characters. These dimensions certainly reveal Hitchcock as a film maker who is fascinated by themes or concerns—or perhaps simply overtones— other than those of thrillers simple and pure. And so there is good reason to raise the question whether these (and other Hitchcock films not specifically discussed above) suggest a Hitchcockian political philosophy.

4

The political philosopher reflects about political life. That reflection may be indulged on a variety of levels. The philosopher may seek the most appropriate means, or may preoccupy himself with ends. Philosophy may spring from purely pragmatic considerations—the grubby stuff of everyday politics—or may be guided by more general ideas, if not ideals. At its best, "political philosophy may be understood to be what occurs when this movement of reflection takes a certain direction and achieves a certain level, its characteristic being the relation of political life, and the values and pur-

---

31 *Ibid.*, p. 380.

32 Almost literally. His next several pictures were all set in closely confined spaces, allowing him to indulge his preoccupation with the fascinating but narrowly technical problems involved in such film making.

poses pertaining to it, to the entire conception of the world that belongs to a civilization."[33] And it is at this level—relative to his view of the world—that we must seek the political philosophy of Alfred Hitchcock.

Our starting point must be the comment of Richard Schickel—"We're living in a Hitchcock world, all right." The Hitchcockian *Weltanschauung*, evident in his films over the past fifty years, is a vision of the world as "essentially a less reasonable place than nice people like to think," a point of view that modern man increasingly has come to accept.[34]

As Schickel summarizes it, Hitchcock's vision is one permeated with anxiety, informed with an appreciation of "how thinly the membrane of civilization is stretched over an essentially irrational existence. . . ." Hitchcock's art "reflects his fear of disorder, in particular the breakdown of rational mental and emotional processes and of those institutions—especially the law—which we depend upon to maintain a sense of security and continuity in everyday life."[35]

Such a view implies quite a profound notion about man's nature and the nature of human society. In addition, it raises most fascinating questions of political philosophy, which is inextricably intertwined with problems of individual nature, social organization and coercion, and a reconciliation of their sometimes competing demands. Corollary questions include an examination of the nature of political activity, of the ideal state, of the role of the state in human affairs, of the justification of state authority, and of the individual citizen's obligation to the state.

These perennial questions of political philosophy, juxtaposed with Schickel's analysis and Hitchcock's films, must inevitably recall the ideas of the only true genius among English political philosophers, and invite (as Durgnat occasionally pursues) specific comparisons between the film maker and the philosopher. I refer, of course, to Thomas Hobbes.

The parallels between Hitchcock and Hobbes are indeed striking. On a fundamental point they would I think, disagree. Were they to sit down for dinner and later talk philosophy, the disagreement would undoubtedly be seen to stem from Hitchcock's perception through his films of a paradoxical weakness in Hobbes' political philosophy. Hitchcock frequently echoes Hobbes, but he also goes beyond him, bringing Hobbes' philosophy into the world of international politics in the twentieh century. Hitchcock's perception of this universal dilemma is accurate, but his solution is highly personal. Hitchcock poses the problem incisively (as well as entertainingly), but each of us must extricate ourselves.

Hitchcock's world is uncannily similar to Hobbes' famous "state of nature," described in *Leviathan*:

---

33 Michael Oakeshott, "Introduction" to his edition of Thomas Hobbes, *Leviathan* (Oxford: Basil Blackwell, 1047), p. ix.
34 Richard Schickel, "We're Living in a Hitchcock World, All Right," *The New York Times Magazine*, October 29, 1972, p. 42.
35 *Ibid.*

Whatsoever therefore is consequent to a time of war, where every man is
enemy to every man; the same is consequent to the time, wherein men live
without other security, than what their own strength, and their own invention
shall furnish them withal. In such condition, there is no place for industry;
because the fruit thereof is uncertain: and consequently no culture of the
earth; no navigation, nor use of the commodities that may be imported by
sea; no commodious building; no instruments of moving, and removing, such
things as require much force; no knowledge of the face of the earth; no account of time; no arts; no letters; no society; *and which is worst of all, continual fear, and danger of violent death;* and the life of man, solitary, poor,
nasty, brutish, and short.[36]

Anxiety, and ultimately the fear of death are essential ingredients in
Hobbes' political philosophy. They drive men to agreement whereby they
place above them a sovereign who will maintain peace, safeguard their
lives, and guarantee enough stability for them to pursue their most basic
desires. This compact is more than simply consent; it is a unity of will.
Each gives to one man (or an assembly of men) sovereignty—absolute
power. "This done, the multitude so united in one person, is called a Com-
monwealth. . . . This is the generation of that great LEVIATHAN, or rather, to speak more reverently, of that *mortal* god, to which we owe under
the *immortal God,* our peace and defence."[37]

While Hitchcock may agree with Hobbes as to the essentially chaotic
and "brutish" condition of man, he cannot, it seems, agree with Hobbes'
solution—mutual subjugation to an absolutely sovereign government. For
Hitchcock, I believe, finds government ultimately inadequate. Even on the
level of everyday, simple political activity, Hitchcock is hardly enamored
of politics. Schickel quotes his remark that politics is "one of the meanest
forms of man's attitude toward his fellow man."[38]

Numerous incidents in the films examined thus far illustrate this notion.
In *The Thirty-Nine Steps,* for example, the fugitive Danay (Robert Donat)
wanders into a political meeting, is mistaken for a candidate, and is thun-
derously applauded after delivering an absolutely nonsensical speech filled
with ambiguities and empty rhetoric. As Durgnat quite rightly notes, the
scene is a comment on "the idiocy of political rhetoric, and of the political
process, in this democracy."[39] In *The Lady Vanishes,* the gentle Miss Froy
says that "one mustn't judge a people by its politicians. After all, we British
are very honest at heart."

That the agents of the state appearing in Hitchcock's films are inept is
rather obvious. Worst of all are those who attempt to carry out one of the
state's most crucial functions—the administration of justice. Even outside

36 Thomas Hobbes, *Leviathan.* Edited with an Introduction by Michael Oakeshott
(Oxford: Basil Blackwell, 1946), p. 82. My italics.
37 *Ibid.* p. 112. Italics in original.
38 Schickel, "Hitchcock World," p. 46.
39 Durgnat, p. 127.

the political films, Hitchcock seems obsessed with the theme of ordinary individuals suddenly being subjected to gross miscarriages of justice. The most obvious representatives of the supposedly legitimate authority of the state—the police—are not only bunglers but maniacs, as witnessed by the recurrence of scenes in which police, in pursuit of suspects who may or may not be guilty (the police frequently have no way of knowing), fire wildly at them and anyone else who happens to get in the way.[40] Their irresponsible use of force is but a small portion of the misuse of authority by a state which so frequently apprehends "the wrong man."

And it will not suffice to say that Hitchcock is simply mirroring the oft-cited American disparagement of politics and politicians. The above examples suggest Hitchcock's belief that the state itself is deficient.

In Hitchcock's more obviously political films, the state fails miserably to protect ordinary individuals suddenly involved in utterly irrational and potentially fatal machinations. Hitchcock's heroes must rely on their own strengths if they are to be vindicated, let alone survive. They are in the same position as man in Hobbes' state of nature, who must "use his own power . . . for the preservation of his own nature; that is to say, of his own life; and consequently . . . [do whatever] he shall conceive to be the aptest means thereunto."[41]

Perhaps the most noteworthy aspect of these films is that the political situation is directly related to *international* politics. And it is in this respect that Hitchcock both reflects and seeks to resolve a paradox inherent in *Leviathan,* one which Hobbes recognizes but does not adequately explicate. Hobbes writes:

> But though there had never been any time, wherein particular men were in a condition of war against one another; yet in all times, kings, and persons of sovereign authority, because of their independency, are in continual jealousies, and in the state and posture of gladiators; having their weapons pointing, and their eyes fixed on one another; that is, their forts, garrisons, and guns upon the frontiers of their kingdoms; and continual spies upon their neighbours; which is a posture of war.[42]

The independent sovereigns of the world—nation-states in our own time— are in a state of nature *vis a vis* each other; the warlike condition of the state of nature is their everyday experience. The reason is simple—there is no sovereign above them. Hobbes recognized this fact yet never fully considered the possible consequences for domestic peace and order of this inter-sovereign, perpetual rivalry. His greatest concern, after the frightful experience of the English civil wars of the seventeenth century, was with the do-

---

40 Durgnat cites such incidents in *Strangers on a Train* and *To Catch a Thief,* and Furhammar and Isaksson note that "East German police shoot wildly in the centre of Berlin . . ." Cf. Durgnat, pp. 221, 249-50; Furhammar and Isaksson, p. 140.

41 Hobbes, *Leviathan,* p. 84.

42 *Ibid.,* p. 83.

mestic peace and the creation of a powerful domestic sovereign. He failed to consider the consequences to the citizen and to the domestic order when the sordid world of international politics begins to impinge upon them. Hitchcock, however, perceives those consequences only too well. Chaos intrudes into ordinary lives, and the domestic sovereign, consumed with the problem of its own survival in a world of competing sovereigns, must necessarily give short shrift to the demands of ordinary citizens. Moreover, in a world where political ideologies are adhered to with theological fervor, Nazism vs. Democracy or Communism vs. Capitalism become Manichean conflicts between absolute good and absolute evil. Thus the agents of these death struggles (whether they are played out in Europe or Korea or Cuba or Vietnam) can justify wiretapping, assassinations, and every other conceivable assault on domestic political civilities in the name of "national security." In the world of *Machtpolitik,* the Roger Thornhills are totally expendable.

While Hitchcock's box-office impulses may have contributed to or reinforced this lunatic dichotomy, as in his pre-war propagandizing, he has also shown, as in *Lifeboat,* an ability to criticize democracy as much as his most recent political films criticize Communist systems. And ultimately Hitchcock is concerned with the common citizen and his increasing awareness that all political systems, having no sovereign above them, must engage in a perpetual state of war which can all too easily engulf their innocent citizen-victims.

Basically, American experience with international politics since 1940 seems to have been one constant state of emergency. The anxieties bred by such a situation have evidently affected our domestic politics, and along with them, a paranoia bred by the international situation and exacerbated by a sudden realization that our own government is not all that it claimed to be. Or rather, that the actions perceived by political leaders to be necessary to save our system have almost totally eroded that which was most worth saving. Such paranoid anxiety can easily lead to the desire for an authoritarian system—the very solution Hobbes opted for in a condition of civil war. Does Hitchcock the political philosopher suggest such a solution?

It would be tempting to dismiss Hitchcock as an incipient totalitarian (or at least authoritarian), and it would be child's play to mass evidence from his personal life. The famous incident of the young Hitchcock being arbitrarily incarcerated as an object lesson—and his subsequent life-long fear of policemen—may go far toward explaining his feelings about law and justice evinced in many of his films. A typical response to paranoid anxiety is a search for rigid control. Hitchcock's total planning of his films is constantly noted—he himself boasts of it. Schickel tells us that Hitchcock does not drive, seldom travels, books the same rooms in hotels whenever he does travel, hates "suspense, shock, even mild surprise," and works for Universal Studios, the most rationalized and controlled in Hollywood.[43]

---

[43] Schickel, "Hitchcock World," p. 22.

Hitchcock's fear of disorder may actually surpass Hobbes' legendary distaste for chaos. Yet the above analysis should indicate that Hitchcock does not trust the state to provide any more order than religion or any other form of organized social control. At one point, Schickel refers to Hitchcock as a post-Christian moralist. God is indeed dead in our own and Hitchcock's world, but equally moribund is that mortal deity Leviathan. Or, if not dead, at least hopelessly inadequate. The disorderly, the unruly, the irrational in man's nature is all too essential a part of twentieth century experience. The absurdity of man's existence is inescapable; and Hitchcock, he tells his interviewers, practices absurdity religiously. Yet in his own life and in his art, he has introduced into the world some element of order, realizing perhaps that here one finds the only cohesion on which to rely.

Hitchcock's political message is that we must recognize the limits of state-imposed order. We must set our own limits and create within them. This is certainly not Hobbes' advocacy of an authoritarian state. It is advocacy of the understanding (intuitive, perhaps) that the membrane of individual civility is as thin as that which is stretched over the general civilization, but that only personal strength and effort can sustain man in this kind of world. At best, man can hope to control only portions of his personal life, and even those he may have to control totally to withstand the forces of his own unreason as well as those of other men in a deficient society. Above all, man must learn to live with the expectation that at any moment the membrane may snap, and chaos ensue. Certainly politics, even (or perhaps especially) the politics of Leviathan, is not a solution.[44]

Hitchcock the post-Christian moralist is also, and always has been, the post-Watergate political philosopher.

---

[44] In *Blackmail* (1929), the forces of disorder run rampant through the British Museum, while the impassive face of an Egyptian deity stares at them; but in *Saboteur* and *North by Northwest,* these forces are loosed against a background of massive governmental symbols.

1976

NATIONAL CINEMA

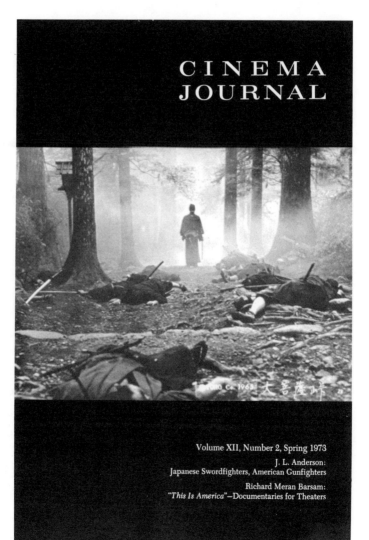

CINEMA
JOURNAL

Volume XII, Number 2, Spring 1973

J. L. Anderson:
Japanese Swordfighters, American Gunfighters

Richard Meran Barsam:
"This Is America"—Documentaries for Theaters

The "Eastern" Writer in Hollywood

John Schultheiss

There have been at least two significant periods in American film history when the Hollywood studios actively recruited the services of so-called "Eastern" writers—those who had established, or were in the embryonic stages of establishing, a literary reputation either as novelists, dramatists, poets, or critics.° The initial period (circa 1919-1922) coincided with the studios' efforts to shift the thrust of silent screen artistry from the movie personality to the well-written story. The second and more famous era of the Eastern writer in Hollywood (roughly the thirties and early forties) occurred because of the desperate need for snappy dialogue and story elements which would take advantage of the motion picture's new dimension of sound. During this latter time almost every noteworthy literary figure came West to write for films. They never succeeded in turning Hollywood into a modern Parnassus, but theirs was an invigorating and exciting presence during one of filmdom's most colorful and flamboyant periods.

The first indication of Hollywood's generally heightened appreciation of the writer's importance in the production of motion pictures was evidenced in the formation by Samuel Goldwyn in June, 1919, of an organizational unit within his studio—The Eminent Authors—for which he said, "I must claim the virtue of absolute novelty."[1] Goldwyn's move was in partial response to the success of the Jesse Lasky Famous Players' emphasis on the star performer, and he sought some competing feature. He also intended to alter the focus of screen creativity by elevating the importance of the story and dramatic structure in the artistic pattern:

> Gradually there grew up within me a belief that the public was tiring of the star and a corresponding conviction that the emphasis of production should be placed upon the story rather than upon the player. In the poverty of screen drama lay, so I felt, the weakness of our industry, and the one correction of this weakness which suggested itself to me was a closer cooperation between author and picture-producer.[2]

Goldwyn decided to draw on writers who had earned a reputation in the

---

°The term "Eastern" writer has sometimes been applied not only to the majority of the involved American writers from non-movie fields, but also to noted British and European authors whom the studios imported to work in various film writing capacities.

[1] Samuel Goldwyn, *Behind the Screen* (New York, 1923), p. 235.

[2] *Ibid.*

established literary arena. At his urging many celebrated authors came to the movie capital.

The first Eminent Authors group consisted of Rex Beach, Gertrude Atherton, Mary Roberts Rinehart, Rupert Hughes, Basil King, Gouverneur Morris, and Le Roy Scott. Later Goldwyn imported writers who were particularly indigenous to the East, all of whom had some connection with the theatre: Clayton Hamilton, playwright and dramatic critic of *The Bookman;* Louis Sherwin, dramatic critic of the New York *Evening Globe;* and playwrights Charles Kenyon (*Kindling*), Cleves Kinkead (*Common Clay*), and Thompson Buchanan, author of several successful melodramas and sentimental comedies.

Other studios began to bolster their staffs with similarly prestigious writing talent, such as Elinor Glyn, Sir Gilbert Parker, Edward Knoblock, Arnold Bennett, Gene Stratton-Porter, Zane Grey, Kathleen Norris, Rita Weiman, and Somerset Maugham.

Robert E. Sherwood, in his "Silent Drama" column of film criticism for the old *Life* magazine, April 14, 1921, noted the phenomenon in a manner which gives an early suggestion that there was something less than respectable about the Hollywood employment:

> The eminent authors who were lured out to Culver City (Cal.) by the seductive scent of the Goldwyn gold, have sponsored a great deal of press matter, in which they have frantically attempted to justify their motives in devoting themselves to this new and somewhat more lucrative form of literary endeavor.

The motion picture had been indicted virtually from its inception as a corporate, mechanical medium, which directed its product toward a mass, 14-year-old mentality. Accordingly, it had been denied the stature of art granted to its literary and musical counterparts. Thus, with Sherwood's mild implication of a sordid relationship between formerly pristine author and commercial film, there began the string of contemptuous statements and the catalogue of creative studies in which the writer is depicted as betrayer of his literary art. The image of the artist who "sold out" would persist for the next three decades. It was an image that most writers themselves believed, and which only the strongest managed to discard.

In the beginning Hollywood's motives were honorable. But, because of a kind of literary arrogance on the part of the writers, and an artistic and organizational intransigence in the studios, the mating did not work out. William C. deMille, in his *Hollywood Saga*, says:

> Few writers of the primitive cinema won academic honors as authors, and as real authors began to drift into the field they seemed to take strange pleasure in their utter ignorance of the medium and its demands. For the most part they regarded their studio experiences as literary slumming and delighted to talk about the "prostitution" of their art, not realizing, poor darlings, that what the studios were offering was honorable marriage. They could not, of course, marry so far beneath them; the most their literary honor

would concede was that, for gold, they would lie awhile with this new Caliban.[3]

The majority of the theatre-oriented, Eastern-based authors simply were unable (or unwilling) to understand and utilize the peculiar dramatic mechanism of the cinema to tell their story. DeMille, a playwright who had come to Hollywood much earlier to adapt literary material to the screen, tells what happened:

> The gentlemen from Broadway decided at once to disregard such picture technic as we had been able to evolve and to follow more closely their rules of the theater. They thought the whole idea was to photograph a play very much as it would be performed on the stage. They disdained the close-up method of telling a story, thereby losing that value of greater intimacy which is one of the screen's advantages over the stage. They played most of their scenes in long ensemble shots which, from a screen standpoint, left many of their characters out of the action at any given moment. In short, while being compelled to retain all the liabilities of picture form, they rejected its few hard-won assets. In addition, they chose to keep all the limitations of stage drama although forced by screen conditions to lose the theater's most valuable elements, the living actor and the spoken word. Their experiments were not successful, largely, perhaps, because the public, having accepted a new technic for pictures, was not pleased by a reversion to theater methods in a medium which had already discarded them in order to find its own more appropriate form of expression.[4]

Those writers who took the trouble to learn something about the new medium in which they were working had a tendency to stress the other extreme—they became intoxicated by the freedom of screen style. "Just because a picture could change its background every few seconds they tended to avail themselves of the opportunity until dramatic action was in danger of being entirely lost in physical movement."[5]

The Belgian writer, Maurice Maeterlinck, was probably the first Nobel Prize winner to be employed by a Hollywood studio. His difficulty in creating powerful literature for the screen was typical of most of the eminent writers. Dramatist Elmer Rice (*The Adding Machine*), who was also employed by the Goldwyn Studios at this time, tells of being given the assignment of revitalizing a story Maeterlinck had written:

---

3 William deMille, *Hollywood Saga* (New York, 1939), pp. 158-159.

4 *Ibid.*, pp. 257-258. Mildred Cram, "Author in Hollywood," *The American Spectator Yearbook* (New York, 1934), p. 184, also comments on this tendency to "theatricize" the film medium: the famous author, "in spite of himself, is apt to work in terms of the theatre until he discovers the tricks of the new trade—how to turn a sequence on sound, how to 'cut away' from a scene, how to reduce dialogue to a minimum, how to catch the elusive and vitally important 'tempo,' the beat and measure of a good picture. The writer trained in the studio carries this 'beat' in his head. He is like the composer who 'hears' an orchestra mentally. The newcomer, unless he is divinely flexible, must undo his technique—be it that of novelist, biographer, playwright or poet—and weave new patterns with new threads."

5 DeMille, p. 259.

It concerned a kindly farmer to whose blissful domain comes a touring banker, seeking a night's shelter. Next morning the banker sees a telltale film upon a pool. Oil! He contrives to dispossess the farmer and take over the land. Disaster descends upon the bucolic family; the wife dies of consumption or of a broken heart (I forget which); the son becomes a criminal, the daughter—need it be said?—a harlot. The farmer takes to the hills, brooding over his wrongs and vowing vengeance. Years later, his moment comes. The banker, now a great oil magnate, goes hunting in the mountains, where he encounters his victim. The avenger levels his gun, but as he is about to pull the trigger love enters his heart; he lowers his weapon and extends his hand in token of forgiveness.[6]

Rice read the story in amazement, unable to believe that a man of Maeterlinck's stature could have produced it. He was "shocked by this evidence of the corrupting influence of Hollywood."[7] The tide of indictments against Hollywood's effect on writers was beginning to gain momentum.

Robert Sherwood, reviewing *The Lost Romance* (1921), saw a similar corruption in the work of Edward Knoblock:

In the main Mr. Knoblock seems to have followed the example of the numerous other writers who have flocked out to Los Angeles of late, and who were careful to check their intellects at the Grand Central Station before leaving.[8]

Many writers accepted Hollywood positions largely on the strength of Goldwyn's promise of free creative scope. But there already existed a scenario department's entrenched bureaucracy which made this impossible. Elmer Rice explains that the practitioners of the established patterns of picturemaking saw in the invasion from the East a threat to their security. Nor did the stars and the directors take kindly to Goldwyn's concept of the writer's importance. The Eastern writers did not enhance their popularity by frequent affectionate references to the world of the theatre.

The proposed revolution in writing came to nothing. All story material was channeled through (Jack) Hawks (story department head), who vetoed every innovation with the comment that it was "not pictures." Everything went into the old sausage machine and it all came out looking and tasting alike. I once sat beside Gertrude Atherton during the screening of a film made from one of her novels. When I asked her opinion she said, "What I like most about it is that there is still a picture to be made out of my book."[9]

The results of Eminent Authors and the first Eastern writer emigration to Hollywood certainly were not totally satisfactory to either the film producers (Goldwyn: "When the tradition of the pen ran athwart the tradition of the screen I am bound to say that I suffered considerably from the

6 Elmer Rice, *Minority Report: An Autobiography* (New York, 1963), p. 177.
7 *Ibid.*
8 Robert E. Sherwood, "The Silent Drama," *Life*, June 2, 1921, p. 804.
9 Rice, p. 179.

impact"[10]), or to the writers (Rice: "Creatively I had accomplished nothing
. . . nothing is more important than independence of thought and freedom
of action"[11]).

Nevertheless, according to film historian Richard Griffith, the experiment
set new standards: "The very presence in their midst of expert writers challenged the indigenous picture-makers to set their sights higher. Never again
could scripts be mere loose scenarios hastily scribbled by studio hacks for
careless directors."[12]

THE SECOND COMING OF THE EASTERN WRITER

The post-*Jazz Singer* flurry for speakable dialogue precipitated a revival
of the quest for quality authors. Many of the best screenwriters who were in
Hollywood during the advent of the sound film could not write good dramatic dialogue, and even for those who could there was still a brand-new
kind of screenplay to be developed. There were no accepted forms, no models to follow. How much or how little dialogue should be used was a matter
of future experiment. There were only a few writers who had written both
for stage and screen, and these bore the brunt of the first months, but the
supply of writers was far from sufficient. Other writers had to be called in
and, for the second time in its history, Hollywood was gorged with famous
dramatists, novelists, critics.

It was within this context that writer Herman J. Mankiewicz, who was
already in Hollywood, sent his famous telegram to Ben Hecht back in New
York: "Will you acccept three hundred per week to work for Paramount
Pictures. All expenses paid. The three hundred is peanuts. Millions are to be
grabbed out here and your only competition is idiots. Don't let this get
around."[13]

So massive and diverse was the writer influx during this famous period
that several literary and artistic circles developed. The slickest of these
cliques was centered at the Garden of Allah Hotel on Sunset Boulevard. Its
members were essentially those writers from the ex-"Round Table" set of
New York's Algonquin Hotel, including Dorothy Parker, Robert Benchley,
Donald Ogden Stewart, Marc Connelly, and such non-Algonquin individuals as F. Scott Fitzgerald, Samuel Hoffenstein, and Edwin Justus Mayer.
This group had expensive tastes and habits and did not hesitate to exhaust
their large salaries in sustaining them.

---

[10] Goldwyn, pp. 242-243.

[11] Rice, p. 186.

[12] Richard Griffith, *Samuel Goldwyn: The Producer and his Films* (New York,
1956), p. 13.

In F. Scott Fitzgerald's *The Last Tycoon* (Penguin Books: Middlesex, England,
1963), p. 149, Monroe Stahr (Thalberg) speaks of the directors in his studio being angry
when he imported Eastern theater talent: " 'Some of them have never forgiven me . . .
It put them on their toes and made them learn their jobs all over, but they never did
really forgive me. That time we imported a whole new hogshead full of writers, and
I thought they were great fellows till they all went red.' "

[13] Ben Hecht, *A Child of the Century* (New York, 1954), p. 435.

A second group was more cosmopolitan. It included Christopher Isherwood, Aldous Huxley, Gerald Heard, and associated actors, musicians, and philosophers, such as Aldous' brother, Julian, Mrs. Bertold (Salka) Viertel, Greta Garbo, Charles Chaplin, Anita Loos, Bertrand Russell, and Stravinsky. The group seemed to have a bohemian cohesion, with interests in pacifism and Hindu mysticism, and came to be localized in the Santa Monica Canyon.

A third group was made up of people more committed to plain writing than urbanity or elegance. These men had their own kind of bohemian existence which revolved around one block on Hollywood Boulevard, the block which contained the Stanley Rose Book Shop and Musso & Frank's Restaurant. Here collected Nathanael West, William Faulkner, Elliot Paul, William Saroyan, and Budd Schulberg.[14]

The writers' second movement West prompted volumes of derisive literature excoriating the Hollywood "system," deploring the movies' treatment of the writer, and denouncing the writer's prostitution of his artistic values by embracing the Hollywood employment—most of the attacks being written by the angered and frustrated writers themselves. Novels such as Horace McCoy's *I Should Have Stayed Home,* Nathanael West's *The Day of the Locust,* Peter Viertel's *White Hunter, Black Heart,* Stephen Longstreet's *The Beach House,* Jay Richard Kennedy's *Prince Bart* are representative doses of vitriol directed towards Hollywood—produced by writers who were quite successful there.

The anguished memoirs and anti-Hollywood novels of the so-called "corrupted" writers—along with the scornful accounts of the decadent Hollywood environment by the "untainted" Eastern establishment critics such as George Jean Nathan or Edmund Wilson—were written mainly from the viewpoint of remorse over the adulteration and sometimes abandonment of the writers' non-movie literary production. But while it was true that there did occur an attrition of some authors' desire and fecundity in this respect, many motion pictures received the benefit of their verve, wit, and style. The Hollywood film was often proportionately rewarded by well-constructed plots and zesty charm.

WHY DID THEY COME?

Edmund Wilson, in *The Boys in the Back Room,* was moved to verse in observing the flight of writers to Hollywood:

> What shining phantom folds its wings before us?

---

[14] Ben Hecht has said: "Once in Hollywood, within a two mile radius you could find two-thirds of the great talent of the world. Poets and painters and philosophers. Lured here by the gold." Quoted in Cecil Smith, "Ben Hecht Returns, Rips Hollywood Apart," *The Los Angeles Times,* August 26, 1956.

For an intimate, first-hand glimpse of the Santa Monica group of artists, by one whose home was the comfortable salon where they collected, see Salka Viertel's engaging and charming autobiography, *The Kindness of Strangers* (New York: Holt, Rinehart and Winston, 1969).

What apparition, smiling yet remote?
Is this—so portly yet so lightly porous—
The old friend who went west and never wrote?[15]

Budd Schulberg, a particularly insightful interpreter of the Hollywood scene, attempted to concretize Wilson's apparition. His observation of the atrophy of some of America's most gifted writers was amplified by his affection for them and by an intense appreciation of their literary capacities. This is how he saw the destructive pattern take place:

> Greatly talented and magnificently paid, they had seemed to have everything. Seeing them in their stylish clothes, with their stylish ladies, listening to the bright polish of their conversation, still respecting their dreams of returning in triumph to their first creative love, their plays, their books, one could not easily foresee the pattern that would trap them all. Yet, almost without exception, ten years later they were bankrupt men, broken financially, creatively, even physically. Alcoholism had spread like plague among them. They were debt-ridden, alimony-ridden and, worst of all, conscience-ridden.[16]

In Schulberg's novel, *The Disenchanted*, the main character, Manley Halliday, is depicted as an amalgam of F. Scott Fitzgerald and other writers who "had talent and got short-circuited."[17] But Halliday is shown as having the awareness to perceive the tragic irony of the Eastern writers' emigration West, and he is fascinated by the psychology that precipitated it:

> The realization that he and Bob (Benchley) and Dotty Parker and Eddie Mayer and Sammy Hoffenstein and perhaps half a dozen others of the old gang had all been brought into the Hollywood fold suddenly oppressed him. There had been so many luncheons and cocktails and all-night sessions when Hollywood had been only a term of derision, when they had vied with each other in witty denunciations of this Capital of the Philistines. No one with any self-respect, he remembered saying, would ever go to Hollywood, except possibly to pursue Billie Dove.
> And fifteen years later here they were, all lured to the Garden of Allah, all on weekly pay rolls or, worse yet, trying to get on. Were they men of inadequate wills who had acquired the authors' cancer—expensive tastes? Or could they, like Manley himself, persuade themselves that this was merely a stop-over on the way back to positive work?[18]

Halliday's questions are at the crux of the syndrome. Sheilah Graham, who saw these emigrés at their destination at the Garden of Allah, was also fascinated by the paradox but just as mystified:

> Why did they do it? No one forced them to go to Hollywood and write and suffer. No one put a gun to their heads. Most of those who went had

---

[15] Quoted in Leslie Fiedler, "What Shining Phantom: Writers and the Movies," *Man and the Movies,* edited by W. R. Robinson (New York, 1969), p. 304.

[16] Budd Schulberg, "Why Manley Halliday is . . . Manley Halliday," *Theatre Arts,* December, 1958, p. 17.

[17] *Ibid.,* p. 16.

[18] Schulberg, *The Disenchanted* (New York, 1950), p. 30.

begged their agents to get them there. I saw them at the Garden lolling around, enjoying the lazy life while hating the producers who made it all possible and, meanwhile, despising themselves.[19]

The explicit, tangible reasons for the Eastern writer's sojourn to Hollywood are fairly easy to ascertain. According to Ben Hecht they were the money, the witty companionship of one's fellow writers from the East who were all making the trip, and the virtual anonymity which spared the screenwriter any critical attacks which might be aimed at a motion picture on which he worked. Hecht explained it this way:

> First, the money. It was easy money. You didn't gamble for it as in the theatre. Or break your back digging for it as in the field of prose. It was money in large sums. Twenty-five- and fifty-thousand-dollar chunks of it fell into your pockets in no time. You got it sometimes for good work, more often for bad. But there was a law in the studios—hire only the best. As a result, the writer who had written well in some other medium was paid the most. . . . Next to the lure of easy money was the promise of a plush Bohemian vacation. Witty and superior folk abounded. The town was loud with wild hearts and the poetry of success. The wit, superiority, wildness had no place in a movie script. But there was happy room for them in the cafes, drawing rooms and swimming pools.
> "You write stinking scripts," said Charlie (MacArthur), "but you meet the people you like to be in a room with."
> The other matters that took you to Hollywood had nothing to do with the movies. They had to do with flaws in yourself—flaws of laziness, fear, greed. . . . The writer intent on "doing his best" has to expose that best to critical blasts that mow him down, two times out of three. And if he wants to keep serving his art, he and his lacerations must lead a sort of a hall-bedroom existence. . . . The movies solved such matters. There were no critics to mow him down. The writer of a movie is practically anonymous. It's a pleasant anonymity.[20]

The writers' premier motivation of money bears reiteration and elaboration through specific examples. Harold Clurman, one of the founders of the Group Theatre, speaks of the attraction which Hollywood had for the young dramatist:

> From success or failure the playwright's escape is Hollywood. . . . The theatre is in the very heart of the marketplace, where a feverish and fabulous exchange of goods seems the essential drama. The playwright cannot but be affected by it. If he has had some success, why not more? If he has had little success, and greater rewards for his efforts are open to him in Hollywood, why not take advantage of the situation? This thought-process is particularly typical of the more recent playwrights, since respect for the stage as a medium and the tradition of the serious playwright as an autonomous artist are rapidly waning. The mortality rate among playwrights under forty is extraordinarily high.[21]

19 Sheilah Graham, *The Garden of Allah* (New York, 1970), p. 221.
20 Hecht, *Charlie* (New York, 1957), pp. 157-159.
21 Harold Clurman, *The Fervent Years* (New York, 1945), p. 169.

This is confirmed by Pauline Kael who gives us

> a picture of Herman Mankiewicz, a giant of a man who mongered his own talent, a man who got a head start in the race to "sell out" to Hollywood. The pay was fantastic. After a month in the movie business, Mankiewicz—though his Broadway shows had not been hits, and though this was in 1926, when movies were still silent—signed a year's contract giving him $400 a week and a bonus of $5,000 for each story that was accepted, with an option for a second year at $500 a week and $7,500 per accepted story, the company guaranteeing to accept at least four stories per year. In other words, his base pay was $40,800 his first year and $56,000 his second.[22]

Clifford Odets, a dramatist who made the transition from the New York stage to films, tells of the monetary problems of the theatrical writer: "I never made a living out of the theatre. A playwright can spend six to eight months writing a play, then make about six weeks salary. Of 13 plays I have written, I made a living out of two, *Golden Boy* and *Country Girl*."[23]
Novelist Nathanael West had the same motive for going to Hollywood:

> I once tried to work seriously at my craft but was absolutely unable to make the beginning of a living. At the end of three years and two books I had made the total of $780 gross. So it wasn't a matter of making a sacrifice, which I was willing enough to make and will still be willing, but just a clear cut impossibility. . . . It is for this reason that I'm grateful rather than angry at the deep mud-lined rut in which I find myself at the moment. The world outside doesn't make it possible for me to even hope to earn a living writing, while here the pay is large . . . enough for me to have three or four months off every year.[24]

The congeries of other psychological, sociological, and philosophical factors which might have been operative in the motivational framework of the writers is much more elusive. At this level of speculation the ideas tend to be of the cryptic nature of Leslie Fiedler's:

> But what ever drew writers to Hollywood? The search for destruction, I am tempted to answer off the cuff, a desire to play Russian Roulette, if not to die —to act out in their own particular lives the fate of the literary art to which they have committed themselves, the fate of books in the world of Hollywood, whose normal temperature is *Fahrenheit 451*.[25]

A literary death wish, if there was one, was perhaps the most depressing explanation. Novelist James Hilton offered a more positive reason:

> The centuries-old bottleneck in the communications system is broken at last; the printed word no longer holds the monopoly. Hence in part the lure that Hollywood has for the writer of books. It is new; it is exciting; and it

22 Pauline Kael, "Raising Kane—I," *The New Yorker*, February 20, 1971, p. 49.
23 Obituary of Clifford Odets, The Los Angeles *Times*, August 16, 1963, p. 8.
24 Nathanael West, "Introduction" to *The Day of the Locust*, Bantam Books edition (New York, 1963), pp. xvi-xvii.
25 Fiedler, pp. 313-314.

enlarges his audience incomparably. If, in doing so, it also simplifies and
sometimes distorts what he has to say, he must make his own reckoning as to
whether, on balance, he would rather say a little less exactly what he wants
to the millions or a little more exactly to the thousands.[26]

Walter Wanger, recognizing this tremendous power of the film medium
to communicate and propagandize ideas, urged the liberal writer to utilize
Hollywood in order to proselytize the American public to his views, to help
him fulfill his social mission of criticizing and reshaping society's institutions.

If there is to be an entente between the liberal and Hollywood, the first
requisite is a realistic, non-snobbish viewpoint on the liberal's part. The motion pictures reach the people whom the liberal needs to convert. ... . The
American motion picture is the medium through which the relationship of
goodwill among men can be established. The intellectual should orient himself to that fact.[27]

Whatever their reasons, the writers did set out for Hollywood to confront an exceptionally formidable moral and artistic challenge.

The Hollywood "System"

What the artist found when he got to Hollywood—in terms of studio
structure, production doctrine and protocol, and establishment attitudes and
treatment of writers—was, he discovered soon enough, a fairly dismal arena
for his talents. In order to establish the environment which to a great extent
determined or contributed to many of the failures experienced there, it
might be useful to review a few of the more colorful indictments of this
Hollywood system.

Budd Schulberg tells about a special aspect of the syndrome:

If mediocrity seemed to be the major muse of the movies, if most pictures
were turned out as mechanically as newspapers were rolled off their presses,
and as quickly tossed aside and forgotten, it was not to be blamed on the
shortcomings of the medium, as many of the middlebrows and even some of
the highbrows claimed. The fault lay in a system of production that was the
logical expression of American commerce in a period when the average family went to the movies—*any movies*—two or three times a week, and each of
the seven major studios was grinding out fifty to sixty pictures a year. . . .
Inevitably some 375 of the 400 films a year would be standard product, slick,

[26] James Hilton, "A Novelist Looks at the Screen," *The Screen Writer*, November,
1945, p. 31.
[27] Walter Wanger, "Hollywood and the Intellectuals," *The Saturday Review*, December 5, 1942, p. 40.
An astute fictionalization of the Hollywood writer, who represents the intellectual's
new role in American culture, is to be found in the character of Shep Stearns, in
Schulberg's *The Disenchanted*. He is depicted as the idealist who will enlighten and
lead the masses out of their economic and political bondage and aid in the construction
of a better social system.

smooth, polished to a high professional gloss, and about as full of real life as the box of popcorn sold with the show.[28]

Detective story and screenplay writer Raymond Chandler gives a synthesis of the Hollywood malaise:

> The overall picture . . . is of a degraded community whose idealism even is largely fake. The pretentiousness, the bogus enthusiasm . . . the all-pervasive agent, the strutting of the big shots . . . the constant fear of losing all this fairy gold and being the nothing they have never ceased to be, the snide tricks. . . . It is like one of these South American palace revolutions conducted by officers in comic opera uniforms—only when the thing is over the ragged dead men lie in rows against the walls and you suddenly know that this is not funny, this is the Roman Circus, and damn near the end of a civilization.[29]

Perhaps the most ornate attack is in Christopher Isherwood's *Prater Violet*:

> The film studio of today is really the palace of the sixteenth century. There one sees what Shakespeare saw: the absolute power of the tyrant, the courtiers, the flatterers, the jesters, the cunningly ambitious intriguers. There are fantastically beautiful women, there are incompetent favorites. There are great men who are suddenly disgraced. There is the most insane extravagance, and unexpected parsimony over a few pence. There is enormous splendor, which is a sham; and also horrible squalor hidden behind the scenery. There are vast schemes, abandoned because of some caprice. There are secrets which everybody knows and no one speaks of. There are even two or three honest advisers. These are the court fools, who speak the deepest wisdom in puns, lest they should be taken seriously. They grimace, and tear their hair privately, and weep.[30]

Finally, Robert Sherwood pens this despairing analysis:

> "What's the use of trying to be artistic?" the film folk justifiably enquire. "If we give them anything really good, they don't understand it. The only thing that isn't over their heads is Sex."
> It is this unshakable conviction which deadens Hollywood, which converts it from the Athens that it might be into the magnified Gopher Prairie that it is. Every writer or actor or artist of any kind who journeys there, however high his hopes or firm his integrity, is bound eventually to arrive at the point where he must utter the same unanswerable question: "What's the use?" And having done so, he must either depart at once, before the California climate dissolves the tissues of his conscience, or he must abandon his idealistic pre-

---

28 Schulberg, "The Writer and Hollywood," *Harper's Magazine*, October, 1959, p. 135.

29 Raymond Chandler, "Letter to Alfred A. Knopf, January 12, 1946," *Raymond Chandler Speaking*, edited by Dorothy Gardiner and Kathrine Sorley Walker (Boston, 1962), pp. 126-129.

30 Christopher Isherwood, *Prater Violet*, Modern Library Paperback edition (New York, 1945), p. 88.

tensions, settle down to a monotonous diet of the succulent fruits of the lotus, and live out his days, in sun-kissed contentment, accomplishing nothing of any enduring importance, taking the immediate cash and letting the eternal credit go.

And, by the way, I'm sure that Omar Khayyám would have loved Hollywood, and that, had he lived there, he would have left behind him no compositions that an Edward Fitzgerald would have bothered to translate.[31]

Writing for motion pictures had been always considered by many people to be essentially inferior to the writing done in other fields. Many critics, especially of the Eastern establishment, have been eager to ascribe a higher literary value to a short story for *The New Yorker* magazine than to a screenplay for a feature motion picture. George Boxley, a characterization of a prominent author (probably Aldous Huxley) writing for films, in F. Scott Fitzgerald's *The Last Tycoon*, voices this idea of lesser literary standards for motion pictures. He is defending a scene he wrote in his screenplay:

> "I don't think you people read things. The men are dueling when the conversation takes place. At the end one of them falls into a well and has to be hauled up in a bucket."
> He barked again and subsided.
> "Would you write that in a book of your own, Mr. Boxley?"
> "What? Naturally not."
> "You'd consider it too cheap."
> "Movie standards are different," said Boxley.[32]

This attitude probably stems from a recognition of the corporate creative process involved in transferring the written word to the screen. Unlike the theatre in which the author's words are sacrosanct, the screen writer's ideas usually defer to the director, who maintains totalitarian control on the set, or to the producer, who usually imposes his own ideas on his writer-employee of how the script should read. This unique tampering with the author's original work tends to mitigate his contribution to the final film, thus denying him claim, in some eyes, to serious artistic consideration. Christopher Isherwood, both a novelist and a screen writer, explains his reasons for recognizing a disparity in the literary quality of each form:

> One must not put it on a par with the novel, for in screen writing the director is boss. The films are a visual operation and in my view one should not really say that one is a writer in films unless one is a writer-director. If a director said to me "Your script is sacred," I would be suspicious of his ability . . . The difference between writing a novel and a screenplay is like passing from the totalitarian world where the writing is all your doing down to the last comma—where you are absolutely responsible—to the extraordinarily

31 Sherwood, "Hollywood: The Blessed and the Cursed," *America As Americans See It*, edited by Fred J. Ringel (New York, 1932), p. 72.
32 Fitzgerald, *The Last Tycoon*, p. 39.

cooperative world of creating a screenplay. . . . One gets tired of absolute power even in the arts.[33]

The literary establishment's cynical view of the screen writer seemed to be held in Hollywood too. Mildred Cram, novelist and screen writer, has bemoaned this paradox:

> There is no prestige attached to being an author in Hollywood. An author (of standing) in London, in Paris, even in New York, enjoys a certain distinction. He is acceptable. He is even desirable. His opinion is worth something. But when he reaches Hollywood, he finds himself curiously, unexpectedly and completely anonymous. The arrival of Joan Crawford at the Metro-Goldwyn-Mayer studios in Culver City is an event. Her lavish car rolls through the gate, onto the lot. Bayard Veiller parks across the street, in Charles Bickford's service station. I may be wrong, but I do not recall ever having seen an author's car within the sacred precincts. I believe the gateman would slam the iron portals in Vicki Baum's face.[34]

Raymond Chandler tells how the "system" tended to debilitate the author's efforts of creation, even in his own eyes:

> It makes very little difference how a writer feels towards his producer as a man; the fact that the producer can change and destroy and disregard his work can only operate to diminish that work in its conception and to make it mechanical and indifferent in execution. . . . That which is born in loneliness and from the heart cannot be defended against the judgment of a committee of sycophants. . . . There is little magic of work or emotion or situation which can remain alive after the incessant bonescraping revisions imposed on the Hollywood writer by the process of rule by decree.[35]

Monroe Stahr, Fitzgerald's otherwise sympathetic embodiment of such a Hollywood production head, Irving Thalberg, says in *The Last Tycoon*: "I never thought I had more brains than a writer has. But I always thought that his brains *belonged* to me—because I knew how to use them. Like the Romans—I've heard that they never invented things, but they knew what to do with them."[36]

A practice which the writers found particularly distasteful, invented by Thalberg, was the mass-production of scripts—the system of assigning multiple writers to work on the same screenplay, most often without each other's knowledge. Fitzgerald described how this worked in *The Last Tycoon*:

> "We have all sorts of people—disappointed poets, one-hit playwrights—college girls—we put them on an idea in pairs, and if it slows down, we put two more writers working behind them. I've had as many as three pairs working independently on the same idea."

33 Quoted in Frances Ring, "Isherwood—A Writer in Many Mediums," The Los Angeles *Times*, August 21, 1966.

34 Cram, pp. 176-177.

35 Chandler, "Writers in Hollywood," *The Atlantic Monthly*, November, 1945, p. 52.

36 Fitzgerald, *The Last Tycoon*, pp. 150-151.

"Do they like that?"

"Not if they know about it. They're not geniuses—none of them could make as much any other way."[37]

William de Mille tells the consequence of such a method:

As a result, the writer naturally lost his sense of artistic responsibility. Constantly rewriting the work of others and knowing that his own work, in turn, would be changed and changed again, he simply did the best he could and took comfort in his salary. Even today the system of multiple authorship continues, which means that in working for the screen, the author as a rule has nothing to gain but money.[38]

ALIENATION AND CONFORMITY

Almost every writer seemed to think that Hollywood work was only a *temporary* fund-raising exercise ("this was merely a stop-over on the way back to positive work"[39]), that once they made enough money back to the maple-shadowed New England farmhouse they would go and write as their own men once again.[40] Budd Schulberg has introduced this element in his novels. In *What Makes Sammy Run?* (1941) Al Manheim visits a poet acquaintance of his, now writing for the movies, who fits the pattern exactly: "he reached the final stage full of teary nostalgia for the glories of his youth and eloquent resolutions to return to New England and his Muse, 'as soon as I finish the MacDonald-Eddy script I have to do when I get back from my vacation.' "[41]

In his novel *The Harder They Fall* (1947), the debilitated Hollywood writer is reintroduced in the figure of David Stempel, a once-famous author. He is telling the narrator, Eddie Lewis: " 'All I need is jus' one good credit, an' some o' this gold. I need more gold, Eddie, and then I'll—go to Mexico, six months, maybe a year, rediscover my soul, Eddie.' "[42] This is a painful vision for Eddie: "The author of *The Locomotive Dream*, one of the bright young hopes of my generation, was employed by the studio that specialized in blood-and-thunder Westerns. For me it was almost like discovering that the writing credit on *The Lone Ranger* was Thomas Mann."[43]

The Eastern writer in Hollywood was to become the archetype of the American artist as a success—a betrayer of his talent for the cheap rewards

---

[37] *Ibid.*, p. 71.

[38] DeMille, p. 285.

[39] Schulberg, *The Disenchanted*, p. 30.

[40] Schulberg, in "Gentle Genius at Large in Jungletown," *Life*, February 28, 1969, p. 6, states that "it was the mode for eastern authors to go west for their two grand a week and then Super Chief it back to the Algonquin Round Table to exchange witticisms at the expense of the ignoramuses who had paid them 25,000 bigs to sit in their offices doing crossword puzzles."

[41] Schulberg, *What Makes Sammy Run?*, Bantam Classic edition (New York, 1961), p. 46.

[42] Schulberg, *The Harder They Fall*, Signet Book edition (New York, 1968), p. 131.

[43] *Ibid.*, p. 126.

of society. Ernest Hemingway immortalized this image in "The Snows of Kilimanjaro":

> He had destroyed his talent by not using it, by betrayals of himself and what he believed in, by drinking so much that he blunted the edge of his perceptions, by laziness, by sloth and by snobbery, by pride and by prejudice, by hook and by crook. . . . It was a talent all right but instead of using it he had traded on it.[44]

It is perhaps this concept which is the basis of Monroe Stahr's statement in *The Last Tycoon*: "We don't have good writers out here. . . . we hire them, but when they get out here they're not good writers."[45]

In a way, this hints at the deeper transformation of the struggling intellectual, pursuing his artistic goals, into the munificently paid writer in Hollywood, well-fed but creatively impotent. This intellectual crisis seemed to occur because the artist, who prior to his Hollywood employment had felt a self-righteous superiority to the materialistic values of society, was now forced to confront the same material temptations he had so easily resisted in theory. Because his material needs were now handily accommodated by his hefty studio paycheck, he found it difficult to muster the creative energy to pursue his former literary urgings. Richard Hofstadter, reviewing the entire problem of the intellectual's place in modern society, summarizes this phenomenon:

> An insistent new note has crept into the writing of the past two decades: one hears more and more that the intellectual who has won a measure of freedom and opportunity, and a new access to influence, is thereby subtly corrupted; that, having won recognition, he has lost his independence, even his identity as an intellectual. Success of a kind is sold to him at what is held to be an unbearable price. He becomes comfortable, perhaps even moderately prosperous, as he takes a position in a university or in government or working for the mass media, but he then tailors himself to the requirements of these institutions. He loses that precious tincture of rage so necessary to first-rate creativity in a writer, that capacity for negation and rebellion that is necessary to the candid social critic, that initiative and independence of aim required for distinguished work in science. It appears, then, to be the fate of intellectuals either to berate their exclusion from wealth, success, and reputation, or to be seized by guilt when they overcome this exclusion.[46]

This idea of the destructive nature of success is touched on in *The Disenchanted*:

> "Why must Hollywood always take the rap? Why didn't Bane have enough guts to stay with his plays?"

---

44 Ernest Hemingway, "The Snows of Kilimanjaro," *The Snows of Kilimanjaro and Other Stories* (New York, 1966), p. 11.

45 Fitzgerald, *The Last Tycoon*, p. 71.

46 Richard Hofstadter, *Anti-Intellectualism in American Life* (New York, 1963), p. 416.

"Temptation," Manley said. "That's writers in America. . . . Your high
mortality on writers, that goes on all the time in America. Y'know why? . . .
American idea of success. Nothing fails like success. Write one bestseller
here, one hit play, Big Success. Do one thing, get rich 'n famous. Writers get
caught up in American system. Ballyhoo. Cocktail parties. Bestseller list.
Worship of Success."[47]

Novelist James T. Farrell (*Studs Lonigan*) makes a similar point:

A large proportion of the literary talent of America is now diverted to
Hollywood. . . . Such talent, instead of returning honest work for the social
labor that made its development possible, is used up, burned out, in scenario
writing. This is a positive and incalculable social loss. And there can be little
doubt of the fact that a correlation exists between the success of this commercial culture and the loss of esthetic and moral vigor in so much contemporary writing. This must be the result when talent is fettered and sold as a
commodity, when audiences are doped, and when tastes are confused, and
even depraved.[48]

There seems to be some doubt, however, that the corruption of the artistic spirit is *necessarily and inexorably* the result of employment in a mass
culture medium, as the Eastern writers were in the Hollywood studios. Edward Shils, in his "Mass Society and Its Culture," maintains:

The mere existence of the opportunity will not seduce a man of strongly
impelled creative capacities, once he has found his direction. And if he does
accept the opportunity, are his creative talents inevitably stunted? Is there
no chance at all that they will find expression in the mass medium to which
he is drawn? The very fact that here and there in the mass media, on television and in the film, work of superior quality is to be seen, seems to be
evidence that genuine talent is not inevitably squandered once it leaves the
traditional refined media. . . . There is no reason why gifted intellectuals
should lose their powers because they write for audiences unable to comprehend their ordinary level of analysis and exposition.[49]

But the nature of creativity is such that it is defeated if anything is substituted for its goal. If an artist in expressing himself succeeds also in giving form to the inarticulate dreams or needs of many people, and is later
rewarded with a million dollars, that need not affect him if his creative
drive is strong. But if he works on something he does not believe in or respect *in order* to make a million, then he and his work deteriorate. It is the
change of goals which is important. Hortense Powdermaker, in her *Hollywood, The Dream Factory,* makes this point:

It is a very different matter for either artist or scientist deliberately to
lower his standard in order to make a lot of money. Corruption of both work
and man is inevitable, and if it extends over any length of time there is no going

47 Schulberg, *The Disenchanted,* pp. 179-180.
48 James T. Farrell, *The League of Frightened Philistines* (New York, 1945), p. 182.
49 Edward Shils, "Mass Society and Its Culture," *Daedalus,* Spring, 1960, pp. 305-
306.

back. The artist who thinks he can beat the game, stay in Hollywood and clean up his million, and then return to his own creative works, is usually fooled. There are well-known examples of writers who finally shook the dust of many years of Hollywood from their typewriters, only to turn out mediocre plays and novels which resemble far more the movie scripts on which they had made their million, than their pre-Hollywood work.[50]

The careers of a Clifford Odets, a Donald Ogden Stewart, a George Oppenheimer, a Daniel Fuchs demonstrate how unfortunately true this evaluation is. For a representative case, one has only to read Fuchs' latest novel, *West of the Rockies*, a pedestrian, unengaging portrait of the neurosis of a Hollywood starlet, to note the disparity between this and his compelling former work. His previous novels (*Summer in Williamsburg, Homage to Blenholt,* and *Low Company*) were written in the thirties and were insightful, moving accounts of Brooklyn tenement life. But from 1937 to the present he has written little except screenplays. There is little question that the long literary hiatus, made possible by Hollywood's economic security (he has explained that money was the reason he originally travelled West[51]), has dulled the skill he displayed long ago.

But if Fuchs is a classic example of the writer who "sold out,"[52] his defection benefited the American cinema. It was suggested earlier that the writer movement to Hollywood was the re-direction of talent from one field to another. The literary world suffered a loss when Fuchs abandoned his books for films—and this, some would say, is the tragedy. But those who acknowledge the films which Fuchs wrote as artistically justifiable projects can take heart in his superb contributions to *The Hard Way* (1942), *Between Two Worlds* (1944), *The Gangster* (1947) based on his own novel *Low Company, Panic in the Streets* (1950) for which he won a Screen Writers Guild nomination, and *Love Me or Leave Me* (1955) for which he won an Academy Award.

Pauline Kael contends that the cinema benefited from the impact of the Algonquin group and *New Yorker* writers who, like Fuchs, took part in the thirties and forties' Hollywood revolution. She admits that all the writers experienced Hollywood as prostitution of their talents, and though many fell in love with the movies and thus suffered from personal frustration, "they nonetheless as a group were responsible for that sustained feat of

---

[50] Hortense Powdermaker, *Hollywood, The Dream Factory* (New York, 1950), pp. 291-292.

[51] Daniel Fuchs, "Author's Preface," *Three Novels* (New York, 1961), pp. v-viii, wrote: "Promptly a barrage fell upon me, friends and strangers and well-wishers, wondering what had become of me, why I had sold out, and so on. . . . I went to Hollywood. The popular notions about the movies aren't true. It takes a good deal of energy and hard sense to write stories over an extended period of time, and it would be foolish to expect writers not to want to be paid a livelihood for what they do."

[52] See John Updike, *Bech: A Book* (New York, 1970), p. 18: "his favorite Jewish writer was the one who turned his back on his three beautiful Brooklyn novels and went into the desert to write scripts for Doris Day."

careless magic we call 'thirties comedy.' "[53] The famous passage concerning the corrupted Eastern writer, from Schulberg's *The Disenchanted*, goes this way:

> "He had two hits running on Broadway at the same time. Even Nathan liked 'em. Popular 'n satirical. Like Barry, only better. The critics kept waiting for him to write that great American play."
> "What happened to him?"
> "Hollywood."[54]

Hollywood destroyed them, but they did wonders for the movies. Kael observes that "the recurrence of the names of that group of writers, not just on rather obscure remembered films but on almost *all* the films that are generally cited as proof of the vision and style of the most highly acclaimed directors of that period, suggests that the writers—and a particular group of them, at that—may for a brief period, a little more than a decade, have given American talkies their character."[55]

It is thus a literary/cinematic dichotomy, if you will, that confronts the observer attempting to evaluate whether any damage or any good was done during that hysterical period. One questions whether to mourn the loss to traditional literature, or to rejoice at the windfall motion pictures received as a result. Moreover, as Kael records in a remarkably complete summation of the entire question, the writers were ambivalent themselves:

> They were ambivalent about Hollywood, which they savaged and satirized whenever possible. Hollywood paid them so much more money than they had ever earned before, and the movies reached so many more people than they had ever reached before, that they were contemptuous of those who hadn't made it on their scale at the same time that they hated themselves for selling out. They had gone to Hollywood as a paid vacation from their playwriting or journalism, and screenwriting became their only writing. The vacation became an extended drunken party, and while they were there in the debris of the long morning after, American letters passed them by. They were never to catch up; nor were American movies ever again to have in their midst a whole school of the richest talents of a generation.[56]

Some Passed By

Each individual author's experience in the Hollywood milieu was, of course, unique. There were varying degrees of success (financial, cinematic) and failure (literary, cinematic) usually depending upon the individual's length of stay and the extent of his artistic and philosophical assimilation into the "system." But there were at least three broad divisions of the multitude of writers who confronted, or had to come to terms with, the Hollywood phenomenon. There were (1) those who refused or else departed al-

---

53 Kael, "Raising Kane—I," p. 48.
54 Schulberg, *The Disenchanted*, p. 179.
55 Kael, "Raising Kane—I," pp. 51-52.
56 *Ibid.*, p. 60.

most immediately, (2) those who stayed and virtually stopped writing for magazine and book publishers, and (3) those who managed to do work of their own while accepting occasional jobs with Hollywood studios.

Of the many writers who had only a brief affair with the Hollywood seductress, a few experiences are illustrative, and their comments are colorful enough to broaden understanding of what it was like. For example, playwright A. E. Thomas (*What the Doctor Ordered*, 1911; *No More Ladies*, 1934) whom the New York *Times* called "the brightest wit among our writers for the stage in the second and third decades of this century," had a short and undistinguished stint in Hollywood. Mildred Cram tells of his frustration:

> A. E. Thomas came. A sheaf of stage successes to his credit. A first-rate wit. A technician. They gave him an office. They paid him every Saturday morning: such a nice, round check. But they neglected to explain the mystery . . . what is a screenplay and why. "Here is a story," they said. "A fine, successful story by a famous novelist. We own it. We paid fifty thousand dollars for it. It won't do for the screen. Re-write it."
> So he did. They said, "Thank you very much," and gave him another story, which he re-wrote, with great care and decreasing enthusiasm. No one spoke to him. No one read what he wrote. No one in the studio seemed to have the slightest interest in him, or in the mounting pages of manuscript on his desk. They gave him a third story, reminding him that it needed "treatment." Then, abruptly, recognizing the peril of his situation, he fled to the healing sanity of Rhode Island. Just in time. As Dana Burnet fled from a submarine story, all the way to France. I. A. R. Wylie. Louis Bromfield. Van Druten. P. G. Wodehouse. Locke. Dozens and dozens of others . . .[57]

James T. Farrell had a long enough exposure to Hollywood to decide that he wanted no part of it. He made reference to an uncompromised personal integrity as the reason for his lack of success there; he felt secure in his judgment of rejecting the more lucrative movie employment for the freedom of literary endeavors: "I am proud not to be rich because I gave myself and my time to creative struggle."[58] In a short story, "$1,000 A Week," Farrell dramatizes the anguish of the screenwriter and has his writer-hero take flight back East (as Farrell did) from the stultifying studio job.

Novelist Thomas Wolfe (*Look Homeward, Angel*, 1929) declined a screenwriting job offer by Irving Thalberg, even though he could have earned more in a year ($40,000) than he had made from all his books. But he later remarked that he would have been willing to sell his novels to the movies:

> I am not only willing but eager for the seducers to make their first dastardly proposal. In fact, my position in the matter is very much like that of the

---

57 Cram, p. 176.
58 Quoted in Rick Dubrow, "Studs Lonigan Writer Discusses His Works," *Hollywood Citizen News*, August 12, 1960.

Belgium virgin the night the Germans took the town: 'When do the atrocities start?'[59]

Wolfe added why he refused the studio job: "I wanted to write; I had work to do. I had writing, and still have, and I think I will always have, that I wanted to get done. It meant more to me than anything else I could do. And I think that is the reason I am a writer."[60]

Ernest Hemingway never wrote for films either—but he had some very definite advice for anyone who was interested in doing so:

> First you write it, then you get into a Stutz Bearcat and drive west. When you get to Arizona, you stop the car and throw the script out. No, you wait until they throw the money in, then you throw it out. Then you head north, south or east but for chrissakes don't go west to Hollywood.[61]

THE WESTWARD MOVEMENT

There was a much larger group of Eastern writers who, in effect, abandoned all other literary activity during many years of Hollywood employment. Some of their Hollywood work was among the best ever achieved.

Robert Benchley was the perfect example of the Eastern literary establishment figure who had begun to construct impressive writing credentials when he left New York for Hollywood. Benchley had been the managing editor of *Vanity Fair* magazine (1919-1920), drama editor of *Life* (1920-1929), and for several years drama editor of *The New Yorker*; he had written several successful humorous books, such as *Of All Things* (1921), *Love Conquers All* (1922), *Pluck and Luck* (1925); he was one of the pivotal figures on the Algonquin "Round Table." Benchley was indeed recognized as a notable humorist and respected critic. But he left the literary world for Hollywood and a job as an actor.

Benchley made no secret of the fact that his work in films was frustrating and depressing. He would have preferred to have been at his old drama desk at *The New Yorker*, but like many impecunious writers he was attracted to the money. Theodore Strauss told of this conflict which Benchley had to resolve: "Whenever he grows nostalgic about his two seats on the aisle, or pines for the old inkwell and the writer's lamp, he merely draws out his son's tuition bills and consoles himself with the thought that after all, youths don't go to college forever and maybe before he's 90 he may be writing about the theatre again."[62] This was the element of self-deception that Hollywood was only a temporary, money-raising status. Benchley himself maintained: "I got into this racket (films) against my will. And I'm still in it against my will. But some day—"[63]

59 Bob Thomas, *Variety*, January 7, 1970, p. 36.
60 *Ibid.*
61 Graham, p. 179.
62 Theodore Strauss, "Colloquy in Queens," The New York *Times*, February 9, 1941.
63 *Ibid.*

At times, Benchley exhibited a painful self-awareness of his evaporated writing career. He turned away from Robert Sherwood at a party:

'Those eyes, I can't stand those eyes looking at me.' Everyone thought he was joking, as he usually was, but he was frowning at Sherwood who had recently won another Pulitzer Prize. 'He's looking at me,' sighed Bob, 'and thinking of how he knew me when I was going to be a great writer. And now he's thinking, Look what he became!'[64]

Benchley, however, is fondly remembered for his series of humorous, well-written short subjects, including *The Treasurer's Report, The Courtship of the Newt, No News Is Good News,* and *How to Sleep,* which won an Academy Award as the best comedy short of 1935.

In 1921 Dorothy Parker, another member of the "Round Table," expressed her opinion of motion pictures in a "Hymn of Hate":

Every few minutes, there is a close-up of the star
Registering one of her three expressions.
The sub-titles offer positive proof
That there is a place where bad metaphors go when they die.
The critics agree unanimously
That the picture removes all doubt
As to whether movies should be classed among the arts,—
Removes all doubt is right. . . .
I Hate Movies:
They lower my vitality.[65]

She was speaking from a position of firm literary repute in the East, from her place as "Constant Reader" for *The New Yorker,* as authoress of books of verse, essays, and short stories: *Enough Rope* (verse, 1926), *Sunset Gun* (verse, 1928), *Laments for the Living* (stories, 1930), *Death and Taxes* (verse, 1931), and a play with Elmer Rice, *Close Harmony* (1924). But in 1929 she was in Hollywood working for the movies she openly despised. Robert Sherwood noted her change of venue: "That ruthlessly wise poetess, Dorothy Parker, was lured to the Metro-Goldwyn-Mayer studio in Hollywood for the purpose of writing dialogue for *Madame X!* If they could get him, they would doubtless turn Eugene O'Neill loose on *Rebecca of Sunnybrook Farm.*"[66]

She remained in Hollywood for twenty years. Her non-movie writing decreased, and her literary focus was diverted. Actually, she did not like to write much anyway—and this factor points out a characteristic that was applicable to so many of the other Eastern writers there at that time. They shared Parker's aversion to the real toil of authorship and were therefore quite susceptible to the allurements of a Hollywood job which seemed to be less taxing. As Pauline Kael says:

---

64 Graham, pp. 107-108.
65 Dorothy Parker, "Hymn of Hate," *Life,* July 21, 1921, p. 10.
66 Sherwood, "Renaissance in Hollywood," *The American Mercury,* April, 1929, p. 434.

In Hollywood, they sat around building on to each other's gags, covering up implausibilities and dull spots, throwing new wisecracks on top of jokes they had laughed at in New York. Screenwriting was an extension of what they used to do for fun, and now they got paid for it. They had liked to talk more than to write, and this weakness became their way of life. As far as the official literary culture was concerned, they dropped from sight.[67]

Parker herself made it clear that her years in Hollywood were not happy ones: Hollywood "was a horror to me when I was there and it's a horror to look back on. I can't imagine how I did it. When I got away from it I couldn't even refer to the place by name. 'Out there' I called it."[68] She was cynical about the writers' motives: "I want nothing from Hollywood but money and anyone who tells you that he came here for anything else or tries to make beautiful words out of it lies in his teeth."[69] She was cynical about the nature and quality of the work:

> We are not authors, we're just workers. Of course, our craft is a respectable one, just as the carpenter's craft, for instance, is respectable. You see, writing for films is just like doing crossword puzzles—except that to do crossword puzzles you have to have a certain knowledge of words.[70]

Yet a sampling of the films Parker helped write indicate that she was involved in some of the screen's most engaging work: *The Moon's Our Home* (1936), *A Star Is Born* (1937), for which she won an Academy Award nomination for best screenplay, *Trade Winds* (1938), *The Little Foxes* (1941), *Saboteur* (1942), *Smash-up—The Story of a Woman* (1947), earning her second Academy Award nomination, this for best original story. She may have hated Hollywood, but motion pictures were enriched through her efforts.

Donald Ogden Stewart was a good friend of both Robert Benchley and Dorothy Parker (Benchley was best man at his first marriage in 1926). His career pattern was nearly identical with theirs. His literary life opened quite successfully. He began by writing a series of parodies for *Vanity Fair* magazine, which he published as a book, *A Parody Outline of History* (1921). He wrote a best seller called *Proper Behavior* (1922) and in the next few years wrote a series of books which definitely established him as a popular American humorist: *Aunt Polly's Story of Mankind* (1923), *Mr. and Mrs. Haddock Abroad* (1924), *The Crazy Fool* (1925), *Mr. and Mrs. Haddock in Paris, France* (1926), *Father William* (1929), and a play, *Rebound* (1930). True to the pattern of others of his Algonquin "Round Table" colleagues, Stewart left for Hollywood, where he was so successful as a screenwriter that he produced no other literary works for 17 years. The films he wrote,

---

[67] Kael, "Raising Kane—I," p. 54.

[68] Quoted in Morton Cooper, "Parker's Pen is Ever Sharp," *Coronet*, May, 1965, p. 103.

[69] Dorothy Townsend, "The Queen of Wisecracks Marshals Her Subjects," The Los Angeles *Times*, June 18, 1962.

[70] "Are Film Writers Workers?" *Pacific Weekly*, June 29, 1936, p. 371.

however, distinguished him as one of the best and most sought-after artists in his adopted medium: *Laughter* (1930) Academy Award nomination for best original story, *Dinner At Eight* (1933), *The Prisoner of Zenda* (1937), *Holiday* (1938), *Love Affair* (1939), *The Philadelphia Story* (1940) Academy Award best screenplay, *Kitty Foyle* (1940), *That Uncertain Feeling* (1941), *Keeper of the Flame* (1942), *Life With Father* (1947).

In an article on Donald Ogden Stewart, writer Gary Carey notes that Stewart's real talent lay in adapting plays to the screen, performing as a kind of play doctor, shaping and pruning other people's work. He goes on to say that "given Stewart's early reputation as a creative writer, it is surprising that he found adaptation so fulfilling that between 1930 and 1942 he never felt the need to return to either the novel or the play as a form of personal expression."[71] Stewart seems to have denied that he was "fulfilled" by his work in Hollywood; he referred to himself as an "example of a talent that for ten years had been going to wrack and ruin amid the alabaster swimming pools of Hollywood."[72] Like the others, he was self-aware: "The horrible catch to it all is that they were ten marvelous years and I enjoyed every minute. But I hadn't become the writer I set out to be when I wrote *Aunt Polly's Story of Mankind* and went about in drunken moments whispering that it was the *Candide* of 1923. I shall spend the rest of my life making up those ten years I wasted so beautifully."[73]

Stewart had supposedly "discovered his conscience," and the vehicle which was to return him to literary prestige was a play, *How I Wonder* (1947). But the depressing result was—as in the case of Daniel Fuchs, Clifford Odets (discussed below), and others—that he was unable to revitalize the literary skills which had lain dormant since 1930. The play was a failure, receiving unfavorable critical notices. The cruelest review was by George Jean Nathan, who specialized in pointing out what he thought were examples of Hollywood's destruction of creative talent:

> Mr. Stewart has been spending the last fifteen years in Hollywood as a writer for the moving pictures. It is apparent that, like many another writer for the moving pictures in Hollywood, he has been thinking. Thinking is the favorite extra-professional exercise for such literati, particularly those who before their fall were on their way to doing creditable work . . . The cerebration, flowering, thereupon develops into the belief . . . that his dramatic rebirth must take the shape of a performance which will be so markedly oppugnant to everything in any manner even distantly associated with the screen that people will be transportedly set back on their tails by his re-divulgation of his old, real, admirable self, for years so lamentably suppressed.[74]

71 Gary Carey, "The Many Voices of Donald Ogden Stewart," *Film Comment,* Winter 1970-71, p. 77.
    Stewart himself gives a very interesting summary of his film writing experiences in "Writing for the Movies," *Focus On Film,* Winter (Nov/Dec), pp. 49-57.
72 Theodore Strauss, "Sad Tale of a Penitent Humorist," The New York *Times,* January 24, 1943.
73 *Ibid.*
74 Carey, p. 78.

ODETS AND OTHERS

When Clifford Odets exploded onto Broadway with *Waiting For Lefty* (1935) and *Awake and Sing* (1935), the description he was generally accorded was "the most promising young American playwright." Ironically, when he died almost three decades and many plays later, the description had scarcely changed. His obituary in the New York *Times* told a somber truth:

> His failure to outgrow the adjective "promising" was a constant source of chagrin to the writer. Subjected for years to much harsh criticism from many friends as a classic case of the artist who had "sold out" to Hollywood, Mr. Odets periodically rebelled against his reputation. Scarcely a year went by without a promise of a new play, a new Broadway repertory company, a new film that he would make his "personal" contribution to the artistically developing movie industry.[75]

Frequently he kept his promises—but the artistic potential everyone expected to materialize was somehow never quite fulfilled.

Whether Hollywood is to carry the major part of the blame for this lack of artistic fulfillment is hard to say, but it did intervene in 1936 when Odets left New York to write the screenplay for *The General Died at Dawn*. He unashamedly admitted that money was his original motive:

> Considering that the writer of plays is so underpaid, is there any wonder that there aren't 10 successful dramatists in the country? And if they don't come to Hollywood and settle down to making good movies and a good living they are likely to starve to death—if the critics don't kill 'em first![76]

Harold Clurman feels that for Odets at this time Hollywood was Sin. "Odets would never reach any maturity as a person until he had exercised his right to sin; and either survived or succumbed to (Hollywood's) effects."[77] But *Newsweek's* short and callous obituary did not find Odets on the survivors' list. It dismisses Odets' later career with a terse: he had "his stature stunted in Hollywood."[78]

Odets painted this image of himself through the tormented figure of Charlie Castle, an artist who sold his soul to Hollywood, in *The Big Knife* (1948). Odets speaks through the Castle personification of the rapacious Hollywood system:

> Isn't every human being a mechanism to them? Don't they slowly, inch by inch, murder everyone they use? Don't they murder the highest dreams and hopes of a whole great people with the movies they make? This whole movie thing is a murder of the people. Only we hit them on the heads, under hair —nobody sees the marks.[79]

---

[75] Obituary, The New York *Times*, August 16, 1963.
[76] Philip K. Scheuer, "Big Knife Sheathed by Clifford Odets," The Los Angeles *Times*, November 9, 1959, p. 13.
[77] Clurman, *The Fervent Years*, p. 170.
[78] Obituary, *Newsweek*, August 26, 1963.
[79] Odets, *The Big Knife* (New York, 1949), p. 135.

In an elegiac piece in the New York *Times* after Odets' death, Harold Clurman wrote:

> Most of Odets' work was a confession. He told us of his anguish at sharing those values in our civilization that he despised. He begged for protection from the contaminations against which he always raged and which he realized infected him.[80]

These comments are strikingly evocative of the image established by T. S. Eliot in "The Love Song of J. Alfred Prufrock": the sensitive, *aware* personality who experiences his own and society's corrosion but cannot escape or help.

His film work reflects a rather uneven effort. Most of the time he was a highly-paid ghost writer, acting as an uncredited rewrite man polishing other writers' scripts. The credits he did take vary from the effective *None but the Lonely Heart* (1944), which he also directed, and the bitter and witty *Sweet Smell of Success* (1957), to an entertaining potboiler such as *Humoresque* (1946), to the rather dismal *The Story on Page One* (1960), another directorial effort, and *Wild in the Country* (1961), an Elvis Presley vehicle.

But, somehow, Odets had a deeper, distinctive maturity which separated him from other writers who got side-tracked. Clurman pinpoints that quality:

> Stronger than the sound of torment that rose from his clash by night was the urgency of hope, a belief in ultimate salvation, a desperately noble affirmation of what was purest in himself and the exalted ideals of his race and his country. Here we find the source of Odets' importance. His work reflected not only his own faltering but the time and place with which he struggled.[81]

Three other careers are significant enough to be included with those who forsook their literary work for Hollywood screenwriting: Edwin Justus Mayer, Samuel Hoffenstein, and George Oppenheimer. These men are not immediately thought of by contemporary readers as authors with especially prestigious literary credentials, because they chose so early to desert their literary careers—before they had a chance to advance beyond the triumph of an initial critical success. But a review of these men's experiences creates perhaps an even heightened remorse in literary observers, because of the incredibly rapid quenching of artistic potential. It could be maintained that those writers who went to Hollywood with firmly established reputations had at least an extended period of time for the fruition of their literary abilities in the original arenas. Mayer, Hoffenstein, and Oppenheimer, however, cut themselves off so early that they represent only an echo of an incipient talent.

Edwin Justus Mayer had a brilliant Broadway success in 1924 with his play *The Firebrand*. Budd Schulberg called him the urbane playwright

---

80 Clurman, "Clifford Odets' Ideals," The New York *Times*, August 26, 1963.
81 *Ibid.*

whose sense of language "enriched the theatre."[82] Mayer never followed up his first success; he went to Hollywood instead. He became one of the best and highest-paid screenwriters, and his film credits reveal a true facility with the medium: *Desire* (1936), *Midnight* (1939), *To Be Or Not To Be* (1942) one of the most memorable screenplays in film history, and *A Royal Scandal* (1945). True to the pattern of the most unfortunate Eastern writers in Hollywood, Mayer was always planning a literary work which never materialized. His effort was to be a book about Pitt the Elder—just as Robert Benchley had plans for a book on Queen Anne—in order to maintain contact with what he considered a more serious and legitimate writing activity than screenplays. Both men died with the books in the research stage.

With his *Poems in Praise of Practically Nothing* (1928), sardonic verse of the Jazz Age, Samuel Hoffenstein created a sensation. Many predictions were made about his future as a prominent man of letters. He supposedly confirmed these opinions by another volume, *Year In, You're Out* in 1930. He was then silent until *Pencil in the Air* (1947). Hollywood occupied the intervening years. He himself felt that his Hollywood work had ruined his literary career, and he was never fulfilled during those years. Sheilah Graham remembers him as one "who always seemed unhappy."[83] Nevertheless, his film writing was noteworthy and commendable, especially: *Dr. Jekyll and Mr. Hyde* (1932) for which he won an Academy Award nomination for best adaptation, *Lydia* (1941), *Tales of Manhattan* (1942), *Flesh and Fantasy* (1943), *Laura* (1944) Academy Award nomination for best screenplay, *Cluny Brown* (1946). Hoffenstein died in 1947, and Ben Hecht gave him a suitable epitaph: "he was not meant for the roughhouse esthetics of Hollywood."[84]

Finally, George Oppenheimer, who, because of critical acclaim accorded to his 1920's comedy, *Here Today*, seemed ready to take his place as a formidable writer but actually decided to try his luck in Hollywood. Among his nearly 30 feature credits are some significant films: *Libeled Lady* (1936), *A Day at the Races* (1937), *I Love You Again* (1940), and *The War Against Mrs. Hadley* (1942), for which he won an Academy Award nomination for best original screenplay. But a life as a serious writer of his own works withered.

Oppenheimer looked back on that former writing career with nostalgia and wondered "what would have happened if, some thirty-three years ago, I had not defected to the west."[85] But once he was in Hollywood, it was difficult to break free:

> I was now convinced that . . . I might as well go back to New York and be at liberty there. I consoled myself with the thought that in New York I

---

[82] Schulberg, "Why Manley Halliday is . . ." p. 16.
[83] Graham, p. 151.
[84] Hecht, "If Hollywood is Dead or Dying as a Moviemaker, Perhaps the Following Are Some of the Reasons," *Playboy*, November, 1960, p. 139.
[85] George Oppenheimer, *The View from the Sixties* (New York, 1966), p. 93.

would be free of the grinding fear and petty tyrannies. I would become a free-lance writer, do plays, stories and books. For a moment it sounded wonderful. Then I realized that to go back would be an admission of failure. In addition I wanted Hollywood with all its rewards and its forfeits, its comfortable living and its mental discomfort. I was hooked.[86]

Later, he elaborates further on Hollywood: "Graustark is no more, its towers razed by reality. Yet, despite its fears and follies, I shall always be grateful to Hollywood. It gave me enough money to escape from it."[87] He admits, however, that nothing he has produced equalled the quality of his very early work: "None of my later projects duplicated the success of *Here Today.*"[88]

FITZGERALD AND FAULKNER

Then there were those who persisted in producing significant literature in spite of their employment at the studios. Unlike many of the others who lost the energy to write, this small group proved that independent creativity was not incompatible with Hollywood work.

William Saroyan wrote his novel, *The Human Comedy* (1943), during the heart of his Hollywood contract days. The novel was published by Harcourt-Brace in conjunction with the movie, for which Saroyan won an Academy Award for best original story. Budd Schulberg wrote *What Makes Sammy Run?* (1941) while he was a Hollywood screenwriter, before he reversed the usual process and fled East.

The most outspokenly bitter of Hollywood critics, Ben Hecht, claims that he never lost his equilibrium—even during the center of the writer influx:

> The first wave of geniuses from Broadway, London, Paris and Berlin was already on hand issuing dinner invitations (black tie), collecting weekly bags of gold and denouncing Hollywood, much as in these pages. For when we started we were all much alike. It was my misfortune to remain unchanged.[89]

Hecht wrote two famous plays, *The Front Page* (1928) and *Twentieth Century* (1933), both with Charles MacArthur; a novel, *A Jew in Love* (1930); and *A Guide for the Bedeviled* (1944) during the years he was one of the most prominent screenwriters with *Underworld* (1927) Academy Award for best original story, *Viva Villa!* (1934) Academy Award nomination for best adaptation, *The Scoundrel* (1935) Academy Award for best original story, *Wuthering Heights* (1939) Academy Award nomination for best screenplay, *Angels over Broadway* (1940) Academy Award nomination for best original screenplay, *Notorious* (1946) Academy Award nomination for best original screenplay.

Rather than being stunted by Hollywood, Lillian Hellman turned her ex-

---

[86] *Ibid.*, p. 123.
[87] *Ibid.*, p. 254.
[88] *Ibid.*, p. 255.
[89] Hecht, *Charlie*, p. 165.

cellent plays into superior motion pictures: *The Children's Hour* (1934, filmed as *These Three,* 1936, with her screenplay), *The Little Foxes* (1941) Academy Award nomination for best screenplay, *Watch on the Rhine* (1943), *The Searching Wind* (1946). She was also writing independent films such as *Dead End* (1937) and *The North Star* (1943) Academy Award nomination for best original screenplay.

Robert E. Sherwood wrote three Pulitzer Prize winning plays—*Idiot's Delight* (1935), *Abe Lincoln in Illinois* (1938), and *There Shall Be No Night* (1940)—plus a Pulitzer Prize winning biography, *Roosevelt and Hopkins* (1948), plus many other plays, throughout the years he was writing films in Hollywood. Many of his films were notable artistic achievements: *The Scarlet Pimpernel* (1935), *The Ghost Goes West* (1936), *Rebecca* (1940) Academy Award nomination for best screenplay, *The Best Years of Our Lives* (1946) Academy Award for best screenplay, *The Bishop's Wife* (1947), *Man on a Tightrope* (1953).

Because of F. Scott Fitzgerald's literary reputation, there has been a tendency to ascribe blame to Hollywood for a general lack of productivity in his later screenwriting years. In fact, when Fitzgerald ended up in Hollywood for the last period (1937-1940), his previous major work was the unsuccessful *Tender Is the Night* (1934). He was not silenced by the "system," but his readership was already unresponsive—in the late 1930's—to a man who was a clarion voice of a by-gone Jazz age. To Fitzgerald Hollywood represented a salvational rather than destructive force.

The definitive work on Fitzgerald's Hollywood years is Aaron Latham's *Crazy Sundays,* but a few comments are relevant here. Unlike his literary counterpart, Manley Halliday in *The Disenchanted,* Fitzgerald was not a film snob. He had expressed in *The Crack-Up* that "as long past as 1930, I had a hunch that the talkies would make even the best-selling novelist as archaic as silent pictures."[90] He plunged into a study of filmmaking that even included a card file of the plot lines of all the pictures he had seen.[91]

But there is little doubt his image of himself had changed. When he went to the studio to work he knew:

> I have now at least become a writer only. The man I had persistently tried
> to be became such a burden that I have "cut him loose" with as little compunc-

[90] Fitzgerald, "Handle with Care," *The Crack-Up,* edited by Edmund Wilson (New York, 1956), p. 78.

[91] Schulberg, "Old Scott: The Mask, The Myth, and the Man," *Esquire,* January, 1961, p. 98.

Joseph Scott, in "F. Scott Fitzgerald—A Taste of Hemlock," *Calendar,* The Los Angeles *Times,* December 19, 1965, writes that "Fitzgerald did not feel like a burnt out case at the start of his 1937 summer trip to Hollywood . . . Critic Maxwell Geismar has suggested that there may have been no place else in the 30s for Fitzgerald to go. 'Perhaps his only remaining deep and instinctive contact with all the myriad phases of life in the United States was with show business.' "

S. J. Perelman, a fellow screenwriter with Fitzgerald in those days, states in Graham, p. 49: "Scott's dream wasn't yet jaded. It was to write something so brilliant that it would securely establish his reputation in Hollywood."

tion as a Negro lady cuts loose a rival on Saturday night. . . . The old dream of being an entire man in the Goethe-Byron-Shaw tradition, with an opulent American touch, a sort of combination of J. P. Morgan, Topham Beauclerk, and St. Francis of Assisi, has been relegated to the junk heap of the shoulder pads worn one day on the Princeton freshman football field and the overseas cap never worn overseas.[92]

In the beginning Fitzgerald was very optimistic:

> I love it here. It's nice work if you can get it and you can get it if you try about three years. The point is once you've got it—Screen Credit 1st, a Hit 2nd, and the Academy Award 3rd—you can count on it forever . . . and know there's one place you'll be fed without being asked to even wash the dishes.[93]

The pessimism and disillusionment came with the rewriting by producer Joseph Mankiewicz of his script for *Three Comrades* (1938), which Fitzgerald considered a mutilation of an honest and delicate piece of work. He wrote Mankiewicz:

> To say I'm disillusioned is putting it mildly. For nineteen years I've written best selling entertainment, and my dialogue is supposedly right up at the top. . . . You *had* something and you have arbitrarily and carelessly torn it to pieces. . . . I am utterly miserable at seeing months of work and thought negated in one hasty week. . . . Oh, Joe, can't producers ever be wrong? I'm a good writer—honest. I thought you were going to play fair.[94]

After this set-back Fitzgerald wrote his daughter Scottie: "You don't realize that what I am doing here is the last tired effort of a man who once did something finer and better."[95] From the promise of a creative endeavor which was to regain for him a stature which was momentarily obscured, Fitzgerald's vision now focused on:

> . . . this amazing business which has a way of whizzing you along at terrific speed and then letting you wait in a dispirited, half-cocked mood when you don't feel like undertaking anything else, while it makes up its mind. It is a strange conglomeration of a few excellent overtired men making the pictures, and as dismal a crowd of fakes and hacks at the bottom as you can imagine.[96]

As for Hollywood itself, he called it "a dump . . . a hideous town, pointed up by the insulting gardens of its rich, full of the human spirit at a new low of debasement."[97]

It was during this dark period that Fitzgerald wrote the Pat Hobby stories, sardonic portraits of a broken-down script writer and a personifi-

---

92 Fitzgerald, "Pasting it Together," *The Crack-Up*, pp. 83-84.
93 Quoted in Andrew Turnbull, *Scott Fitzgerald* (New York, 1962), pp. 289-290.
94 *Ibid.*, p. 290.
95 Quoted in Arthur Mizener, *The Far Side of Paradise* (Boston, 1965), p. 312.
96 Turnbull, p. 293.
97 *Ibid.*, p. 317.

cation of what he feared he himself might become—analogous to the Charlie Castle caricature in *The Big Knife*, which was Clifford Odets' autobiographical comment. But Fitzgerald's contribution to literary history during this Hollywood period was to be accomplished through his old medium, the novel. Hollywood proved to be the source of perhaps his greatest literary achievement, *The Last Tycoon*. John Dos Passos tells of the salutary interaction between Fitzgerald and Hollywood:

> Hollywood, the subject of *The Last Tycoon*, is probably the most important and the most difficult subject for our time to deal with. Whether we like it or not it is in that great bargain sale of five- and ten-cent lusts and dreams that the new bottom level of our culture is being created. The fact that at the end of a life of brilliant worldly successes and crushing disasters Scott Fitzgerald was engaged so ably in a work of such importance proves him to have been the first-rate novelist his friends believed him to be.[98]

Budd Schulberg confirms this evaluation of Fitzgerald: "He had drawn upon Hollywood for subject matter, for technique and finally for moral insight. To learn of his struggles there, his 'Crazy Sundays,' but also his hard-working Mondays, is to reaffirm one's faith in the stamina of genius."[99]

In 1939 critic Edmund Wilson wrote that he had been worried that novelist Nathanael West had fallen victim to Hollywood. Wilson put it this way —in reaffirming West's vitality:

> Nathanael West, the author of *Miss Lonelyhearts*, went to Hollywood a few years ago, and his silence had been causing his readers alarm lest he might have faded out on the Coast as so many of his fellows have done. But Mr. West, as this new book happily proves, is still alive beyond the mountains, and quite able to set down what he feels and sees—has still, in short, remained an artist.[100]

The vehicle which had sustained West's artistry was *The Day of the Locust*, a disturbingly surrealistic vision of the marginal Hollywood of the has-beens and the would-bes. It is one of the best novels ever written about Hollywood, and it was produced from the epicenter of West's employment as studio screenwriter. He wrote enduring literature concurrently with his movie work, which he did not find an obstacle to his creativity. He did not mind the "oaters" he wrote for Republic Pictures—he could easily write lines like, "Pardner, when you say that, smile." It was "relatively painless and I can concentrate on what I want to write for myself."[101]

Thus Fitzgerald and West did some of their best literary work while writ-

---

98 Quoted in Francis Downing, "The Disenchantment of Scott Fitzgerald," *Commonweal*, November 10, 1950, p. 118.

99 Schulberg, "F. Scott the Scriptwriter," *Life*, May 7, 1971, p. 9.

100 Edmund Wilson, "The Boys in the Back Room," *Classics and Commercials* (New York, 1962), pp. 52-53.

101 Quoted in Joseph Blotner, "Faulkner in Hollywood," *Man and the Movies*, p. 301.

ing for the movies. As Carolyn See writes: "In Hollywood dreams sometimes do come true, and this was certainly another seductive aspect of the
city for those writers who may have come here to sell their souls but never
got around to it."[102]
William Faulkner is a famous example of a writer who preserved his literary effectiveness during periodic stays in Hollywood writing films. Of
course, he had no illusions about the nature of his studio work: "The way
I see it, it's like chopping cotton or picking potato bugs off plants; you
know damn well it's not painting the Sistine Chapel or winning the Kentucky Derby. But a man likes the feel of some money in his pocket."[103] And
frequently he became fed up with the diversion from his real love, his books.
He wrote once:

> I think I have had about all of Hollywood I can stand. I feel bad, de-
> pressed, dreadful sense of wasting time, I imagine most of the symptoms of
> some kind of blow-up or collapse. I may be able to come back later, but I
> think I will finish this present job and return home. Feeling as I do, I am
> actually becoming afraid to stay here much longer.[104]

But Faulkner rejects the claim that Hollywood is the evil force which
aborts a writer's creative aims:

> Nothing can injure a man's writing if he's a first-rate writer. If a man is
> not a first-rate writer, there's not anything can help it much.[105]
> I get sick of those people who say if they were free (of Hollywood) what
> they'd do. They wouldn't do anything. It's not the pictures which are at fault.
> The writer is not accustomed to money. Money goes to his head and destroys
> him—not pictures. Pictures are trying to pay for what they get. Frequently
> they overpay. But does that debase the writer?[106]

Faulkner certainly was not debased by the Hollywood money. He stayed
in Hollywood only long enough to earn subsistence for an extended period
of private writing back home in Mississippi. And his body of work during
(1932-1955) and after (1955-1962) the Hollywood years is proof that there
was no corruption of his talent. His work during that time included *Absalom, Absalom!* (1936); the Snopes trilogy: *The Hamlet* (1940), *The Town*
(1957), *The Mansion* (1959); *Go Down, Moses* (1942); *Intruder in the
Dust* (1948) and several others. These superb pieces of literature were
created along with some memorable film work, such as *To Have and Have*

102 Carolyn See, "Will Excess Spoil the Hollywood Writer," Los Angeles *Times
West Magazine*, March 26, 1967, p. 36.
    Her unpublished Ph.D. dissertation for the University of California at Los Angeles,
The Hollywood Novel: An Historical and Critical Study, is a remarkably comprehensive
survey of Hollywood in fiction.
103 Blotner, p. 294.
104 *Ibid.*, pp. 295-296.
105 "Interview of William Faulkner," *The Saturday Review*, July 28, 1962, p. 19.
106 Quoted in Stan Swinton, "Faulkner Hits Writer Alibis," *Hollywood Citizen-News*,
March 8, 1953.

Not (1945) and *The Big Sleep* (1946). Perhaps his ability to write without embarrassment or condescension for the audience of *The Saturday Evening Post* as well as for the intellectual shows a healthy lack of self-consciousness. It is hard to think of another American writer who could do so.

It is perhaps right and fitting that William Faulkner, the exemplary figure for all artists of conscience and discipline in Hollywood, should give the prescription for individuality:

> There's some people who are writers who believed they had talent, they believed in the dream of perfection, they get offers to go to Hollywood where they can make a lot of money, they begin to acquire junk swimming pools and imported cars, and they can't quit their jobs because they have got to continue to own that swimming pool and the imported cars. There are others with the same dream of perfection, the same belief that maybe they can match it, that go there and they resist the money. They don't own the swimming pools, the imported cars. They will do enough work to get what they need of the money without becoming a slave to it . . . it is going to be difficult to go completely against the grain or the current of a culture. But you can compromise without selling your individuality completely to it. You've got to compromise because it makes things easier.[107]

Faulkner's words were the secret of survival in Hollywood, and he proved by example that it was an effective formula. Accordingly, Budd Schulberg feels that Hollywood has been wrongly made a symbol of the writer's personal weaknesses:

> There were Hollywoods before Hollywood was even discovered. There were people who went there and met it on its own terms and beat it.
>
> The challenge of doing a good movie, of doing a good piece of work, isn't something to be ashamed of. The only thing to be ashamed of is to be sucked in and to let yourself be dependent on that contract and paycheck. That's when you're lost.[108]
>
> One can go to Hollywood without succumbing to Hollywood, and one who is interested in writing truly can move back from the film into the novel, where he may find another, more ranging kind of esthetic experience.[109]

A Contemporary View

The Hollywood environment which the Eastern writer faced during his heyday has, of course, faded along with many other aspects of the former

---

[107] Quoted in Blotner, p. 303.

[108] Quoted in Harvey Breit, "Talk with Mr. Schulberg," The New York *Times Book Review,* November 5, 1950, p. 28.

    Schulberg made an allied point years before in *What Makes Sammy Run?,* pp. 209-210: "The trouble with Hollywood is that too many people who won't leave are ashamed to be there. But when a moving picture is right, it socks the eye and the ear and the solar plexus all at once and that is a hell of a temptation for any writer. . . . Hollywood may be full of phonies, mediocrities, dictators and good men who have lost their way, but there is something that draws you there that you should not be ashamed of."

[109] Schulberg, "Why Write It When You Can't Sell It To the Pictures?", *The Saturday Review,* September 3, 1955, pp. 5-6.

studio set-up. Economic imperatives, which forced an end to the policy of retaining an army of writers under contract, have made the contemporary writer's context almost incomparable with the past. Unfortunately two similarities remain: the writer's work is still subject to the exigencies of budget and front office caprice; and his contribution to a film is usually overlooked, while the felicities in the script are attributed by critics to others—most often to the director.

In defense, writers have attempted various ways to preserve the integrity of their work and retain some influence over the shaping of the final film. Solutions have included becoming a producer or director in order to gain more control, and—the current most common procedure—the formation of independent units in "package" arrangements, by which producer, director, writer, and stars team up for film production.

But the modern writer, who expends his talent on scripts for which a producer reserves artistic control, still faces frustration and creative heartbreak. The end of the studio system has not guaranteed him the autonomy which he desires. Furthermore, Pauline Kael, while recognizing that critics "tend to ignore the contribution of the writers—and the directors may be almost obscenely content to omit mention of the writers," nevertheless does not harbor much hope that the writer as director or producer is an efficacious remedy:

> The Hollywood writer is becoming a ghostwriter. The writers who succeed in the struggle to protect their identity and their material by becoming writer-directors or writer-producers soon become too rich and powerful to bother doing their own writing. And they rarely have the visual sense or the training to make good movie directors.[110]

In the present time, in spite of the cataclysmic re-alignments which have enveloped Hollywood since the 1930's and 1940's, the writer still confronts a moral dilemma and financial temptation; sometimes when he starts out planning to take his place at the side of Robert Sherwood and William Faulkner, he often discovers that he has ended up between Pat Hobby and Sammy Glick.

---

[110] Kael, *Kiss Kiss Bang Bang* (Boston, 1968), p. 59.

1971

Eastern Writer Academy Award Nominations and Winners

To illustrate that many authors who had earned their reputations in essentially non-movie fields were artistically successful by film industry standards, regardless of the subsequent fate of their independent writing careers, the following is a list of those Academy nominations and awards won by Eastern writers. The listings are for the years 1927-1950, the span of time most properly applicable, very broadly considered, to the employment of the Eastern writer in Hollywood. * denotes winner. "co-" means the credit is shared.

1927-28. *The Patent Leather Kid*, First National: Rupert Hughes (Original Story). *Underworld*, Paramount: Ben Hecht (Original Story).

1929-30. *All Quiet on the Western Front*, Universal: George Abbott and Maxwell Anderson (Co-Achievement Dell Andrews).

1930-31. *Laughter*, Paramount: Donald Ogden Stewart (Co-Original Story Harry d'Abbadie d'Arrast and Douglas Dory).

1931-32. *Arrowsmith*, Goldwyn, UA: Sidney Howard (Adaptation). *Dr. Jekyll and Mr. Hyde*, Paramount: Samuel Hoffenstein (Co-Adaptation Percy Heath). *What Price Hollywood*, RKO Radio: Adela Rogers St. Johns (Original Story).

1932-33. *Lady for a Day*, Columbia: Robert Riskin (Adaptation). *State Fair*, Fox: **Paul Green (Co-Adaptation** Sonya Levien). *Rasputin and the Empress*, MGM: Charles MacArthur (Original Story).

1934. *It Happened One Night*, Columbia: Robert Riskin (Adaptation). *The Thin Man*, MGM: Frances Goodrich and Albert Hackett (Adaptation). *Viva Villa*, MGM: Ben Hecht (Adaptation).

1935. *Broadway Melody of 1936*, MGM: Moss Hart (Original Story). *The Scoundrel*, Paramount: Ben Hecht and Charles MacArthur (Original Story). *Lives of a Bengal Lancer*, Paramount: John L. Balderston (Co-Screenplay Achmed Abdullah, Grover Jones, William Slavens McNutt, and Waldemar Young).

1936. *After the Thin Man*, MGM: Frances Goodrich and Albert Hackett (Screenplay). *Dodsworth*, Goldwyn-UA: Sidney Howard (Screenplay). *Mr. Deeds Goes to Town*, Columbia: Robert Riskin (Screenplay). *My Man Godfrey*, Universal: Morrie Ryskind (Co-Screenplay Robert Riskin).

1937. *In Old Chicago*, 20th Century-Fox: Niven Busch (Original Story). *A Star Is Born*, Selznick-UA: Robert Carson (Co-Original Story William A. Wellman). *Captains Courageous*, MGM: Marc Connelly (Co-Screenplay John Lee Mahin, and Dale Van Every). *Stage Door*, RKO Radio: Morrie Ryskind (Co-Screenplay Anthony Veiller). *A Star Is Born*, Selznick-UA: Robert Carson and Dorothy Parker (Co-Screenplay Alan Campbell).

1938. *Blockade*, Wanger-UA: John Howard Lawson (Original Story). *You Can't Take It With You*, Columbia: Robert Riskin (Screenplay).

1939. *Love Affair*, RKO Radio: Mildred Cram (Co-Original Story Leo McCarey). *Gone with the Wind*, Selznick-MGM: Sidney Howard (Screenplay). *Ninotchka*, MGM: Charles Brackett (Co-Screenplay Walter Reisch and Billy Wilder). *Wuthering Heights*, Goldwyn-UA: Ben Hecht and Charles MacArthur (Co-Screenplay).

1940. *My Favorite Wife*, RKO Radio: Bella Spewack and Samuel Spewack (Co-Original Story Leo McCarey). *Angels over Broadway*, Columbia: Ben Hecht (Original Screenplay). *The Great McGinty*, Paramount: Preston Sturges (Original Screenplay). *The Grapes of Wrath*, 20th Century-Fox: Nunnally Johnson (Screenplay). *Kitty Foyle*, RKO Radio: Dalton Trumbo (Screenplay). *The*

Philadelphia Story, MGM: Donald Ogden Stewart (Screenplay). *Rebecca,* Selznick-UA: Robert E. Sherwood (Co-Screenplay Joan Harrison).

1941. *Meet John Doe,* Warner Brothers: Richard Connell (Co-Original Story Robert Presnell). *Citizen Kane,* Mercury-RKO-Radio: Herman J. Mankiewicz (Co-Original Screenplay Orson Welles). *Hold Back the Dawn,* Paramount: Charles Brackett (Co-Screenplay Billy Wilder). *The Little Foxes,* Goldwyn-RKO-Radio: Lillian Hellman (Screenplay).

1942. *The Pride of the Yankees,* Goldwyn-RKO-Radio: Paul Gallico (Original Story). *Wake Island,* Paramount: W. R. Burnett (Co-Original Screenplay Frank Butler). *The War Against Mrs. Hadley,* MGM: George Oppenheimer (Original Screenplay). *Mrs. Miniver,* MGM: James Hilton (Co-Screenplay George Froeschel, Claudine West, and Arthur Wimperis). *The Pride of the Yankees,* Goldwyn-RKO-Radio: Herman J. Mankiewicz and Jo Swerling (Screenplay). *The Talk of the Town,* Columbia: Irwin Shaw (Co-Screenplay Sidney Buchman).

1943. *Action in the North Atlantic,* Warner: Guy Gilpatric (Original Story). *The Human Comedy,* MGM: William Saroyan (Original Story). *The North Star,* Goldwyn-RKO-Radio: Lillian Hellman (Original Screenplay). *Holy Matrimony,* 20th Century-Fox: Nunnally Johnson (Screenplay). *Watch on the Rhine,* Warner: Dashiell Hammett (Screenplay).

1944. *Lifeboat,* 20th Century-Fox: John Steinbeck (Original Story). *Hail the Conquering Hero,* Paramount: Preston Sturges (Original Screenplay). *The Miracle of Morgan's Creek,* Paramount: Preston Sturges (Original Screenplay). *Two Girls and a Sailor,* MGM: Richard Connell (Co-Original Screenplay Gladys Lehman). *Double Indemnity,* Paramount: Raymond Chandler (Co-Screenplay Billy Wilder). *Gaslight,* MGM: John L. Balderston (Co-Screenplay Walter Reisch and John Van Druten). *Laura,* 20th Century-Fox: Samuel Hoffenstein (Co-Screenplay Jay Dratler and Betty Reinhardt). *Meet Me in St. Louis,* MGM: Fred F. Finkelhoffe (Co-Screenplay Irving Brecher).

1945. *A Medal for Benny,* Paramount: John Steinbeck (Co-Original Story Jack Warner). *The Lost Weekend,* Paramount: Charles Brackett (Co-Screenplay Billy Wilder). *Pride of the Marines,* Warner: Albert Maltz (Screenplay).

1946. *The Strange Love of Martha Ivers,* Wallis-Paramount: John Patrick (Original Story). *To Each His Own,* Paramount: Charles Brackett (Original Story). *The Blue Dahlia,* Paramount: Raymond Chandler (Original Screenplay). *Notorious,* RKO-Radio: Ben Hecht (Original Screenplay). *Anna and the King of Siam,* 20th Century-Fox: Sally Benson (Co-Screenplay Talbot Jennings). *The Best Years of Our Lives,* Goldwyn-RKO-Radio: Robert E. Sherwood (Screenplay).

1947. *Smash-Up—The Story of a Woman,* Wanger-U-I: Dorothy Parker (Original Story Frank Cavett). *A Double Life,* Kanin-U-I: Garson Kanin (Co-Original Screenplay Ruth Gordon). *Gentleman's Agreement,* 20th Century-Fox: Moss Hart (Screenplay).

1948. *A Foreign Affair,* Paramount: Charles Brackett (Co-Screenplay Billy Wilder, and Richard L. Breen). *The Snake Pit,* 20th Century-Fox: Millen Brand and Frank Patros (Co-Screenplay).

1949. *Come to the Stable,* 20th Century-Fox: Clare Booth Luce (Motion Picture Story).

1950. *Father of the Bride,* MGM: Frances Goodrich and Albert Hackett (Screenplay). *Adam's Rib,* MGM: Garson Kanin (Co-Story and Screenplay Ruth Gordon). *Sunset Boulevard,* Paramount; Charles Brackett (Co-Story and Screenplay Billy Wilder and D. M. Marshman, Jr.).

A Quantitative View of Soviet Cinema

Steven P. Hill

The history of Soviet cinema has been extensively described in English-language books and articles on the subject by Babitsky and Rimberg, Dickinson and de la Roche, Leyda, Macdonald, and others.[1] These writers have concentrated on the qualitative history of motion pictures in the USSR, describing the work of specific major film-makers and the characteristics of specific major films, studios, and administrative policies. If these studies have any limitation, it is on the quantitative side—a meager and scattered presentation of statistical information on overall film production in the Soviet Union year by year.

Such a limitation is quite understandable, because Soviet administrators and economists for many years did not make a habit of releasing detailed statistical data on production achievements or failures. Indeed, many Soviet economic studies published in the Stalin period deliberately neglected factual evidence in favor of theoretical quotations cited and interpreted from the scriptures of Marx, Lenin, and Stalin—a practice sometimes referred to as "quotationism."

The noted Russian historian of early Soviet cinema, Lebedev, makes this kind of scattered reference to quantity of production, mentioning in one place "if in 1922 the number of released features and semi-features did not surpass nine titles, then in 1924 it rises to forty-two," and in another place "the release of fictional, live-actor films [in] the 1924/25 fiscal year [was] 70 [and in] 1930 [was] around 120 films."[2] Some of Lebedev's figures, despite their approximate and apparently non-comparable nature (calendar vs. fiscal year, all genres vs. only fictional, etc.), have been taken over directly by Babitsky and Rimberg (see pp. 69, 245). And when Babitsky and Rimberg quote various sources' production statistics for the 1930s, they do so with a necessary reservation: "At the end of the Second [Five-Year] Plan the decline in production was matched by a decline in the publication of

---

[1] Paul V. Babitsky and John Rimberg, *Soviet Film Industry* (Praeger: New York, 1955); Thorold Dickinson and Catherine de la Roche, *Soviet Cinema* (Falcon Press: London, 1948); Jay Leyda, *Kino* (Macmillan: New York, 1960); Dwight Macdonald, "Soviet Cinema, 1930-38," *Partisan Review,* July, August, 1938; Winter, 1939.

[2] Nikolai Lebedev, *Ocherk istorii kino SSSR,* 2nd ed. (Iskusstvo: Moscow, 1965), pp. 152, 270.

production statistics. In 1937 apparently only 25 full-length features were completed of the 123 that had been scheduled for release by Soviet planners" (p. 240).

This quotation gives a good idea of the situation encountered by earlier historians, who were often able to cite only approximate, incomplete, and heterogeneous data.[3] But the situation has changed since the recent appearance of a new source of information. This is the four-volume "copyright catalog," *Sovetskie khudozhestyennye fil'my* (henceforth *SKF*),[4] which, although containing no statistics, does furnish detailed credits and annotations for "each" Soviet fictional (literally, "artistic") film released from 1918 through 1963. Using this source it is possible to analyze production and distribution for any given year or period of years (the films are grouped in the catalog by year of production, and the release date is also indicated). The present article will concentrate on the early period from the Revolution to World War Two (1918-40), when Soviet cinema was making great artistic and social strides, as well as undergoing the slow and difficult transition to sound. This also seems to be the period which, for a variety of reasons, has been least documented by systematic statistical data.

For the inter-war period, 1918-40, the *SKF* catalog registers nearly 1,600 titles (they are numbered serially, from 1 to 1,590). The author checked all of these and tabulated (see below) the number of features produced and the number released in each calendar year. Since a film's year of production and year of release do not always coincide, the two are given separately. The ratio of silent to sound films is also noted. The data covers only *fiction features produced and released in the Soviet Union;* it thus excludes documentary and educational films, films less than five reels (50-70 minutes) in length, imported films, and unreleased (banned) films.

Unreleased or banned films could not be included, because the *SKF* catalog registers only films actually released in the USSR. Hence the omission of several pictures over the years, the most notable of which are Dzigan's *First Cavalry* (adapted from Vishnevsky), Eggert's *Harbor of Storms* (Balzac), Eisenstein's *Bezhin Meadow* (Turgenev-Rzheshevsky), Kalatozov's

---

3 Reference should also be made to a relatively rare Soviet data source, dating from 1940, which was evidently not noted by some previous historians. This anonymous graph of production statistics ("Sovetskoe kino v tsifrakh," inserted after p. 80, *Iskusstvo kino,* No. 1, 1940) can be compared with some findings of the present article above, since it deals with sound fiction features released in certain years: 5 in 1931, 16 in 1932, 20 in 1933, 27 in 1934, 21 in 1935, 49 in 1936, 45 in 1937, 41 in 1938, and 52 in 1939. Although these figures are usually close to those of the present compilation, they coincide in only one year (1932); the greatest discrepancy is for 1936 (49 vs. only 31 according to the present compilation). Overall the Soviet graph indicates 276 sound fiction features released from 1931 through 1939, as compared with 245 in the present compilation—a difference of about 13 percent. This would not be too much of a surprise, considering that many branches of many film (and other) industries make a common practice of "puffing up" their own production and attendance figures.

4 Edited by A. V. Macheret, N. A. Glagoleva, and others (Iskusstvo: Moscow, 1961-68). This is the same valuable new reference book used by Jay Leyda in his article "Between Explosions" (*Film Quarterly,* summer, 1970, pp. 33-38).

Nail in the Boot, Kavaleridze's *Prometheus* (Shevchenko), Obolensky and Kuleshov's *Theft of Sight,* Preobrazhenskaya's *Only Joy,* Room's *Strict Young Man* (Olesha), and Yutkevich's *Light Over Russia* (Pogodin). Nonetheless, the statistics of the present article are consistent and thus comparable from year to year, in that they always represent only films which were shown publicly. The data would need to be increased by some factor (3%, 5%?) to gain an estimate of the total films created in a given year. Compare one extreme case cited by Babitsky and Rimberg (p. 88): of the 135 films allegedly produced in 1927/28, 13 were banned—in other words, almost 10% of that fiscal year's production would not be registered in the *SKF* catalog (unless, of course, some of them were released after all, in a later year—the history of Soviet cinema has known several such cases).

Question marks in the table indicate very fragmentary data for 1918-21, when the chaos of the Revolution and Civil War all but precluded film production, except for some newsreels, short "agitation" films, and features produced by private entrepreneurs (particularly in the territory not yet under Soviet control.)[5] Those Soviet films which were made have for the most part not been preserved, and contemporary documentation on them is meager.

Beginning with 1922, the year in which celluloid became available again and reconstructed Soviet studios began to produce fiction features in a somewhat organized way, there was a steady annual increase in film-making throughout the 1920s (see table). The seven Soviet features released in 1922 were entitled *Trio* (directed by Narokov, Moscow), *In the Revolution's Whirlwind* (Chargonin, Moscow), *The Exile* (Barsky, Georgia), *Thou Fate, Russian Woman's Fate* (Svetlov, Petrograd), and *There is No Happiness on Earth, Father Serafin,* and *Sorrow without End* (all three by Pantaleyev, Petrograd). The growth pattern reached its peak in 1928, when 112 features were produced and 109 released, setting a Soviet record which was not to be equalled or surpassed until the 1960s.

The middle 1920s were a boom period for Soviet cinema. Operating under the limited free enterprise allowed by Lenin's New Economic Policy (1921-27), shrewd studio executives like Moses Aleinikov at Mezhrabpom-Russ, Boris Mikhin and Ilia Trainin at Sovkino's First Studio (formerly the Hanzhonkov Studio), and Pavlo Nechesa at VUFKU (the Ukranian studio) concentrated their resources on turning out entertainment for the mass audience. Such a policy was quite logical at this time, since the studios were responsible for financing themselves from box office receipts. Close government control and sponsorship was to come later.

EARLY COMEDIES AND CO-PRODUCTIONS

Mezhrabpom-Russ became known as the number one commercial studio,

---

[5] The appendix to the *SKF* catalog (vol. 3, pp. 249-306) registers 352 fiction films (of all lengths) privately produced in 1918-21. This surprisingly large "unknown land" of Russian cinema had remained almost untouched by historians until Leyda began to study them in his article cited above.

PRE-WAR SOVIET FEATURE FILMS

Year	Productions			Pct. Sound	Releases			Pct. Sound
	Silent	Sound	Total		Silent	Sound	Total	
1918-21	16?	0	16?	0.0%	13?	0	13?	0.0%
1922	9	0	9	0.0	7	0	7	0.0
1923	20	0	20	0.0	13	0	13	0.0
1924	37	0	37	0.0	38	0	38	0.0
1925	58	0	58	0.0	62	0	62	0.0
1926	89	0	89	0.0	70	0	70	0.0
1927	104	0	104	0.0	89	0	89	0.0
1928	112	0	112	0.0	109	0	109	0.0
1929	80	0	80	0.0	106	0	106	0.0
1930	108	3	111	2.7	91	3	94	3.2
1931	71	7	78	9.0	77	6	83	7.2
1932	45	18	63	28.6	54	16	70	22.9
1933	15	14	29	48.3	27	15	42	35.7
1934	27	27	54	50.0	24	21	45	46.7
1935	7	30	37	81.1	16	29	45	64.4
1936	0	43	43	100.0	2	31	33	93.9
1937	0	35	35	100.0	0	42	42	100.0
1938	0	38	38	100.0	0	42	42	100.0
1939	0	54	54	100.0	0	43	43	100.0
1940	0	40	40	100.0	0	47	47	100.0
Subtotals by periods:								
1918-29	525	0	525	0.0%	507	0	507	0.0%
1930-35	273	99	372	26.6	289	90	379	23.7
1936-40	0	210	210	100.0	2	205	207	99.0
Totals	798	309	1107	27.9%	798	295	1093	27.0%

with outstanding comedies like *The Three Million Case* (by Jacob Protazanov, the best "popular" director, a kind of Russian George Cukor) and *The Doll with Millions* (Serge Komarov), science-fiction (Protazanov's *Aelita*), adventure serials (Theodore Otsep's *Miss Mend*), even sex, sadism, and horror (Constantine Eggert's *The Bear's Wedding* and *The Lame Nobleman*). Mezhrabpom-Russ featured the first major Soviet "star," Igor Ilyinsky (the Russian Robert Morley), whose name alone brought in large audiences— and still does today, in revivals of his silent comedies with added soundtracks. Money was the name of the game in scripting as well as casting: several scenarios capitalized on the theme of getting rich quick, through winning a lottery, finding a missing inheritance, and the like (*Doll with Millions*, Boris Barnet's *Girl with the Hatbox*, Protazanov's *Tailor from Torzhok*, etc.). This type of escapism evidently reflected the hopes of many

Soviet movie-goers in those days before the final elimination of free enterprise in Stalin's Five Year Plans (1928 and after).

Nor had the Stalinist "Iron Curtain" yet fallen in the middle 1920s, and many Western films were imported into the USSR. Charlie Chaplin and Douglas Fairbanks, Sr. (as well as his German counterpart, Harry Piel) outsold domestic productions in Soviet theaters. Western influences in filmmaking were very discernible, dating back to 1923 when Ivan Perestiani's *Red Imps* transferred James Fenimore Cooper to the Russian Civil War setting and became the first box office hit produced within the USSR. Working in Soviet Georgia with its "exotic" tradition, Perestiani went on to make a whole series of romanticized melodramas like *The Case of Tariel Mklavadzeh* (1926). Lev Kuleshov made many of his early films with American or Western characters, settings, and plots. Two of them, *Mr. West* and *The Merry Canary*, featured Vsevolod Pudovkin. Kuleshov eventually lost favor with the studios when he refused to cast glamorous leading ladies instead of his plain wife Alexandra Hokhlova (the Russian Zasu Pitts).

When Fairbanks and Mary Pickford visited the USSR in mid-1926 (having already discovered *Battleship Potemkin* in Berlin), Kuleshov's student Komarov scored a casting coup by making an Ilyinsky comedy with Pickford in a guest appearance (*The Kiss of Mary Pickford*, 1927). Less well known, perhaps, is that during their visit Pickford and Fairbanks also attended a Mezhrabpom screening of the Gothic chiller *Bear's Wedding*—on which they bestowed the same high praise as they did on *Battleship Potemkin*. Mezhrabpom-Russ extended the foreign influence by setting up two coproductions with Germany, Gregory Roshal's *The Salamander* (1928, with Bernhard Goetzke and Natalie Rozenel) and Otsep's *Living Corpse* (1929, with Pudovkin and Marie Jacobini).

Sovinko (formerly Goskino), the government-sponsored complex of studios under the overall charge of Constantine Shvedchikov, tended a bit less toward commercialism than did Mezhrabpom. It was at Goskino that young "highbrow" film-makers like Serge Eisenstein began their careers, developing a style of what we now call "prop-art" (propaganda for the artist's sake, a combination of "formalism" and "agitation"). But even Eisenstein acknowledged the commercial trend of the time. At the first studio discussion of *Battleship Potemkin*, when the young director was criticized for abandoning his "pure" style of *Strike* (a "Brechtian" film made for the intellectual elite, Eisenstein offered to compromise:

> "I think . . . it is more important for the thing [*Potemkin*] to get across and make an impression. In the final analysis there would not be a repetition of what happened with *Strike*—despite the fact that it was praised at first, it is doing poorly in theaters. Further on I will learn to adjust myself to the demands of the audience" (*Bronenosets Potemkin* [Moscow, 1969], p. 205).

The first downturn came in 1929, when the number of feature productions fell by 29%, from 112 to 80. This drop-off was less perceptible in releases: more than forty 1928 productions were not shown until 1929, smoothing out the pattern of films released (this was also true in some other years —see table). The 1929 downturn signaled the start of an erratic production graph which was to plague the USSR's film industry for the next quarter of a century, hindered as it was by the conversion from imported to domestic equipment and celluloid during the industrialization drive (begun in 1928), the intensified censorship and political purges which crippled the arts at various times (especially the late 1930s), the destruction and dislocation of World War Two, and the Stalinist standstill in the arts for nearly a decade after the war.

The year 1929 was also significant in another respect: it was the last year of completely silent cinema in the USSR. About three years behind Hollywood, the Soviet Union began making sound features in 1930, when it released three variety films called *Sound Collected Program No. 1, No. 2,* and *No. 3* (directed by Room, Ekk, and others at two Moscow studios, Mosfilm and Mezhrabpomfilm). There were six more sound features produced and released in 1931, in the following order: *Road to Life* (Ekk, Mezhrabpomfilm), *Golden Mountains* (Yutkevich, Leningrad), *Alongside Us* (Bravko, Mosfilm), *Mechanical Traitor* (Dmitriev, Mezhrabpomfilm), *Alone* (Kozintsev and Trauberg, Leningrad), and *Tommy* (Protazanov, Mezhrabpomfilm).

Whereas America had practically completed the transition to sound by this time (so that 1930 can be conveniently regarded as the start of the all-sound era in America), the Soviet Union was to experience a considerably longer transition period, stretching over the years 1930-36. During this time the number and proportion of sound features increased relatively slowly from year to year (see table), reaching half of the total output only in 1934. The following year might in fact be regarded as the first full-fledged year of the sound era in the USSR, since 1935 was the first in which the *majority* of Soviet features were "talkies" (81% of all productions, 64% of all releases).

SOUND AND SOCIALIST REALISM

It is interesting that this periodization of Soviet cinema based on the technical criterion of silent *vs.* sound happens to coincide closely with the often-mentioned periodization according to "cultural politics." Thus, the starting point for the purges and artistic repressions carried out by Stalin's administrators was the assassination of Kirov in December, 1934; and the recognition of "socialist realism" as the obligatory method for Soviet cinema occurred at the January, 1935, Conference of Film Workers. And so by both technical and political criteria, 1934 can be regarded as the end of one epoch in Soviet cinema, and 1935 as the beginning of another.

The last year in which silent features were produced was 1935. Of these last seven productions, five were released the same year: *Beyond the River* (Berishvili, Georgia), *Laurels of Miss Ellen Grey* (Zheliabuzhsky, Yalta), *Ball and Heart* (Yurtsev, Mosfilm), *Seven Hearts* (Tikhonov, Turkmenistan), and *I Will Return* (Ledashchev, Turkmenistan). The remaining two were thus the last Soviet silent films: *Jigit* (Ganiev, Uzbekistan) was released May 7, 1936, and *Game of Love* (Sharif-zade, Azerbaijan) May 19, 1936. As could be expected, the regional studios made the transition to sound more slowly than did the central ones in Moscow and Leningrad: six of the final seven silent features were regional productions.

The growth rate of Soviet sound films starting from scratch in the 1930s proved to be much less rapid than the rate of silent films had been a decade earlier (starting from about the same level). The increasing percentage weight of sound films was achieved not so much by the yearly increase in their absolute number as by the decrease in the number of silent films. This can be seen by comparing the last year of all-silent cinema (1929) with the first year of all-sound cinema (1936 or 1937). There was an increase of 43 in the number of sound productions between 1929 and 1936, but a decrease of 80 in the number of silent productions; likewise, there was an increase of 42 in the number of sound releases between 1929 and 1937, but a decrease of 106 in the number of silent releases. Thus total Soviet film output during the slow transition to sound dropped to half of what it had been at the end of the all-silent era. This low level, an average of slightly over forty features annually, was then maintained in the last few years before the war.

It is interesting to note the relationship between production and release of films during the conversion period. Almost all of the early sound features were released immediately after production (i.e., in the same year), as can be seen from the table: 3 of 3 in 1930, 6 of 7 in 1931, etc. This shows the influence of market factors: sound film, being in demand, were put into theaters as soon as they were ready. Contrast this with the supply and demand of the late silent films: a substantial part of those produced in 1930 (34 of 108) was not immediately released—partly in order to make room for 18 silent films carried over unreleased from 1929. This same overlapping pattern was repeated in every following year in a drawn-out attempt at "inventory clearance" of the more and more outdated silent films.

The totals at the bottom of the table are also of interest. We see that over 1,100 features in all were produced and released by the Soviet Union before World War Two, an average of slightly more than 48 per year. Of the total, about 800 were silent and about 300 sound; the proportion of sound productions was nearly 28% of the total. The totals show a discrepancy between the total number of productions (1,107) and the total number of releases (1,093); this is explained by the delayed release of 14 films produced in 1940—12 were released in 1941, 1 in 1943, and 1 as late as 1959 (*The Old Jockey* by Barnet at Mosfilm).

Comparing the total number of Soviet fiction films of *all lengths* produced in the pre-war period (1,590 according to the *SKF* catalog) with the number of *feature-length* fiction films extracted by the present study (1,107), we see that about seven-tenths (69.6%) of all pre-war Soviet fiction films were of feature length (defined as five or more reels). This ratio, extracted from the data for 1918-40, might be useful in making preliminary estimates of features produced in more recent periods.

As an example, the last serially-numbered film in the latest volume (1958-63) of the *SKF* catalog is No. 3,413; thus we can subtract the pre-war total of 1,590 from it, obtaining 1,823 as the total number of fiction films of all lengths which have been produced in the years 1941-63. Applying the same 70% ratio, we could make a rough estimate that 1,250-1,300 Soviet features have been produced in that time span.

The wartime and postwar years under Stalin saw production drop to a fantastic low of 10 features produced and 10 released in 1951; and the modern era under Khrushchev and Brezhnev-Kosygin saw production rise rapidly once again until it attained the now stable figure of about 120 features annually by the mid-1960s.[6]

---

[6] In recent years more information about film production has been made available through yearbooks. The latest of these, which has been appearing annually since 1964, is called *Ekran 64, Ekran 65,* etc. A previous series was published under the title *Ezhegodnik kino* between 1955 and 1961.

Although a systematic analysis of this and other modern trends does not enter into the scope of the present article, it does offer promise as the subject for a separate study.

1972

Japanese Swordfighters
and American Gunfighters

J. L. Anderson

Like so many Japanese critical terms, *gendai-geki* and *jidai-geki* are simultaneously precise and loose categorizations for the two major mega-genres of Japanese films. *Gendai-geki* generally refers to motion pictures which have a setting contemporaneous with the time of filming. *Jidai-geki* is not the Japanese equivalent of such general English language terms as historical drama, costume drama, or period drama. It primarily refers to films set in the latter part of the Tokugawa era, from the early 1600's to 1867. Stories with earlier historical settings are also *jidai-geki* but these are rare. The proper period of the *jidai-geki* ends with the beginning of the Meiji Restoration in 1868.

Jidai-geki plots usually center on swordsmen of fictional, legendary, or actual historical origin. These same heroes often appear in the popular printed fiction of the Tokugawa and Meiji periods. This kind of adventure story still has many readers in Japan.

In addition to these literary sources, *naniwabushi, kodan,* and other kinds of oral narrative transmitted by individual storytellers are other major *jidai-geki* sources. Unlike the Kabuki theater which moved from its popular origins to become an aesthetic entertainment, these balladmongers today remain common entertainers without any aura of fine culture. Kabuki furnishes almost no film stories but many of its plot elements reoccur in *jidai-geki*. These same plot elements are equally common to traditional ballads, popular fiction, and *Shinkokugeki* (New National Drama) which took heroic tales set in the late feudal era and staged them with representational realistic techniques borrowed from *Shimpa* and *Shingeki*. *Shinkokugeki* did not try to rework Kabuki plays into its realistic style. Instead its playwrights fashioned their scripts from the more violent stories of the oral narrative traditions. The emphasis was on maximum melodramatic thrills. The highlights of *Shinkokugeki* performances are elaborate athletic swordfights that exploit all possible gory variations in a manner that suggests berserk Grand Guignol.

In contrast, Kabuki swordfights—not nearly as numerous as those of *Shinkokugeki*—are a form of dance called *tachimawari*. In classic *tachima-*

wari, the hero may brandish a sword but his opponents are armed symbolically with sticks, flowering branches, or umbrellas. Their actions are only graceful hints of the "real" thing. There is no physical contact between fighters because the presentational Kabuki style demands that each actor maintain his own integral theatrical space. When "hit," a victim does a flip in the air and walks off stage. If the hero is supposed to be fighting a large gang, a "dead" opponent will immediately re-enter and fight again. The fight ends in a tableau not unlike a movie freeze-frame.

While indigenous literature and drama give narrative elements and some staging techniques to the *jidai-geki,* much of its essential form derives from the international cinema, particularly the American Western. The people of Japan have always liked Westerns.

In the late 1910's and early 1920's, the Japanese especially favored William S. Hart. Hart's sentimental realism appealed to the Japanese more than the flashier optimism of Tom Mix or the epic heroes of *The Covered Wagon.* Like a traditional Japanese swordsman, Hart was often an outcast caught up in his own troubles rather than an avenger seeking to help others. His films had an oppressive, enclosed-world quality that was at variance with the expansive postcard landscapes of other Westerns. Often Hart's films projected a *déjà vu* that was a direct equivalent to a swordsman's realization that times were also passing him by. Hart's ruthless skill with a weapon and his fits of violence crossed with anger were closer to the behavior of traditional Japanese heroes than Mix's horsemanship, fist fights, stunts, and Sunday-school morality.[1]

In the history of the Japanese film, the *jidai-geki* occupies a similar but larger place than the Western does in the American film. It has long been a staple commercial item; it is a uniquely national film genre that has reinforced a national myth; it has dramatized the nation's fundamentalist code of ethics as nostalgic allegory; it has inspired some of the greatest motion picture achievements of the country and has also been a major source of trash; it has been a means to exploit vicarious bloodletting; and its basic structure is an Augustan exercise which refines a few basic elements within limited narrative and stylistic parameters.

As the shoot-out and saloon fight create the dramatic highlights of the Western, the *jidai-geki* has its equivalent in *chambara,* the violent, realistic swordfighting scenes derived from *Shinkokugeki.* As *chambara* is the hallmark of *jidai-geki,* the defining quality of *chambara* is explicit violence.

---

1 My conclusion here stems from the fact that Hart was a major box office attraction in Japan and his best pictures arrived, somewhat delayed, around 1920. The causal connections proposed here have only the proof of simple logic and not of decisive, direct evidence.

Protagonists and Conflicts

The *jidai-geki* usually focuses on a man with a sword. Traditionally, there are three major types of sword heroes whose differentiation, in part, reflects feudal social structure. First are the *samurai*, those exalted warriors whose code of *bushido* represents standards to which swordsmen of all kinds may aspire. But as *jidai-geki* are primarily tales of dislocation, the *samurai* in films are seldom part of the established order. Most of them have lost the lords to whom they owed hereditary allegiance. Many have become *ronin*—masterless *samurai*. Impoverished and denied their ancestral place in the world, these warrior outcasts wander from place to place, seeking refuge, employment, or revenge.

A second variety of swordsman is the *kyokaku* or sword-carrying commoner. These are men who have no hereditary right to carry swords but somehow, through purchase or usurpation, they have acquired weapons and the skill to use them. To a *kyokaku*, the sword is a means to the stature and power denied him by birth. Often chivalrous *kyokaku* are identified as defenders of their helpless fellow commoners.

The third and lowest group of swordsmen are *yakuza* who are professional gamblers engaged in all kinds of illicit enterprises. Their survival in a treacherous underworld depends on their sword power. The *yakuza* is less of a loner than the *ronin* or *kyokaku*. He is typically the leader or a member of a gang which is organized along the strict lines of their legal superiors: the feudal lord and his *samurai*. Like the *kyokaku*, the *yakuza* occasionally rises to the challenge of fighting for the meek.

The core conflict in many European and American narrative forms is essentially moralistic and partially allegorical: good vs. bad. The good may be totally manifest in the protagonist and in his associates as they forcibly confront those who represent evil. In its most primitive manifestation we get the black hats against the white hats; those who kick dogs against those who pet them. The good-bad confrontation may also be internal. In its most simple aspect, we see the black and white sides of a "rounded" character as good and bad inclinations fight it out inside one person. By the end of these stereotyped stories, morality has made its play. The good and bad receive their just rewards which are often directly proportional to their goodness and badness. When the good do not get sufficient reward or when it becomes evident that they will not inherit the earth, we sometimes think we have a tragedy.

In much Japanese fiction and particularly in *jidai-geki*, the essential conflict has a different dialectic: the confrontation between *giri* and *ninjo*. *Giri* refers to duty or obligation; *ninjo* to feeling or personal inclination. In simplistic psychoanalytical terms, *giri* might relate to the superego which moderates *ninjo*, instinct. The basic conflict in traditional *jidai-*

geki usually arises because the protagonist faces (or faced) a complicating choice between what he is obliged to do and what he would like to do. The major plot of *Ronin-gai* (*The Street of Ronin;* Masahiro Makino, 1929),[2] has the hungry hero picked up and kept by a woman pickpocket who loves him. The feeling is not mutual. He sees her only as a means to stay alive until his luck changes. After several weeks, he is about to run away without repayment when he learns that she has been arrested. He rushes to her and—with his swinging sword—frees her from the police. Both now realize that although he could not love her he has now honorably met his obligation to her. They separate.

In Japanese films, *giri* is not based on abstract commitment or on natural law. It is tangible. *Giri* implies active relationship. Obligations are acquired because an obligee at one time performed deeds which the obligor must eventually repay. One therefore owes *giri* to one's parents, one's relatives, one's lord, one's employer, one's group. They in turn may owe *giri* to the individual.[3]

The nature of the obligation is often bound by the kind of societal relationship that exists between parties. It particularly depends on whether one is in a socially defined inferior or superior position to another. It is not inherently a simple dominance-submission relationship. *Giri* describes a relationship that is ideally more feudal than authoritarian because it implies mutual responsibilities.

As feudal Japan was a highly hierarchical society, interpersonal relations tended to break down into rigid superior-inferior (*oyabun-kobun* in Japanese terms) relationships. This was especially the case between lord and *samurai* when military necessity required unflinching allegiance to the neglect of any reciprocity of feelings or responsibilities. There remained, however, a vague assumption that demands on the inferior's obligation must be tempered with human considerations. The *oyabun* ideally could not make unreasonable requests of his *kobun*. A superior was expected to temper his demands with *ninjo*.

In reality and fiction, Japanese seldom discuss *giri* and *ninjo* in abstract terms. *Giri-ninjo* considerations are part of an invisible framework which structures the actions of all performers. One way to illustrate the critical place of *giri-ninjo* conflict is to view it as the manifestation in dramatic form of the prime historical confrontation of the Tokugawa per-

---

[2] The format for citing films is: the original Japanese title followed in parentheses by my translation of the title or by the American release title; then the director of the film and the year of release in Japan. Except when they appear in the Japanese title of a film, names of persons are in European order with the surname last.

[3] The discussion of *giri* here is not necessarily descriptive of Japanese reality at any time. I am describing the *giri-ninjo* conflict as it has operated within the context of Japanese motion pictures.

iod. The rigid demands of a decaying military system are in opposition to individual emotions and the desire for reciprocal, money-based responsibilities of an emerging burgeois society. The modern relevance of this is that such conflicts continue to influence the behavior of twentieth century Japanese.

Consequences of Choice

The source of core action in *jidai-geki* is often in the consequences of the protagonist's choice between his inescapable responsibilities and his conflicting personal inclinations. For instance, *Dojo Yaburi* (*Defeating the Champion;* Seiichiro Uchigawa, 1964) begins with one of the most common rising actions of *jidai-geki*: a *samurai* abandons his perfunctory feudal responsibilities to run away with his beloved who was forced to become a concubine. The body of the film is the story of their pursuit by their respective masters.

At the start of *Hiken Yaburi* (*Breaking the Swords;* Kazuo Ikehiro, 1969), a *samurai* takes on the thirty-six swordsmen who murdered his uncle and kills them all single-handed. He has an equally skilled friend who belonged to the same clan as the assassins but refused to participate in the murder. The friend is expelled from his clan for not coming to the aid of the killers. From this arise intricate complications until the two roving friends are eventually forced to fight it out.

Apart from the neat conflicts between *giri* and *ninjo,* a central assumption in most *jidai-geki* is that one may also be forced to choose between two opposing *giri.* This conflict is further complicated when one considers: should one weigh one obligation against another without considering how one feels? Honoring any obligation to another may violate one's own personal inclinations. In dramatic form, a *giri-ninjo* conflict involves more than obligation to other persons. It implies that one must also be loyal to one's private feelings. The tension is in the kind of compromise involved in any choice. Unlike the traditional irreconcilability of Western good and bad, *giri* and *ninjo* can be—perhaps, ought to be—congruent. Conflict arises not because the two must inherently be in opposition but because specific *giri* and specific *ninjo* are incompatible in a specific situation.

The *giri-ninjo* conflict in *jidai-geki* can be a liberating theme. In a culture with a strong sense of fate, the confrontation between formal duty and feeling for others offers something revolutionary: the possibility of choice. Even if free choice is not exercised because the compulsions of *giri* are so great, the protagonist senses an alternative. He is aware of the possibility of choosing even if he cannot exercise that freedom.

Concurrent with this awareness of choice, there is sometimes a deterministic recognition that one's present low circumstances are not necessarily the result of conscious personal decision. Uncontrolled outside forces turned the protagonist into outcast *ronin* or *yakuza*. Now, removed from the normal social structure, the swordsman at last can be free to choose. Ultimately, the swordsman can fall back only on himself to justify his actions. If he does what *giri* would compel it is because he personally has responsibility for incurring that obligation. Over the years—this is one of the constants of *jidai-geki*—the swordsman has been a proto-existential man who finds his life meaningful only in his relations with other. Minute by minute he defines who he is. He cannot justify himself in terms of divine support, natural law, or abstract concepts of moral right. Because of this, his alternatives are seldom clear cut. He is constantly accommodating himself to the realities of the world around him. The *jidai-geki*, unlike many Occidental narratives, suggests that life is not the attaining of ideals but rather the continual compromising of ideals.

At its most extreme, freedom for the swordsman leads to the nihilism of such archetypal heroes as Chuji Kunisada and Sazen Tange. In such pictures as *Ooka Seidan* (*Ooka's Trial;* Daisuke Ito, 1928), *Tange Sazen* (Kunio Watanabe, 1937), and *Hien Iai-giri* (*Duel at Hien;* Hideo Gosha, 1966), the *ronin* named Sazen sacrifices everybody—enemies, friends, bystanders, lovers, and police—who would hold him back from his determined goal. In the character of Sazen Tange, *giri* and *ninjo* are united. He chooses to be dominated by one obligation which is also his single *ninjo*: revenge. According to the particular plot of a picture, Sazen seeks either to destroy his father's murderers or to avenge himself against those who have ousted him from his clan.

Acting from Impulse

Jidai-geki heroes, no matter what their social standing, seem dominated by the *bushido* tenet that stresses the necessity to decide immediately upon a certain course and then follow it without wavering no matter what the end. Consequences of an action are not to be thought out in advance, they are to be accepted after one is committed to action. Because acting immediately from pure first impulses is obviously so difficult, many *jidai-geki* are structured on the complications which arise from the reluctance to respond spontaneously. Olivier's movie vision of *Hamlet* as the man who couldn't make up his mind and got into worse trouble seems very Japanese.

From an orthodox *bushido* viewpoint, *Chushingura*, the famous tale of the forty-seven loyal *ronin* which is a major Kabuki play and a frequent movie story, has heroes who are less than exemplary retainers. They are faulted because their revenge of their master (who was forced to commit suicide) took so long and was so well thought out.

The inclination to move directly from first impulse—often violent—coexists in Japanese films with an opposing cultural norm that calls for the control of feelings. Although most movie characters share the common trait of endurance and sublimation, traditional *jidai-geki* differs from traditional *gendai-geki* in that its protagonsists reach a breaking point and burst into physical action. Emotion runs stronger and is more visible in *jidai-geki* because the period film is built on the strongest dramatic outlet for emotion—massive violence. The swordsman, unlike contemporary Japanese, has the means in hand to express his immediate brute feelings.

In contrast, *gendai-geki,* particularly those of the 1930-50 era, are populated with modern characters who at the end finally contain their *ninjo.* Acceptance of life and its oppressive obligations is the common resolution of the dilemmas presented in many films with contemporary settings. The typical narrative structure of Japanese motion pictures reinforces this mood of endurance because a story seldom comes to a gigantic conflict in which all is resolved. Small climax follows small climax as life flows on.

Especially in the years before the war, *gendai-geki* accented personal frustration. The demands placed on an individual—the many *giri* to which he or she had to respond—were overwhelming. As one could not resolve these problems according to one's innermost inclinations, one settled for the most correct pattern of outward behavior.

The traditional *gendai-geki* tends to be depressing. Until recently, when a moviegoer felt that his misery did not need company, he went to a *jidai-geki* for a little uplift. Given a down disposition, *gendai-geki* had the bathos he craved. A pervasive sad quality might be the basis for both popular and critical success of a film. The public appeal of a picture often seemed to depend on how well a film maker brought off the feeling of the world closing in on his characters. Even the most "serious" artists in Japan prefer a controlled pathos rather than a tragic explosion.

Many writers have pointed out that the common Japanese translation for "tragedy" is *higeki* which is a word that connotes little more than "sad drama." There is a distinctive Japanese catharsis which comes not from high tragedy and the noble emotions of the Occident but from situations that explore the beauty of melancholia. Like classical European catharsis, the Japanese form may produce homeopathic relief. But the specific effects differ. The audience does not come away purged and free and somewhat more aware of the possibilities of self. The Japanese catharsis is less of a deliverance. It stems from an imploding of emotion in which the individual merges with the pathos of the work and comes out somehow more aware of the world and where he is in it. The aim of a work is to explore what is, not what might be.

In their most conventional aspects, *gendai-geki* and *jidai-geki* represent in film the two opposing philosophic tendencies found in other Japanese dramatic forms. This is the division between drama of acceptance and of protest. *Gendai-geki* traditionally presents the former; *jidai-geki* the latter.

Although suicides are common in Kabuki and in popular novels, they are less frequent in *jidai-geki*. When a suicide occurs in a Japanese narrative it becomes not a desparate, final act of degradation but rather a conclusive great gesture. It is structured as a means to resolve the unreconcilable, as an act of ultimate protest, or as the final proof that the doer is capable of the noblest deeds. If a moral attitude must be taken, one does not blame the person who killed himself. Instead, one condemns those who drove the person to commit suicide. As in other kinds of events in Japanese films, the seeds of action are more social than psychological.

Because the typical *jidai-geki* demands violence which is entertaining, suicide is often too stark an ending for its male protagonists and too ennobling for its antagonists. The incidence of suicide is much greater in *gendai-geki*. Yet suicide was an evident fact of life in feudal Japan. *Jidai-geki* suggest that it was more a fact of a woman's life. The three most specific "causes" of suicide are to preserve one's chastity or image of purity, to show the intensity of one's love, and to sacrifice oneself for another.

Palpable violence against others sets the general tone and carries the action of *jidai-geki* throughout its history. The average *jidai-geki* has a larger bodycount than all but the bloodiest American films. Its only major rival is the Western of the 1925-1950 period that featured Indian attacks.

In addition to duels and to *chambara* battles, murders are common in *jidai-geki* and must be revenged. Murderers are seldom brought to legal justice. Death of any kind seldom comes as poetic justice or as retribution from on high. Expansive moral or symbolic implications of death are infrequent. When a major character dies at the end of a film the event may have no transcendental significance. Death is often little more than a formal device to terminate the story.

Revenge is a common theme. As in traditional drama and fiction, it seldom involves more than the direct personal touch. Revenge is taken by one human on another. There is no divine punishment. A quirk of fate seldom does in the wrong-doer. In the most typical Occidental revenge motif, the wronged person sets out to avenge himself in the exemplary manner of Jean Valjean.[4] This kind of revenge occurs in *jidai-geki* but more frequently the avenger is a person who is related by blood or allegiance to the wronged party. He acts for another out of *giri*. A definitive revenge story is that of Sazen Tange who jilts his lovers, steals from friends and strangers, and kills dozens in order to bring retribution to the murderers of his father. Nothing else matters to him as he loses an arm, an eye, and finally his life.

---

4 Film makers have nevertheless transferred the Hugo novel to Meiji Japan in at least two motion picture versions: *Jyan Barujan* (*Jean Valjean*; Tomu Uchida, 1931) and *Resu Miseraburu* (*Les Misérables*; Daisuke Ito and Mashiro Makino, 1952, in two feature-length parts.)

While living men seek revenge in *jidai-geki,* a convention descended from Tokugawa literature requires that a wronged woman undertake vengeance after she is dead and can return as a ghost. The archetypal Japanese ghost story—there seems to be no other plot—is about the ghost of a woman who punishes her sexual offenders. The nineteenth century Kabuki play *Yotsuya Kaidan* (*Yotsuya Ghost Story*) which presents this standard form has been adapted to film many times.

In recent years there has been an increase in live heroines who are out for deadly revenge—usually for rape—as in *Irezumi* (*Tattoo;* Yasuzo Masumura, 1966). Occasionally, a girl has to do a swordsman's job as in *Hitokiri O-Katsu* (*O-Katsu, Killer;* Nobuo Nakagawa, 1969) when O-Katsu avenges her father's fatal torture, the debasement of her sister-in-law, her brother's murder, and her hometown's impoverishment.

Settings and Heroes

Important aspects of *jidai-geki* become more visible when the genre is compared to the American Western film. Similarities should not necessarily be interpreted as the influence of one upon another although saying this does not deny the specific influence that Westerns have had on certain Japanese film makers. The *jidai-geki* most familiar to overseas audiences are those of Akira Kurosawa who clearly acknowledges his interest in Westerns while maintaining perfect Japanese authenticity in his work.[5]

Few *jidai-geki* present the wide open spaces of the old-style Western. The Japanese setting has always tended to close in on the swordsman. When their action is restricted to a small town or an interior location, recent adult or television Westerns may also evoke similar feelings of geographic containment. Even with such spatial restrictions, grand territorial struggles dominate the Western: claim jumping, railroad rights-of-way, opening of stagecoach or Pony Express routes, fencing in open range, taking over water rights, moving cattle over large distances, foreclosures on ranches, criminal trespassing. The swordsman is more involved with intangibles. In *jidai-geki,* persons rather than property are more likely to be violated. Even the *yakuza* who has his gambling "territory" sees it more as people than as space.

In earlier pictures, the Westerner might run into hostile Indians aroused because of the invasion of their land. This is something the Japanese never face, for their confrontation with the indigenous Ainu took place long be-

---

[5] That the influence between two cultures can be mutual is evident in the various transformations of Kurosawa's *jidai-geki* into American settings. His *Rashomon* (1950) became Martin Ritt's *The Outrage* (1964); *Shichi-nin no Samurai* (called both *The Seven Samurai* and *The Magnificent Seven,* 1954) became John Sturges's *The Magnificent Seven* (1961); and *Yojimbo* (*Bodyguard,* 1961) became Sergio Leone's Spanish-Italian Western, *Fistful of Dollars* (1964).

fore the *jidai-geki* swordsmen arrived. There is no racial or cultural basis for groups fighting it out as in old cowboy and Indian movies. *Jidai-geki* group confrontations are between social units of the same society.

When the man with a gun rides out of town at the end of a picture, it is usually a triumphant movement. The image of his travelling toward the far horizon is optimistic. He moves toward the unknown but to a possible *El Dorado*. The final image of the solitary swordsman walking into the distance indicates that he is an exile from the familiar world and an outcast from the social situations which give him stature as a man. If abstract retribution is ever indicated in *jidai-geki*, it comes when circumstances force a person—as good as dead—to undertake an endless journey. Roads in *jidai-geki* lead to nowhere.

The expansive natural landscapes within the body of a Western film contrast with the closer views of blossoming flowers, pools of reflecting water, butterflies soaring the wind, and solitary naked bushes of the conventional *jidai-geki*. The world of nature in the Western not only provides the stage for the action but also functions as an encompassing symbol which suggests freedom or escape or undetermined possibilities.

The bits of nature built into a *jidai-geki* usually work like precise literary similes because the images are not so important in themselves but for what they refer to. They become public signs which indicate the emotional states of characters or the pervading mood of a scene. Such images do not seem open to widely variant readings but function as a vocabulary with specific designations. Thus, the rings of water made by a frog's leap into a pond indicate the death of a man, falling cherry blossoms the ephemeral existence of a *samurai*, and the rising sun the start of a new life. The illumination is not novel or insightful but reaffirming and ritualistic.

The worth of a *jidai-geki* hero is not determined by absolute or internal measurement but by his visible status among a group of people. When he is a *yakuza*, leader, the hero relies on his loyal followers. When the swordsman is a single *ronin* or a vagabond *yakuza*, he is then much more alone than the man with a gun. The Westerner may find allies in the law, new friends, or like-minded people. The swordsman lives in a world where such casual support is seldom available.

In the past three decades, the most famous loner has been *samurai* Musashi Miyamoto[6] who discovers that despite his love and loyalty, he can-

---

6 The Musashi of the movies comes from Eiji Yoshikawa's novel, *Miyamoto Musashi*, published in the 1930's. Hiroshi Inagaki made the first film version in three full-length parts in 1940; Kenji Mizoguchi did an introspective single feature version in 1944; and Inagaki remade his original in color and two parts in 1954 and 1956. The first part of the Inagaki color version played in the United States as *Samurai*. Tomu Uchida in 1965-66 attempted the definitive version in five separate features—each two hours long. Musashi also appears as an antagonist in films which center on his arch rival Kojiro.

not rely on kinship or any other kind of traditional obligation. He re-
solves to go it alone. Musashi perfects his swordsmanship and himself
through extreme discipline, practice, aesthetic activity, sacrifice, and medi-
tation. He maintains his personal image with a Zen coolness that is uncommon among *jidai-geki* swordsmen.

Like the man with a gun, the swordsman spends a lot of his time drink-
ing in public places. Fights often break out in such places although the
jidai-geki hero usually first steps outside with his sword. The saloon is also
the place where heroes meet women. In America, the saloon woman's
basic occupation is conventionally disguised as hostess or entertainer. Japanese have always openly acknowledged prostitution by public house
women in their films even if they did not detail the specifics.

Prior to the end of the Second World War, lovemaking scenes of every
kind had to be very circumspect although couples disappeared behind
closed doors or went upstairs. On camera, things could not go much beyond
a glance between partners. Hand or shoulder holding marked the extreme.
The national government censor prohibited kissing scenes and such offending shots were cut from imported films. The Japanese did not kiss on
screen until 1946. Since then, particularly in the past decade, Japan has
moved rapidly toward explicit sex in movies. Several film makers are now
fully competitive with the Europeans and Americans in revealing the
physical manifestations of love and in moving toward the definitive presentation of copulation.

Women and Weapons

The common basis for an understanding between a saloon woman and
an American man with a gun has been what Robert Warshow in his essay, "The Westerner," called "her quasi-masculine independence."[7] Both he
and she are proud that nobody owns them. In *jidai-geki*, the hero and the
prostitute are often attracted for the opposite reason. She, more often
than not, is a semi-slave who has been purchased by a brothel owner. His
freedom is restricted by strong *giri*. Both are owned. Their total love can
be consummated only when they break their individual bonds.

The Westerner sometimes leaves his saloon woman for a good girl. Often
the obvious implications are that he is forsaking his former, looser way of
life. This seldom happens in *jidai-geki*. More often, the girl, whether prostitute or virgin, departs from her lover because the compulsions of physical
force or of obligation make her leave. The hero of the Western frequently
has a woman who does not understand why he does what he does. The

One of these is Inagaki's *Sasaki Kojiro* (*Kojiro Sasaki*, 1967) which is a color remake
of his two-part black and white version of 1950.

7 *The Immediate Experience*, 1962.

Japanese hero is more likely to have a woman who understands his actions all too well.

Sometimes, especially when the hero's love lies elsewhere, the saloon woman is simply somebody the Westerner can talk to. He sees her as more compassionate than passionate. The swordsman also runs into mother substitutes in public houses but they are usually much older and they have teeth, not hearts, of gold.

The totally innocent heroine—the conventional school marm or rancher's daughter in a Western—also appears in the *jidai-geki*. Most likely she is a girl on the verge of being sold into prostitution or turned into a courtesan. The film maker seldom condemns prostitutes as persons or prostitution as an institution. He suggests only that nice girls don't. If they do, it is because they have become victims of circumstance.

Jidai-geki has its share of merchants' and aristocrats' thoroughly virginal daughters. If the swordsman fails to deliver such a girl from her antagonist, she protects herself with a handy dagger normally concealed in her kimono sleeve. She has been trained to deliver this to the throat of her attacker. If she fears that she cannot repulse an attack, she uses the dagger on herself. But before she cuts, she may bind her legs tightly together so that no matter how violent her death spasms, her body will be found in unblemished modesty. Should the swordsman save her from her assailant or from suicide, romantic complications normally follow.

Chaste girls seldom become rivals of more experienced women. Although *jidai-geki* has its rival lovers, there is a more familiar triangle that sometimes appears in Westerns. Instead of having to choose between two loving rivals, the choice for a person—hero or heroine—is between one's only beloved and a heavy to whom one is somehow obligated. Often love is abandoned because the protagonists are compelled to do other things.

There is more direct personal violence in *jidai-geki* than in the Western. The conventional swordsman kills more enemies than the gunslinger. Moreover, between opposing guns there is usually protective space. A gunman stands off and fires. Yards away somebody falls. For each killing, a swordsman needs close contact.

The swordsman fights only with his sword. Strength, endurance, cunning, skill, and life are all at stake at once. The Westerner splits the stakes. He engages in two distinct kinds of duels. The fatal confrontation is the gun fight. The test here is more skill than endurance. One well placed shot and the loser dies. The other form of combat in the Western is the fist fight in which opponents test each other's physical strength. These body struggles do not customarily end in death although results can be fatal if they fight for possession of a weapon.

Widespread destruction of property—usually in a saloon—is common in the Western hand-to-hand confrontation. As men batter their opponents' bodies, they enjoy an orgy of smashing tables, chairs, bottles, stair railings, and mirrors. Swordsmen revel similarly in demolition. Frequently they miss each other with their swords. Their blows crash into the surrounding setting. In anger, frustration, or ecstasy, they whack away at the world around them. They have a particular fondness for slashing through the thin wood and paper partitions of Japanese architecture. The severable door is as much an expendable stock property in the *jidai-geki* as the breakaway bottle and chair are in the Western.

A sequence in Akira Kurosawa's *Yojimbo* suggests the importance of the devastated setting in *jidai-geki*.[8] The protagonist (Toshiro Mifune) is an impoverished *ronin* who comes to a town which is divided into two warring factions. Sensing a chance for profit and fun, he allies with one side, then another. So free is he that he sets up battles between both sides for his own amusement. On one level, he becomes an "arranger" of familiar fighting action as if he were a film director staging a scene. After one particularly efficient fight in which he quickly kills six swordsmen, the hero steps back to survey the scene. It does not look desolate enough so he artfully cuts through doors, bags of rice, and other properties until he achieves the total destruction that marks the end of a *chambara* fight.

Honor, Alertness, and the Law

In addition to group confrontations, man to man fights are obligatory in both genres. This kind of personal contest is usually preceded by a verbal showdown in the Western. One person tries to get the other to initiate physical action: to draw or hit first. Winning consists of beating the other man to the gun or in eventually countering the adversary's initial blow.

Among *yakuza*, there is a tendency to attack without prior verbal confrontation. Swords speak. A *samurai*, however, is more likely to show restraint. He places his hand in a ready position on his sword and challenges with a peculiar staccato speech pattern in which he sharply clips each word. *Yakuza* sometimes try to imitate this but it is apparently something *samurai* are born with.

A single defeat does not necessarily mean dishonor in a Western. It is often more a question of how one fought. With swordsmen, the measure of a man's fighting depends less on manner, much more on the resolution. Winning every time counts above all else.

An important judgment to be made when a fight occurs in a Western concerns who started the quarrel. It is assumed that one party is at fault.

---

8 In this film Kurosawa integrates traditional elements of the American Western into the *jidai-geki*. The picture functions in part as a parody of the most common conventions of both genres.

Dispute over placing this blame frequently brings on yet another fight. Another kind of judgment prevails in *jidai-geki*. As fighting of any kind disturbs a natural harmony and the prevailing equilibrium, all participants must share the blame. Japanese film makers generally support the maxim, "*kenka ryoseibai*"—"in a quarrel both sides are wrong."

A frequent dilemma for the man with a gun is his reluctance to strike behind a person's back even though he knows he will have to take on an opponent later under less favorable conditions. To attack from behind is to violate, if not the code of the real West, then the code of the Western movie. The swordsman may not attack from behind with full honor, but if he does, the stronger onus is on the person attacked, for he has not been cautious enough.

Whatever the circumstances, both sets of heroes must always be ready. The gun and the sword should always be worn. Failure to carry a trusted weapon leads to trouble. Film makers build many plots on such oversights. Beyond having their weapons handy, the swordsman and the man with a gun must be able to perceive danger everywhere. Acute awareness is a supreme quality in both.

In Japan, this hypersensitivity to peril reaches its extreme in the stories of Zatoichi, a totally blind *yakuza* who is an expert swordsman.[9] Zatoichi has an uncanny ability to sense his enemies' moves. His ears, nose, and intuition are super keen. Even his skin can detect the disturbances in the air caused by the tiniest movements of his opponents.

Apart from affirming the actual importance of sheriffs and U. S. marshalls in the historic West, the dramatic function of a law officer in the Western personifies the conflict between justice or natural goodness and the general lawlessness of the setting. Traditionally, when somebody comes up against a Western law officer, it signifies a clash between good and evil. A variation in this moral confrontation occurs when the abstract code and its representative are in conflict within a single character such as a corrupt or frightened sheriff.

A swordsman is much less likely to be a law officer than is the hero of a Western.[10] In many stories, the Japanese acts in violation of official law and in opposition to its representatives if only because the violent use of

---

9 During the 1960's, the Dai-ei Company ground out two or three Zatoichi pictures every year as major productions with Shintaro Katsu in the title role. Representative works are *Zatoichi Monogatari* (*The Story of Zatoichi;* Kenji Misumi, 1962); *Zatoichi Kyojotabi* (*The Flight of Zatoichi;* Tokuzo Tanaka, 1963); *Zatoichi Kenkatbi* (*The Fighting Journey of Zatoichi;* Kimi Yasuda, 1964); and *Zatoichi Chikemuri Kaido* (*Zatoichi's Bloody Trail;* Kenji Misumi, 1968).

10 If a *jidai-geki* protagonist is an officer of the law, this fact is usually disguised until a climactic moment although this kind of disguise is a more frequent device in Korean and American fiction.

the sword was generally proscribed in the Tokugawa era. No matter what the legal violation, the hero's conduct is seldom justified or resolved. It is accepted. On some occasions, "proper" behavior patterns as well as the formal forces of the law are in irreconcilable conflict with the actions of the swordsman. There is less an assumption in *jidai-geki* that ideal human behavior should somehow conform neatly to established laws.

An inherent but seldom explicit first principle of *jidai-geki* is that the swordsman is an anarchist opposed to the established order. But concurrently, there are unvoiced restrictions on his behavior. In the situations where the Westerner might become apprehensive about breaking the law, the swordsman cares less about legality and more about disturbing the existing social harmony. Disturbance of normal equilibrium is an obvious starting point for most Occidental and Japanese narratives.

The antagonists of *jidai-geki* are less likely to be representatives of metaphysical evil although there is seldom doubt about their individual badness. Their actions clearly violate man's natural inclination toward right conduct. When the Japanese villain loses, the event traditionally is neither a symbolic triumph of justice nor a victory of abstract good over bad. It is simply that one wrongdoer has been done in. One specific local oppression has ended.

The plot of a Western often derives from the archetypal dilemma of *The Virginian,* who, at one point, presides over the lynching of his thieving friend. He must decide between personal loyalty and a code which demands death for cattle rustling. The choice is between a human relationship and an impersonal code. The typical Japanese hero faced with his *giri-ninjo* conflict chooses less between a personal and an abstract relationship and more between two kinds of human relationships. His choices are essentially interpersonal.

Something inside *jidai-geki* heroes compels them to impetuous violent behavior. With uncommon exceptions, only heavies are so inclined in Westerns. The typical swordsman can be cool in the face of a challenge but he enjoys losing his cool, too. Despite this low tolerance of inaction, there are significant differences among swordsmen. The extremes are Musashi Miyamoto and Chuji Kunisada. Both fight when they sense the slightest threat. But when faced with his own indecision or internal uneasiness, *samurai* Musashi prefers to meditate or undergo some other self-discipline. The commoner Chuji attempts to resolve everything by immediate action. He relieves personal tensions by seeking a fight. Belief comes when he again survives a fatal battle. It does not matter what the triumph brings. Victory itself is sufficient.

Ultimately, the Japanese and American heroes in these films fight for their personal honor. Although the man with a gun may overtly battle for justice, he also fights to preserve his honor which he defines as his own image of what he should be. The swordsman also fights for his honor but it is less self-defined. He is more concerned with how he appears to others. This makes him no less honorable than the American. It may even make him less liable to self-deception for he must measure himself against standards which are not his own.

No matter what others may think, the man with a gun generally knows if he is the best in battle. Sometimes he is wrong. The swordsman has to keep proving his skills both to the public and to himself. Sometimes he loses. The Western plot traditionally presents more complicated and stronger conflict than the hero's open attempt to maintain his reputation for gun fighting. Only within the past two decades has there been key conflict based on the athletic matching of gun skills between protagonist and antagonist. The standard structural device for this is the neurotic younger rival—as in *The Gunfighter*—who challenges the melancholic established gunman in hope of winning instant reputation.

The *jidai-geki* has always had the skill-challenge theme. The typical swordsman is obsessed with protecting his public standing from the shame of defeat. The obsessions of the man with a gun are frequently complicated by his feeling of guilt about fighting. He suffers for not living up to his code. The distinction between the two genres here—shame vs. guilt—is almost too simple. As in previous observations in this essay, I am suggesting tendencies, not perfect differentiations. Even the most uncomplicated film will not conform to all of the attributes I have described as typical.

Changes in the Genre

As the *jidai-geki* and the Western have developed, the swordsman and the man with a gun have moved outside their conventional behavioral modes. Those who make the modern *jidai-geki* suggest that the *giri-ninjo* conflict is an oversimplification of life. More and more, they inject other social, philosophical, and political concerns into their works. Similarly, in the American Western the once necessary dramatic conflict between good and bad has shaded into a gray which acknowledges a more complex basis for human behavior. Most typically, and in distinction to the socio-political consciousness of contemporary *jidai-geki*, the makers of Westerns adopt a psychological orientation to probe the inner workings of their characters. The result is the "adult" Western. In a sense, the recent Western and *jidai-geki* have both moved to a more palpable dramatic realism. What they have lost is fundamental mythic power. We get less legend and more case history.

By the late 1950's, the content of *jidai-geki* broadened to such an extent that the term now lacks much of the defining quality of earlier years. But the core of the tradition remains. It centers on Tokugawa swordsmen regardless of such distinctions as epic, serious, historical, or regular *jidai-geki*. If the earlier swordsman hero was aware of the necessity for choice within a *giri-ninjo* value system, the more recent swordsman usually faces a wider range of choice as he may elect from different value systems. The newer heroes seem more governed by modern concepts of self-interest. If a swordsman was previously aware of the possibility of freedom, he may now actually try to experience that freedom. The possibilities are still that whatever the choice, the dramatic consequences of freedom will be tragic.

With increasing frequency, nihilistic heroes now have the redeeming virtue of not simply helping but of liberating the oppressed. Senkichi Taniguchi, in his 1960 *Kunisada Chuji*, has his hero spend most of his time raiding government rice warehouses and distributing grain to the peasants who grow it. In *Sengoku Gunto-den* (*A Story of Civil War Highwaymen;* Toshio Sugie, 1960), a *samurai* who is betrayed by his corrupt peers organizes a band of mounted outlaws. They ride off to rob thieving officials. The spoils go to the poor. Within this context, the wildest violence becomes permissible because it leads eventually to justice. What is new to *jidai-geki* is the inherent assumption that a hero's violence must be continually justified in a broad social context. In earlier films, violence for violence's sake might be enough.

There is now more emphasis on self-realization and less consideration of one's image before others. There is no question that the heroes of Kurosawa's *Yojimbo* and Inagaki's *Miyamoto Musashi* answer only to themselves. Whereas earlier protagonists' actions were commonly governed by considerations of their stance in an immediate group or community, the new swordsman is equally responsible to abstract ideas and to the standards of an intangible, larger society. Hideo Gosha's *Kedamono no Ken* (*The Sword of the Beast;* 1965) is as ferocious a *jidai-geki* as any ever made but its basic conflict stems from an intellectual *samurai*'s unsuccessful attempt to reform his corrupt lord. *Roku-nin no Ansatsusha* (*Six Assassins;* Eisuke Takizawa, 1954) presents a swordsman's conflict between his duty as a *samurai* to revenge the death of a friend and his realization that such old ways must end in the new Japan.

Within a narrative tradition that has always been loaded with violent situations, recent *jidai-geki* follow the international trend toward explicit, detailed bloodletting in films. The most conventional way to stage a sword fight is to suggest that a sword strikes so quickly and cleanly that it makes no gory mess. Many are killed but the swordsman keeps it neat. The shift now is to much more blood and entrails. Sometimes this horror shocks and repels for dramatic effect. Other times the violence is simply there gratuitously. It works only as a crowd pleaser.

Kurosawa, in a scene that parodies this modern inclination, created one of the bloodiest single gestures in *Tsubaki Sanjuro* (1962). In the climactic fight, the hero and his opponent strike simultaneously. The hero moves so precisely that his sword punctures just enough of his enemy's heart. Blood spurts out in a fifteen foot geyser. Onlookers (in the film) gasp as if at Yellowstone.

Liaisons between a swordsman and his women are increasingly explicit even though *gendai-geki* carry most of this contemporary burden. Apart from scenes in a copular mode, sex angles form basic story premises in more and more films. These plots often derive from classic themes in Japanese erotic literature.

The sexual roles of women have undergone a major change in a few latter-day *jidai-geki*. They are no longer submissive objects. They use sex to achieve the goals which the swordsman wins with his sword. But the majority of *jidai-geki* have not altered the conventional role of a woman. In her most familiar characterization, she is an innocent in love or in distress. If employed in a brothel, she is at least innocent of other ways of the world. Usually, she needs protection. In return, she offers promises of affection.

In her other conventional guise, the *jidai-geki* woman becomes a substitute for a male in the manly arts if only for a few heroic moments. A habitual *jidai-geki* message is that a woman, after all, is only a woman, but a good sword is something else. Women have no other potential than to be objects of passive comfort which must be protected or to be pseudomales who can hold their own in a *chambara* world and then become women again. *Nuregami Botan* (*Wet Haired Beauty*; Tokuzo Tanaka, 1961) presents an archetypal exploration of the latter direction. A woman *yakuza* is an expert swordswoman and the leader of a gang of several thousand gamblers. She is loved by an apparent clod whom she continually betters in various tests of martial skills. One day while taking a bath, she is attacked by a rival gang. Her would-be lover and swordsman saves her in a climactic scene which mixes a little skin and a lot of sword. She marries him and becomes a good wife. Later, her fighting skills will be useful in educating her sons.

Kabuki has its *onnabudo* (woman *samurai*) roles yet the swordswoman was an infrequent character in *jidai-geki* until a cycle of such films began in the late 1960's.[11] In most of these, a heroine substitutes for the standard

---

11 During the American Occupation there was a curious mixture of traditions when *Shinkokugeki*-style sword plays were crossed with the American strip tease. These live productions featured athletic swordswomen. The familiar gesture of the theatrical sword fighter who slips one shoulder out of a kimono to free his/her leading sword arm for a fight is as good a way as any to bare a bosom.

swordsman figure in a familiar plot. *Nuretsubame Katate-giri* (*One Armed Slaying Bird;* Kimiyoshi Yasuda, 1969) presents a female Sazen Tange (one arm, one eye) and *Makka na Nagaredori* (*Red Wanderer;* Teiji Matsuda, 1969) has a heroine as blind as Zatoichi. Both are destined for sequels. Television created the *Osen Torimono-cho* (*Osen: A Detective Story;* 1968-69) series about a simple servant girl who is secretly a great avenger.

In an inevitable meeting of genres, a *samurai* merged with the Western in *Koya no Toseinin* (*Wilderness Wanderer;* 1968) which Junja Sato filmed with a bi-national cast. A Japanese cowboy rides through a broad made-in-Japan American landscape. He is out for revenge against those Americans who murdered his *samurai* father and mother while they were on a trip to the United States. This new kind of *ronin* learns how to handle weapons from an old gun slinger. Once he is sure of his ability to outshoot the best, he guns down the killers one by one.

With the rapid expansion of television after the late 1950's, the average number of annual per capita visits to film theaters in Japan fell from eight per year in 1960 to about three per year in 1969. By this time, 85 percent of all households had at least one television set.[12] Overall, the total number of features produced remained relatively stable at around 400 during this decade for as major companies cut back their feature output independents filled the gap.

Although *jidai-geki* never regained their pre-war dominance, they rose to a post-war high of about 37 percent of total feature film production in the mid-1950's. In 1959, this proportion slipped to 28 percent then continued to fall below 21 percent in 1962 to 14 percent in 1964. By the end of 1969, the percentage of *jidai-geki* was down to eight.[13]

In 1968-69, the ratio of *jidai-geki* to *gendai-geki* among Japanese-produced television shows was higher than the corresponding proportion of films made for theatrical release. A fair surmise is that the role played in popular entertainment by the traditional *jidai-geki* movie is now taken, in part, by *jidai-geki* made especially for television and by the heavy importation of television Western series made in the United States. The present interest in the American Western on television far exceeds what this kind of film used to draw in Japanese theaters.

Partially due to the universal requirements of weekly television series

---

[12] The following recapitulation of the total number of movie theaters in Japan indicates the expansion and contraction at the exhibition end of the business.

1930	1,392	1950	c.3,000	1955	4,707	1965	4,649
1941	2,466	1952	3,921	1960	7,457	1968	3,814
1945	845						

[13] At least seven displaced Japanese *jidai-geki* directors occasionally work in Hong Kong and Taiwan on Chinese swordsman films. Despite the objections of local directors, Chinese producers claim the Japanese shoot more efficiently than native Chinese and stage more exciting sword fights.

which demand that continuing characters stumble into sudden trouble rather than face rising complications which grow out of their own past, many television *jidai-geki* protagonists exhibit a major shift in basic motivations. The new swordsman in such series as *Kaettekita Yojimbo* (*The Return of the Bodyguard*), *Shingo Juban Shobu* (*The Ten Contests of Shingo*), and *Kaze* (*The Wind*) is much less concerned with personal loyalty, revenge, or any other selfish interest. Instead, this new hero, aroused by an overpowering concern for justice, has become a public avenger who fights for the right outside the normal channels of the law. This direction derives from the *yakuza* story formula in which gamblers such as Chuji Kunisada defend the poor only *after* a personal *giri* tie is established. In contrast, the television protagonist is an ombudsman with a sword who actually seeks out people in trouble. Despite this, the familiar conflicts of *jidai-geki* remain. These are no longer the immediate personal problems of the hero but of the people he freely helps.

A *Jidai-Geki* Aesthetic

Amid these shifts in emphasis, *jidai-geki* in general continue to function within a Japanese narrative tradition in which the pervading attitude is phenomenological acceptance. Things are presented as wholes without analysis or definition. Description, not explanation, is the dominant mode. The film makers' emphasis on "what is" may often be at the expense of tight formal construction. Dramatic flow may even stop to contemplate something or to savor a mood. Formal structure is often further obscured by a tendency toward a baroque narrative whose load of details hides the simple basic patterns of a work.

Because most *jidai-geki* are primarily composed of archetypes, conventions, and other familiar elements, it is easy for a Japanese audience to get into the world of the work. Even when the specific story and characters are not direct repeats of the past, the audience still arrives at the film with certain shared expectations and with an awareness of the basic components of the genre. The important dramatic values are not based on novel or surprise elements but in the subtleties of execution and in the arrangement of familiar materials. The *raku* pottery of Japan offers a precise analogue. It is restricted to one basic shape, two sizes, and two glazes. What one is usually concerned with in *raku* is: what are the permutations of the set components?

The familiar qualities of a Japanese film come not only from the narrative elements—stock situations, traditional characters, and conventional plots—but also from the shape of things seen and heard. *Jidai-geki* abound in common images which, within a Japanese aesthetic, are not senile clichés. They are instead durable essentials whose placement within a work leads not necessarily to new meaning or new experience but to amplification of the old.

The Japanese unities are not those of plot, time and place, character, viewpoint, or thesis but are rather those of mood, tone, rhythm, effect. The American film maker will often ignore tone and mood to maintain plot consistency. The Japanese does the opposite. For him, plot functions as a subordinate to other narrative values. Japanese realism and referents to reality are based on a minimum of formal plot elements such as motivation, causal relationships, plausibility. This a-logical structure tends to give a documentary or reality flavor even to the most presentational style or "unrealistic" content. The tempo, the mood, and the structure that is hard to parse flow as in life itself. Thus situations and even acting need not conform to conventional "life-like" dramatic criteria. The storyteller gives first attention to those things which contribute to the reality of the feeling engendered and not to the reality of the events enacted.

The prevailing psychology of Japanese motion pictures is essentially Jamesian and descriptive. Motivation is not as important as the action itself. Gesture precedes the emotion. This is immediately evident in yet another hallmark of Japanese cinema: scenes in which characters suddenly burst into crying. In these, the character cries first, then he is sad.

Connections in a Japanese narrative are associative and modular rather than linear and unified. One component simply relates to another which relates to another which relates to another like links in a chain. The essential relations are between any two adjoining elements. This contrasts with the classic European construction in which patterns are woven throughout the length of a work with unifying threads running from the start to the finish.

If Godard claims that his works can have "a beginning, middle, and end but not necessarily in that order," Japanese suggest that their films might have no beginning and no end but three middles, not necessarily in that order. The chances are that even a melodrama will not rise to a high climax but unroll simply from small event to small event. When the film is over, there may be little sense of conclusion and with this, less sense of a moral or message. The viewer comes away, not pondering, but having felt.

1973

Towards a Historiography of American Film

Charles F. Altman

During the past decade the literature on the nature and history of the American film has more than doubled. Major new books now appear once a month, rather than once a year as they did during the fifties, or scarcely once a decade as in the twenties and thirties. For the film historian this situation is both exciting and dangerous. Exciting because new facts and analyses are constantly being offered: forgotten films are rediscovered or reconstructed, documents are sifted and published, novel hypotheses about the development of the American film are extended and explored. Such an abundance of new material also presents a danger, however, for it appears at so fast a pace that we have difficulty assimilating it all. If ever there was a time when it was possible to know everything there was to know about American film, and to present it in a single book, surely that time has passed.

Faced with an overabundance of material we must constantly make choices—in our courses, in our writing, and in our viewing habits. What we at times forget is that each one of these choices is laden with implications of far-reaching importance. What material should be taught with *The Grapes of Wrath*? Another film directed by John Ford? Another scripted by Nunnally Johnson? Shot by Gregg Toland? Produced by Darryl Zanuck? Starring Henry Fonda? Or should we read Steinbeck's novel? Or see another film of the same era, the same theme, the same narrative structure, the same studio, or the same genre? Perhaps we should mimeograph the facts and figures concerning the film's distribution. Whatever decision we make—and we all make decisions like this one on a regular basis—we have simultaneously decided against many other alternatives, thus implicitly choosing one mode of historical explanation over another.

What are the modes of historical explanation commonly employed in dealing with the American film? Just what facts do we bring to bear on the study of cinema? How are these facts to be used? As basic as these questions may seem, they have not often been asked publicly by historians of American film. Clearly, however, today's abundance of historical material forces us to consider these questions. No longer can a film historian deal with all the facts, nor can he pretend that they are objective phenomena divorced from a particular way of looking at them. Film history has now reached its second stage: from the *who, what, where,* and *when* we have moved to the *how* and *why;* from *establishing* facts we have progressed to *explaining* facts. Along with this change American film history has broken down into separate schools, each having its own object and methodology, each depending on a different hypothesis about the fundamental determinants of cinema production and distribution, each proposing its own valorizations, its own canon, its own periodization.

To write film history is to establish a *theory of coherence* of filmic events. Film historiography will provide us with a typology of such theories and with an analysis of their potentials, their shortcomings, and the often unsuspected subsidiary effects of their application. This essay can only provide a beginning in the direction of a proper American film historiography. The field is sufficiently broad and confused to prohibit any definitive statement at this time. Nevertheless, I hope that the following pages will serve to draw attention to an important area, to provide a tentative typology of modes of history writing commonly practiced in the field of American film, and to point to some of the problems associated with their use. This analysis is meant to be suggestive and not exhaustive, thought-provoking rather than conclusive.

The method I will employ is the following: for each of the thirteen approaches to American film history which seem to me most important and most fully constituted at this time I will provide a label, followed in parentheses by the periods to which this approach has been most commonly applied. Then there is listed a representative bibliography of books and articles which reflect the approach in question. The summary which follows defines the mode of explanation characteristic of the approach, gives an example or two, and points out the dangers which each type of writing appears to court. After having dealt with each approach separately I will suggest some of the ways in which film historiography is related to notions of periodization and to the choice of a canon of films.

Three qualifications require mention at this point. First, my definition of history has been broad and inclusive. For the purposes of this essay, "criticism" is any activity which concentrates on the relationship of the film image to other images in the same film; "history" is any activity which relates a particular film's images to something outside that film: earlier films, the mode of projection, the actors' preparation, the studio's organization, and so on. Second, the history about which I write is the history of narrative films in commercial distribution. I have not considered experimental, non-narrative, or documentary films—in spite of their importance—because I believe that their historiography is largely separate from that of the commercial narrative film (with certain exceptions which I will mention). Third, for the sake of convenience I will tentatively adopt the following:

to 1905	archaeology
1905-14	silent short
1915-27	silent feature
1927-34	coming of sound
1934-41	Hollywood's golden age
1941-48	the war and its effects
1948-55	Hollywood beleaguered
1955-62	blockbuster years
1963-	new Hollywood

This periodization will probably be accepted in its entirety by almost no one (in fact I will later offer some specific criticisms), but as much as any single periodization could it seems to represent the divisions made by American film historians. With these qualifications in mind we will progress to a typology of American film history writing.

Production

The most basic distinction separates those approaches which concentrate on the *production* of the film image from those which stress the *distribution* of that image. In one case we are dealing with the *determinants* of the film image, in the other with its *destiny*. The following ten approaches are primarily concerned with production.

1) *technology* (archaeology, coming of sound, Hollywood beleaguered)

Baudry, Jean-Louis. "Cinéma: effets idéologiques produits par l'appareil de base." *Cinéthique* 7-8 (1970), 1-8. Reprinted as "Ideological Effects of the Basic Cinematographic Apparatus." *Film Quarterly* 28 (Winter 1974-75), 39-47.

Ceram, C. W. (Kurt Marek). *Archaeology of the Cinema*. New York: Harcourt, Brace & World, 1965.

Comolli, Jean-Louis. "Technique et idéologie: caméra, perspective, profondeur de champ." *Cahiers du cinéma* 229 (May 1971), 4-21.

Deslandes, Jacques. *L'histoire comparée du cinéma*. 2 vols. Paris: Casterman, 1966/68.

Dickinson, Thorold. *A Discovery of Cinema*. London: Oxford University Press, 1971.

Fielding, Raymond. *A Technological History of Motion Pictures and Television*. Berkeley: University of California Press, 1967.

Geduld, Harry. *The Birth of the Talkies*. Bloomington: Indiana University Press, 1975.

Hendricks, Gordon. *Origins of the American Film*. New York: Arno, 1971.

Macgowan, Kenneth. *Behind the Screen: The History and Technique of the Motion Picture*. New York: Delacorte, 1965.

Mitry, Jean. *Histoire du cinéma*. 3 vols. Paris: Editions universitaires, 1967-73.

Ogle, Patrick. "Technological and Aesthetic Influences upon the Development of Deep Focus Cinematography in the United States." *Screen* 13 (1972), 45-72.

Ramsaye, Terry. *A Million and One Nights: A History of the Motion Picture*. New York: Simon and Schuster, 1926.

Sadoul, Georges. *Histoire générale du cinéma*. 6 vols. Paris: Denoël, 1948-75.

Perhaps the first type of history to be widely practiced, technological history attempts to chronicle the invention and commercialization of the mechanical apparatus necessary for the production and projection of the film image. Zootropes and phenakistoscopes, panchromatic film and cinemascope, Muybridge and Edison, Lumière and Pathé—this is the technological historian's domain. Without the technology of moving picture production and projection there would of course be no film history. The primary model of technological history is thus diagrammed as follows:

apparatus → image

However obvious this causal relationship may seem, it nevertheless has been subjected to criticism in recent years. The normal assumption of the technological historian is that technology grows out of technology. It may be speeded up by external phenomena (especially other technological developments; e.g., radio and television), but as a general rule the technological historian considers technology as the initial link in the chain of image production. A growing number of French theoreticians now contest that notion (see the Baudry and Comolli articles cited above), suggesting that the technological apparatus itself reflects a choice among many different types of device which might have been perfected. The eventual decision as to which device should be developed is not made by a single individual, these critics maintain, but by the ideological system in which the inventors labor. Their model is thus:

ideology → apparatus → image

We find ourselves here faced for the first time with a notion which will recur frequently in the pages which follow. In literary criticism, which all too often serves as the model for film criticism, it is assumed that the flow of energy and influence is from author to text to reader. This assumption is strongly supported by the fact that literary authors are usually individuals who are relatively uninfluenced by their audience. American films, quite to the contrary, have most often been made as commercial products by a studio constantly concerned about audience reaction. The net effect of this situation has been to provide the American film industry with a feedback system far more influential than that which most literary authors possess (though authors of serials, dime novels, and other popular genres have sometimes approximated Hollywood's system). Instead of a simple linear model which reads as follows:

film authorship → image → audience

we need a model which completes the production/distribution/feedback loop:

⌐→ film authorship → image → audience ⌐
└── industry ← ideology ← society ←────┘

As this model makes clear, any given creative intention can properly be seen not only as the source of the image, but also as the result of a complex network of relationships which involves the audience, society as a whole, the film industry, and the ideology which they reflect. Considered in this light, our technological histories of the cinema remain too narrow in scope because they fail to acknowledge technology's complex position within a capitalist (or socialist, or Marxist) system.

2) *technique* (silent short, golden age, blockbuster years)
    Barr, Charles. "CinemaScope: Before and After." *Film Quarterly* 16 (Summer 1963), 4-24. Reprinted in *Film Theory and Criticism: Intro-*

ductory Readings, ed. Gerald Mast and Marshall Cohen. New York: Oxford University Press, 1974.

Eisenstein, Sergei. *Film Form.* Trans. and ed. Jay Leyda. New York: Harcourt, Brace & World, 1949.

Fell, John. *Film and the Narrative Tradition.* Norman: University of Oklahoma Press, 1974.

Niver, Kemp. *The First Twenty Years: A Segment of Film History.* Los Angeles: Artisan (Locare Research Group), 1968.

The following all concern the early work of D. W. Griffith:

Bitzer, G. W. *Billy Bitzer: His Story.* New York: Farrar, Straus & Giroux, 1973.

Gunning, Tom. "Griffith, Biograph, and the Development of Film Language." *UFSC Newsletter Supplement,* Vol. 5, No. 2 (1974), 1-4.

Henderson, Robert. *D. W. Griffith: The Years at Biograph.* New York: Farrar, Straus & Giroux, 1970.

Meyer, Richard. "The Films of David Wark Griffith: The Development of Themes and Techniques in Forty-two of His Films." *Film Comment* 4, No. 2-3 (1967). Reprinted in *Focus on D. W. Griffith,* ed. Harry Geduld. Englewood Cliffs: Prentice-Hall, 1971.

Niver, Kemp. *D. W. Griffith: His Biograph Films in Perspective.* Los Angeles: John Roche, 1974.

Petric, Vlada. *D. W. Griffith's "A Corner in Wheat."* Cambridge, Mass.: University Film Study Center, 1975.

Pratt, George C. *Spellbound in Darkness: A History of the Silent Film.* Greenwich, Conn.: New York Graphic Society, 1973.

Stern, Seymour. "*The Birth of a Nation:* The Technique and Its Influence." In *The Emergence of Film Art,* ed. Lewis Jacobs. New York: Hopkinson & Blake, 1969, pp. 58-79.

Long the mainstay of academic film history, the technical approach seeks to determine the history of particular techniques. Who first used the close-up, the iris, deep focus? Where is parallel editing first used for social commentary? Is lighting used for psychological effect before Griffith? Almost everyone who has written at length about the early history of film has participated in the often oversimplified search for "firsts" which characterizes this technical approach. In fact there seems to be an unspoken rule of film history whereby important technical innovations are assumed to grow out of recent technological innovations: the periods which receive the greatest technical attention always follow those which are seen as technologically important. Griffith tests the new Biograph camera, thus discovering new solutions to old problems; Lubitsch and Clair lead the way in counterpointing the newly acquired sound track against the old visual; Mamoulian builds his career on a series of experiments conducted with the technological innovations of the thirties; Welles and Toland add faster lenses to pancromatic film and discover deep-focus photography; Ray learns to cope with cinemascope. Out of these clichés technical film history is forged.

The fact that the technical approach is often most prominent in the writing of directors (e.g., Eisenstein, Clair) and cameramen (e.g., Bitzer, Niver) tells us something important about the context implied by technical history. Consider Eisenstein describing a problem of montage or Bitzer explaining how he and Griffith created the iris: from these passages arises the sense of a plan, a purpose, an overall conception within which a given technique is only the solution to a particular problem. We might diagram the situation this way:

conception → problem → technique → image

Seen from this point of view the technical approach is a very exciting one, with much to contribute to the *auteur* theory, genre study, or studio approach. Unfortunately, this *prospective* technician's approach, which connects the technique to the problem that engendered it, is rarely met in the pages of technical film history. Instead, we are given a *retro*spective critic's approach which, abandoning all notions of context and foregoing any concept of textual unity, seems to borrow its methodology from art history.

More perhaps than any other field, art history has remained retrospectively teleological in its approach to history. We know what techniques caught on in the cubism of the teens, so we have only to follow history upstream to discover the technical experiments of Braque and Picasso in 1908. Today's accepted practice is the *telos,* the goal which gives all previous activity its meaning. This nineteenth-century positivist approach is now slowly receding in the world of art history, as it must in the field of film history as well, lest we succumb to the temptation to reduce all films to the sum of their innovations. Reputations have in fact been ruined by the overzealous application of this approach. I think particularly of Rouben Mamoulian, whose innovations (slow wipes, point-of-view shots, use of color) were so highly acclaimed in the thirties that few of his other many qualities as a director were noticed. Inevitably, however, the techniques of the thirties were "surpassed" (a key word in this falsely evolutionary scheme), carrying the director who had been so closely identified with them into near oblivion. One wonders whether the patronizing attitude often exhibited today toward early Griffith or Mamoulian will one day extend to Welles and Altman: we keep them around somewhat like senile grandparents, not for what they are now but because long ago they spawned the splendid present generation.

3) *personality* (silent feature, golden age)

Anger, Kenneth. *Hollywood Babylon.* New York: Delta, 1975.

Arvidson, Linda. *When the Movies Were Young.* New York: Dover, 1969 (originally 1925).

Brown, Karl. *Adventures with D. W. Griffith.* New York: Farrar, Straus & Giroux, 1973.

Brownlow, Kevin. *The Parade's Gone By.* New York: Knopf, 1968.

Durgnat, Raymond and John Kobal. *Greta Garbo.* New York: E. P. Dutton, 1965.

Griffith, Richard. *The Movie Stars.* New York: Doubleday, 1970.

Jeanne, René and Charles Ford. *Les Vedettes de l'écran.* Paris: Presses Universitaires de France, 1964.
Mailer, Norman. *Marilyn.* New York: Grosset and Dunlap, 1973.
Morin, Edgar. *Les Stars.* Paris: Seuil, 1972 (3rd ed.).
Schickel, Richard. *His Picture in the Papers: A Speculation on Celebrity in America, Based on the Life of Douglas Fairbanks, Sr.* New York: Charterhouse, 1973.
. . . *The Stars.* New York: Bonanza, 1962.
Wagenknecht, Edward. *The Movies in the Age of Innocence.* Norman: University of Oklahoma Press, 1962.

To the above list could be added countless biographies of stars, as well as books entitled *The Films of Xxxxx.* The cult of personality in American cinema needs little introduction, it seems, for to the average academic film historian star-gazing represents the very weakness which carefully researched and reasoned historical writing seeks to overcome. The populace worships personalities; it is up to the academy to raise the film experience to a higher plane. This attitude grows out of the more general phenomenon whereby the "legitimate" theater (and other "high" arts) has often been regarded as superior to cinema. The theater has actors and actresses, trained in their profession and schooled in the dramatic classics, while the cinema has "stars," often inept performers saved from oblivion by a collusion between some publicity department and the eager masses. It is only natural, then, that books reflecting film's personality cult should be written not by professional film historians, but by free-lancers and journalists (Griffith, Schickel), nostalgics (Wagenknecht, Jeanne and Ford), people who "were there" (Arvidson, Brown, and those interviewed in Brownlow), social scientists, and eccentric artists (Morin, Anger).

Given this general situation, it is clear that the personality approach to film history needs rehabilitation, not criticism. Academicians have long tried to repress the fact of stardom in American life and film; we are perhaps ashamed to admit that we are, as a population, highly susceptible to charismatic personalities, whether we are schooled in the classics or not. The star system is a Hollywood fact of life (at least it was from the silent feature to the blockbuster period); instead of relegating it to columnists and fans we need to analyze it with the same patient care we devote to other endeavors. As Schickel's book on Douglas Fairbanks, Sr., suggests, the concept of stardom has spread throughout American life, and perhaps constitutes one of Hollywood's strongest and most consistent attractions. It is not an aspect of film history which we can lightly ignore.

What would it mean to take the problem of personality seriously? First, we would have to give up the aesthetic principles inherited from literary "new criticism." The Hollywood star-vehicle is anything but a self-contained aesthetic universe. The very concept of stardom implies continuity (and for the public, synonymy) of screen life and daily life. A star's image is the result of every contact which he/she has had with the public: previous films, newspaper coverage (gossip as well as fact), television or newsreel appearances, records, even product endorsements, family background, and apocryphal jokes. This is why it is perfectly legitimate for personality/star studies to include material of the widest possible range (songs for Judy Garland, pin-up pictures for Marilyn Monroe, articles on James Stewart's war record). Beyond studies devoted to a single star we need more historical research on the varying approaches to personality and stardom at different times and in different places. Where is the book which details the cult of personality from Biograph's insistence on anonymity to Fox's "one-girl-at-a-time" policy to Hollywood's interaction with television? It is time that academic film history accommodated this important approach.

4) *film and the other arts* (silent short, golden age)

Bazin, André. *What is Cinema?* Trans. and ed. Hugh Gray. Berkeley: University of California Press, 1967. Vol. I contains "Theater and Cinema," pp. 76-124, and "Painting and Cinema," pp. 164-72.

Blanchard, Gérard. *Histoire de la bande dessinée: une histoire des histoires en images de la préhistoire à nos jours.* Verviers: Marabout, 1974.

Bluestone, George. *Novels into Film.* Berkeley: University of California Press, 1968.

Fell, John. *Film and the Narrative Tradition.* Norman: University of Oklahoma Press, 1974.

Lacassin, Francis. *Pour un neuvième art: la bande dessinée.* Paris: Union générale d'éditions, 1971.

Lindsay, Vachel. *The Art of the Moving Picture.* New York: Liveright, 1970 (originally 1915).

Magny, Claude-Edmonde. *L'âge du roman américain.* Paris: Seuil, 1948.

Nicoll, Allardyce. *Film and Theatre.* New York: Crowell, 1936.

Ropars-Wuilleumier, Marie-Claire. *De la littérature au cinéma.* Paris: Armand Colin, 1970.

Seldes, Gilbert. *The Seven Lively Arts.* New York: Sagamore, 1957.

Vardac, A. Nicholas. *Stage to Screen: Theatrical Method From Garrick to Griffith.* Cambridge: Harvard University Press, 1949.

The last of the four methods commonly applied to the study of early cinema consists of a systematic comparison of the film medium to its visual, literary, and dramatic neighbors. The general presupposition shared by most historians of this persuasion is that film is in some way conditioned by the other arts. That is:

other arts → image

Like many approaches, this method is heavily influenced by the fact that film history was born virtually with the invention of cinema. Early critics had no significant predecessors to compare Porter and Méliès to, so they looked to the other contemporary arts for their *comparanda*. Little has changed in this practice today: the film most often compared to other arts is early film; the arts most often referred to are contemporary arts. Yet some of the most obvious instances of direct influence occur later and involve arts long dead. The costume drama of the thirties needs to be related to nineteenth-century European book illustration and painting; the late forties and early fifties are strongly influenced by early American painting, thanks to the lead of Minnelli and Mamoulian. Likewise, the early Western must be compared not only to the turn-of-the-century dime novel, but also to the medieval epics from which the Western borrows its value system, character types, and plot patterns (a comparison already suggested by Bazin).

More important still, we need to avoid the assumption that film only borrows from the other arts, without contributing to them. Though this approach may make some sense during the early years of film's development, it is surely of limited value during Hollywood's studio years. For reasons of convenience (in teaching as well as in writing), much attention has been focused on adaptations of well-known literary texts, usually novels or plays. The choice of this type of comparison necessarily packs the jury—"obviously" Steinbeck's *Grapes of Wrath* influences Ford and not vice versa. Who can doubt that the American school of novelists known as "hard-boiled" are a primary influence on American film, particularly the *film noir*? After all, aren't a number of these films just adaptations of their novels? Why study the Hollywood musical after 1945? Isn't it just a series of celluloid transcriptions of Broadway successes? Wrong in both cases. As Magny has shown in one of the most brilliant and neglected books on American film, the modern American novel (Fitzgerald, Dos Passos, Faulkner, Hemingway), contemporaneous with the heyday of the studio system, is in fact heavily influenced by film techniques, themes, and values, as is the "hard-boiled" school. Likewise, three of Broadway's greatest musical successes (*Porgy and Bess, Oklahoma, Carousel*) were directed on stage by none other than Rouben Mamoulian, who cut his teeth on such film musicals as *Applause, Love Me Tonight, The Gay Desperado,* and *High, Wide and Handsome* (the latter scripted by Oscar Hammerstein). Technique after technique in the stage versions can be seen to derive from Mamoulian's experience in Hollywood.

Perhaps a greater danger still is represented by John Fell's recent book on *Film and the Narrative Tradition*. Fell presents a great deal of fascinating material, but he often handles it in a manner which reflects the profession's lack of concern with historiographical problems. Though his major focus is the "cannibalization" of other forms by the cinema, he arbitrarily limits himself to late nineteenth-century source material. Fell quotes numerous popular novels, for example, to show that "transitions in space could be attended to with general variations on 'Meanwhile, back at the ranch'" (p. 73), implying some sort of connection between the conventions of turn-of-the-century prose and subsequent parallel editing in films. But why choose these novels when the technique has been a part of the Western narrative tradition for at least three thousand years? Fell credits Jack London with introducing a "three-dimensional frame of reference" into our visual perception. What then must we say about the systematic development of perspective in the Italian *quattrocento*? In order to show that "Victorian writing is especially interesting for its filmlike predispositions" (p. 54), Fell often quotes twentieth-century critics who use cinematic terminology to describe nineteenth-century novels. But the same critical/cinematic language has been applied to the Bible and Homer, to the medieval epic and the picaresque novel. It makes perfect sense to mention parallels between Boucicault's staging and the split screen of early films, but why must the field of inquiry be limited to late nineteenth-century theater? What about the medieval iconographic tradition which opposed Virtues to Vices or Dives to Lazarus? What about Thomas Nast's "Tammany Hall" series of political cartoons?

The main problem with Fell's method is that he has simply transferred the game of technical firsts to a larger field. Instead of imitating Eisenstein's concern to relate technique to function and ideology ("Dickens, Griffith, and the Film Today," in *Film Form*), Fell—and many others like him—reduces the problem of intermedia relationships to a list of technical borrowings. We used to argue whether Griffith or Ince was the first to use composition in depth. Now Fell would show us that Winsor McCay's cartoons predated their work in the use of this important technique. The trouble with this approach to film history is that it simply opens a new can of worms. Doesn't Breughel compose in depth? And what of Vermeer's open doors? We need to decide what it is we are claiming. Either the mode is *influence,* for which we need to prove the film maker's familiarity with this alleged source material, or the mode is *analogy,* for which our field of inquiry may be much wider.

5) *chronicle* (every period from archaeology through new Hollywood)

Casty, Alan. *Development of the Film: An Interpretive History.* New York: Harcourt Brace Jovanovich, 1973.

Crowther, Bosley. *Vintage Films.* New York: Putnam's, 1977.

Higham, Charles. *The Art of the American Film: 1900-1971.* Garden City, N.Y.: Doubleday, 1973.

Knight, Arthur. *The Liveliest Art: A Panoramic History of the Movies.* New York: Macmillan, 1957.

Mast, Gerald. *A Short History of the Movies.* New York: Bobbs-Merrill, 1976 (2nd ed.).

McVay, Douglas. *The Musical Film.* New York: Barnes, 1967.

Solomon, Stanley. *The Film Idea.* New York: Harcourt Brace Jovanovich, 1972.

As a general rule, the chronicle approach tends to be restricted to general film histories, and to picture-books which provide short essays on the "classics" of film. Two major concerns govern the employment of this method: the desire to establish (or reaffirm) a given canon of "major" films, and the natural, indeed necessary, impulse to combine film history with analysis of specific exemplary films. In general, the more a historian has been influenced by "new critical," phenomenological, or formalist methodology, the more likely he is to want to build his general history around a series of interpretations. The chronicler then fits other relevant topics

around the basic catalogue of masterpieces, obeying the publisher's pre-
scribed space limitations. Here we find ourselves face to face with one of
the disturbing facts about American film publication: all our general histories are conceived as introductory texts. In France, the histories written by
Georges Sadoul and Jean Mitry (see section one above) have reached six
and three volumes, respectively, without leaving silent film. Likewise, Roger
Manvell and Rachel Low devote four volumes to the *History of the British
Film* from 1896 to 1929 (London: Allen & Unwin, 1948-50). In this country, general histories are published only for a far more secure market. It is
their duality of purpose which forces most American general histories to
subscribe, at least in some measure, to the chronicle approach. Students
must be given analysis as well as history; they must be initiated into film
through the best possible films, those which we all agree to be landmarks of
film history.

The most obvious problem with this approach is one which it shares with
its literary model—the study of "peak" literature, the masterpieces which
rise above the age to provide touchstones for the culture. A film history
structured around analyses of important films implies more than it says.
Readers are likely to take a series of separate events arranged in chrono-
logical sequence as a historical chain rather than as unconnected films.
Post hoc ergo propter hoc is the type of logic which tends to be applied to
the chronicle. This is all the more true in that a general film history which
also serves as an introductory text can assume no knowledge on the part of
the reader. Concrete comparisons of a film to its predecessors can only be
made to previous entries in the book's catalogue. The limitations of the introductory general history thus become an invitation to falsify history ever
so slightly in order to make necessary and important points about the development of a given technique, theme, or structure.

6) *social* (coming of sound, golden age, the war)
   Bergman, Andrew. *We're in the Money: Depression America and Its
      Films*. New York: New York University Press, 1971.
   Deming, Barbara. *Running Away from Myself*. New York: Grossman,
      1969.
   Jacobs, Lewis, *The Rise of the American Film*. New York: Teachers
      College Press, Columbia University, 1968 (originally 1939).
   White, David M. and Richard Averson. *The Celluloid Weapon: Social
      Comment in the American Film*. Boston: Beacon, 1972.

To this list might well be added a growing number of articles, a voluminous bibliography on the documentary, and an increasing array of studies
devoted to film's treatment of women, blacks, or other minority groups.
Wherever the social approach is found, however, it must be distinguished
from another with which it is often combined: the sociological approach,
concerned not with society's effect on film but with film's effect on society.
In its simplest form the social history of film assumes the following relationship:

society → image

As is often the case, the dangers of this approach grow out of its obvious validity. Who could deny that *All through the Night, Ministry of Fear,* or *Sherlock Holmes and the Voice of Terror,* all of which concern Nazi infiltrators during the Second World War, spring out of the social conditions of wartime? *Scarface* and *Gold Diggers of 1933* clearly draw much of their subject matter and general attitude from current social problems (prohibition, the depression). In choosing to deal with such seemingly obvious relationships, however, social history betrays its general failure to evaluate *exact* relationships between society and film. Films "reflect" society, we say, taking shelter behind the ambiguity of the phrase. Instead of analyzing the relationship between society and cinema, most social historians have treated film as an unmediated transposition of social reality. (Bergman provides perhaps the most obvious example of this tendency.) Outside of Marxist journals like *Jump Cut* (and the documentary tradition, where social history has achieved greater sophistication), one rarely finds an examination of the ways in which film distorts, transforms, and problematizes social reality. If film is a *window* on the world (a favorite metaphor of social historians), it is also a *frame,* a highly selective medium with its own rules and traditions.

Even the most obvious of relationships leaves room for doubt. Most critics agree that there is a causal connection between periods of great stress like the depression or the war and the production of "entertainment" movies (e.g., musicals and screwball comedies). At the same time, however, these are the years of social realism, of documentary and newsreel influence, and of many important problem films. The question must be asked: is the relationship between society and the film image a positive or a negative one? Does film reflect society or does it compensate for it? Whatever we decide about this difficult question, we must admit that these two hypotheses constitute antithetical subdivisions of the general social approach.

Two other problems are of particular importance in the writing of social history. First, we must make very certain that the society/image relationship is significant and primary, rather than just a reflection of some other more general phenomenon. If we were to apply a social argument to the nostalgic films of the seventies (what the French call "la mode *retro*"), we might well be tempted to relate this nostalgia to the simultaneous end of the Vietnam war and the beginning of the economy's "stagflation." The end of the war freed us to consider other subjects; economic problems helped to define the new topic as the "good old days." As enticing as this argument might be made to seem, it overlooks one important fact: attention to cultural memory is a permanent feature of American history and cinema. A major motif of the genre films which comprise the majority of American sound film production is the cultural past. Relating "la mode *retro*" to the end of the Vietnam war invites us to take secondary determinants for primary ones.

A second and very basic problem of social history involves the notion of periodization. Many of our presuppositions about film history grow naturally out of political and literary history. The parallels, however, are at best confusing, because the history of cinema is too short to support a proper parallel with political or literary history. In France or England we might speak of a literary period according to the reign of a monarch (Elizabethan age, Victorian period, Napoleonic era, century of Louis XIV), but the corresponding American periods are much shorter (prohibition, the New Deal, the war, McCarthyism, the Eisenhower years). These periods are simply too short to support a cinema history based on the period-style model provided by literary history. In Hollywood, change takes time: a few months to imitate a competitor's success, a few years to reflect a serious economic change, a decade before a talented assistant gets to direct his film, maybe a generation before a major change in literary taste or world politics makes itself fully felt. And what is a generation? Approximately one-third of the entire history of American cinema. How is it possible to pinpoint six- or seven-year periods when some directors may stay in the same studio for decades, never changing their fundamental approach, while others come and go in two or three years? Given the micro-miniaturized scale of film history, we must be particularly careful with months, let alone years, and must resist the temptation to confuse periodizations derived from film's internal history with those borrowed from film's social determinant.

7) *studio* (silent feature through Hollywood beleaguered)

Balio, Tino. *United Artists: The Company Built by the Stars*. Madison: University of Wisconsin Press, 1976.

Baxter, John. *Hollywood in the Thirties*. New York: Barnes, 1968.

Capra, Frank. *The Name above the Title*. New York: Macmillan, 1971.

Crowther, Bosley. *The Lion's Share: The Story of an Entertainment Empire*. New York: Dutton, 1957.

Dunne, John G. *The Studio*. New York: Farrar, Straus & Giroux, 1969.

Fordin, Hugh. *The World of Entertainment: Hollywood's Greatest Musicals*. Garden City, N.Y.: Doubleday, 1975.

French, Philip. *The Movie Moguls*. Baltimore: Penguin, 1971.

Higham, Charles. *Warner Brothers*. New York: Scribners, 1975.

Thomas, Bob. *King Cohn: The Life and Times of Harry Cohn*. New York: Putnam, 1967.

Of all the problems of film history, the one least well provided for by methodologies borrowed from other disciplines is the question of cumulative authorship. In painting, studio composition was a common Renaissance practice, but for lack of information art history has rarely gone any farther than to distinguish between a work painted by an artist alone and one on which his studio collaborated. Even in the latter case, the painting is usually classified with the major artist's paintings, often accompanied by a note indicating which parts he is believed not to have done. In other words, the concept of cumulative authorship is handled by the assumption of a hierarchy within which a given individual had both the first and the final word. This approach, consonant with what we know of the historical facts, thus brackets the notion of collaboration and concentrates instead on individual authorship. In literature a similar situation obtains. An author may be inspired by another's idea, given material by a friend, aided stylistically by a colleague, edited by his press, and forced by public response to make revisions, yet current practice permits—in fact requires—us to forget all this outside participation. Individuals write literature, not teams.

We thus come to the cinema sadly lacking in any method of making sense of Hollywood's peculiar brand of collaboration. This is all the more serious in that the production of a Hollywood film involves far more than actors, technicians, and director; behind the scenes there is a veritable army of support personnel concerned with problems as varied as acquiring "properties," checking copyrights, verifying period authenticity, and securing publicity. In fact the very size of the operation permits us to make a preliminary distinction among studio studies. The first type usually involves a great deal of archive work, as well as interviews with executive officers; its basic assumption seems to be the following:

studio money decisions → image

A second approach concentrates on the interaction among the actors, the director, and the crew (and in some cases the producer). This model assumes the following relationship:

studio aesthetic decisions → image

In many cases our best view of this second approach is provided not by studio studies as such but rather by attempts to chronicle the making of a single picture. For example:

Kael, Pauline. *The Citizen Kane Book*. Boston: Little, Brown, 1971.

Knox, Donald. *The Magic Factory: How MGM Made An American in Paris*. New York: Praeger, 1973.

McClelland, Kirk. *On Making a Movie: Brewster McCloud*. New York: Signet, 1971.

Ross, Lillian. *Picture* (on *The Red Badge of Courage*). New York: Rinehart, 1952.

Schary, Dore. *Case History of a Movie* (on *The Next Voice You Hear*). New York: Random House, 1950.

Both approaches, financial and aesthetic, are useful but incomplete, as two examples will quickly demonstrate. Tino Balio's recent study of United Artists (though actually more a distribution than a production study, given UA's special nature as a nonproducing company) reveals many of the values and the problems of the financial approach, while Hugh Fordin's popularized account of the Freed unit at MGM is more concerned with the aesthetic side of things. Balio works from the enormous collection of documents donated to the University of Wisconsin's Center for Film and Theater Research. This fact proves to be both a blessing, for it permits Balio to be unusually thorough and accurate in his claims, and a pitfall, for there was too much to do simply in collating all of UA's papers for us legitimately to expect Balio to go any farther. Yet what we need is precisely something which would transcend archival material. Throughout the book, films are labeled as "products," and treated as such, for that is the way they are treated in the financial papers deposited in Wisconsin. We long in vain for Balio to capture the complex relationship between financial and artistic decisions; given the nature of his materials he cannot possibly do so.

Fordin's book goes to the opposite extreme: it is largely dependent on interviews with Arthur Freed and other MGM personnel. Again and again a serious scholar is frustrated by the book's lack of references and notes, its refusal to identify sources for figures, quotes, judgments. As a lasting history of the production unit responsible for the most highly acclaimed series of musicals in Hollywood's history, *The World of Entertainment* will not do. Yet it does do something which Balio's book does not. It gives a glimpse, however limited, of MGM's chain of command, of the order of decisions on individual films, of the criteria (both financial and aesthetic) by which decisions were made. This is the kind of information which we so desperately need if we are ever to take questions of authorship past the level of theory. Thanks to Frank Capra's autobiography we know that he had far more power at Columbia than any director at MGM. What we need now are studio studies which will consider documents as well as eye-witness statements in order to show each studio's differing mix of financial and aesthetic decisions, each studio's (or period's) differing chain of command, and the various orders in which decisions were made and changed.

8) *auteur* (golden age through new Hollywood)
    Sarris, Andrew. *The American Cinema: Directors and Directions, 1929-68.* New York: Dutton, 1968.

Many other *auteur* studies might be cited, including dozens dealing with single directors, but Sarris is certainly the one who has most persistently and creatively applied the *politique des auteurs* to American film. In his introductory essay to *The American Cinema* ("Towards a Theory of Film History") he states his position quite plainly: "Ideally the strongest personality should be the director, and it is when the director dominates the film that the cinema comes closest to reflecting the personality of a single artist. A film history could reasonably limit itself to a history of film directors" (p. 24).

Sarris's position has been sufficiently discussed, so I will limit my comments to two points. First, Sarris's statement—and the *auteur* theory in general—depends on a hypothesis which we do not yet have the means to prove or disprove. Until we know more about the actual decisions made in individual movies, we will have to consider the importance of the director a hypothesis, not a given. Certainly the musicals starring Astaire and Rogers, or produced by Freed, or choreographed by Kelly have a unity—and a continuity—which is created by someone other than the director. Second, Sarris seems to be interested solely in reflections of the personality of a single artist. I too am interested in such reflections, but I am also interested in reflections of a community, and if I had to suggest which I thought I was more likely to find in Hollywood it would have to be the latter.

In the introduction to his *Short History*, Gerald Mast reveals another of the potentially dangerous assumptions which lurks beneath the surface of the *auteur* theory. He says:

> A study of eighty years of film history has led this author to make one basic assumption: no great film has ever been made without the vision and unifying intelligence of a single mind to create and control the whole film. Just as there is only one poet per pen, one painter per canvas, there can be only one creator of a movie. The *"auteur* theory" is as valid for films as for any other art. (p. 3)

I pass over the truth value of this statement. I disagree with Mast (was there really a single *auteur* for the Pyramids, the Parthenon, Chartres cathedral?), but that is unimportant here. Suppose Mast is right, then what kind of history will he write? A history about great films (for which reason I have identified his *Short History* with the chronicle approach). Now I have nothing against such a history, but *a* history of film is not *the* history of film, and the latter must certainly include many films, individuals, and experiences which no one would classify as great.

Furthermore, the *auteur* approach to history, particularly as it is practiced by Sarris, tends to designate not only great films, but great directors as well. A director's entire corpus tends to get treated in the same way, according to a single judgmental phrase. At the same time, all diachronic relationships are lost except those which fit easily within the perimeters of the individual director's career. This bracketing of historical concerns grows out of the fact that *auteur* history is usually criticism first and history only second. French *nouvelle critique*, strongly influenced by American "new criticism," was born in France simultaneously with the *auteur* theory. All three approaches are devoted to close analysis of individual works and based on an assumption of textual independence. In one sense, then, the *auteur* theory, like "new criticism" and its French equivalent, is part of a reaction against history and thus remains uncomfortable with historical thinking. Nevertheless, the *auteur* theory has already contributed greatly to the rehabilitation of many important figures in American film history. Before it can make further steps, however, other figures besides the director will have to receive serious consideration as potential *auteurs,* and some method will have to be found to reintroduce historical relationships into more than the development of single *auteurs.*

9) *genre* (silent feature through blockbuster years)
   Kaminsky, Stuart. *American Film Genres: Approaches to a Critical Theory of Popular Film.* Dayton, Ohio: Pflaum, 1974.
   Solomon, Stanley. *Beyond Formula: American Film Genres.* New York: Harcourt Brace Jovanovich, 1976.
To these two general studies (published, like the general histories, with a textbook market in mind) must be added scores of studies devoted to specific genres. Some of the best are:

Clarens, Carlos. *An Illustrated History of the Horror Film.* New York: Putnam's, 1967.

Kitses, Jim. *Horizons West.* Bloomington: Indiana University Press, 1969.

McArthur, Colin. *Underworld U.S.A.* New York: Viking, 1972.

Thus far we have considered approaches which look to something outside the filmic text as the major determinant of the film image: technological developments, other arts, the society, the studio as a whole, the director, and so forth. The generic approach to film history accepts another hypothesis:

film → image

That is, the shape of a film is not determined by its director, cameraman, or producer, nor by their society or studio, but by previous films. Previous films have such a strong effect that film makers tend, knowingly or not, to replicate previous efforts with only slight variation. Films of a given genre are thus most fruitfully compared to other films of the same genre.

Two separate impulses support this hypothesis. The first is an empirical one made by nearly every regular filmgoer: films, and especially American films, do tend to look alike. Name any movie and the average movie buff can name another "just like" it. Whether we wish to speak of formulas, of cycles, or of genres, this strong sense of similarity is one which must be dealt with. The second type of supporting evidence is a historical observation made by many different writers: the financial structure of Hollywood during the studio years encouraged the imitation of any successful film, thus leading to the creation of a formula for success. Based on these two common sense observations, generic history chronicles the rise and fall of American film genres.

Or does it? Logic as well as experience suggest that given genres do not spring full-grown from the head of Zeus. Generic film study, however, rarely takes the development of the genre into account. Either we have generic *catalogues* (the one for the musical often reads: operetta, Berkeley, Astaire and Rogers, Garland/Kelly or Minnelli/Donen, Broadway adaptations) or generic *criticism* (which takes the genre as a fixed synchronic unit and attempts to describe its structure and functioning). Neither of these approaches is without value; indeed, genre history cannot be written without them. But neither constitutes, strictly speaking, generic film history. A proper generic film history would not only describe the configurations basic to the genre's major period, but it would outline the development of the genre as well, in many cases tracing it into other genres or media. Current practice privileges the treatment of directors who work often within a given generic tradition (especially Ford and the Western); there is nothing wrong with this approach as long as it does not serve as a substitute for full treatment of the genre conceived as a broad category having its own history.

10) *ritual* (golden age through Hollywood beleaguered)
    Alloway, Lawrence. *Violent America: The Movies 1946-1964.* New York: Museum of Modern Art, 1972.

Braudy, Leo. *The World in a Frame: What We See in Films.* Garden City, N.Y.: Anchor, 1976.

Cawelti, John. *The Six-Gun Mystique.* Bowling Green: Bowling Green Popular Press, 1971.

McConnell, Frank. *The Spoken Seen: Film and the Romantic Imagination.* Baltimore: Johns Hopkins University Press, 1975.

Wood, Michael. *America in the Movies.* New York: Delta, 1975.

Wright, Will. *Six Guns and Society: A Structural Study of the Western.* Berkeley: University of California Press, 1975.

The ritual approach is an important and growing alternative to (and sometimes combination of, as in Wright) the social and generic approaches. The normal social/sociological model of production and distribution is

society → image → audience behavior

with some critics emphasizing the process of producing the image (e.g., Bergman, see section six above), others that of its distribution and influence (e.g., Jowett, see section thirteen below). The ritual model reads otherwise:

society → audience → image

That is, the audience, conditioned by the society of which it is a part, is the ultimate source of the image (usually through the intermediary of a given generic pattern). By its response to different types of film, the audience in the long run dictates the nature and content of the movies it wants to see. Even the standard studio approach has always assumed a circular pattern (emphasized in Handel's classic work analyzing the way *Hollywood Looks at Its Audience;* see section twelve below):

studio → image → audience
audience research ←

Only the ritual approach, however, goes so far as to claim that the audience actually maintains ultimate control over the film's image.

According to Braudy, "Genre films essentially ask the audience, 'Do you still want to believe this?' Popularity is the audience answering, 'Yes.' Change in genres occurs when the audience says, 'That's too infantile a form of what we believe. Show us something more complicated'" (p. 179). In other words, the ritual approach is an attempt to relate generic form to social situation, thus creating a "functionalist" approach similar to those espoused by Malinowski (ritual), Freud (dreams), and Huizinga (play). Each one of these seminal thinkers discovered a new type of meaning by assuming a function for an activity previously considered a useless pastime or entertainment. American cinema—or at least certain aspects of it—thus becomes "a means of reaffirming certain basic cultural values, resolving tensions and establishing a sense of continuity between present and past" (Cawelti, p. 73). In this sense, ritual history is a metahistorical approach, for it attempts to unite not only given historical events but also different historical models (generic, social, sociological).

Perhaps the most serious problem of ritual history is its tendency to encourage abuse. The hypothesis of a ritual function, like the hypothesis of a single *auteur*, feeds our desire to find unity and meaning in Hollywood cinema. In the latter case we may be tempted to create our own unity, in the former our own meaning. Wright's attempt to link various Western sub-genres to the development of American economic systems will strike many as willful. On the other hand, Cawelti's claim that cinema violence serves as an *ersatz* for a country powerful enough to impose its will by force but too polite to do so has a ring of truth about it. Establishing plausible relationships and limiting ourselves to them will take a great deal of research and not a little restraint. Equally important is the fact that society and film genres have their own histories. Respecting both while establishing "ritual" relationships is a neat trick. It remains to be seen whether these pitfalls will nullify the avowedly intriguing nature of the approach.

Distribution

The complexities involved in distributing a Hollywood film are staggering in comparison with the distribution problems of any other industrial or aesthetic product. Furthermore, film historians have traditionally been and continue to be interested in more than the purely physical, legal, and financial details of film distribution. We might thus divide the following three distribution approaches into two groups: *pre-audience,* i.e., those problems which arise between the time the image is constituted and actual audience viewing (legal and industrial approaches), and *post-audience,* i.e., considerations regarding the effect of rather than the preparations for film viewing (sociological approach).

11) *legal* (archaeology, coming of sound, Hollywood beleaguered)
Carmen, Ira. *Movies, Censorship and the Law.* Ann Arbor: University of Michigan Press, 1966.
Conant, Michael. *Antitrust in the Motion Picture Industry.* Berkeley: University of California Press, 1960.
Randall, Richard S. *Censorship of the Movies.* Madison: University of Wisconsin Press, 1968.
In general, the legal and industrial approaches can be distinguished by the limits of the industry: industrial history concerns the industry's inner workings, while the legal approach concentrates on actions initiated outside the industry, such as law suits, antitrust proceedings, and censorship. Histories of censorship offer something of an exception since the Hays Office was, strictly speaking, within the industry. Nevertheless, in order to achieve continuity in their treatment of film censorship most historians have chosen to deal with the actions of the Hays Office along with those initiated by the government.

The potential problems of legal history belong to a general category to which I have already referred. It is tempting to take the lawmaker or the censor as an absolute figure, one who makes his own decisions, independent of other influences. Yet, as revisionist historians have shown, even the most consistent legal decisions often reflect social or political concerns. Why, for example, did it take 11 full years to decide the famous antitrust suit of

United States vs. Paramount Pictures, Inc., et al. (filed on July 20, 1938; final decision on July 25, 1949)? It is curious, to say the least, that the decision should coincide with the investigations of the House Un-American Activities Committee. Though legal history has as its main subject the establishment and enforcement of laws governing film exhibition, it must not avoid consideration of possible economic, social, or political determinants in the making and application of those laws.

In a similar fashion, the historian of censorship must not forget that the Production Code not only limits Hollywood's rights and possibilities, it also reflects Hollywood's values and concerns. A history of film censorship which neglected to demonstrate the close ties relating the structure of genre films to the strictures of the Production Code would miss an essential point: the Code not only prohibits certain patterns and images, it also guarantees that others will occur (e.g., punishment of crime, perpetuation of the family unit, upholding of moral standards). These are to a great extent the same values which existed beforehand. The Production Code is thus not only a conditioner of the industry, it is also conditioned by it. Legal history must reflect this reciprocal relationship.

12) *industrial* (every period, from archaeology to the present)

> *The American Film Industry.* Ed. Tino Balio. Madison: University of Wisconsin Press, 1976. Includes articles by Russell Merritt ("Nickelodeon Theaters 1905-1914: Building an Audience for the Movies"), Carl Laemmle ("The Business of Motion Pictures"), Mae Huettig ("The Motion Picture Industry Today," i.e., during the war), Thomas Guback ("Hollywood's International Market"), and other important articles written from a studio or industrial point of view.

> Balio, Tino. *United Artists: The Company Built by the Stars.* Madison: University of Wisconsin Press, 1975.

> Gomery, J. Douglas. "The Coming of Sound to the American Cinema: The Transformation of an Industry." Unpublished Ph.D. dissertation, University of Wisconsin-Madison, 1975.

> Guback, Thomas H. *The International Film Industry: Western Europe and America since 1945.* Bloomington: Indiana University Press, 1969.

> Hampton, Benjamin B. *History of the American Film Industry from its Beginnings to 1931.* New York: Dover, 1970 (originally 1931).

> Handel, Leo. *Hollywood Looks at Its Audience.* Urbana: University of Illinois Press, 1950.

As Tino Balio's valuable collection of articles uses the term, "industry" means everything relating to the nonaesthetic aspects of production and distribution. The term thus includes the approaches which I have referred to as technological, studio, legal, and industrial. My usage of the term is quite a bit more restricted: it means all the distribution aspects of the industry which are internally controlled: audience research, publicity, theater chains, programming, financial documentation, and any other problems relating to the industry's distribution concerns. The presuppositions governing this approach run as follows:

image → distribution network → audience (→ money)

Emphasis normally is put on the distribution network itself and on all decisions relating to it.

In many ways this important approach is only beginning. We have precious few extended studies of the film industry, perhaps because most of us possess few of the tools necessary for the formulation of industrial history. It is hard to see how anyone could write this type of history properly without a strong background in economics, an ability to find and decipher legal and financial documents, and a general knowledge of technology, studio operation, and legal or practical restrictions. The industrial historian must not only have access to many types of documents, he must be able to smell out self-serving accounts and poor memories; he must not restrict himself to the documents in a particular collection but seek out the interviews and the conflicting evidence without which the whole picture cannot be painted. Frankly, this is a tall order. Perhaps we are wrong to expect a full industrial history from a decade which is just beginning to train industrial historians. It will undoubtedly take many years to discover the necessary documents and methods. In the meantime we should no doubt concentrate on preserving the memories of those who made Hollywood's industrial history, in the form of oral accounts. The American Film Institute has already begun the task of collecting oral histories, but with an emphasis on aesthetically oriented personnel. If we are ever to have a full industrial history of American film, it is essential that this focus be broadened.

13) *sociological* (coming of sound to new Hollywood)

Jowett, Garth. *Film: The Democratic Art.* Boston: Little, Brown, 1976.

Sklar, Robert. *Movie-Made America: A Social History of the American Movies.* New York: Random House, 1975.

Tudor, Andrew. *Image and Influence: Studies in the Sociology of Film.* New York: St. Martin's, 1975.

As I use the term, "sociological" applies to cinema's effect on the society as a whole, whereas "social" suggests society's effect on film. The basic presupposition of the sociological approach is as follows:

image → audience → social behavior

Implicit in this formula is the notion that film, as a group entertainment form, changes not only individual lives but also the goals according to which those lives are lived and the standards according to which they are judged. No other approach so openly proclaims the importance of Hollywood cinema in shaping twentieth-century America.

However captivating and powerful their hypotheses may appear, sociological historians have found it difficult to maintain the approach throughout an entire book. Robert Sklar sets out to show how movies "shape the character and direction of American culture as a whole" (p. vi). What fascinates him about the movies is their "ability to exercise cultural power" (p. vi), as his title implies. Yet I come away from Sklar's book dissatisfied:

his analyses are interesting, his examples well chosen, and his scholarship
sound, but relatively few pages are directly devoted to showing, as the dust
jacket announces, "How the movies changed American Life." In sum, Sklar's
thesis—the basic hypothesis of the sociological method—is more interesting
than the book. Instead of writing separate essays on the periods where he
genuinely detects a specific influence of film on American life, he has decided to cover all periods, filling in with non-sociological material when he
has no specifically sociological analyses to offer. *Movie-Made America* can
thus be advertised by the publisher as "*The* history of the American Movie,"
thereby encouraging course adoptions and sales, but betraying the essential nature of Sklar's work. As a general history the book is inadequate,
filled with gaps and odd choices of material; as an anti-history comprised
of separate attempts at sociological history it is far more satisfying. It is
unfortunate that *Movie-Made America* had to attempt both.

Garth Jowett's hypotheses are not significantly different, but his book
differs radically from Sklar's. Jowett's purpose is to examine "the dramatic
alterations in both the communications infrastructure and the leisure patterns of the American people when the motion picture was introduced into
the United States" (p. 3). Whereas Sklar's book reads like a cross between
cultural history and literary criticism, Jowett's work is clearly that of a social
scientist. *Film: The Democratic Art* is full of fascinating tables covering
such areas as liquor expenditure, radio ownership, and theater seating capacity. Though Sklar and Jowett often use the same data, borrowed from
industry sources, government figures, or previous studies, Jowett usually
quotes the data in full, letting the figures speak for themselves, while Sklar
leaves out the data but explains its significance. Whereas Sklar sometimes
seems to neglect his overall sociological thesis, Jowett often forgets that
films are aesthetic systems which cannot be summed up by so many facts
and figures. The sociological film historian must maintain a careful balance
between emphasis on the film text and the social context. Sklar and Jowett
come at the sociological approach from entirely different directions; they
thus represent the two dominant tendencies of sociological history as well
as its two most obvious pitfalls—too little and too much sociology.

Periodization

Thus far I have taken for granted a periodization which divides 80 years
of American cinema into nine unequal periods. The time has now come to
reconsider that division. We immediately discover that this periodization
(or any other in current use) grows out of a hopeless confusion of methods.
Most periods are delimited on one end by an approach entirely different
from that used to establish the other limit. The "archaeology" period (to
1905) is largely defined by technological concerns, while the "silent short"
period (1905-14) is separated from its "silent feature" successor (1915-27)
by a change in the industry's distribution methods. The technologically defined "coming of sound" period (1927-34) proves an embarrassment to
many historians.

The generally accepted tripartite division of American (and world) film history into silent, classic sound, and modern sound periods, provides no convenient place for the important changes which transformed Hollywood in the late twenties and early thirties. Even Gerald Mast, probably the most self-conscious periodizer among American general historians, must make room for an extra chapter on the coming of sound to complement his four-part division of American film. And when does this transitional period end? With the rise of a new set of directors and stars? With the last major innovations in the sound field? A convenient date has often seemed to be provided by the change in enforcement of the Production Code which took place in 1934. The period which follows ("Hollywood's golden age," 1934-41) is thus delimited on one end by legal concerns and on the other by the changes in social structure and subject matter occasioned by the advent of war. Or is the date of 1941 to be seen as a technical landmark (the beginning of the deep-focus years, rung in by Welles and Toland)? Or is it the year when Hollywood opened its camp to influential European expatriates (Hitchcock, Renoir)?

And why does the period of "the war years" last from 1941 to 1948? Do these years represent the heyday of the *film noir*? Is 1948 the year when HUAC invaded Hollywood? (Actually, the so-called Hollywood Ten were indicted in 1947.) Or the year of the Paramount antitrust decision? (But the final word didn't come until 1949.) Or the beginning of television's increasingly persistent threat? (Then why does *Ziegfeld Follies* bother to have Red Skelton make fun of TV commercials as early as 1946?) Whatever our justification for picking 1948 as the initial year of the "Hollywood beleaguered" period, it will differ from our reasons for the next delimitation. Though this period is often defined largely by the technological innovations (Cinerama, CinemaScope, 3-D) through which Hollywood sought to regain its audience, its end may conveniently be designated by the beginning of a new distribution strategy—the "blockbuster." Throughout the second half of the 1950s and until the *Cleopatra* fiasco in 1962 scores of high-budget epics were treated to enormous publicity campaigns and exclusive showings in selected big city theaters. If this period is defined by distribution practices, however, the following one gains its unity from social concerns (violence, sexuality) and changing studio organization (rise of independents).

No two film historians will agree on a single periodization, and the one I have presented is just as idiosyncratic as the next. The main flaw in this (or any other current) periodization, however, is not a lack of judgment or precision but a specific methodological failing. The periodizations which we now have derive from general film histories rather than unified approaches; they thus reflect an embarrassing mixture of criteria which may be perfectly acceptable as presentational devices in course textbooks but certainly must not be accepted—as they have generally been—as the standard of professional film historians. We have often assumed that film history is a unified field which requires only a single periodization, valid for historians, critics, and theoreticians alike. Nothing could be farther from the truth. Instead of dividing three-quarters of a century into three, four, or nine watertight compartments—a procedure which is reassuring in its neatness, but provides only an approximate fit to historical phenomena—we need to recognize that each type of history writing implies its own periodization. From time to time, periods defined by one approach will coincide with those suggested by another, but far more often overlapping will occur. Indeed, it is precisely this lack of coincidence which gives cinema its dynamic quality, its constantly changing face.

In order to preserve this complexity and the energy which it generates, American film history must derive its general history from periodizations developed by each separate approach, rather than fit each approach to a compromise periodization borrowed from general histories. In other words, proper film history depends on a two-part approach: 1) an analytic process whereby each method of history writing must evaluate its own materials, develop its own history of American film, and eventually derive its own periodization; and 2) a synthetic process whereby general historians build these analyses into a coherent whole, thereby discovering the complex web of relationships—different in every period—which tie each aspect of film history to the next. Any year from 1927 to 1934, for example, might be cited as a watershed in American film making; the problem is not to choose a single most acceptable date, but to render, in the clearest but most complete way possible, the complexity of a medium in which every year provides a new watershed.

The Canon

What films do we watch? In a field where no single individual can ever hope to see more than a fraction of even one country's total output, certainly there can be no more important question—for historian and critic alike—than that of film choice. Just as periodization ultimately depends on historiographical concerns, so the films we see and show are chosen for reasons which derive directly from historiographical decisions. An American film survey course might include Griffith's *Lonely Villa* because it provides a particularly good example of cross-cutting, Le Roy's *I Am a Fugitive from a Chain Gang* for its social interest, Capra's *You Can't Take It with You* as an example of screwball comedy, Preminger's *Man with the Golden Arm* because it was instrumental in challenging the Code's prohibition on the subject of drug addiction, and *Hatari!* for the Hawks *auteur* qualities which it reveals. Decisions are made according to a wide range of criteria (to which one would have to add popularity, availability, and cost), all of which contain complex variables that need to be analyzed. On the surface, this is not bad; obviously we must see, study, and show films for a variety of reasons. The problem arises when a particular approach so dominates a given period of American film history that a disproportionate number of the films available and mentioned in standard sources are chosen by a single criterion.

The canon of early silent shorts which prevails today, for example, is the result of complex factors: copyright law, far-seeing librarians, evolving taste, and chance, to name but a few. Still more important, however, is a historiographical concern. The prevalent historical method applied to the early silent short is overwhelmingly the "technical" approach. It is not surprising, therefore, that our canon of Griffith Biographs is directly dependent on a standard of technical innovation. As Kemp Niver, who transferred the Library of Congress collection of paper prints to film, explains in the introduction to his *D. W. Griffith: His Biograph Films in Perspective* (see section two above), "The fifty films we finally selected are not necessarily the best films Mr. Griffith made for Biograph, but, rather, each is an example of what appears to be his earliest experiment with some camera use or directing and/or editing technique" (p. i). A similar concern seems to preside over the works on Griffith by Bitzer, Gunning, Henderson, Meyer, Petric, Pratt, and Stern mentioned in section two above. Now it is well-known that the discovery of new techniques was an important aspect of early film endeavor, but we cannot afford to have any period so dominated by a single approach to the determination of a canon.

With each new approach to history writing the canon for a given period is extended or modified. When the French formulated their *politique des auteurs* many forgotten films were saved from oblivion. The current interest in studio and genre studies continues to produce new canons (visible in new courses, new books, new film series: the Hitchcock or Hawks retrospective is now giving way to series devoted to the Hollywood musical and specific studios), as personality cults and interest in deep-focus photography did twenty years ago. Every statement we make about American film ultimately depends on the canon we work with. It is essential that we become more aware of the strong ties which link film choice and historiography if we wish our sample of American film production to be a legitimate one.

1976

The Movies Become Big Business: Publix Theatres and the Chain Store Strategy

Douglas Gomery

During the 1920s the American film industry developed into a strong oligopoly. Ownership of a large theatre circuit provided each vertically-integrated Hollywood firm with significant monopoly power. Historian Lewis Jacobs, using a demand-oriented model, argues that since patrons were willing to pay high prices to see first-run films, the large film producer-distributors purchased theatre chains to control access to their customers. Such an explanation is one-sided: were theatres acquired regardless of expense? I think not; motion picture capitalists sought profit and growth, and hence were quite conscious of costs. Second, Jacobs's (implicit) model ignores issues of business organization. How did Hollywood utilize their new theatre holdings to garner higher profits? In this article I argue that during the 1920s the U.S. film industry became a complete "big business" by adopting the strategy of the chain store. Hollywood-owned circuits increasingly presented a more standardized product, on a national level, at decreasing cost—all directed by a central authority in New York. Exhibition was the branch of the industry which could most easily adopt "big business" practices, and thus accumulate the greatest excess profits. Sam Katz, president of the Publix circuit, pushed most strongly for the chain store system, and by 1929 Publix had become the most powerful theatre organization in U.S. film industry history.

I

During the 1920s chain stores became a significant force in the U.S. economy. They came first in the form of grocery stores (A&P, Grand Union, Kroger), next variety stores (Woolworth, McCrory, Kresge), and then chains for drugs, auto parts, gas stations, and clothing. (Here I define a retail chain as multiple ownership of four or more outlets with centralized control.) During the 1920s chain units rose from 29,000 to 160,000. Sales skyrocketed: for chain drugstroes the increase was 125 per cent; for clothing stores growth topped 400 per cent. Grocery chains were the largest. By 1925 A&P's red-fronted stores had become one of the dominant icons of American life. In 1912 this chain had only 400 outlets; twenty years later there were 15,700. In 1930 A&P's sales topped one billion dollars and accounted for about one-tenth of all food sold in the United States. Business historian Alfred D. Chandler argues that chain store strategy was the major U.S. marketing innovation between 1900 and 1930.[1]

The chief advantage for a chain operation lay in cost reduction through scale economies and monopsony power.[2] Chains could spread fixed costs over more operations and purchase inputs at lower prices. To maximize such savings, chains relied on what was labeled "scientific management." Here large circuits would secure trained managers, experts and other skilled labor to operate the firm at peak efficiency: no waste, rapid turnover, maximum profits and growth. To assure that a standardized product would be sold in a "clean and dependable atmosphere," the chain's managers, operating from a central office, divided up the firm's activities, and had each department perform its specialty at maximum efficiency and minimum cost. Gradually the managers would internalize more and more of the transactions, increase the speed and regularity of operations, and continue to lower costs. Simultaneously the chain would purchase more outlets, grow more powerful, and garner more monopsony power for necessary inputs. Costs would fall even further. Chains advertised widely and developed trade-marks for instant recognition. Large accounting departments provided managers with a continuous flow of information in order to circumvent unneeded expenses. Greater profits facilitated new financing, and chains quickly moved to capture new markets during the 1920s.[3]

The growth of chains of movie theatres, like retail stores, began on the regional level. As late as 1920 there still existed wide differences in movie exhibition. Picture palaces were still the exception, not the rule, and the strategy for live entertainment-movie presentation varied from city to city. Gradually , during and after World War I, certain regional chains had taken on increasingly more power, and hence a definable set of exhibition strategies arose. The most successful was the Balaban & Katz (hereafter B&K) system. Perfected in Chicago between 1917 and 1923, it enabled B&K to overtake all its larger rivals and thus dominate the Chicago market as well as the rest of Illinois and most of Iowa and Nebraska. In short B&K developed chain store organization for movie exhibition within the city of Chicago.

The B&K system involved the complete operation of exhibition— standardized and controlled from a central office. Like other exhibitors B&K wished to present the most popular films. However, since B&K entered the exhibition market relatively late, other Chicago exhibitors held exclusive contracts with the major Hollywood producers. B&K had to build its chain with states-rights, subsequent-run, and First National films. Consequently, B&K concentrated on the non-filmic factors of exhibition, fashioned a strategy centered on five important inputs, and thus developed a large comparative advantage over its competitors.[4]

First B&K recognized the important socioeconomic changes taking place in Chicago (and other American cities). The construction of mass transit in the late nineteenth and early twentieth centuries enabled middle and upper-middle class (in terms of income) residents of U.S. cities to flee to the new "streetcar suburbs." Consequently, B&K did not build its first large theatre, the Central Park, downtown, but on Chicago's far west side in Lawndale. Chicago's elevated system had reached Lawndale in 1902, and what had been a semi-suburban area inhabited by a few thousand people, in fifteen years grew to become a crowded urban neighborhood of a hundred thousand people.[5]

Following the prosperity of the Central Park, B&K sought another outlying location and selected a site at the business center of the far northside neighborhood, Uptown. Here B&K built the Riviera in 1918. Now B&K controlled picture palaces which could draw from Chicago's north and west sides. To reach all areas of the city, B&K needed to build on the south side and in the central business district, the Loop. The south-side theatre, the Tivoli (c. 1921), came first. Again B&K located in the largest outlying business center, the south-side equivalent to Uptown. With the huge profits from these theatres, B&K built the Chicago Theatre in the Loop. Once this matrix of four palaces was in operation, B&K could draw from all parts of the city. No Chicagoan needed more than 30 minutes to reach a B&K theatre using the "el" or a streetcar. Thereafter B&K added theatres, reducing the required travel time to 15 minutes. Simultaneously B&K gained control of all the large theatres in the Loop. Thus by 1925 B&K monopolized movie exhibition in Chicago, not by owning all of the theatres, but by controlling large picture palaces in the major outlying business centers and in the Loop.[6]

The "show" in a B&K theatre began before anyone saw a film, or even live entertainment; the building itself served as an important part of the "moviegoing" experience. *Moving Picture World* argued that the Riviera was not as much a theatre as a baronial hall, a place to hold teas or benefit balls. Here were buildings in which B&K's upwardly mobile patrons could feel at home in a palace fit not so much for a seventeenth-century king as a twentieth-century business tycoon. In addition, the exterior of B&K theatres served as a massive advertisement. A huge electric sign identified the theatre. These signs were sometimes three stories high and flashed their message in several colors. Behind the sign an ornate stained glass window and the theatre facade reproduced many of the motifs of the interior. In an era when electricity had been common for only twenty years, the exterior sign was quite a novelty. In contrast, the facades and stained glass windows of B&K theatres served to remind Chicagoans of conservative institutions like churches or banks.

Inside, the foyers were as spectacular as the exteriors and able to accommodate a waiting crowd large enough to fill the theatre. Decoration included massive chandeliers, sometimes costing $25,000 each, a painting gallery, elaborate drapery, and space for a pianist to entertain those waiting. No B&K ticket holder needed to stand outside in inclement weather. Numerous ushers serviced the patrons and an intricate network of passageways enabled eight thousand people to enter and exit with relative comfort and speed. In the auditorium B&K prided itself on excellent sight lines, comfortable seats, and good acoustics. The lighting in the auditorium was varied throughout all performances to supplement the mood of the films or live performance. B&K did not ignore a theatre's auxiliary services. Restrooms were spacious, clean and decorated with paintings and sculpture. In addition B&K provided free babysitting. Mothers could leave their children in the care of a trained attendant and a nurse, and enjoy the entertainment. Playrooms were large, well-equipped, indoor playgrounds. B&K advertised this service widely.[7]

The third aspect of the B&K formula was quite special during the 1920s: air-conditioned theatres. Prior to the Central Park, the nation's first air-cooled movie house, most theatres closed during the summer, or opened to small crowds. Engineers tried to perfect a safe cooling system with adequate power, but available chemical refrigerants proved too dangerous for crowded theatres. Researchers made important progress during the first decade of the twentieth century and by 1911 had developed the technology to safely cool large buildings. Here technological change centered in Chicago because firms in this city still slaughtered and processed most of America's meat.[8]

B&K placed the newly developed carbon dioxide air-cooling systems in the Central Park and Riviera. The cool air entered into the auditorium through vents in the floor and rose to the ceiling to be removed by exhaust fans in the roof. In 1921 engineers installed an improved system in the Chicago Theatre which included a humidity control using an air washer and cleaner, and a special heater. By 1925, motion picture trade papers constantly noted how air-conditioning seemed to explain the large grosses of B&K theatres. B&K's advertising department continuously reminded Chicagoans of the coolness of its theatres, usually by adding icicles to the names of the theatres in newspaper movie listings. Chicago's Health Commissioner even argued that the B&K's theatres had better air than Pike's Peak and recommended all Chicagoans to go to a B&K theatre several hours each week. Such advertising spurred public acceptance and helped the box office; during the summers B&K frequently experienced larger grosses than during winter months.[9]

Fourth, B&K's system was highly labor intensive, sometimes requiring more than one hundred employees in each house. Most famous were the ushers. B&K recruited corps of male college students, dressed them in red uniforms with white gloves and yellow epaulets, and demanded extreme politeness to all customers (with no tips). B&K regulated and monitored quite closely all actions of its employees. For example, ushers were admonished to refer to a patron as a gentleman, lady, or child, never old man, girl, or boy. Ushers could never shout at customers, and always ended any request with "thank you." Ushers and doormen made up one-third of a theatre's staff. Musicians accounted for another third, and projectionists, stage staff, and maintenance the rest.[10]

Rigid control over employees served important functions. First it guaran-

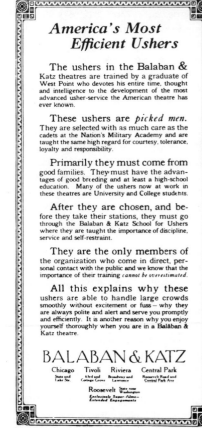

The ushers were part of the show at the Balaban & Katz theatres. From the Theatre Historical Society Collection.

teed a conservative public image—much like a bank or fine hotel. Second it kept labor costs low since most employees were either young, black, and/or female. Labor costs were closely scrutinized and standardized. For example, B&K developed charts specifying precisely the number of janitors it would take to clean any given floor area. Employees provided more than simply service and a good image, however. Ushers maintained "spill cards" to record the number of patrons in all parts of the theatre. At any time the chief usher and the manager of the theatre knew how many vacancies existed, could instantly move new patrons to those seats, and plan how to avoid empty seats for future shows. In that way B&K kept its theatres optimally filled, and thus maximized box-office revenue.[11]

Finally B&K presented more than motion pictures. A vast corps of musicians accompanied the films; live stage entertainment filled one-third of the show's two hours. In fact, before B&K had access to popular films it was able to hire important vaudeville entertainers and insure a constantly attractive entertainment package to its customers. In that way B&K could avoid sustained periods of poor grosses and guarantee a constant flow of revenue. In time B&K became more famous for impressive stage attractions, orchestras, and organists than for any movies it presented.

For musicians and organists B&K developed local stars. B&K stage spectacles offered revues with elaborate settings and intricate, multicolored lighting effects. The stage show stood by itself as a separate presentation unit of a vaudeville-movie entertainment package. In 1919 B&K tried presentations which interrupted the narrative of the film, but abandoned these experiments after one year. Thereafter B&K tested different combinations of live talent, and in 1923 settled on the pure presentation: a separate, unique musical revue, not tied at all to the film. Such shows were expensive, costing about five thousand dollars each to set up. To maximize income and minimize costs, B&K rotated shows. Thus, each presentation unit played one week at the Chicago Theatre, then a week at the Riviera, then a week at the Tivoli. Expenses were split on the basis of theatre size and run status, so B&K charged off 50 per cent of the expenses to the Chicago Theatre, 30 per cent to the Tivoli, and 20 per cent for the Riviera. Costs fell as B&K took over more theatres. Yet repetition did not hurt business; as many patrons as usual turned out at the Tivoli even though the show had already appeared a week at each of two other theaters.

II

In November 1925 B&K merged with Famous Players, and Sam Katz brought his management team to New York to institute the Balaban & Katz system for the Publix chain.[13] Immediately Katz set in place the five-factored strategy that worked so well in Chicago. Simultaneously Katz started to run Publix like a "legitimate business." First he took all power from the house managers and centralized it in New York. Wanting to create a logo as famous as that of A&P or Woolworth, Katz changed the name of many theatres to Paramount. In short, he adapted the principles of chain store operation to the B&K system to create the national Publix chain.[14]

In order to maximize the cost savings which accrue to chain operations, Katz pushed for rapid growth. In five years Publix expanded from approximately 300 to 1200 theatres.[15] Publix did construct theatres, but most of its growth came from merger or direct takeover. By 1930 Publix dominated film exhibition in the South, from North Carolina to Texas, as well as in Michigan, Illinois, Minnesota, Iowa, the Dakotas, Nebraska, and New England. In addition, through Famous-Players Canadian, Publix also controlled Canada. Over two million people attended Publix theatres each day. Publix employed more musicians than any other organization in the world—an estimated 12,000. At its peak during the 1930–31 movie season, Publix was the largest motion picture circuit in film history.[16]

Katz supervised all operations. His assistants controlled everything from planning music to advertising, from booking films to acquiring new theatres. (See Chart 1.) The day-to-day activities were handled by four regional managers. Under the regional managers came divisional managers, district managers, and the local house managers. Within this structure, power flowed from the top. Katz, his New York staff and the four regional managers selected all films for rental, developed and routed all stage shows, picked and trained employees, determined advertising policy, secured supplies, and monitored all expenses.[17]

Chart 1*

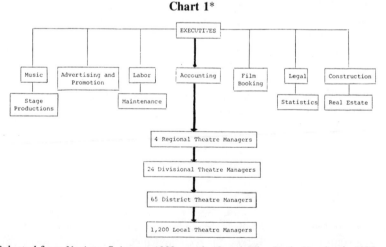

*Adapted from *Variety*, 7 August 1929, pp. 9–10 and *Film Daily Yearbook, 1927*, p. 665. This is not the official company chart; I created it to simplify the division of labor and management for Publix Theatres (1926–1932).

All booking was done from New York. Since Paramount did not make enough films to fill Publix screen-time, Publix bargained with and obtained favorable terms from the other major producer-distributors. Publix's central buyer relied on data from previous years, which had been compiled in massive detail, and suggestions from managers at all levels. The actual scheduling began six to eight weeks in advance. The regional managers and the booker prepared master booking sheets and then sent them down the line to be commented upon at each level. The divisional, district and local managers added the "local" touch, eliminated regionally offensive films, and returned the sheets to New York for final approval. Then Katz held numerous meetings to deal with any last minute contingencies. Executive managers at all levels were recruited from the areas they supervised, and visited their territories several times a year. Katz thought experienced local managers made the best executives since they had firsthand knowledge of the "needs" of their communities.[18]

All deluxe first- and second-run Publix houses presented stage shows. Specialists prepared Publix unit-shows in New York, selecting all props, costumes, performers, and lighting cues. By 1928 Publix had thirty-three such units on the road. A local manager's only responsibility was to make sure shows began and ended on time. New York executives also hired all organists and pit orchestra members. These musicians did not move with the presentation units, however, Publix could employ the most popular talent, mount expensive shows, and spread the cost over several hundred theatres. Publix effected huge cost savings from economies of scale—as had the Keith-Albee and Orpheum vaudeville circuits in previous years.[19]

Each unit was organized around a central theme or motif. Although none can be judged as typical, the "Say It With Flowers" unit of April 1929 illustrates many of the features of Publix stage shows. The setting was the garden of a summer house, complete with a stage band in brilliant red British military uniforms. Six women in white satin hoopskirts performed an opening dance, after which master of ceremonies Ben Black introduced a female vocalist who sang "All I Want To Know." The stage band followed with a novelty arrangement of "Sweethearts on Parade"; a male comic did a bit with Black; and the six dancers from the opening number encored. All performers appeared in the finale of the thirty-minute show, dancing and singing around a maypole in the garden. The whole stage was covered with multicolored lights, contrasting with the streamers from the maypole. A stage band, several "acts," and a spectacular ending formed the basic structure of all Publix unit shows. Frank Cambria, head of the Publix stage department, and his assistants developed seasonal themes as well as ones tied to current public fads such as the radio or airplane.[20]

When Sam Katz moved to Publix, he not only instituted the same labor policy that had worked so well for B&K but went several steps farther. He closely supervised the selection and training of all employees and even established a school to train local managers.[21] Publix managers were expected to take an active part in the civic activities of their communities and file regular reports detailing the nature of this participation. All duties performed were recorded; all instructions and emergencies anticipated. Nothing was left to chance. Using such methods Katz guaranteed that the name Publix meant courteous, costless service to all patrons.[22]

In Chicago B&K advertised widely, but with no more frequency than its competitors. Now in a national market Katz determined Publix could not rely on "word of mouth." Advertising and publicity became vital inputs. Katz's experts formulated numerous ambitious advertising programs in order to sell the Publix and Paramount names. The central Publix slogan became: "You don't need to know what's playing at a Publix House. It's bound to be the best show in town."[23] All advertising copy was prepared by Publix specialists at the New York office and sent down the line in the form of a manual, along with the film and stage show. This manual contained model ads, sketches, suggestions on how to place the ads, descriptions of "stunts" to promote the theatre's program, and even publicity stories to be planted in the newspaper. The major Hollywood producers supplied a similar press kit, but the New York office required Publix managers to use the in-house manual. Each Publix local manager simply selected the material appropriate to his or her market and then executed the advertising campaign within a budget specified from New York. Since each local advertising budget was balanced only once a month, the local manager had some flexibility in advertising appropriations. However, in order to conduct any elaborate advertising the local manager had to secure permission from the Publix New York office.[24]

Publix buyers in New York purchased all supplies and equipment, and allocated materials from regional warehouses. Of course Publix bought in bulk. In addition, rather than just accepting the going price in any one territory, Publix experts searched the United States for the lowest rate. Supplies were issued against manager's requisitions, but were not allowed to exceed certain budgeted amounts. The New York office reviewed all requests for equipment and repairs, and local managers needed authorization from New York for all major outlays.[25]

By now it is obvious that Publix kept careful control on all expenditures at its theatres. Each theatre had a weekly budget detailing all costs. Local managers had to submit weekly reports of actual expenditures, and these figures were carefully scrutinized by accountants in the home office. Any overage had to be explained in a written report. In addition, local managers recorded all nonfinancial aspects of their operations and forwarded such records to the New York office. Here Publix accountants constructed elaborate charts to serve as guides for future decision making. For example, for all deluxe Publix houses, assistant managers recorded the temperature and humidity from the orchestra floor, balcony, lobby and outside every hour on

30,222 in
Two Days!

Into this Paradise of luxury, color and enchantment they came, more than 30,000 in two days, Saturday and Sunday, thrilling with new excitement at every step! The spaciousness of the place! The superb height and dignity of the Grand Hall as they entered! The decoration and equipment throughout, so beautiful that each detail made people halt to admire it alone! And then, a *show worthy of the setting!* These thousands are telling more thousands and they are all coming back, week after week, for there is nothing like the Paramount in all New York for sheer luxury and unprecedented entertainment values!

Continuous 10:45 A. M. to Closing.

Popular Prices!

The
Home of
Paramount
Pictures

Paramount
THEATRE

Located in
the Paramount
Building,
Times Square.

Movie patrons in the twenties went to movie theatres as well as to the movies.
From the Theatre Historical Society Collection.

the hour for the complete operating day. Publix experts then evaluated this data against ideal standards and issued new orders concerning use of the heating and air-conditioning. Local managers also had to hold to strict timing of the theatre activitties. Publix made heavy use of the "spill cards" perfected by B&K in Chicago. Publix real estate experts planned, built, and acquired all new theatres. Specialists calculated traffic patterns, population densities, income distributions, and recreation habits before a theatre site was even considered. When Publix purchased a deluxe.theatre, air-conditioning was immediately added, and other modifications made so that the house fit the Publix standard.[26]

III

The coming of sound changed the Publix system very little. Filmed "stage-shows"—vaudeville shorts—replaced live acts. Orchestras and organists were retained in only the largest theatres. In March 1928, the Publix stage-show circuit reached its acme. Each unit played a guaranteed 33 weeks per year plus 4 weeks vacation. Sam Katz, always quite cost conscious, quickly reasoned that vaudeville acts recorded on sound motion pictures could present the most popular musical entertainment at a huge cost reduction. Thus he lobbied hard for Paramount/Publix to adopt sound.[27] By June 1929 Paramount was producing a continous supply of sound vaudeville shorts, and Katz began to disband the stage-show units, and lay off musicians, organists, and stagehands. Only the Paramount Theatre in New York and the Chicago Theatre retained live stage shows on a consistent basis. By September 1929 the transformation was complete. Publix's products were all-sound, more standardized, more easily monitored, and more profitable.[28]

With this new profit base Paramount/Publix corporation began to expand toward complete monopoly. Between September 1929 and May 1930 Publix acquired 500 more theatres. In June 1929 Paramount/Publix purchased 50 per cent of the newly formed Columbia Broadcasting System (CBS). Still Zukor and Katz wanted more economic power. On 1 September 1929 Paramount/Publix agreed to merge with Warner Bros. to form Paramount-Vitaphone. This new combine would control over 1,700 theatres, six motion picture studios, CBS, the Columbia Phonography Company, and Warners' vast holdings in music publishing. Three giants, RCA, the newly merged Fox-Loew's, and Paramount-Vitaphone would then dominate five entertainment industries: motion pictures, vaudeville, music publishing, radio, and phonograph.[29]

The Paramount/Publix-Warner Bros. merger never took place. The new administration of President Herbert Hoover threatened to sue for antitrust violations. This proposed merger signaled the apex of Paramount/Publix power. Business continued to be fine in 1930: Publix grossed $113,000,000; film rental for Paramount reached $69,000,000. However, Paramount/Publix's consolidated balance sheet was heavy with debt. In five short years

Publix's expansion had generated $30,000,000 of obligations in the form of bonds and guaranteed repurchase agreements.[30] Late in 1930 box office revenues began to decline drastically. Zukor and Katz scrambled to meet short-term deficits; still Katz stubbornly clung to the expansionary philosophy which had generated all the debt. However, during the Great Depression chain store methods could not keep costs low enough to generate sufficient revenue to cover Publix's vast number of mortgages. Sam Katz became Paramount/Publix's scapegoat and was forced to resign in October 1932. Still the Katz system, in a modified form, would be used by Paramount/Publix well into the 1950s.[31]

IV

Prior to 1920 movie exhibition was primarily a regional, not national, operation. Business practices tended to be those modeled on partnerships or small corporations of the nineteenth century. Following the lead of Publix, movie exhibitors adopted the methods of large modern corporations. Like chains in other industries, Publix operated in a national market using coordinated advertising and an identifiable trademark. Scale economies, and monopsony power enabled it to significantly reduce costs. Publix hired the most popular live entertainment, and motion pictures, and sold the package using innovations first developed in Chicago. Expansion proceeded in an orderly fashion: costs fell, profits rose, more theatres were acquired. Other chains copied Publix's methods. The coming of sound altered operations little; the Great Depression would force changes. However, by then vertically integrated movie chains were "big business" in size and operating technique, and thus able to survive the Depression, dominate U.S. film exhibition for the next twenty years, and serve as the cornerstone of Hollywood's monopoly power.

NOTES

[1] Alfred D. Chandler, *The Visible Hand* (Cambridge: Harvard University Press, 1977), pp. 233–237; Thomas C. Cochran, *200 Years of American Business* (New York: Delta, 1977), pp. 116–117; William E. Leuchtenburg, *The Perils of Prosperity* (Chicago: University of Chicago Press, 1958), p. 192; Godfrey M. Lebhar, *Chain Stores in America, 1859–1962* (New York: Chain Store Publishing Co., 1963), pp. 24–64.

[2] Monopsony power results when a firm is one of a limited number of buyers of a certain input, and thus can bargain for a lower purchase price.

[3] Walter S. Hayward and Percival White, *Chain Stores*, 3rd ed. (New York: McGraw Hill, 1928), pp. 1–14, 571; William S. Darby, *Story of the Chain Store* (New York: Dry Good Economist, 1928), pp. 41–59; Chandler, pp. 208, 236–239; Godfrey M. Lebhar, *The Chain Store: Boon or Bane* (New York: Harper & Brothers, 1932), pp. 25–32.

[4] Many inputs made up any exhibitor's product; B&K did not hold a comparative advantage in them all. For example, although B&K utilized large-scale advertising,

and by all accounts was successful at it, it did not innovate any new advertising techniques.

[5]Paul F. Cressey, "Population Succession in Chicago: 1898–1930," *American Journal of Sociology*, 44 (1938), p. 59; Homer Hoyt, *One Hundred Years of Land Values in Chicago* (Chicago: University of Chicago Press, 1933), pp. 225–229; Chicago Plan Commission, *Forty-Four Cities in the City of Chicago* (Chicago: Chicago Plan Commission, 1942), pp. 27–28; *Exhibitor's Herald*, 15 June 1918, p. 22.

[6]Chicago Historical Society, Arthur G. Levy Collection, "Largest Motion-Picture Theatres in Chicago and Vicinity," 12 July 1935, (mimeo), n.p.; Michael Conant, *Antitrust in the Motion Picture Industry* (Berkeley: University of California Press, 1960), pp. 154–155; Chicago Recreation Commission, *The Chicago Recreation Survey*, 1937, Vol. II, *Commerical Recreation* (Chicago, 1938), pp. 36–37; Hoyt, *One Hundred Years*, pp. 227–231, 262.

[7]*Moving Picture World*, 5 October 1918, p. 67; R. W. Sexton and B. F. Betts, eds., *American Theatres of Today* (New York: Architectural Book Publishing Co., 1927), p. 1; "Uptown Theatre," *Marquee*, 9 (Second Quarter, 1977), pp. 1–27; Theatre Historical Society, *The Chicago Theatre* (Notre Dame, Indiana: 1975), n.p.; *Motion Picture News*, 9 April 1921, pp. 2485–86; John W. Landon, *Jesse Crawford* (Vestal, New York: The Vestal Press, 1974), p. 37.

[8]Fred Wittenmeyer, "Cooling of Theatres and Public Buildings," *Ice and Refrigeration*, July, 1922, pp. 13–14; Oscar E. Anderson, *Refrigeration in America* (Princeton: Princeton University Press, 1953), p. 223; Margaret Ingeles, *Willis Haviland Carrier* (New York: Country Life Press, 1952), p. 64.

[9]"Air Conditioning System in Motion Picture House," *Ice and Refrigeration*, LXIX (November, 1925), pp. 251–52; "Heating, Ventilating and Cooling Plant of the Tivoli Theatre," *Power Plant Engineering*, 26 (1 March 1922), pp. 249–255; *Variety*, 9 September 1925, p. 30; *Variety*, 10 June 1925, p. 31.

[10]Arthur Mayer, *Merely Colossal* (New York: Simon and Schuster, 1953), p. 71; Ira Berkow, *Maxwell Street* (Garden City: Doubleday, 1977), p. 201; David Wallerstein, interview held in Slinger, Wisconsin, 28 August 1977; "Uptown Theatre Personnel List," *Marquee*, 9 (Second Quarter, 1977), p. 28; Carrie Balaban, *Continuous Performance* (New York: A. J. Balaban Foundation, 1964), pp. 54–55, 95.

[11]*Exhibitor's Herald and Motography*, 21 December 1918, p. 25; Barney Balaban and Sam Katz, *The Fundamental Principles of Balaban and Katz Theatre Management* (Chicago: Balaban and Katz, 1926), pp. 69–73.

[12]*New York Times*, 18 September 1966, p. 18; *Variety*, 12 April 1923, p. 30; *Variety*, 12 July 1923, p. 27; *Variety*, 1 November 1923, p. 26; *Variety*, 8 November 1923, p. 21; *Variety*, 8 December 1922, p. 37; *Variety*, 29 March 1923, p. 30; *Variety*, 23 September 1925, p. 32.

[13]This merger was part of a general trend toward vertical integration in the U.S. film industry between 1925 and 1930. Paramount/Publix was the largest, and, I think, the most important of the new combinations.

[14]*Variety*, 28 October 1925, p. 27; Mason Miller, "Famous Players in Transition Period," *The Magazine of Wall Street*, 23 April 1927, p. 1178; *Variety*, 26 June 1929, p. 5; "Review of Operations—Paramount Famous Lasky," *Commerical and Financial Chronicle*, 21 April 1928, p. 2490.

[15]It is impossible to more than estimate the number of theatres in the Publix chain at any one time because of extremely complicated real estate arrangements and sometimes secret deals.

[16]U.S. Congress. Senate. Temporary National Economic Committee. *The Motion Picture Industry–A Pattern of Control*, Monograph 43. 76th Congress, 3rd session, 1941, pp. 10, 12, 15; *The Film Daily Yearbook, 1931* (New York: Film Daily, 1931),

pp. 823–844; *The Film Daily Yearbook, 1927* (New York: Film Daily, 1927), pp. 649–671; *Variety,* 7 August 1929, pp. 3–4, 50; *Wall Street Journal,* 11 June 1927, pp. 1, 4.

[17]Howard T. Lewis, ed., *Cases on the Motion Picture Industry* (New York: McGraw-Hill, 1930), p. 516; Mayer, *Colossal,* p. 102; *Variety,* 7 August 1929, p. 10; *Film Daily,* 26 August 1927, pp. 1, 4.

[18]Joseph P. Kennedy, ed., *The Story of the Films as Told by Leaders of the Industry* (New York: A. W. Shaw, 1927), p. 275; Lewis, *Cases,* pp. 516–519; Mayer, *Colossal,* pp. 106–111; Jesse L. Lasky, *I Blow My Own Horn* (Garden City: Doubleday, 1957), p. 241; U.S. Congress, *A Pattern of Control,* pp. 10–15.

[19]*Variety,* 7 August 1929, p. 10; *New York Times,* 10 July 1927, p. 24; *Film Daily,* 21 November 1926, pp. 1, 18; *Film Daily,* 8 April 1926, pp. 1, 6; *Barrons,* 11 November 1926, p. 10; Lewis, *Cases,* p. 519; Kennedy, *Story,* pp. 276–77; Ben M. Hall, *The Best Remaining Seats* (New York: A. N. Potter, 1962), pp. 207–209.

[20]*Variety,* 10 April 1929, p. 41; A. Raymond Gallo, "Presentation Acts," *The Motion Picture Almanac, 1929* (New York: Quigley Publications, 1929), pp. 129–130; Balaban, *Continuous Performance,* pp. 94–95.

[21]Katz eventually dropped the school; other circuits were hiring away recent graduates, while contributing nothing to the cost of education.

[22]*Variety,* 18 January 1961, p. 4; *Film Daily,* 14 January 1926, p. 1; *Film Daily,* 26 February 1926, p. 1; *Film Daily,* 30 July 1926, pp. 1–2; Lewis, *Cases,* pp. 519–520; Kennedy, *Story,* pp. 266–270.

[23]*Variety,* 7 August 1929, p. 4.

[24]*Variety,* 7 August 1929, p. 10, 189; *New York Times,* 25 June 1927, p. 15; Mayer, *Colossal,* pp. 107–108; Lewis, *Cases,* pp. 520–521.

[25]Mayer, *Colossal,* p. 105; Lewis, *Cases,* p. 521.

[26]Kennedy, *Story,* pp. 265, 270–272; *Variety,* 7 August 1929, p. 10; *Variety,* 18 January 1961, p. 4; Lewis, *Cases,* pp. 521–522.

[27]Legally the Paramount Famous Lasky Corporation and Publix were two distinct entities until 24 April 1930. Then the name was formally changed to the Paramount Publix Corporation.

[28]*Film Daily,* 8 April 1929, p. 1; *Film Daily,* 16 April 1929, pp. 1, 4; *Variety,* 14 May 1930, p. 4; *Variety,* 29 May 1929, p. 30; *Variety,* 26 Spetember 1928, p. 19; *Variety,* 7 August 1929, p. 10; Hall, *Seats,* pp. 251–53.

[29]*Variety,* 12 September 1928, p. 57; *Variety,* 11 July 1928, p. 4; *Barrons,* 21 October 1929, p. 15; *Barrons,* 26 May 1930, p. 9; *Variety,* 19 June 1929, p. 65; *Variety,* 28 August 1928, p. 27; *Variety, 11 September 1929,* p. 5; *New York Times,* 22 September 1929, II, p. 14; *Barrons,* 26 August 1929, p. 29; *Variety,* 2 October 1929, pp. 1, 4; *Variety,* 16 October 1929, p. 35.

[30]*Barrons,* 7 November 1932, p. 16; *Barrons,* 28 October 1929, p. 15; *Variety,* 9 October 1929, p. 6; *Moody's Manual of Industrials, 1932* (New York: Moody's Investor Service, 1932), p. 2427; *Moody's Manual of Industrials, 1933* (New York: Moody's Investor Service, 1933), p. 3048.

[31]*New York Times,* 3 November 1932, p. 31; *Film Daily,* 18 November 1930, pp. 1, 4; *Film Daily,* 10 April 1931, pp. 1–2; *Film Daily,* 20 August 1931, p. 1; *Variety,* 18 March 1931, p. 20; *Variety,* 29 April 1931, p. 7.

Dividing Labor for Production Control: Thomas Ince and the Rise of the Studio System[1]

Janet Staiger

Thomas Ince was a classic case of a stage actor who, during a brief period of unemployment in 1910, turned to the fledgling movies as a source of income. Yet his long-term impact on filmmaking would be very great indeed. Working first for IMP and then Biograph, he returned to IMP when promised a chance to direct. He completed his first film in December 1910. Ince soon tired of the one-reel format, however, and accepted a position in the fall of 1911 to direct for Kessel and Bauman's New York Motion Picture Company. He headed to Edendale, California, where a small group of people were already making films. The studio at that time was a converted grocery store: one stage (without even a muslin overhang), a scene dock, a small lab and office, and a bungalow which served as a dressing room. Ince wrote, directed, and cut his first film within one week.[2] From these beginnings, by 1913 he had a fully developed continuity script procedure; by 1916 a one-half million dollar studio on 43 acres of land with concrete buildings. There were a 165-foot electrically lit building (which was unique), eight stages 60 by 150 feet, an administration building for the executive and scenario departments, property, carpenter, plumbing, and costume rooms, a restaurant and commissary, 300 dressing rooms, a hothouse, and a natatorium—and 1,000 employees and a studio structure which was essentially that associated with the big studio period of later years.[3] Why?

Previous historians have provided only partial answers. Lewis Jacobs attributes Ince's innovations to the need to standardize large-scale productions through "formula" pictures and publicity: "Essentially a businessman, he [Ince] conducted himself and his film making in businesslike fashion. . . . Planning in advance meant better unity of structure, less chance of uneven quality, and economy of expression." Kalton Lahue, in *Dreams for Sale*, writes, "Ince kept [his studio] functioning at peak efficiency by holding a tight rein on everything that was done." Eric Rhode notes that Ince "was among the first film-makers to adapt his craft to the latest ideas in industrial management and to set up the assembly-line type of production."[4]

What historians describe without outlining structure is the division of labor under the control of a corporate manager. Nor do they indicate the steps Ince took in progressing to his final system. Using Paul A. Baran and Paul M. Sweezy's monograph *Monopoly Capital* as a large framework, Harry Braverman, in *Labor and Monopoly Capital,* sets up a model and explanation of how and why labor is divided. As a model it is stochastic rather than deterministic—some amount of variation may occur, but on the whole, the model should account for an individual instance of the historical change and development of a labor structure.

Braverman's Model of Labor in Monopoly Capital

According to Braverman, in the most basic capitalistic situation, humans have a potential labor power which they sell to the capitalist who, in turn, hopes to derive from their labor power the greatest possible surplus. But this potential labor power is affected by: 1) "the organization of the process" and 2) "the forms of supervision over it."[5] By selling his/her labor power, the worker is no longer in control of his/her labor time; that control is ceded to the capitalist who has purchased the labor time and the potential of labor power. Naturally, given the profit maximization motive, the capitalist will seek to gain as much as possible from that potential in time and power.

However, unlike physical capital, the results of this purchase are uncertain. The original method of the capitalist was to "[utilize] labor as it [came] to him from prior forms of production," which usually was the craft or domestic system of labor.[6] The capitalist subcontracted for the work he wanted accomplished. But certain problems arose with this system: "irregularity of production, loss of materials in transit and through embezzlement, slowness of manufacture, lack of uniformity and uncertainty of the quality of production."[7]

The first means of striving for control of these variables was to centralize the employment, which provided some control over the irregularity of production through the threat of loss of employment. This initial step, however, had no effect on the other problems. It is here that division of the labor process develops as a second means of solving the other areas of uncertainty.

The division of labor process "begins with the *analysis of the labor process . . .* the separation of the work of production into its constituent elements."[8] Assigning a worker to repeat a single segment of a total task produces three advantages according to Adam Smith: 1) increase in dexterity, 2) saving time, and 3) "the invention of a great number of machines which facilitate and abridge labor."[9] A fourth advantage, saving costs, was pointed out by Charles Babbage. Since the task was segmented, only the worker who was doing the most difficult part of the work had to be paid for his/her skill rather than paying all the workers for the most difficult part— which was what happened under the older craft system. Braverman asserts that these principles have led to separating the worker's brain from his/her hands and that division of labor promotes an almost systematic elimination of skills required for a person to work.

This division of labor was the second of three steps in monopoly capital's quest for organizing and supervising the potential for labor time and power. The third was "scientific management" which was "the control over work through the control over the *decisions that are made in the course of work.*"[10] This advancement in management was initiated, in particular, by Frederick Winslow Taylor, whose work (often called "Taylorism" and typified by the efficiency experts of the first part of the twentieth century) began to be widely disseminated after 1890.

The effects of division of labor and scientific management were multiple—all leading to the separation of the planning phase and the execution phase. This separation destroys an ideal of the whole person, both the creator and the producer of his/her ideas.[11] Practically, this results in certain characteristics which appear consistently in divided labor.

First, there is a physical separation between the conception and production phases.

> The concept of control adopted by modern management requires that every activity in production have its several parallel activities in the management center: each must be devised, precalculated, tested, laid out, assigned and ordered, checked and inspected, and recorded throughout its duration and upon completion. The result is that the process of production is replicated in paper form before, as, and after it takes place in physical form.[12]

Second, not only is conception and execution divided, but specialization results in both planning and producing. Thus there develops the modern corporation which is characterized by: 1) corporate managers, 2) "producing activities which are subdivided among functional departments, each having a specific aspect of the process for its domain,"[13] and 3) extensive development of the marketing process.

Ince had several models of organizing work available to him. He had worked in the theater and might have chosen a labor structure similar to that. Or he might have followed Griffith's (and most of the rest of the industry's) lead: group units which shot from a brief outline.[14] Instead, he seems to have followed the lead of modern industry. Ince, however, is not unique. He is an innovator, perhaps ahead of others in some respects but not by much. His contributions to the production structure of the film industry need to be placed in perspective by examining the conception/execution process and the labor division in his production unit.

The Separation of Conception and Execution

The first part of this structure is Ince's separation of the conception and production phases of filmmaking. To repeat Braverman's observation:

> The concept of control adopted by modern management requires that every

activity in production have its several parallel activities in the management center. . . . The result is that the process of production is replicated in paper form before, as, and after it takes place in physical form.[15]

For Ince and filmmaking, this replication is in the continuity script. The framework for the continuity script already existed in the scenarios of the period. In nearly every issue of *The Moving Picture World* descriptions of how to write scenarios are given budding screenwriters. Even as Ince was beginning to direct, an article in 1911 advises:

> Follow the cast of characters with the scenario proper. Divide the scenario into scenes, giving each change in the location of the action a separate scene— that is, whenever the plot renders it necessary for the operator to change the position of his camera, as from an interior to an exterior view, begin a new scene. Number the scenes consecutively to the end of the play. At the beginning of each scene, give a brief but clear word picture of the settings of the scene; also the position and action of the characters introduced when the picture first flashes on the screen. . . . Now carefully study out the needed action for each scene; and then describe it briefly, being careful to cut out every act that does not have a direct bearing on the development of the plot.[16]

The article continues to describe many of the characteristics we now associate with classical Hollywood cinema.

Ince had traveled to Edendale in October 1911. According to a trade paper, in June 1912 Ince split his studio into two production units because his staff was increasing in size and becoming unwieldly. At this time Ince was writing scenarios, shooting footage, and editing the films, and the company was averaging one two-reel film per week. Under this new system Ince would direct the two- and three-reel Western dramas and Francis Ford, John's older brother, would shoot Western comedies and smaller-cast dramas.[17] A later commentator, George Mitchell, attributes the detailed continuity script to Ince's desire for control over what Ford did.[18] This speculation seems plausible: if management desires to control uniformity and quality of product, some means of supervising the individual work tasks must be devised. But there may be more to it than that. The continuity script also provides efficiency and regularity of production. Describing the Ince studio eighteen months later, W. E. Wing wrote:

> To the writer the most striking feature of Inceville . . . was its system. Although housing an army of actors, directors and subordinates, there is not a working hour lapses in which all the various companies are not at work producing results. We failed to see actors made up and dressed for their various roles, loafing about the stages or on locations; perturbed directors running here and there attempting to bring order out of chaos, while locations waited and cameramen idly smoked their cigarettes, waiting for the "next scene."
> With preparations laid out in detail from finished photoplays to the last prop, superintended by Mr. Ince himself, far in advance of action, each of the numerous directors on the job at Santa Ynez canyon is given his working script three weeks ahead of time.[19]

Ince's scenarios had, by 1913, become what are now labeled continuity scripts. A good number of these scripts, as well as scenarios for Griffith and Sennett films, are available in the Aitken Brothers Papers at Madison, Wisconsin.[20] The earliest Ince script available is for *The Raiders,* which was shot in late 1913. This one is as fully developed as later ones, containing the constituent parts of all of his continuities.

Each script has a number assigned to it which provides a method of tracing the film even though its title might shift. A cover page indicates who wrote the scenario, who directed the shooting, when shooting began and ended, when the film was shipped to the distributors, and when the film was released. This entire history on paper records the production process for efficiency and waste control.

The next part is a list of all intertitles and an indication as to where they are to be inserted in the final print. The location page follows that. It lists all exterior and interior sites along with their scene numbers, providing efficiency and preventing waste in time and labor. These continuities were apparently used during the filming process since pencil lines are drawn through the typed information.

The cast of characters follows. The typed portions list the roles for the story and penciled in are the names of the people assigned to play each part.

A one-page synopsis follows and then the script itself. Each scene is numbered consecutively and its location is given. Intertitles are typed in, often in red ink, where they are to be inserted in the final version. The description of mise-en-scène and action is detailed. Penciled over each scene is a scribble (presumably marking the completion of shooting), and sometimes on the side is a handwritten number—possibly the footage length of the scene. Production stills for advertising often accompany the script.

Occasionally there is the typed injunction: "It is earnestly requested by Mr. Ince that no change of any nature be made in the scenario either by elimination of any scenes or the addition of any scenes or changing any of the action as described, or titles, without first consulting him." The usual anecdotes of a stamped phrase "shoot as written" or "produce this exactly as written" were not confirmed by any of these scripts.[21] Rather, contemporary accounts suggest tht Ince, his production manager, the scenarist, and the director discussed and revised the script until it was in final shape for shooting.[22] The continuities include detailed instructions such as special effects and tinting directions for the intertitles. Later, when Ince gave up cutting the films, notes to the editors are added.

Finally, and very significantly, attached to the continuity is the entire cost of the film, which is analyzed in a standard accounting format. The first section is labor costs, which account for eighty to ninety percentage of the direct costs of production. The second part is costs for expendables such as props, scenery, rentals, and music. In addition, the precise number of feet of negative and positive film is indicated along with a breakdown of cost per reel and per foot.[23]

All of this demonstrates that Ince's use of the continuity script resulted in a two-stage labor process—the work's preparation on paper by management followed by its execution by the workers. The five problems associated with optional systems—irregularity of production, loss of materials, slowness of manufacture, lack of uniformity, and uncertainty of quality—are controlled by that management. This standardization of the work process was used by Ince's publicity department as a mark of quality and uniformity of the film product: "Ince" becomes a brand name through its advertising.

The Division of Labor

The second major part of this structure is the growth of division of labor as planning becomes specialized in the hands of the corporate managers. When Ince began directing, some division of labor already existed for certain tasks, but the jobs were still flexible. Often the scenario might come from any one of the group.[24] Ince himself performed several of the functions which were to be separated out and bracketed as specific tasks: he was the organizer of the work (the producer), the controller of the final script (the scenario editor), the head of shooting (the director), and the film cutter (the editor). As the company expanded operations, he relinquished parts of his work and became a supervisor, utilizing control methods through middle management heads to maintain operations as he wanted them.

The first function to be transferred was the basic writing of the script. By spring 1912 Richard Spencer was in charge of writing the scenarios, and *The Moving Picture World* called the Edendale scenario department the "most highbrow motion picture institution in town."[25] Ince, of course, still worked on the scripts with Spencer. C. Gardner Sullivan, who was to write many of the scenarios, was hired during this period. By 1915, the writing had been split: Spencer was chief story editor and Sullivan headed the scenario department which included six writers.[26]

The next of Ince's functions to go was the actual direction of the films. After Francis Ford was placed in charge of a second unit in 1912, the direction staff increased rapidly, and Ince gradually stopped directing. By 1914, Inceville had eight directors, and by 1915, Reginald Barker headed a group of nine with five or six production units shooting simultaneously. Ince was now titled "Director-General" for the company.[27] The third function which Ince relinquished direct control of was that of actually cutting the films, a task he had delegated to others by 1915.[28] Ince still retained final control through continuity script directions and final examination of each produced film.

The division of labor did not involve Ince's work alone; the steady growth in studio facilities and in scale of production concurrently resulted in additional segmenting of other film production functions. The management of such a complex organization required more professional abilities and, in the Spring of 1913, George B. Stout became Ince's financial head. After reorganizing the administrative system, Stout turned over the controls to Gene Allen and then transferred to Mack Sennett's studio which Ince nominally controlled as West Coast head for Kessel and Bauman. There, Stout also proceeded to divide Sennett's labor by breaking his studio into ten departments based on work functions.[29] Ince's photography unit expanded rapidly, and set and construction demanded an art supervisor. In 1915, the New York Motion Picture Company aligned with the newly formed Triangle Film Corporation, and Ince, as well as Griffith and Sennett, became vice-president of the corporation. An expansion period followed, and more specialists were hired: a former chief cameraman from Universal was employed "to superintend the development of negative films"; Victor Schertzinger began writing musical scores to accompany the films; and Melville Ellis, described as a "designer and fashion expert of International reputation," was hired for the costume department.[30]

One aspect has been left out of this description of the growth of division of labor and that is the situation of the actors and actresses. Stunt people and stock players were replaceable workers. But what about the stars? At an exhibitors' convention both the stars and Ince's control as a mark of quality and uniformity were the central advertising themes. So the stars were not as interchangeable as were the other players.[31] Instead they seemed to serve a function similar in nature to Ince's: product differentiation. For that reason, it would be important that a star be tied to a particular studio so that the star's "unique" qualities would be associated only with that studio's films. At the time of Triangle's formation, Ince disclosed that his idea was "to get stars, teach them the tricks of the camera and then keep them at salaries high enough to restrain them so that they cannot work first for one company and then for another."[32] Even at this time the star as worker was often "bound" to the studio through multiple-year contracts in order to reduce fluctuation in the studio's image. Although a worker, in the sense of being an interchangeable part in the script, the star is also a quality or substance in the product itself and fulfills the function of a means to differentiate the pictures of one company from another.

One way to comprehend the growth of the entire studio structure is to recall the initial description of the new studio that Ince built in Culver City in late 1915, at the same time that he was renovating Inceville in Santa Monica: the 165-foot electrically lit building, the eight stages 60 by 150 feet, an administration building for executive and scenario offices, property, carpenter, and costume buildings, 300 dressing rooms, a hothouse, a natatorium, and so forth. But as impressive as that description is, Ince does not seem to have been unique. While he had the best scenario department, others also had them; Keystone, too, was divided into task sections. A special issue of *The*

Moving Picture World in 1915 describes the growth of the West Coast production companies and lists the New York Motion Picture Company as just one of many whose facilities were expanding.[33] The highly mobile employment patterns in the industry, the widespread publicity, and evidence of the organization of other studios make it clear that Ince was not unusual; that, in fact, most studios were structured somewhat like his.[34]

A Revised Perspective

By 1915 the major divisions of labor had been segmented. A pyramid of labor was the dominant structure with a top manager, middle-management department heads, and workers. This fulfills Braverman's description of a fully organized modern corporation in which "the producing activities are subdivided among functional departments, each having a specific aspect of the process for its domain . . ."[35]

This development was more important to the long-term structure of the film industry and to the development of the form and the style of the films that industry was to produce than was the impact of any individual film or director. In the 1910s several models for organizing motion picture labor competed for acceptance, but the model based on a well organized factory, brought to its fruition by Ince, eventually succeeded in dominating. While his system was attacked as potentially producing "mechanical picture[s],"[36] its economical advantages seem to have won over any artistic fears.

Yet we should not create in Ince another great man of history. While he was an innovator of the continuity script, the industry as a whole was departmentalizing its production units. Earlier historians' comments that the continuity script led to economical and efficient production are correct, but the script is only part of the system of the creation of the product. The continuity script works because it is an external manifestation of a more fundamental structure inextricable from modern corporate business—the separation of the conception and production phases of work and the pyramid of divided labor. It is this fundamental structure which explains Ince's production organization, a structure which earlier historians have failed to foreground.

A question that derives from this is, was there a simultaneous standardization of the product? To answer this question would require an extensive analysis of Ince's films—both the well-known and the lesser works. But it is clear that in the broader model of division of labor and scientific management, the film industry by 1915 had the structure it was to follow for the next fifty years.

NOTES

[1]This paper is a result of a seminar in social and economic problems in American film history conducted by Douglas Gomery, Fall 1977, at the University of

Wisconsin-Madison. I would like to thank the members of the seminar for their suggestions and help in formalizing these ideas. I also appreciate further research leads given me by members of the Society for Cinema Studies at the 1978 conference where a draft of this paper was read.

[2]George Mitchell, "Thomas H. Ince," *Films in Review*, 11 (October 1960), 464–68; "The 'IMP' Company Invades Cuba," *The Moving Picture World*, 8, no. 3 (21 Janauary 1911), 146. (*The Moving Picture World* will be abbreviated *MPW* hereafter.)

[3]Kalton C. Lahue, *Dreams for Sale: The Rise and Fall of the Triangle Film Corporation* (South Brunswick and New York: A. S. Barnes, 1971), pp. 61, 65–6, 71; "Los Angeles Letter," *MPW*, 25, no. 8 (21 August 1915), 1301; "Forty-Three Acres for Incity," *MPW*, 27, no. 6 (12 February 1916), 958.

[4]Lewis Jacobs, *The Rise of the American Film: A Critical History* (New York: Harcourt, Brace, 1939), pp. 162, 205–6; Lahue, *Dreams for Sale*, p. 46; Eric Rhode, *A History of the Cinema: From Its Origins to 1970* (New York: Hill and Wang, 1976), p. 58.

[5]Harry Braverman, *Labor and Monopoly Capital: The Degradation of Work in the Twentieth Century* (New York: Monthly Review Press, 1974), p. 54.

[6]Braverman, p. 59.

[7]Braverman, p. 63.

[8]Braverman, p. 75.

[9]Adam Smith quoted by Braverman, pp. 76–7.

[10]Braverman, p. 107.

[11]For a Marxist analysis of these effects, also see Ernst Fischer, *The Essential Marxist*, trans. Anna Bostock (New York: The Seabury Press, 1970), pp. 15–51.

[12]Braverman, p. 125.

[13]Braverman, p. 260.

[14]Peter Milne, *Motion Picture Directing* (New York: Falk, 1922), p. 136.

[15]Braverman, p. 125.

[16]Everett McNeil, "Outline of How to Write a Photoplay," *MPW*, 9, no. 1 (15 July 1911), 27.

[17]"Doings in Los Angeles," *MPW*, 12, no. 10 (8 June 1912), 913; "Doings in Los Angles," *MPW*, 14, no. 1 (5 October 1912), 32.

[18]Mitchell, pp. 469–70.

[19]W. E. Wing, "Tom Ince, of Inceville," *The New York Dramatic Mirror*, 70, no. 1827 (24 December 1913), 34 [also in George C. Pratt, *Spellbound in Darkness*, revised ed. (Greenwich, Connecticut: New York Graphic Society, 1973), pp. 144–45].

[20]Aitken Brothers Papers, Scenarios, Manuscript Collection (Wisconsin Center for Film and Theater Research, Madison, Wisconsin), Boxes 1–9.

[21]Milne, p. 140; Jacobs, p. 204; Arthur Knight, *The Liveliest Art: A Panoramic History of the Movies* (New York: Macmillan, 1957), p. 38; Edward Wagenknecht, *The Movies in the Age of Innocence* (Norman: University of Oklahoma Press, 1962), p. 175; Lahue, *Dreams for Sale*, p. 45; Rhode, p. 58.

[22]Wing, p. 34; Milne, p. 140; William S. Hart, *My Life East and West* (Boston and New York: Houghton Mifflin, 1929), pp. 206–7.

[23]For example, *The Iron Strain* (1915) costs were $2737.56 per reel (six reels) and $2.73 per foot.

[24]Mitchell, p. 468.

[25]"Doings in Los Angeles," *MPW*, 15, no. 7 (15 February 1913), 668.

[26]Wing, p. 34; Jean Mitry, *Histoire du cinéma: Art et Industrie, Vol. I: 1895–1914* (Paris: Editions Universitaires, 1967), p. 440; Mitry, *Vol. II: 1915–1925*, pp. 88–9; Hart, p. 213; Lahue, *Dreams for Sale*, p. 40.

[27]"William S. Hart," *MPW*, 22, no. 7 (14 November 1914), 920; Mitry, *II*, pp. 88–9; Lahue, *Dreams for Sale*, p. 40; Ad, *MPW*, 25, no. 2 (10 July 1915), 333.

[28]Lahue, *Dreams for Sale*, p. 45.

[29]Kalton C. Lahue, *Mack Sennett's Keystone: The Man, the Myth, and the Comedies* (Cranbury, New Jersey: A. S. Barnes, 1971), p. 244.

[30]Mitchell, pp. 472–3; Mitry, *I*, p. 440; "Los Angeles Letter," *MPW*, 25, no. 9 (28 August 1915), 1466; "Ince's Big Picture Completed," *MPW*, 27, no. 10 (11 March 1916), 1638; "Los Angeles Letter," *MPW*, 25, no. 8 (21 August 1915), 1301; "Triangle Appoints a General Manager," *MPW*, 25, no. 8 (21 August 1915), 1303; "Triangle Opening Announced," *MPW* 25, no. 10 (4 September 1915), 1622; "Manufacturers' Exposition," *MPW*, 25, no. 5 (31 July 1915), 820.

[31]"Manufacturers' Exposition," *MPW*, 25, no. 5 (31 July 1915), 820; Aitken Brothers Papers, Scenarios, Boxes 1–9.

[32]"Los Angeles Letter," *MPW*, 25, no. 7 (14 August 1915), 1144.

[33]George Blaisdell, "Mecca of the Motion Picture," *MPW*, 25, no. 2 (10 July 1915), 216.

[34]Aitken Brothers Papers, Correspondence, Boxes 10–14.

[35]Braverman, p. 260.

[36]Milne, p. 136.

1979

PROFILES
OF FILMS

CINEMA
JOURNAL

Memories of Mr. Magoo

Howard Rieder

Early in 1949, John Hubley asked Jerry Hausner if he might try to help him find a voice for a new cartoon character, a nearsighted little man named Mr. Magoo. Hausner remembers it this way:

> Jim Backus had just come out from New York with the Alan Young Show. He was already fairly well-known as the voice of Hubert Updyke, the richest man in the world.
>
> We had been friends for over twenty years. I spoke to Hubley about Backus and he wanted to meet him. I arranged a luncheon at the Smoke House Restaurant, next door to the UPA studio in Burbank. Hubley spoke of this new character he was trying to find a voice for. He didn't want to have to ask Backus to audition for him because it might be an affront to an actor as well established as Backus.
>
> Hubley asked Backus if he could recommend someone to play the part. Backus asked what he was like, what he looked like. Hubley said, "Well, I haven't any pictures with me, but if we could wander over to UPA I will show you some sketches and a rough storyboard."
>
> We walked over and looked at it. Backus studied the character, and when Hubley said he was nearsighted and lived in his own little world, Backus said he could do it. He said, "My father lives in his own little world, never quite seeing things the way they really are. It isn't that he's nearsighted, but his whole attitude toward life is a kind of personal isolation toward the rest of the world."
>
> Backus mentioned that he used to do a character called the Man in the Club Car. It was the character of the businessman, the tycoon, the loudmouth talker that you meet in a railroad train who offers all kinds of information on world events and who is filled with misinformation. He began to use this voice and it was the voice that ultimately became Mr. Magoo.

The genesis of the character of Mr. Magoo was explained in a letter to the writer by John Hubley:

> The character was based upon an uncle of mine, named Harry Woodruff, at least insofar as my relationship to Magoo was concerned. Jim Backus, who was

introduced at an early stage, formulated a concept based upon his father, a Cleveland businessman and owner of a prosperous pump works. My Uncle Harry was a division head of a large national insurance company.

Magoo, we decided, would always make an appraisal of a situation in one glance. . . . His stubborn rigidity was such that, having made a snap judgment, nothing could convince him he was wrong. Don't you know people like that? They become determined to act on the erroneous judgment, no matter what. This can lead to great comedy (or tragedy).

Jerry Hausner was chosen by Hubley to play the part of Waldo, and he was present at the recording session for the first film, *Ragtime Bear*. Recalling this, he says:

> We went into the studio with two pages of dialogue. We read all of the speeches that had been written down. Then Hubley did something that no other animated cartoon director has ever done in my presence. He said, "Let's do it again and ad lib around the subject. Throw in any wild thoughts you might have."
>
> We did another version of it. Backus began to go crazy and have a good time. . . . He invented a lot of things and brought to the cartoons a fresh, wonderful approach.
>
> In the second cartoon there were no other voices besides Backus'. I think Backus was alone in the studio.
>
> The morning after, very early, I got a telephone call from John Hubley. He said, "I've been up all night and I'm worried. I'm very concerned because I had a recording session with Jim Backus last night and he didn't come off as funny as he did in the first one. I can't understand. We're losing what we had in the first one. I suddenly got a thought. You and Backus are close friends. You appreciate each other."
>
> Actually, Backus is the kind of man that needs an audience. Put him in a recording studio alone and it's like locking Danny Kaye in a broom closet.
>
> Hubley said, "I'm going to set up another recording session and we're going to do it over. I have no part for you, but I will pay you to come to the studio and be there so that Backus will have someone to talk to."
>
> We did that, and it changed everything.

DEVELOPMENT OF STYLE

As the series progressed, dialogue became increasingly important in the Magoo series. Pete Burness points out ironically that after being associated for six years with the mute characters of Tom and Jerry, he began to work with what is probably the most talkative animated cartoon character in history. However, as incessant as the Magoo chatter may seem to audiences viewing the films, the creators of Magoo endeavored to develop high points of indignation and contrast them with quiet moods of pleasure or misery.

This was developed in the writing of the dialogue and polished in the direction of Backus in the studio. Burness comments that they always tried to get a change of color, and rise and fall. This change of mood and pace was necessary to keep the dialogue from lapsing into a continuous haranguing of the high, strident voice that was characteristic of Magoo, and which could be grating over long periods.

To the casual observer, the Mr. Magoo cartoons might appear to be similar in style to *Gerald McBoing-Boing, Madeline, Rooty Toot Toot,* and others UPA has done. This is not completely so. Magoo cartoons have a unique style of their own, closer to the Disney representational type than any other produced by UPA.

Commenting on the differences between Gerald McBoing-Boing and Magoo, Robert Cannon (who directed the Gerald series) said that Magoo is a three-dimensional character "set in space." He is flat, part of the overall design of the frame, but his movements, or his path of movement within the frame, are "design in motion." For Gerald, all but the essential background details are removed. For Magoo, a kind of baroque art treatment is used, loaded with gingerbread.

In animation, UPA worked for crispness in movement to match the crispness in drawing. Pete Burness, who directed most of the Magoo series, put it this way: "We developed strong, definite, clearly readable poses, with a minimum of follow-through." Magoo's animation amounted to about a halfway point between the extreme literalism of Disney and the stylized animation of the more off-beat UPA films. Burness adds:

> We got as much design value or high styling as we could into the backgrounds, but we tried to keep the characters representational.
>
> There was a consistency in color, as well as in design and animation. Our semi-representational styling was not compatible with a textured, colored area. Practically all colored areas were flat color. This is part of the technique.
>
> But there were times when a texture was part of the story. If you wanted a stone wall or stucco wall, or even the ground, you would never paint it as such. The artist would take a sponge and simulate a texture. He would never take his brush and carefully render a three-dimensional, representational image. Many times on interiors we used colored papers, textured and patterned papers, even wallpaper samples.

CROTCHETY LIKE W. C. FIELDS

The character of Mr. Magoo has been compared with the late W. C. Fields. Burness recalls:

> We had been working with him for a short period, and it occurred to us that he had a lot in common with W. C. Fields. After we had made three or four pictures, we felt that there was a great deal in common. We got W. C. Fields pictures and ran them and studied them just to see what they would suggest. We wanted to see if there were dimensions that we were missing that we could put into Magoo.

Asked whether there was any specific element of the characterization derived and incorporated into Magoo as a result of screening the Fields films, Burness said this did not happen. He explained the basic difference:

> W. C. Fields was terribly suspicious of the whole world and hated much of it. Magoo loved the world. He loved people. He was a man of principles and he would defend and fight for those principles. . . . He was similar to Fields in that neither one of them had patience with weaknesses or inequities as they saw them. Of course, Fields was basically a con man. Magoo was terribly civic minded. . . .

We studied the Fields pictures in terms of the way Magoo walks through a situation, which in many cases was the same way Fields would move through a situation.

Jerry Hausner added these contrasts between Magoo and Fields:

Fields was a loud, boisterous, irascible, irritated man. . . . Magoo was well thought of, a kindly person. He was courtly, Victorian. He always took his hat off to ladies he met. Even if he bumped into a tree and thought it was a lady, he would take his hat off. W. .C. Fields always had conflicts with little kids. Magoo would never do anything like that. He would always be trying to help.

Stephen Bosustow, principal owner of UPA Inc. from 1943 to 1960 said that he felt they had noted similarities with Fields at the very beginning:

W. C. Fields used to hate kids. He would take a pass at them. Well, we had a running gag with Magoo in which he carried a cane and would lash out at what looked like dogs, crying, "Down! Down!" He really wouldn't hit a dog, but would hit what to him looked like a dog. Sometimes it was a fire plug, sometimes something else.

Robert Cannon, who directed two of the Magoos, confirmed that this piece of business—Magoo swatting at objects—was taken from W. C. Fields. Cannon also felt that Backus picked up elements of Fields' laugh.

A number of changes took place over the ten years of production of short subjects starring Mr. Magoo. These changes were influenced primarily by the individuals working on the series at different times. The first change came shortly after Magoo's introduction. Having directed the first two films, John

Hubley asked to be taken off the project so he could do new things. He continued to function as supervising director of all films in the studio, and on the next few Magoo pictures worked closely with Burness. Commenting directly on the changes, Burness said:

> It was felt that Magoo should have a warmer side. In the first one he was almost completely disagreeable and ill-tempered. It was felt by many of us that it would be a good characteristic . . . if he would have a warm, sentimental side. I felt this was true and proceeded on this assumption. . . .
>
> John Hubley, who had more to do with the creation of Magoo than anyone else, was in disagreement with this.
>
> I have later wondered if I was right. I have wondered because he got progressively warmer until he was weakened. It should have been used with discrimination. He might break out from time to time in a sentimental mood, but I believe that his basic character would have been stronger if he had continued crotchety, even somewhat nasty. I think there was a certain dilution of his character in making him too sweet.

John Hubley commented on this point:

> I feel that as the series developed the formula became somewhat mechanical. There were too many nearsighted gags, not enough situation comedy and character conflict. His motivation became unclear. In earlier shorts he was doggedly trying to get some rest, or prevail upon a lackadaisical friend to engage in energetic sport, or to file a claim for insurance on a bogus policy. Always involved in a pulsing, dynamic action.

Magoo was a human being, not an animal character. He could not undergo the physical destruction Tom and Jerry and Bugs Bunny indulge in. He must

Background and overlay for *When Magoo Flew*, February 1955, directed by (Wilson) Pete Burness.

be "saved" from destruction logically and never destroy himself. Elaborating on this difference, Pete Burness said:

> Violence is a thing that is associated with most other cartoon series; their whole approach to story is based on violence; characters destroy each other. The pattern is that the character is burned to a crisp or chopped into pieces. Then, in picking up the next sequence, he is as good as new. It's a kind of magic thing that works well in *Tom and Jerry* and *Bugs Bunny*. But Magoo, being a human being more than a magic kind of cartoon character, doesn't work well with this kind of violence. . . . He behaves almost like a live character actor.

OFTEN IN DANGER

At the same time, one of the comedy elements which Burness feels works particularly well in the development of a humorous situation in a Magoo film is the element of suspense created when Magoo is in danger of being hurt, particularly when he is in danger of falling. This device worked effectively in both *Trouble Indemnity* and *When Magoo Flew*, the latter an Academy Award winner. In the first instance Magoo was wandering about on the girders of an unfinished building; in the second, he was walking on the wings, body, and tail of an airplane in flight. Burness regards this as a particularly normal kind of comedy technique, often used in silent films.

Burness felt the high point of the series was represented by *When Magoo Flew*. It was one of those happy films when everything was right.

> It was a good premise. It was developed well. The premise came from a writer who is not in the cartoon business, Barbara Hummer. She had seen the Magoos and was amused by them. She had this story idea of Magoo getting on an airplane by mistake. He wants to go to the neighborhood movie, but takes the wrong street and goes to the airport. To Magoo it looks like a theater. He goes in, and in his usual bullheaded way, gets on a plane. When he sees the "Fasten Seat Belts" sign flash he thinks it's the title of the picture. He remarks about loving airplane pictures. Then he gets out on the wing and wanders around. . . .
> Up to this point all of our cartoons had been made for the regular Academy size screen. But Columbia had expressed an interest in making a picture in CinemaScope, and if it turned out well they wanted a whole series in Cinema-Scope. This was an exciting thing. . . . I knew this picture would be scrutinized very carefully by Columbia, and I also felt that it had a good strong story. In practically every instance, where necessary, I risked the wrath of the production office by reshooting or making other changes. As a result we came out with a fine picture. Everyone did a beautiful job on it. It was well written, well designed, nicely colored, excellently animated, and beautifully scored.

A later episode directed by Rudy Larriva, departed from the normal all-animation technique. And although it reached for the notion of danger, it was not a success, according to Pete Burness:

> A story idea came up which involved some film clips of live action. The film was called Magoo's Private War.
> In this film Magoo is a civil defense warden. He takes his duties very conscientiously. He stumbles on a theater where they are premiering a big feature about war, airplanes, and space ships.

Drawn especially for *Cinema Journal*, these sketches by John Hubley represent his present recollection of the earlier, more "crotchety" Magoo.

As part of the promotion, they have large mock-ups in front of the theater of airplanes and searchlights.

Magoo mistakes this for an air raid and goes to work. He gets into the theater during the newsreel. They cut to the screen and we see men and tanks on maneuvers. Battleships fire their big guns and dive bombers cross the ocean. Magoo thinks this is part of an attack. It was a wild sort of thing. . . .

Columbia thought this was a wild, crazy, amusing film and they howled. But it laid an egg. Nobody knows why. The audiences didn't react to it at all. But the group at the studio who screened the film thought it was very funny.

An analysis of Mr. Magoo's character and its appeal was made by a Yale University professor of psychology in the *Quarterly of Film, Radio, and Television*. Milton J. Rosenberg looked at him this way:

In all of his adventures, Mr. Magoo has been in a desperate situation. He is virtually blind, pitifully weak, and very small. He is handicapped also by a majestic inability to understand the dynamics of the world through which he stumbles. Yet every time we encounter him, he is face to face with malignant and inimical forces of both inanimate and animate orders. Shysters, confidence men, and bandits try to do him in or bleed him dry. His near-blindness inevitably carries him to a point just short of irredeemable destruction. . . .

Mr. Magoo's survival in the face of danger is inexplicable. It seems to us a sheer gratuity, totally unrelated to any source of power in the man himeslf. But is that true? *Is Magoo just plain lucky?* Or is there perhaps some secret power that he *does possess*, some obscure but trustworthy magic of his own devising? Is this survival a gift of inscrutable fate, or does he earn it?

Running through all the Magoo cartoons, there is, I believe, a secret intimation that it is not fate that has saved Magoo but rather that he has saved *himself.* How has he done this? Here the artists of UPA unconsciously voice a hope that lies deep and not fully known within each of us. Magoo has saved himself—and we may save ourselves—by complete allegiance to a set of social values and moral conceptions.

The values Magoo lives by are those of yesterday's self-made man. In comic guise, he is a personification of the verities of a social era contiguous with our own. He is American individualism in its purest moral form.

A clue to this question is provided by Pete Burness:

There are many philosophies and religions that feel you make your own destiny. You create your own good fortune by your attitude and the forthrightness of your point of view. We always felt this was Magoo's prime characteristic. The near-sightedness was just a device. The important thing was Magoo's absolute self-confidence, the absolute certainty he feels that he is right at all times.

1969

Frame from *Magoo's Canine Mutiny*, March 1956, directed by Pete Burness.

Dixon, Griffith, and the Southern Legend: A Cultural Analysis of *The Birth of a Nation*

Russell Merritt

At about 8:30 Saturday night, April 17, 1915, the manager of Boston's luxurious Tremont theatre called for police protection. Minutes before, he had closed the box office window when a band of Negroes had come to buy seventy-five cent tickets. Now his lobby was flooded with several hundred angry protesters who had followed the original delegation through the Boston Common and down Tremont Street. Their leader, National Equal Rights League secretary William Monroe Trotter, said the protesters would not leave until he and his original party were permitted to go inside. The harried manager was determined to keep Trotter's friends out. He had received a telephone call warning him about a Negro plot to disrupt the 8:30 showing. The Negro conspirators, he was told, planned to enter the theatre, charge the projection booth, and tear the film out of the projector. The manager hoped he had nipped the plot in the bud. Within minutes, two hundred Boston policemen arrived and forced the Negroes behind police lines.

Meanwhile, inside the Tremont theatre, the audience watched D. W. Griffith's *The Birth of a Nation*. Griffith's first full-length film had been arousing controversy since its Los Angeles premiere three months earlier, but this was the first time Negroes had actually demonstrated. Minutes after the film began, a Negro in the tenth row threw a rotten egg at the screen and was immediately arrested. Sixty plainclothesmen and uniformed police prevented further incidents until the final curtain. But as the house lights came up, a dozen incendiaries and "stink bombs" poured down from the balcony and rear of the theatre. The audience raced out of the main exits only to meet the crowd of disgruntled Negroes held outside by the police. The wild scene that followed kept two hundred and sixty policemen busy, and by eleven o'clock eleven men were arrested including the Reverend Dr. Aaron Puller and William Trotter. Police were instructed to keep a twenty-four hour guard around the Tremont, and, in response to the demonstration, Mayor James Curley forced the theatre to cancel *The Birth of a Nation's* Sunday performances.[1]

---

[1] All the major Boston newspapers—notably *The Christian Science Monitor, The Boston Evening Transcript,* and *The Globe*—began to cover *The Birth of a Nation* and its effects after the black demonstration. For accounts of the riot and its aftermath,

We are still learning how to interpret that riot and the film that caused it. Griffith's Civil War epic holds all silent film box office records. By 1931, the film had earned $18 million, and by 1946 when the last count was taken, more than 200 million people had seen it. No one knows how many more have seen it since then.[2] Yet the film continues to arouse storms of bitter controversy.

Today we usually hail *The Birth of a Nation* as an important landmark in film narrative technique. In praise of its spectacle and Griffith's contribution to film grammar, there is hardly anything new to say. These are the aspects of the film that are best known, the only aspects most people know. No one who writes on film history fails to pay homage to Griffith's brilliant talents as a craftsman and inventor.[3]

That praise is well-deserved, but it tends to place the unimportant things at the center and the important at the outer edges. Griffith's craftsmanship alone no more explains *The Birth of a Nation*'s peculiar appeal than Homer's metrical skill explains the magic of the *Iliad*. Griffith made his film because he had a story and a vision he wanted to share. He attracted his

see the issues of April 18, 1915 through April 26, 1915, especially *The Sunday Globe* April 18, 1915; *The Globe* April 19, 1915; *The Christian Science Monitor* April 19, 1915; *The Boston Evening Transcript,* April 19, 1915; and *The Boston Post,* April 19, 1915.

[2] See Benjamin Hampton, *A History of the Movies* (New York, 1931), p. 130 and Milton Mackaye, "The Birth of a Nation," *Scribner's Magazine* CII (November, 1937), p. 40 for financial earnings. Original attendance records are more reliable than financial statistics. The film had unprecedented first runs in all American major cities. From its Los Angeles premiere at Clune's Auditorium on February 8, 1915, until its final performance at New York's Liberty Theatre on January 2, 1916, the movie had been seen by a nation-wide audience of 5 million people (*New York Times,* January 2, 1916, section VIII, p. 8). It ran for forty-five weeks in New York City, thirty-five weeks in Chicago, and twenty-two weeks in Los Angeles. *The Columbus Dispatch,* April 22, 1917 estimated that one out of every nine people in the United States had seen Griffith's film. *The Brooklyn Eagle,* June 24, 1917, claimed a national audience of 10 million people; a world audience of fifty million. Since then, estimates of attendance have ranged from 200 million (Seymour Stern, "Griffith: 1–'The Birth of a Nation' " *Film Culture,* no. 36 (Spring-Summer, 1965), p. 147) to 300 million (Aitken and Nelson, *The Birth of a Nation Story,* p. 67).

[3] The standard studies of *The Birth of a Nation* include Milton Mackaye, "The Birth of a Nation," *Scribner's Magazine,* CII (November, 1937), pp. 40-46, 69; Iris Barry, *D. W. Griffith: American Film Master* (New York, 1940), pp. 20-22, 34-37; Lewis Jacobs, *The Rise of the American Film* (New York, 1939), pp. 171-88; Terry Ramsaye's chapter entitled "The Birth of a Nation," in *A Million and One Nights,* vol. 2 (New York, 1926), pp. 635-44; Richard Griffith and Arthur Mayer, *The Movies* (New York, 1957), pp. 30-39; and A. Nicholas Vardac, *Stage to Screen* (Cambridge, Mass., 1949), pp. 223-26.

James Agee cut through the usual critical cant with fresh insight about Griffith's personal gifts and limitations in his obituary of Griffith for the *Nation,* Sept. 4, 1948, reprinted in *Agee on Film,* vol. 1 (New York, 1958), pp. 313-18. See Edward Wagenknecht, *The Movies in the Age of Innocence* (Norman, Oklahoma, 1962), pp. 99-109 for a scholarly approach to the film with an analysis of previous critics' work. For valuable, hitherto inaccessible, primary material buried underneath unreadable prose and extremely shaky scholarship, see Seymour Stern, "Griffith: 1–The Birth of a Nation" *Film Culture,* XXXVI, Spring-Summer, 1965.

audience and aroused his antagonists not only because of the film's style, but because the drama itself was one contemporary Americans anxiously wanted to see.

My concern here is with the sources, the dynamics, and the impact of that narrative. For all the attention lavished on *The Birth of a Nation*, this has been the aspect most consistently ignored or misunderstood. Most of the audience that came out of the Tremont theatre that night in 1915, for instance, believed Griffith's story was historically true, that *The Birth of a Nation* was a nostalgic, but essentially accurate description of the Civil War years and their aftermath. Social reformer Dorothea Dix called it "history vitalized. Go see it," she wrote, "for it will make a better American of you."[4]

Booth Tarkington, Burns Mantle, and assorted historians agreed that it was eminently worth seeing for its educational value.[5] In New York, secondary school teachers took their advice and brought their classes to special film showings while ministers throughout the country endorsed the movie from the pulpit. In Cambridge, Massachusetts, the rector of the Harvard Street Unitarian Church gave three sermons on *The Birth of a Nation*. "The film," he claimed, "must be preserved and our histories rewritten."[6]

Delighted by the response, Griffith told a *Photoplay* reporter that soon history books would be altogether banished from the classrooms, replaced with films such as his.[7] Meanwhile, Griffith's collaborator, Thomas Dixon, secured the *imprimatur* of President Wilson himself, who in his earlier years had written voluminously on American history. After he saw it, Wilson is supposed to have said: "It is like writing history in lightning. My only regret is that it is all so terribly true."[8]

---

4 Quoted from a four-column advertisement for the film in the Boston *Globe*, April 9, 1915. See also *Boston Sunday Post*, April 4, 1915 and *Boston Post*, April 6, 7, 8, 1915.

5 Boston *Globe*, April 9, 1915. The Boston advertisement listed Rupert Hughes, Booth Tarkington, Richard Harding Davis, George Peabody, Dorothea Dix, Hugh Johnson, Burns Mantle, Thomas J. Walsh, Representative Claude Kitchen, and the Reverends Charles Parkhurst and Thomas Gregory among those who endorsed the film.

6 The Cambridge (Massachusetts) *Chronicle*, May 15, 1915, cited in Stern, "Griffith I," p. 209. The New York *American*, April 18, 1915, carried a feature article by the Rev. Thomas G. Gregory, "The Rev. Dr. Wise Sees 'The Birth of a Nation,'" that claimed the film taught "good will, the deep and cordial affection and devotion between whites and blacks" through its "beautiful and touching scenes."

The April 9, 1915 *Globe* advertisement claimed that eleven New York school principals—including three parochial school principals—made special arrangements to show the film to their schools.

7 Cf. Henry S. Gordon, "The Story of David Wark Griffith, Part V," *Photoplay* (October, 1916), p. 93, and William K. Everson, "Griffith and Realism: Apropos *The Birth of a Nation* (1915)" *Cinemages* 5 (June, 1955), p. 14.

8 This famous remark was first quoted in the New York *Post*, March 4, 1915. After the stormy New York and Boston runs had begun, the White House retracted its endorsement of the film in a letter from the President's press secretary to Representative Thomas Thatcher of Massachusetts. See Arthur Link, *Wilson: The New Freedom* (Princeton, New Jersey, 1956), pp. 253-254 for the Wilson correspondence. For an excellent scholarly account of Wilson's entanglement with *The Birth of a Nation*, see Thomas Cripps, "The Reaction of the Negro to the Motion Picture *Birth*

Much of what Griffith filmed is historically accurate, but the illusion of general historical truth and perspective is largely the product of Griffith's art. *The Birth of a Nation* is not an historical document any more than are Walt Whitman's war poems or Shakespeare's history plays. Whether Griffith knew it or not, the initial and determining impulse behind his film was not historic truth, but the dramatization of a familiar legend.

The Southern Myth

In its classical form, the legend of the Old South is more or less familiar to everyone. Whether in Stephen Foster's folk songs, *Gone With the Wind*, the Uncle Remus stories, or the novels of Thomas Nelson Page, the legendary South has charmed and haunted our country since the days of Thomas Jefferson. It is America's historic Arcadia, where the lion lies with the lamb. The wise old men, the patriarchs of the plantation, have earned the respect and love of almost all who know them. Their children are the innocent youths, the lovers who grow up on the land—modern musketeers who duel, hunt, ride, and rescue young ladies.[9]

Though the myth can be traced as far back as the 1830's when *The Southern Literary Messenger* was founded (1834) and John P. Kennedy wrote *Swallow Barn* (1832),[10] the legend as we know it today began in the 1880's at the tail end of the Reconstruction.[11] Confronted with an impoverished land, a topsy-turvy social order, and an alien government imposing unwanted domestic legislation, Southern writers turned to the ante-bellum South to remind themselves and the world what had been taken from them. Poets and playwrights wrote of a golden land ravaged by the war, carpetbaggers, and scalawags: pictures that amply justified the South's fierce resistance to the Northern occupation.

In its long post-war heyday, the Old South rose again and again in magazine fiction, between the covers of sectional novels, in music sheets, and on the American stage.[12] Modern adaptations of *Uncle Tom's Cabin* were runaway favorites throughout the eighties, the novel's abolitionist motives

of a Nation," *The Historian*, XXV (May, 1963), pp. 348-49. Raymond Cook details Dixon's involvement with the White House in his biography of Dixon, *Fire From the Flint* (Charlotte, North Carolina, 1968), pp. 169-173.

[9] Theodore L. Gross, *Thomas Nelson Page*, Twayne's United States Authors Series (New York, 1967), p. 80. Other major studies of the literature about the Old South are William Taylor, *Yankee and Cavalier* (New York, 1961), Francis Pendleton Gaines, *The Southern Plantation*, Columbia University Studies in English and Comparative Literature (New York, 1925), Rollin G. Osterweis, *Romanticism and Nationalism in the Old South* (New Haven, 1949), and Paul H. Buck's chapters on Southern literature in *The Road to Reunion: 1865-1900* (Boston, 1937).

[10] Taylor, *Yankee and Cavalier*, pp. 123-55; Osterweis, *Romanticism and Nationalism*, throughout "Part One—The Emergence of Southern Romanticism."

[11] Kenneth Stampp, *The Era of Reconstruction: 1865-1877* (New York, 1965), pp. 3-25; Buck, *The Road to Reunion*, 196-235; Wilbur J. Cash, *The Mind of the South* (New York, 1941) stresses the South's predisposition towards fantasy during these years in his chapter "Of the Frontier the Yankee Made." See particularly pp. 126-33.

[12] Paul Buck, *The Road to Reunion: 1865-1900* (Boston, 1937), pp. 196-235.

softened by contemporary producers and its plantation scenes enriched by "darkie musical numbers." Dion Boucicault's *The Octoroon,* a plantation drama of the fifties, was second in popularity only to Uncle Tom after the War. Meanwhile, Thomas Nelson Page, the South's most popular post-war writer, reached the best seller list with his plantation novel *Red Rock* and his magazine stories collected under the title of *The Old Dominion.*[13] Ushered in by Uncle Remus and Miss Ravenel, the familiar plantation characters wandered through the pages of uncountable national magazines, while Americans from all parts of the country sang about them in songs from minstrel shows and vaudeville routines.[14]

By 1914 most Southern writers considered the job finished and the legend dried up. In the years between the novels of Page and Harris, and the appearance of *The Birth of a Nation,* the Old South's literary prospect became one of weedy hybrids and scrubby second-growth imitations. Nothing of quality had been written about the Old South for more than fifteen years. Southern writers in general, like Southern readers, were growing tired of the Old South, more impressed with the tenant farmer and mill hand of the New South. A booklist compiled from Francis P. Gaines' *The Southern Plantation* reveals that from 1910 to 1915, the number of plantation novels and plays had dwindled to less than half the number written in the five years before that.[15] But Griffith faced a special challenge. The devoted son of Colonel "Roaring Jake" Griffith, who had ridden with Wheeler at Chickamauga and fought against Sherman in the march to Atlanta, he felt that he had discredited the family name. After five years at Biograph, the would-be poet and playwright was only partially convinced he belonged to an honorable profession.[16] The familiar story is that the idea of a Civil War epic transformed him into an impassioned filmmaker burning with social purpose. This is probably overstated but, in its essentials, doubtless true. Billy Bitzer, Griffith's closest friend on the Majestic-Reliance lot, remembered the new enthusiasm on the set when Griffith started filming *Birth*:

> Where heretofore he was wont to refer to starting on a new picture to "grinding out another sausage," and go at it lightly, his attitude in beginning on this one was all eagerness. He acted like here we have something worthwhile.[17]

Not only was Griffith set to defend the Old South's storybook "history," he

13 Gaines, *The Southern Plantation.* For a full listing of the writers working this mine and the stories they produced, see his chapter, "The Development of the Tradition in Literature," especially pp. 74-89. Gaines claims the vogue peaked in the 1880's and early 1890's, citing the popularity of Harris, Page, and F. Hopkinson Smith's influential plantation novel, *Colonel Carter of Cartersville* (New York, 1891).

14 Gaines, *The Southern Plantation,* pp. 95-127.

15 Gaines, *The Southern Plantation,* pp. 74-89.

16 For Griffith's pre-film career, see Russell Merritt, "The Impact of D. W. Griffith's Motion Pictures from 1908-1914 on Contemporary American Culture," unpublished dissertation (Harvard University, 1970), pp. 1-44; 301-309.

17 G. W. Bitzer, "D. W. Griffith," unpublished manuscript at the Museum of Modern Art, New York, p. 9.

would also demonstrate that the motion pictures, the disreputable orphan of the arts, could recount the legend more eloquently and sway a wider audience than even the South's finest novelists. In one broad sweep he would redeem both his homeland and his profession, making a name for himself in the arts at last.

Griffith's immediate source was the notorious Reconstruction melodrama, *The Clansman*, a prime specimen of the skid row depths to which the Southern romance had sunk. Its author was Thomas Dixon, Jr., from North Carolina, a professional Southerner, sometime preacher, novelist, and fervent Negrophobe. Dixon's story was familiar to Griffith as both a novel and a play. The Kinemacolor Company had earlier tried to turn *The Clansman* into a movie, starring Griffith's wife; as a play in 1906, it had attracted Griffith's attention because of the widely-publicized Negro agitation.[18]

But the first part of *The Birth of a Nation* was largely Griffith's own. Dixon's play had recounted the horrors of Reconstruction; for the Civil War, Griffith was thrown back on his own resources, and what emerged was an extraordinary mix of traditional Southern motives cast in a fresh form.

Griffith's Genteel Family

Griffith brought to the legend a personal point of view that colored his story and he tailored it to his audiences as Page and Harris had suited the legend to theirs. The feature of the legend Griffith found most appealing was the emphasis on the closely-knit home, an absolute faith in the values of family life. Always a central part of the Southern myth, Griffith turned the family into his story's mainspring.

When Griffith wants to show us what the Old South is like in *The Birth of a Nation*, he need go no further than the porch of the family estate. What he finds there sums up life's worthwhile pleasures: a family completely at ease, using its spare time to talk, play, and be together. The narrative begins on the modest estate of Ben Cameron in Piedmont, South Carolina. There, we discover, everyone knows and accepts his place—not only the slaves, but the children and parents too.

The true focal point is the Southern woman. She presides over the family like a local household goddess, "the prophetess and high priestess of her people."[19] Griffith once told an interviewer about his play, *The Treadmill*, "It says that not man is God, but woman, the poor mother of the skies."[20] He seldom ranked her much lower than that. As usual in the myth, she is idealized past the point of credibility. She is the epitome of what incenses modern feminists: the Southern belle, the obedient and playful child, the passive and devoted mother. But she is also the very essence of the Griffith family: the hardworking motor that keeps it running. She hustles and

[18] James Hart. *The Man Who Invented Hollywood* (Lousiville, 1972), p. 89.

[19] Thomas Dixon, Jr., *The Clansman* (New York, 1905), p. 362.

[20] Quoted in Ezra Goodman, "Flashback to Griffith," *P.M.* (May, 1948), reprinted in Goodman, *The Fifty Year Decline and Fall of Hollywood* (New York, 1962), p. 18.

bustles about the household, managing family chores as we might expect, but (more important) she is the one from whom originate the virtues which define the family at large. The qualities that endear the Camerons to us on that front porch are essentially feminine: gentleness, Christian virtue, playful friendliness, tidiness, and a soft-spoken preference for the refined. The men illustrate these qualities as well as the women. Ben and his brothers, all spruced up, innocently tease their sister or frolic with their Northern friends, while Dr. Cameron, "the kindly master of Cameron Hall," plays with the puppies and kittens.

The woman-centered home was a perpetual obsession with Griffith. Not only in *The Birth of a Nation*, but in most of his films, especially the Biographs, Griffith venerated all the family stood for. Over and over again we come across Biograph titles like *For a Wife's Honor* (1908), *The Planter's Wife* (1908), *His Wife's Mother* (1909), *The Girls and Daddy* (1909), *Wanted: A Child* (1909), *The Honor of His Family* (1909), *The Two Brothers* (1910), *Her Father's Pride* (1910), *The Three Sisters* (1911), and *Her Mother's Oath* (1913). Griffith's first film, *The Adventures of Dollie* (1908), a story about gypsies kidnapping a baby girl, is set "on the lawn of a country residence" where "we find the little family, comprising father, mother, and little Dollie, their daughter."[21]

The happy family is always a closely knit family. Members play together (*A Country Doctor*), fight together (*A Feud in the Kentucky Hills*), mourn together (*What Drink Did*), read at the hearth together (*The Drunkard's Reformation*), are robbed together (*The Girls and Daddy*), die together (*In Old Kentucky*), laugh together (*Muggsy's First Sweetheart*), endure poverty together (*The Two Paths*), and do charity work together (*Simple Charity*). In his films about the Jones family—*The Smoked Husband* (1908), *Mr. Jones at the Ball* (1908), *Mr. Jones Has a Card Party* (1909), *The Joneses Have Amateur Theatricals* (1909), and *Mr. Jones' Burglar* (1909)—Griffith introduced what is probably the first family comedy series. In his exquisite Billy Quirk-Mary Pickford comedies he set the standard for the girl-next-door romance. Even before *The Birth of a Nation* was released, Griffith was filming a story about a mother and her baby called *The Mother and the Law*—later, of course, part of *Intolerance* (1916), where the central image would be a mother rocking her cradle.

In *The Birth of a Nation*, threats to the South are inseparable from threats to the family. Our first extended view of Austin Stoneman, the tyrannical anti-Southern "Master of Congress" shows him seated at a desk in his cluttered Washington study. The study becomes, in effect, a kind of anti-home. Instead of a wife, Stoneman keeps a mulatto mistress "of sinister animal beauty" and, ignoring his sons and daughter, spends most of his time with political cronies. In "this strange house on Capitol Hill" (head title, reel 7)

---

21 Quoted from the descriptive trade *Biograph Bulletin*, Number 151. A set of these bulletins from 1903 to 1913 is in the Museum of Modern Art Film Library, New York City. A microfilm duplicate set is in Harvard University's Widener Library, Cambridge, Mass.

"where his daughter [Elsie] never visits" (title, 87), Stoneman schemes with Charles Sumner for control of the Senate (87-94), and after Lincoln's assassination sets up headquarters for Reconstruction government (509-540).[22] Political acquaintances, mulatto friends, businessmen, and government officials hustle in and out continuously, in obvious contrast to the Cameron family tranquility. Worst of all, the Camerons' stable family structure has been turned upside down. In Stoneman's library, the head of the household submits to the mulatto maid.

The Family Epic

The Civil War and its aftermath gave Griffith an opportunity to expand this vision of the family and its antagonists to heroic proportions. The South as a whole becomes a kind of family in *The Birth of a Nation,* an informal folk society made up of front porches, picket fences, dirt roads, slave shacks, and family balls held in the living room. The enemy threatening this idyllic community is harder to describe; at first glance it appears to be that familiar Southern hobgoblin, the Northern metropolis. The twentieth century filmmaker had no need to be as tactful as Page or Harris had been twenty years before. He makes a point of associating Stoneman's corrupt library with the North, and paints withering miniature portraits of General Sherman burning homes on his march through Atlanta and General Grant, the cigar-puffing Philistine (cf. 260-263 and 417-418). On a grander scale, the North seems possessed by a spirit basically different from the South's. The Yankees have created a highly institutionalized society, a collection of impersonal, usually sinister organizations that almost always mean trouble. We remember the North for its Abolitionist meetings (2-7), Puritan slave marts (1), Government offices (114-115), Ford's Theatre (444-498), the Stoneman apartment (8;439-43; 396-410), and military hospitals (376-95, 413-15). When the North transplants itself in the South, it breeds more organizations—the detested Freedman's Bureau (586-600) and the reconstructed South Carolina legislature (682-710).

Yet Griffith is particularly careful to notice that this strange spirit is only an extrinsic part of the North. When Griffith talks about the Reconstruction and carpetbaggers, he does not usually want us to think of Northerners; he prefers to regard carpetbaggers simply as aliens, a vague group of outside agitators who properly belong to neither North nor South. Wherever he can —in the North-South love affairs, on the Civil War battlefields, and in Dr. Cameron's Yankee hideout—he accepts Page's dictum that Northerners and Southerners are essentially the same, fundamentally part of the same family. The Pennsylvania home where Stoneman's children live (10-22; 116-

---

[22] A print of *The Birth of a Nation* is in The Museum of Modern Art Film Library, New York City (copyright number LP 6677). All references to the film are made from this print. I have also made use of Theodore Huff, *A Shot Analysis of D. W. Griffith's The Birth of a Nation* (Museum of Modern Art, 1961) when referring to specific scenes. Although there are minor differences between the print used by Huff in his study and the Museum's print, I have nevertheless used his system of scene numbers for convenience in my text.

126) is patterned directly on the Cameron's Southern plantation. Elsie and her brothers, teasing and running after one another, enjoy the same spirit that endears Ben and his family to us. The brave homesteaders who protect Dr. Cameron from the hordes of marauding blacks come from the North, too (title, 1065), close kin to the Yankee soldiers who save Ben's life during the Civil War (360-65).

Stoneman himself is only superficially committed to the frosty anti-Southern spirit, and that is what makes him such a curious figure. The crippled statesman has been given two roles to play, the second diametrically opposed to the first. He is not only the "Master of Congress"; he is also a loving father who can respond to those reliable family values, the values of the Old South. Despite the attention he gives his mistress and evil enterprises, he still mourns the death of his son (257) and spends at least part of his leisure with his daughter, Elsie (8-9). He has raised, meanwhile, the best kind of Southern children, and their spirit is not lost on their father. Towards the end, it is, of course, Stoneman's sense of family honor that redeems him from the mad folly of Reconstruction. When his leering Black protégé wants to marry his daughter, Stoneman finally comes to his senses. Stoneman the family man easily overwhelms Stoneman the Yankee politician.

In other words, if the North is the home of General Grant and General Sherman, Griffith emphasizes more often and more forcibly that it is also the home of Abraham Lincoln and those generous families who give the South needed supplies. This sinister spirit—this threat—may have infected the North, but it is no more natural to the North than to the South. The country itself is potentially a homogeneous family; everyone who belongs shares the Old South's ideals and dreams.

We have called the legend of the Old South the mainspring of Griffith's film, but Griffith did more than simply resurrect an old myth. In the first part of the film he loyally followed the tradition his forebears had established—recreating the myth to reconcile North and South, claim the Negro as the Southerner's loyal friend, and emphasize the horrors of the war. But as he entered the second half of *The Birth of a Nation*, Griffith was brought into the sphere of a darker, more modern influence and began to cultivate the legend for an original purpose.

Griffith had based his film on two stories by Thomas Dixon, Jr.: Dixon's novel, *The Clansman* (Doubleday, Page, and Company, 1905) and the play, also called *The Clansman* (unpublished script, 1905), that Dixon adapted from it.[23] In the part of the film we have examined, Dixon's influence was

---

23 Many film historians claim Dixon's Reconstruction novel, *The Leopard's Spots* (New York, 1903) was also a source for *The Birth of a Nation;* this is incorrect. The error may be traced back to the original 1915 playbills and souvenir programs for *Birth* which, eager to flaunt the film's literary pedigree, cited both *The Clansman* and *The Leopard's Spots* as the film's sources.

There is no evidence that Griffith ever read *The Leopard's Spots,* despite certain similarities between that novel and the film. These similarities exist because when

erratic. He had provided Griffith with the novel's fictional characters and suggested individual scenes, but the overall conception was Griffith's own. In the second part of the film Dixon as much as Griffith became the man behind *The Birth of a Nation*. His stories were the main sources for Griffith's Reconstruction plot and the racist themes that give the second half its distinctive flavor. The film's historical tableaux and extended historical footnotes were also Dixon's work. Reading *The Clansman* is like going through *The Birth of a Nation* in a bad dream, so far is it removed from Griffith in skill and scope, yet it is fair to say that without Dixon, Griffith could not have finished his film.

Enter Tom Dixon

Dixon's novel is a lurid Southern romance purporting to cover the effects of Reconstruction in the Carolinas from 1865 to 1870. It takes up Ben Cameron's story after he has been wounded at Petersburg and put into a Federal hospital. He recuperates quickly, thanks to the loving care of nurse Elsie Stoneman, and soon returns to his home in Piedmont, North Carolina. No horror of a Civil War hospital could prepare Ben for the tragedy he finds at home. His impoverished community has been victimized by the Radical government, its families put under the heel of former slaves. The freedman has bankrupted the state and defied his former master; with the help of the carpetbagger he has attempted to turn the South into a jungle. In Darwinian terms, Ben's venerable father explains the situation to a Northern critic:

> "For a Russian to rule a Pole," he went on, "a Turk to rule a Greek, or an Austrian to dominate an Italian is hard enough, but for a thick-lipped, flat-nosed, spindle-shanked negro, exuding his nauseating animal odour, to shout in derision over the hearths and homes of white men and women is an atrocity too monstrous for belief. Our people are yet dazed by its horror. My God! when they realize its meaning, whose arm will be strong enough to hold them? . . .
> "This Republic is great . . . because of the genius of the race of pioneer white freemen who settled this continent, dared the might of kings, and made a wilderness the home of Freedom. Our future depends on the purity of this racial stock. . . .
> "Yet may we not train the Negro?" asked Stoneman.
> "To a point yes, and then sink to his level. . . . The issue, sir, is Civilization! Not whether a negro shall be protected, but whether Society is worth saving from barbarism."[24]

The Ku Klux Klan from this point of view is the white man's only hope. It rushes down from the hills, "the resistless movement of a race," to redeem the South and drive away the barbarian. The novel ends as Ben, now the Grand Dragon of the South Carolina Klan, saves a former Federal of-

---

Dixon adapted *The Clansman* for the stage, he incorporated certain characters and episodes from *The Leopard's Spots* which Griffith later kept intact in his film.

[24] Dixon, *The Clansman*, pp. 290-2.

ficer from the enemy's clutches (in the play, Ben saves his Northern sweetheart, Elsie, and her father). The Klan disarms the Negro militia and Klan-supervised elections disenfranchise the Negro and restore Southern whites to the government. "Civilization has been saved," says Ben at last, "and the South redeemed from shame."[25]

Dixon was no isolated crackpot, but a representative spokesman of his time. So well-known were his works that when *The Birth of a Nation* first appeared, critics invariably discussed it as his film, usually ignoring Griffith altogether. Dixon's arch-enemy, W. E. B. DuBois, referred to the film as "Tom Dixon's latest attack on colored people;" his close friend, former classmate Woodrow Wilson, granted Dixon the special favor of a White House screening.

Thomas Dixon had first risen to prominence in the eighteen nineties when, as an ordained Baptist minister from North Carolina, he electrified congregations in Boston and New York with his fiery evangelism and gospel of social Christianity.[26] In 1891 he was made pastor of the Twenty-Third Street Baptist Church in New York City, and by 1900 was reportedly attracting larger congregations than any other Protestant preacher in the country.[27] The millionaire John D. Rockefeller, one of Dixon's great admirers, offered to share half the expenses in building Dixon a million dollar "People's Temple" in downtown Manhattan.

Although Dixon declined Rockefeller's offer, he resigned in order to reach a still larger, nationwide audience through writing. Within three years he had published the rabid anti-Negro Reconstruction novel, *The Leopard's Spots* (1903) which made him a best-selling author overnight. *The Clansman*, his next novel, was even more successful.

In both these novels, Dixon rode the back of current fears spawned by the large migration of Southern Negroes to Northern cities, the waves of immigrants pouring in from Eastern Europe, and the abiding popularity of alarmist social theories. Dixon wrote at a time when Chicago began to segregate its schools and Harlem was transformed from an upper-class suburb into a Negro slum. Mounting waves of race riots in the North and lynchings in the South had punctuated ten years of Jim Crow legislation. When Dixon's play *The Clansman* opened in Charleston, South Carolina, in September, 1905, a New York *Evening Post* reporter described the audience:

> The people have not come to be amused—and that is a feature which is startlingly evident to every close observer. . . . Every reference to the maintenance of the power of the white race is greeted with a subdued roar . . .
> When the cause of the carpetbagger and the Black League seemed in the ascendant, there was hissing. But it was not such hissing as one hears di-

---

25 Dixon, *The Clansman*, p. 374.

26 Maxfield Bloomfield, "Dixon's *The Leopard's Spots:* A Study in Popular Racism," *American Quarterly* XVI (Fall, 1964), p. 389. For the life of Dixon, see also Raymond A. Cook, "The Man Behind The Birth of a Nation," *The North Carolina Historical Review* XXXIX (Autumn, 1962), pp. 519-40, which was later expanded as a chapter in his *Fire from the Flint*.

27 Bloomfield, "Dixon's *Leopard's Spots*," p. 389.

rected toward the eyebrows of the villain in the ordinary melodrama. The whole house, from pit to roof, seethed. At times the actors could not go on.[28]

Dixon's audience had grown up on a brand of Social Darwinism which gave intellectual veneer to their white supremacy standards. This familiar theory maintained that societies, like individuals, were organic and capable of different peaks of growth before decline. It had already been used to justify America's colonial policies in the Philippines and Hawaiian Islands. Dixon was simply exploiting the other side of the proposition. If the superior Anglo-Saxon could elevate the inferior native to his standard, couldn't the semi-barbarian drag the Anglo-Saxon down to his? Dixon, along with Henry Adams and Charles Pearson, saw danger signals. The white American was beset on all sides by barbarian peoples ready to taint his blood and corrupt his civilization. Was the white man strong enough to thwart these invaders? While Jack London manned the western barricade and warned America about the imminent "Yellow Peril," Dixon exposed the homemade "Black Peril" boring from within.[29]

Griffith Versus Dixon

Dixon had discovered an ingenious and extremely effective means to dramatize the fears of Northern city dwellers concerned by their new black neighbors. He simply took over the old Southern legends, so familiar to his Northern audiences, and used them to illustrate the Negro's social and political incompetence. Dixon's Reconstruction became a testing ground to see what the Negro was really like when left to roam at large. The familiar picture of the postwar years now took on new implications for twentieth century America. The Negro's allegedly bestial behavior during Reconstruction could now be interpreted as a warning for the country as a whole and the North in particular—an argument for strict segregation laws (such as the effort in 1910 to re-establish the New York state law barring interracial marriage), the renewed talk about Negro colonization, and restrictive immigration laws.

Griffith, as we have seen, emphasized other facets of the legend in the first part of his film. In his description of the old South in which Dixon's influence was only incidental, he painted the traditional portrait of the Negro—the mischievous simian imp, absolutely devoted to his master. In these scenes, there are only a few hints of Dixon's new bestial firebrand. Griffith, in fact, dwelt not on the Negro in Arcadia, but on the Negro's master and mistress; the filmmaker had no axe to grind except to show, as did Page and Harris, the uselessness and horrible cost of war.

When he came to adapt Dixon's material, he did not object to Dixon's

---

[28] Cf. Rayford Logan, *The Negro in American Life and Thought:—The Nadir 1877-1901* (New York, 1954), and Gilbert Osofsky, "Progressivism and the Negro: New York, 1900-1915," *American Quarterly* XVI (Summer, 1964), pp. 153-68 for the plight of the urban Negro in the Roosevelt years and the Negro's attempts to cope with it.

[29] Bloomfield, "Dixon's *Leopard's Spots*," pp. 390-93, has an excellent analysis of Dixon's first novel as a Social Darwinian tract.

social theory, but insisted on toning down the anti-Negro bias. He modified Dixon's most vicious portraits and balanced the bad, "bestial" blacks with sympathetic "faithful darkies." In addition, he deleted the disgusting scene in which a white mother and her daughter are raped by a Negro gang and commit suicide to preserve their "honor." He replaced it with a similar, but far less inflammatory scene from Dixon's play. In the play, a single Negro attempts to attack a girl—Ben's sister, but fails when she jumps off a cliff. The alteration spared Griffith's audience the spectacle of an actual rape scene and softened Dixon's racial focus by making the attack the work of one individual instead of a black mob.

Griffith found Dixon's racial theories less troublesome than the writer's other perversions of the Southern myth. Most shocking to Griffith was Dixon's manifest sympathy for the metropolis and the enterprising business-man. *The Clansman,* like all Dixon's novels, reveals his partiality towards the industrious white collar worker. As a man who had risen from ploughing fields on his father's farm, Dixon extolled the virtues of hard work. "Cava-lier fiddlesticks. There are no Cavaliers in my country," says Ben to his sweetheart. "We are all Covenanter and Huguenot folks. The idea that Southern boys are lazy loafing dreamers is a myth."[30]

Dixon's Southern heroes are doctors, cotton merchants, teachers, lawyers and congressmen. Ben studies to become a lawyer (as had Dixon) and his sister's fiancé organizes the Eagle and Phoenix Company Cotton mills. Griffith found such common enterprise utterly incompatible with his image of the aristocratic South. There *were* Cavaliers in his country; the white collar worker belonged in the North where there were industries and cities to accommodate him. Working for a living, even after the war, was not appropriate for a Southern gentleman. Griffith might show Ben putting a "Boarding" sign outside the plantation on a pillar (438) in order to show the South's willingness to get back on its feet. But in contrast to the novel, no boarders ever come to the film's plantation and Griffith tactfully omits all further mention of money-seeking enterprise in the Cameron household.

Secondly, Griffith drastically revamped Dixon's Klan to conform to his vision of a Southern folk society. He found Dixon's Klan over-organized, too much like a large corporation to be an authentic folk movement. Dixon had described a highly institutionalized Klan, carefully patterned after age-old family clans of Scotland. In hushed tones, Dixon unveiled the Klan's elab-orate power structure and complex communications network and chron-icled its supposed history. Ben commutes to Nashville, Tennessee, to meet General Bedford Forrest (1821-1877), one of the Klan's actual founders, and learns from Forrest how to recruit men in the Carolinas and recite the age-old rituals. At the Klan meeting the Grand Scribe quotes from the South Carolina Klan's historic charter.

Griffith wanted to create a homier and more informal terrorist society. He filtered out almost all Dixon's historical and ritualistic mumbo-jumbo. What

---

30 Dixon, *The Clansman*, p. 129.

little ritual remains centers mostly about the death of Ben's sister rather than ties with a legendary past. Ben himself is for Griffith the Klan's founder, inspired not by General Forrest, but by white children frightening pickaninnies with a bed-sheet (746-755); and as for the Klan's organization, Griffith mentions only that whole families participate. The women sew the uniforms and keep them hidden; the old folks and children faithfully keep Klan secrets to themselves (792-93). Like the Confederate Army, Griffith's Ku Klux Klan is a folk organization, spontaneously organized and easily run.

The second part of *The Birth of a Nation* is, then, an uneasy collaboration between two Southerners who shared similar, but by no means identical, points of view about the South. In the weeks these two men collaborated together in a loft on Union Square, New York, these differences were not submerged but incorporated together into an expanded, frequently contradictory, interpretation of the myth. Both Dixon and Griffith left their distinctive marks on the finished product; neither dominated the other.

New Meaning for the Civil War

The rivalry between the playwright and his director is particularly apparent in the scramble to assign meanings to the Civil War and Reconstruction. Dixon expresses his attitude towards the war in the historical tableaux and extended historical footnotes presented at periodic intervals throughout the film. For us, those tableaux are the faded, mildly comic relics of a nineteenth century theatrical tradition; but for Dixon they spell out a social interpretation of the war he had developed with painstaking care from his studies at Johns Hopkins.[31]

They explain, for instance, why a film about the destruction of the South should be called *The Birth of a Nation*, that curious title which was apparently another one of Dixon's contributions.[32] As the tableaux make clear, the Civil War was infinitely more than a mere historical landmark. It was the act indispensable for a vital Union, or in Dixon's words, "The agony which the South endured that a nation might be born."[33]

Lavish displays of miscellaneous historic moments—"The Bringing of the

---

[31] That Dixon, rather than Griffith, wrote and conceived the tableaux is further suggested by comparing the opening tableau (the Puritan minister blessing the African slaves) and p. 124 of *The Clansman:* "The South is no more to blame for negro slavery than the North. When a slaver arrived at Boston, your pious Puritan clergyman offered public prayer of thanks." See also the detailed description of the black barbarians in the 1871 South Carolina legislature, p. 270. In no other Griffith film about the South does this notion occur; blacks in Griffith's stories are comic, not terrifying.

[32] The famous story about Dixon shouting the title change from *The Clansman* to *The Birth of a Nation* during a New York preview was first printed in Ramsaye, p. 641. The story is at least partially apocryphal; the film was referred to as *The Birth of a Nation* long before the New York City, March, 1915 preview. A full-page advertisement in *The Los Angeles Daily Times,* February 9, 1915 reads in part: "ALL THIS WEEK The Clansman—or—THE BIRTH OF A NATION Produced by D. W. Griffith."

[33] Playbill for *The Clansman,* Liberty Theatre, New York (1095) quoted in *The Birth of a Nation* (title, 507).

Africans to America" (1), "President Lincoln Signing the [Draft] Proclamation of 1861" (114-115), and "The Abolitionists . . . Demanding the Freeing of the Slaves" (2-7)—illustrate the major events leading up to the war. Dixon's abiding theme, expressed in the titles that accompany these pictures, is an exposé of the country's divisiveness caused by the blacks and by creeping Federalism. The tone is set by the first title: "The Bringing of the Africans to America planted the first seed of disunion" (title, 1).

The seed, we learn, has landed on fertile ground. Before 1865, the country is a mere variant of a feudal kingdom, a collection of thirty-four quarreling states irremediably divided by unnamed but all-important political differences (cf. scenes 85-86). The Civil War acts as the great national watershed in which those squabbling states are tempered finally into one sovereign nation. The "soul of Daniel Webster calls out after Petersburg: 'Liberty and union, one and inseparable, now and forever.'" Exhilarated by the advent of a united people, Dixon celebrates the war as the glorious military event required to start the new national epoch.

At Appomattox, the power of the "sovereign states" has been decisively crushed, but for the first time all the states are joined together. The loss of their sovereignty, "established when Lord Cornwallis surrendered to the individual colonies in 1781" (title, 84), is the sacrifice the Southern states make that the nation might be born. But for that sacrifice, Dixon argues, America might never have emerged from its pre-war feudalism.

We should expect that this is the birth of the American nation, but we underestimate Dixon's social concern. The Civil War has solved only the country's political problem. The country cannot take on authentic national identity until it is racially "united" too.

The black continues as a source of national disunity. Just as the black slave helped "sow the seed" of the Civil War, so the black freedman threatens "America's Aryan birthright." As Abraham Lincoln said in *The Clansman*, "We can never attain the ideal Union our fathers dreamed, with millions of an alien, inferior race among us, whose assimilation is neither possible nor desirable. The Nation cannot now exist half white and half black, any more than it could exist half slave and half free."[34]

Griffith's metropolitan and Reconstruction threats bubble up into national importance—jeopardizing the creation of an "American civilization." From a taut challenge to the family ideal to an overt threat against the South, the sinister force suddenly erupts as the spirit of barbarism and chaos, symbolized by "crazed" reconstructed blacks who want to rule the country. Where once civilized if misguided Northerners like Stoneman controlled the Negro, by the film's climax the "African" victimizes all Americans. As the film title so charmingly puts it, "the former enemies of North and South are united again in common defense of their Aryan birthright." (title, 1076)

A second war must be waged before America can evolve into an organic society. The second struggle, even more titanic than the first, pits an undi-

---

34 Dixon, *The Clansman*, p. 47.

vided Anglo-Saxon "people" against a sinister, lost minority whose very existence threatens the majority with heretical doctrine and racial corruption. In contrast to the first struggle, no one hesitates to fight the second war which in its intensity and quasi-religious symbolism takes on the aura of a crusade. Once the struggle has been won, Dixon argues, Americans can look forward to the advent of the hard-fought, long-awaited national millennium.

Griffith Versus War

Griffith states Dixon's case feebly. Coming away from *The Birth of a Nation,* we easily forget the "logic" of Dixon's historical and social tract because Griffith stumbles too often over the fine points. Although Griffith may have had no overt quarrel with Dixon's interpretation of the Civil War, the scenes that are most typically his portray the war as a "bitter, useless" enterprise, a "breeder of hate." Typically, Griffith lingers over the battlefield dead and families in mourning; the war episodes he chooses to photograph—notably, the burning of Atlanta and the guerrilla raid on Piedmont—are the ignoble catastrophes of war, not the glorious victories. Consistent with the battles in his Civil War Biographs and in *Intolerance,* the wrong side usually wins and the right side suffers terrible losses. More sensitive to the anti-interventionist feelings of 1915 America than to the "birth-pangs" interpretation of the Civil War, Griffith sent a war message quite distinct from that contained in the tableaux:

> If in this work we have conveyed to the mind the ravages of war to the end that *war may be held in abhorrence,* this effort will not have been in vain. (Introductory title).

Further, throughout the story he assures us that Negroes are not all alike. Loyal Negroes, as noted before, counterbalance reconstructed Negroes in a way they do not in either Dixon's novel or play. Dr. Cameron's "faithful souls," for instance, battle evil blacks with the intensity of Southern whites. In short, Dixon in the tableaux wants to set up an Aryan nation, but Griffith does not want to offend "any race or people today." The viewer cannot decide from the garbled evidence whether the reconstructed Negro threatens the South (and hence the country) because he is ignorant or because he is black.

Inconsistencies such as these cloud our theoretical understanding of Dixon's social and political theory, but no one can forget how Griffith illustrates his text. By the film's climax, Piedmont's Reconstruction has become an image of white civilization fighting against barbarian darkness. Storms of Negro firedrakes howl lawlessly in the streets, while white families huddle helplessly in their homes. A reconstructed Negro has already driven Ben's "pet sister" to suicide, and now another threatens Ben's sweetheart. Meanwhile, Negro militia wildly beat at the doors and windows of Dr. Cameron's refuge where "North and South" desperately fight side by side. Inside the cabin, to save her from the barbarian hordes, Dr. Cameron makes ready to dash his daughter's brains out (shot 1130). The South's struggle by this point has rallied all civilized Americans together. Together, North and South beat back the invasion, but only in the final tableaux does that struggle take on its ultimate meaning.

Few people have seen the first of these final tableaux. In 1915, the N.A.A.C.P. managed to have censored the entire sequence from all existing film prints, and the out-takes were never preserved. Traces of the tableaux remain, however, in early notes and outlines of *The Birth of a Nation* kept in the Museum of Modern Art, and several people who remember seeing the tableaux have obligingly filled in the blanks.[35]

According to these sources, the sequence after the Klan's victory offered originally the final solution for the nation's race problem. America's Negro population has been lined up at New York harbor. With a title describing it as "Lincoln's solution," Griffith and Dixon proceed to envision the mass deportation of Negroes "back to Africa." One by one, the Negroes are loaded onto the ships, and as the sequence ends, the country's ten million Negroes leave for the jungle, never to return. One wonders, incidentally, if the Camerons' faithful darkies, somehow forgotten in those last wild moments, were also put on the boat.

The Klan's work is done. The Camerons have been rescued, the Negro deported; all threats to the Southern way of life removed or converted. At last, the old South is finally restored. While the scent of magnolia and peach blossoms is still fresh and the Southern gentlemen return to their plantations, Griffith ends his legendary romance. In the closing minutes of the film, he finally draws out the larger allegory into full view. From out of nowhere the God of War suddenly descends. In a blaze of fury and energy, the pagan god hacks away at defenseless victims cringing below, and a title appears, even more visionary:

> Dare we dream of a golden day when the bestial War shall rule no more. But instead—the gentle Prince in the Hall of Brotherly Love in the City of Peace. (title, 1371)

The God of War now dissolves into the image of Jesus Christ. Ben and Elsie see a beautiful city in the distance, the people gaily dancing in the streets. As Ben and Elsie stare in amazement, Griffith recalls Webster's words:

> *Liberty and union,* one and inseparable, *now and forever.*

---

35 Cf. title cue-sheet for *The Birth of a Nation* in the Griffith papers on file in the Museum of Modern Art. See also Stern, "Griffith: I," p. 164. This vanished tableau, too, bears Dixon's distinctive mark. Dixon frequently advocated mass black deportation as the only tenable solution to the country's race problem. Thomas Dixon, Jr., "Why I Wrote 'The Clansman'" *The Theatre* VI (January, 1906), p. 22: ". . . Lincoln, up to the day of his death, urged Congress to colonize the negroes. This nation must yet return to Lincoln's plan, or, within fifty years face a civil-racial war, the most horrible and cruel that ever blackened the annals of the world." Dixon's Lincoln in *The Clansman* advocates this plan, pp. 45-49. For still more of the same, see Dixon's *The Leopard's Spots* (New York, 1902), pp. 433-439.

Griffith, in contrast, seems never to have heard of the idea in his other films. Black deportation is advocated in no other Griffith work I have examined.

In this final allegorical effusion, Griffith has spiraled out from his portrayal of the South to a universal vision for mankind. In an incredible and unconvincing *tour de force,* Griffith has related the restoration of the old South to contemporary dreams of peace and isolation. Just as Dixon's plea for racial and social unity attracted American city dwellers in the throes of assimilating Negroes and immigrants, Griffith's plea for peace is designed for a country on the brink of war. The restoration of the old South has been made "the golden day when bestial War shall rule no more," a "City of Peace" safe from the cares of the outside world. Griffith has not only reshaped the country into the image of the old South; together with Dixon he has made the old South and its values an elixir for modern political and social problems.

Attacks on the Old Legends

Ingenious and insistent though they were, the two Southerners were fighting another lost cause. The legendary South, of course, would not rise to overwhelm those chaotic Reconstruction ideals and unite the country. That evil spirit Griffith found so intolerable—so conducive to war and civil strife—had won already. Reconstruction values, not Griffith's family ideals, were becoming the country's values. Stoneman's political ambition, Silas Lynch's desire for education and racial equality, the carpetbagger's love for enterprise—to appreciate them fully, we need to remember they were becoming in effect the impulses behind industrialism, civil rights, "the Eastern Establishment," the sexual and social revolution; in short, a central part of twentieth century progress.

As we have seen, by 1915, when Griffith released *The Birth of a Nation,* the legend itself had already become old-fashioned. In the same years *The Birth of a Nation* enjoyed its greatest popularity (from 1915 to 1926), Southern writers like Ellen Glasgow and James Branch Cabell were taking hard and introspective looks at the South. The growing popularity of the new writers and their broad swipes at the old legends helped prepare for the later and deadlier blows dealt by Thomas Wolfe, DuBose Heyward, William Faulkner, James Agee, and Erskine Caldwell.

And how are we to interpret that Negro riot in front of the Tremont theatre which forced the country's most popular film to close down for one day in Boston? Are we to interpret it as a sign of the despair Negroes felt in the face of the continuing indignities hurled against them? They had strong reason to be angry. Griffith's Civil War epic showed that it was still possible to capitalize on racist themes to attract enormous audiences. More than one historian has called the first fourteen years of the twentieth century the nadir of American civil rights. *The Birth of a Nation's* success unquestionably reflected the Negro's abiding unpopularity among the American whites.

But a people in abject despair do not riot. By 1915 the black American, like other minorities, had begun to organize. The N.A.A.C.P. had been founded in 1909, followed two years later by the Urban League. Although he was still a forgotten man in national politics, the Negro was growing increasingly powerful in local affairs. His voice could not be as conveniently ignored in 1915 as when Dixon first published his fanatical racist novels. The newly-founded N.A.A.C.P., led by Jane Addams and W. E. B. DuBois, was able to force censor boards in New York, Boston, Ohio, Washington, D.C., and elsewhere to delete the most inflammatory anti-Negro passages from *The Birth of a Nation,* while newspapers in virtually all the major American cities included furious debates about the film's historical accuracy.[36] Four months after the film's premiere, the Negro magazine *Crisis* could claim a partial victory because "the latter half [of the film] has been so cut, so many portions of scenes have been eliminated, that it is a mere succession of pictures, sometimes ridiculous in their inability to tell a coherent story."[37]

The film was banned in its entirety from commercial theatres in Chicago, Cleveland, St. Louis, Topeka, and San Antonio. Gov. Frank Willis killed it in Ohio, and later the film was outlawed everywhere in Illinois and Michigan. Agitators at work against the picture in New York, Boston, Baltimore, San Francisco, and Dallas obliged managers to scissor out the most offensive scenes.[38] Absolute equality was still far away, but in 1915, as this response indicates, there was a new awakening of interest in the Negro citizen in the United States.

In the post-war years, Dixon found himself an anachronism. While he continued to write, publishing some ten books in the 1920's and 1930's, he never again made the best-seller lists. He made five films without Griffith,[39] but none of them was successful, and he returned to write propaganda literature shortly thereafter.

Dixon's arguments, reiterated over and over again, took on the mildly comic flavor associated with the literary relics of a bygone era. The leading actress in the 1920 road show of Dixon's *The Red Dawn* had the audience in the aisles; their laughter was loudest in the most serious scenes.[40] In two

---

[36] Thomas Gordon Hitchens, "The Critical Reaction to D. W. Griffith's The Birth of a Nation" (unpublished ms., University of Iowa, 1956) has conducted a thorough investigation of these responses in contemporary newspaper and magazine reviews. For a cross section of the Negro response, see Boston Branch of the N.A.A.C.P., *Fighting a Vicious Film: Protest Against 'Birth of a Nation'* (Boston, 1915); "Fighting Race Calumny," *Crisis,* X (June, 1915), 40-44, 87-89; and the *Afro-American Ledger,* May 22, 26, June 5, July 31, August 7, September 25, and December 25, 1915. Thomas Cripps (see footnote 8) synthesizes the most important primary material (pp. 344-362).

[37] The *Crisis,* X (October, 1915), p. 296.

[38] Goodwin Berquist and James Greenwood, "Protest Against Racism: 'The Birth of a Nation' in Ohio," *Journal of the University Film Association,* XXVI (1974), pp. 39-44; Cripps, "The Reaction of the Negro," p. 359; *Motion Picture News,* December 4, 1915; July 28, 1917; May 14, 1918; and *Exhibitors Trade Review,* May 10, 1919.

[39] They were entitled *The Fall of a Nation* (The Dixon Studios, 1916), *The One Woman* (Dixon Studios, 1918), *Bolshevism on Trial* (Dixon Studios, 1919), *The Way of a Man* (Paramount, 1920), and *The Mark of the Beast* (Dixon Studios, 1923). For details, Raymond Cook, *Fire from the Flint,* pp. 184-198.

[40] Cf. chapter one in Gladys Hurlbut, *Next Week, East Lynne!* (New York, 1950).

respects, however, his work possesses an enduring value independent of his reputation as a writer. He was the first "mob novelist" to dramatize the Negro problem as a national rather than a sectional issue and to insist that its solution was a matter of grave concern for all Americans. He was also the first writer to revamp the Negro stereotype from the shuffling darkie into the spectre of the black radical.

Griffith himself continued to make popular films throughout the balance of the decade and into the early 1920's, making such critical and popular successes as *Hearts of the World* (D. W. Griffith, Inc., 1918), *Broken Blossoms* (United Artists, 1919), and *Way Down East* (United Artists, 1920). He returned to the old South once more in 1923 when he made *The White Rose*, but the familiar legend had lost its magic for him by then. The film failed at the box office and critics complained of its wooden, creaky plot.[41]

Today, the old legend has not quite died, but it continues to wither. Griffith probably used the legend's sentimental conventions better than anyone else, and some of them remain charming and poignant; but just as often the conventions strike us as awkward and cheap. The stereotypes no longer count for very much; audiences today are more often amused than outraged by them.

These limitations, though, do not explain all our unfavorable reactions to *The Birth of a Nation*. Griffith's extraordinary power upsets us too. Modern audiences, always a little smug when looking at the past, are somewhat tongue-tied before Griffith's film. We are troubled that Griffith can so successfully build the Klan into a glorious Armada, and that he can so convincingly transform the Negro into a grotesque. Griffith's ultimate achievement in *The Birth of a Nation* is the intensity with which he forced and continues to force his tattered themes and values upon us. He brought to the old South a sweep and scope, a visual grandeur, a vitality and spirit that gave the legend the most eloquent expression it has ever had. He had surpassed even Thomas Nelson Page in attracting an audience to hear the old story. He foresaw that his film would still be shown when Page's novels went out of print.

Fifty years later we have not escaped the technical impact of his work, nor have we as a nation stepped beyond the shadow of his theme.

---

41 For the critical response, see Eileen Bowser (revision of Iris Barry) *D. W. Griffith: American Film Master* (New York, 1965), p. 70. Ezra Goodman's 1947 interview with Griffith reprinted in his *The Fifty Year Decline and Fall of Hollywood* (New York, 1961) gives a hellish picture of Griffith's last years, hiding in his hotel room, afraid to answer phone calls or open letters.

1972

The Evolution of Eisenstein's *Old and New*

Vance Kepley, Jr.

1

Soviet cinema is often shaped by Communist Party politics rather than audience tastes, and when the dictates of the Party leadership change, the film industry may be left in a difficult position. From Lenin's death in 1924 to Stalin's ultimate triumph in the power struggle that followed, the Soviet Union experienced a period of uncertainty, and Bolshevik policy was subject to radical alterations. Sergei Eisenstein's *Old and New* is an example of a film caught in the complexities of changing Soviet agricultural policy.[1] Originally, the film was to be a simple lesson on the need for the Soviet peasantry to join collective farms, but it was in production from 1926 to 1929, the very years in which Soviet farm policy was undergoing major changes. Eisenstein responded to the fluctuating political climate, and the finished film emerged as a sophisticated examination of ancient Russian tradition and Marxist modernism.

In order to understand the complexities of Eisenstein's subject and the difficulties he faced during production, some historical background is necessary. Russia has always been a land of dichotomies. The vast Russian plain, one-sixth of the world's land surface, stretches into both Europe and Asia. Forces of Western European civilization have been at odds with Slavic and Eastern Orthodox traditions, resulting in the split between the Westernizers and the Slavophiles. An additional schism exists between the urban-based, autocratic government and the rural peasantry, which has always resisted interference from far-off St. Petersburg or Moscow. The primary concern of the peasants has always been their attachment to the land,

---

[1] For those who have not seen the film, a plot synopsis is in order. Marfa Lapkina, a peasant woman in a poor village, is determined to overcome the backward farming methods of the area. The local kulaks refuse to help her. When a Soviet agriculture specialist proposes the formation of a dairy cooperative, Marfa is an enthusiastic supporter, but most peasants are suspicious and refuse to join. The backward peasants try to fight a drought by forming a religious procession, but they fail. When a cream separator is introduced to the villagers, it proves a success and wins many converts to the cooperative. After some difficulty the peasants save enough money to purchase a cooperative bull, Fomka, but jealous kulaks poison him. The cooperative seeks to acquire a tractor, but bureaucratic inertia delays its delivery. Due to Marfa's efforts, it finally arrives; the pompous tractor driver is humbled, and the villagers are united in their efforts for a successful cooperative.

Old and New is available for rental in 16mm from Macmillan Audio Brandon Films.

I wish to thank Betty Kepley and Peter Sarapuka for translations of Russian sources and Professors Steven P. Hill and Robert Carringer for much advice and assistance.

reflected in the myth of "Mother Russia." When the Bolsheviks gained power in 1917 they were an essentially urban movement with Western European intellectual roots. They would have preferred immediate nationalization of all farmland, but Lenin understood the old peasant suspicion of governments. Since the government was too weak at that point to enforce collectivization, Lenin sanctioned the system of individual land holdings of the peasants, and he recognized that the ideal of collectivization would have to wait until the new socialist state was on more solid footing.

Lenin's New Economic Policy (N.E.P.), initiated in 1921, was an additional concession to practical considerations. N.E.P. was a semi-capitalist system designed to allow the Soviet Union time to recover from the economic chaos of the Civil War. N.E.P. permitted the peasants to solidify their private holdings and sell grain on the open market. The wealthier peasants, the kulaks, became even stronger as a result of N.E.P. concessions, and the Bolsheviks recognized them as a threat to the future of socialism. The Bolsheviks, however, intended N.E.P. to be a temporary measure, and they realized that eventually socialism would have to be taken into the countryside.[2]

All these historical and economic factors came to a head at the same time that Eisenstein was making *Old and New*. The middle and late 1920's was a period of serious dissension within the Bolshevik Party, and from this struggle Stalin emerged as the unchallenged power in the Soviet Union. Even before Lenin's death in 1924, Stalin had begun laying the groundwork for his ascension by forming a triumvirate within the Politburo with G. E. Zinoviev and L. B. Kamenev. Within a year after Lenin's death, they had forced Trotski to resign as Commissar of War, thus ending any potential danger of a Bonapartist movement.[3] With Trotski weakened, Stalin could direct his energies against other Politburo members who might represent threats to his power, and the sham nature of the triumvirate became apparent. In striking at his fellow Politburo members, Stalin exploited the debate over Soviet agriculture within the party.

The inner circles of the Communist Party were divided into two groups on the rural issue. The left wing of the Politburo was represented by Stalin's allies, Zinoviev and Kamenev. They believed that a stable socialist state could not be maintained unless the countryside was modernized. They urged the government to encourage the rapid collectivization of farmland to coincide with immediate industrialization of the Soviet economy. A right-wing opposition soon crystallized headed by N. Bukharin, M. Tomski, and A. Rykov. While they accepted the principle of modernization of the econ-

---

2 Theodore H. Von Laue, *Why Lenin? Why Stalin? A Reappraisal of the Russian Revolution, 1900-1930* (2nd. ed.; Philadelphia: J. B. Lippincott, 1971), Chapter II, discusses many of the ancient factors of Russian life that the Bolsheviks faced. Alec Nove, *An Economic History of the U.S.S.R.* (London: Penguin Press, 1969), pp. 84-5, outlines the basis of N.E.P.

3 Isaac Deutscher, *Stalin: A Political Biography* (2nd. ed.; New York: Oxford University Press, 1966), pp. 265-97.

omy, they opposed collectivization for the immediate future. They felt that the state should continue to encourage individual farm holdings and appease the kulaks in order to meet the pressing need to supply grain to the cities.[4]

With the lines clearly drawn, Stalin was able to play one side against the other while trying to find a practical solution to the farm problem. Stalin decided that it would be necessary to delay collectivization until the Soviet economy was more fully revived under N.E.P. This also gave him the chance to undermine the positions of the other two triumvirs, who were identified with the left-wing, pro-collectivization faction of the Politburo. Stalin threw his support to the rightist faction, but he was careful to appear as something of a conciliator. The issue came to a head at the important Fourteenth Party Congress in 1925. The resolution on agriculture which was outlined at the preliminary Fourteenth Party Conference in October called for continued support of the individual efforts of the peasants, with a provision warning against the kulaks gaining undue power included as a concession to the leftist faction. When the full Congress met in December, the leftists were denounced by Stalin and it was obvious that collectivization was defeated.[5]

In the aftermath of the Congress, Stalin was able to cripple the left wing. When Zinoviev and Kamenev recognized that Stalin had abandoned them, they sought to form an alliance with Trotski to protect their position. Stalin had already removed several Zinoviev supporters from key party positions, and when he saw the alliance forming around his arch-enemy Trotski, he moved swiftly against it. By October, 1926, Stalin had forced Zinoviev, Kamenev, and Trotski out of the Politburo. When Trotski led a counterdemonstration on the tenth anniversary of the November Revolution, he was banished to Alma A **ta** and Kamenev and Zinoviev were forced to issue renunciations of their views.[6] Stalin had shattered the illusion of the triumvirate and asserted his personal authority.

The defeat of the leftist group allowed Stalin to direct his energies against the right wing of the party, and again the agriculture issue provided the opportunity. Although some cooperative farms had been established under N.E.P., 97 percent of the sown acreage was still in individual holdings.[7] A crisis occurred when the cities experienced a serious grain shortage in the winter of 1927-8. The grain shortage was partly the result of a work slowdown by peasants and withholding measures by the kulaks. The rightist faction of the Politburo, Bukharin, Rykov, and Tomski, was identified as the pro-kulak group, and the grain shortage left them in public disfavor. This was the opportunity that Stalin needed. Although Stalin had supported the rightist faction, he had been careful not to be identified too closely

4 *Ibid.*, pp. 298-304.
5 Leonard Schapiro, *The Communist Party of the Soviet Union* (New York: Vintage Books, 1960), pp. 293-5.
6 Deutscher, pp. 307-11.
7 Nove, p. 150.

with them. Stalin claimed that the kulaks, and, by implication, the pro-kulak faction, were to blame for the grain shortage. He initiated emergency measures to extract grain from the countryside, and he declared that it was time to "strike hard" against the kulaks. By the beginning of 1929, Stalin had forced the rightist faction to issue confessions of ideological guilt, and Trotski had been banished from the Soviet Union.[8] Stalin had triumphed over friend and foe alike.

The four-year period from 1925 to 1929 was thus a time of crisis for the young socialist state. The split within the party and the question of the future of the Soviet economy resulted in a general uncertainty about what lay ahead. Stalin was playing at power politics in his maneuvers on the agriculture issue, but he was also responding pragmatically to legitimate economic factors. In 1925 Stalin recognized the need to give N.E.P. additional time. By 1929, however, Stalin could not continue to concede to the wishes of the kulaks, who were demanding higher grain prices, without losing the crucial support of the urban proletariat. The grain shortage of 1928 had been a timely crisis which precipitated a necessary shift in policy. Before 1929 was out Stalin announced both the First Five-Year Plan for industrialization and the collectivization of the farms.[9] In doing so he made the ominous statement, "We must smash the kulaks, eliminate them as a class . . ."[10] After four years of debate, the turmoil of collectivization was about to begin.

2

When Eisenstein undertook his film on Soviet agriculture, he had to come to terms with the various historical forces which shaped the lives of the peasants. The peasant relationship to the land, the old dichotomies and struggles in Russian life, and the complex process of forming Soviet agricultural policy in the 1920's were factors influencing Eisenstein's handling of his subject.

There was little in Eisenstein's background to qualify him as an authority on Russian agriculture. He was born of well-to-do parents in Riga, an old Hanseatic city which was closer to Western Europe in culture than to old Russia. He spent much of his youth in another city modelled on Western standards, St. Petersburg, and like many products of gentile Russian families, he learned French and German as a child.[11] His thoroughly urban background and training as an engineer would seem to preclude his grasping the nuances of peasant culture, but he was a man of enormous intellectual curiosity. His voluminous reading and his capacity to do thorough research were his qualifications for undertaking *Old and New*.

When Eisenstein initiated the project, he was determined to do exhaustive

---

8 Deutscher, pp. 313-7.
9 Schapiro, pp. 378-82.
10 Quoted in Deutscher, p. 320.
11 Eisenstein's background is discussed in Marie Seton, *Sergei M. Eisenstein: A Biography* (New York: A. A. Wyn, 1952), Chapter I.

research on both the economic aspects of farming and the culture of rural Russia. As Marie Seton said, "scientific fever possessed him," and he searched through documents of the Commissariat of Agriculture, examining records and reports.[12] He hunted through newspapers and books on Soviet agriculture to the point of consulting A. A. Zorich's brochure, *About Cauliflowers.* He cited the resolution on agriculture of the Fourteenth Party Congress, and from what he assumed was the party line on agriculture, he took the original title for the film, *The General Line.* A very important source was a book of sketches of a rural village, O. Davydov's *Maklochania.* The book includes a discussion of a dairy cooperative which served as a prototype for the one depicted in *Old and New.* Davydov tells of the farm acquiring a cream separator and pooling funds to purchase a cooperative bull, and both incidents appear as episodes in *Old and New.*[13] In fact, the cream separator as a symbol of modernization so fascinated Eisenstein that he kept an advertisement of an American separator on the wall of his Moscow apartment. In addition to this intellectual research, Eisenstein was anxious to get a sense of the visceral quality of village life. In order to do this, he, his co-director Grigori Alexandrov, and their cameraman Eduard Tisse went to live in a village for a month before beginning production.[14]

Although Eisenstein's preparation for the film acquainted him with the history and culture of the Russian peasantry, he could not have anticipated the shifts in agricultural policy within the party. He began work on the film in the spring of 1926, but did not complete it until the fall of 1929, the exact period in which the debate over Soviet agriculture was being waged. The inability of the artist to contend with changing historical forces is evident in the history of *Old and New.*

Eisenstein and Alexandrov began work on their agricultural film, then referred to as *The General Line,* in May, 1926. They completed the first draft on May 23 and reworked that into a more concise scenario which they submitted to their studio, Sovkino, on June 30. They then worked out a contract with Sovkino which specified that shooting should begin on October 1, 1926, and terminate on February 1, 1927. Eisenstein began shooting *The General Line* on schedule, and shooting progressed through the winter of 1926 at Rostov-on-Don, Baku, and the northern Caucasus. But in January, 1927, Sovkino instructed Eisenstein to stop shooting *The General Line* in order to begin making *October* for the tenth anniversary of the November Revolution.[15] For the rest of the year Eisenstein was involved in his celebrated race to finish *October* before the November 7 anniversary date and before Pudovkin presented *The End of St. Petersburg.*

The chronology of the first phases of production of *The General Line* indicate that work was progressing smoothly on the film until the order

12 *Ibid.,* p. 94.
13 N. Zorkaia, *Portrety* (Moscow: Iskusstvo, 1966), p. 85.
14 Seton, p. 95.
15 Editors' notes in S. M. Eisenstein, *Izbrannye proizvedeniia v shesti tomax,* ed. S. I. Iutkevich, *et al.* (Moscow: Iskusstvo, 1971), VI, 531.

came to begin production of *October*. The anniversary was certainly a memorable occasion for the young socialist regime, and it is not surprising that Sovkino would want to have its famous young director involved in a commemorative film. On the other hand, recalling a film crew from location on a moment's notice was not a matter to be taken lightly by a film industry which was not abundantly wealthy. It seems very likely that Sovkino was concerned about the shape of the Communist Party's agricultural policy at the time. When the order to postpone *The General Line* was given, Stalin was still adhering to a policy of encouraging individual farm production and appeasing the kulaks. A film calling for collectivization and depicting kulaks as incorrigible villains could represent an embarrassment if Stalin's stance became the long-range policy, and at that point there was no indication that Stalin would change his position. A film in honor of the November Revolution must have seemed much safer to Sovkino; it would rally public support for the film industry and allow the regime to maintain an image of unity even while Stalin was trying to undo Trotski and others within the party.[16]

In fact, the title, *The General Line*, was one of the most ironic misnomers in the history of cinema. It was precisely the dissension within the inner ranks of the Bolsheviks which precluded the establishment of a general line on agriculture. Although Eisenstein considered the decision on agriculture of the Fourteenth Party Congress to be the inspiration of the title, this was a curious claim. The Congress did not endorse collectivization; it sanctioned individual holdings.[17] *The General Line* was on unstable ground from the beginning.

After *October* was finished, Eisenstein returned to *The General Line* in the spring of 1928. Again the date is significant. This was after the winter grain shortage which had inspired Stalin's shift in attitude toward the peasants. Kulaks were once again officially labelled as villains, and there was no worry about portraying them as such in the film. Eisenstein returned to the film with a second scenario which he and Alexandrov completed in April of 1928, and shooting on the film continued from July to November of that year. The film was then edited and presented to Sovkino, where it was given approval in February, 1929. But the authors were still not satisfied, and they decided to do more work on the film. They travelled to the collective farm "Giant" near Rostov-on-Don, where they shot additional footage.[18] This material was then incorporated into the film, and it was ready for release before the spring was out.

Eisenstein and Alexandrov considered the production completed and

---

16 It is widely held that Eisenstein had to delay release of *October* in order to edit Trotski's role out of the film; see Seton, pp. 100-1. This may or may not have been the case. But it is certain that the tenth anniversary of the November Revolution coincided with the Party's most serious split. As we have seen, Trotski was leading a counterdemonstration on November 7, 1927, in direct defiance of Stalin.

17 Schapiro, pp. 293-5.

18 Editors' notes in Eisenstein, *Izbrannye proizvedeniia* VI, pp. 531-2.

were preparing to travel to the West when an additional delay occurred. They received a call from none other than Joseph Stalin asking them to drop in for a chat. Stalin complained that the conclusion of the film was inappropriate. He told them, "Life must prompt you to find the correct end for the film. Before going to America, you should travel through the Soviet Union, observe everything, comprehend it, and draw your own conclusions about everything you see."[19] As a result of this request, a shooting crew was assembled, and they travelled through rural areas for the next two months shooting location footage. The additional work done on the film may not have greatly altered the shape of the film, but it did delay its release until October of 1929.[20]

Why did Stalin choose to interfere personally at this point? Was it worth the added delay and expense to incorporate some more rural footage into the film? Had Stalin determined at that point to announce collectivization in the fall, and did he want the film's release delayed until that time? This is difficult to determine, but there is some interesting circumstantial evidence. The film opened on October 7, 1929, and it had been retitled *Old and New* so as not to be identified with the agriculture policy of the Fourteenth Party Congress. Besides opening in three Moscow theaters, the film was shown simultaneously in 52 other cities throughout the Soviet Union in areas as widely separated as Sevastopol, Archangel, and Vladivostok.[21] This distribution indicates that it was recognized as an important and timely film which should be widely seen. More importantly, the film was designated to be shown in conjunction with an official event scheduled for October 14. This was "Collectivization Day," an all-out public relations effort to sell the idea of collectivization,[22] and *Old and New* was part of this campaign. Assuming Stalin knew in May that he would be announcing collectivization in the fall, he may then have decided that a more timely premiere of the film would be advantageous.

Back in December of 1928, before the final revisions in the film had been made, Eisenstein and Alexandrov noted that of the 10 months invested in production of the film, there had been only 120 working days. They claimed that 180 days had been lost to bad weather, moving, and the "struggle for the existence of *The General Line.*"[23] They are not clear on what that struggle entailed. There may or may not have been factors that militated against the continuation of one film project over such a long period of time; there may have been interference from Sovkino during production. Soviet critic Viktor Shklovski recounts an incident in which Eisenstein had to contend with outside interference during production, although the

19 Quoted in Jay Leyda, *Kino: A History of Russian and Soviet Film* (2nd. ed.; New York: Collier Books, 1973), p. 269.

20 Leyda, p. 269.

21 *Izvestiia*, October 5, 1929, p. 4.

22 *Ibid.* The total public relations commitment to "Collectivization Day" can be seen in *Izvestiia*, October 13, 1929, which is entirely concerned with collectivization.

23 *Izvestiia*, December 6, 1928, p. 5.

subject was economic rather than political. The financial overseers of the film industry had to check on Eisenstein's progress before they would allocate additional funds for production. With an impish rebelliousness, Eisenstein concocted a "carnival film about abundance" to show the economists. Footage of plentiful harvests, cattle, sheep, and milk was thrown together and presented to the economists as representative of Eisenstein's work on the film. They were apparently impressed by Eisenstein's little joke, as they promptly approved the additional funds.[24]

Whether there was any interference beyond this apparently routine checking is unclear. But Eisenstein was certainly aware of the debate over collectivization, and that this put his film in a potentially vulnerable position. How did he respond to the evolution of Soviet agricultural policy over the three-year period in which *Old and New* was in production? The answer to this lies in the changes that he made in the conception of the film, reflected in the various scripts that he and Alexandrov prepared. The script versions indicate that he maintained the same general shape and intent of the film, and most of the original scenes are retained from the earliest version. The alterations that he did make are significant, however, because they often reflect compromises that Eisenstein made with the changing political environment.

3

The first script version that Eisenstein and Alexandrov submitted to Sovkino in June, 1926, suggests a more dramatic depiction of the material than the finished film.[25] The script opens by establishing an immediate tension between the peasants and the prosperous landowners.

120 million peasants—and . . .
A few thousand landowners.
MUCH land to the landowners—
LITTLE to the peasants.

Such cannot exist.[26]

This situation erupts into violence as the peasants mass for an attack on the landowner's estate.

The guns of the landowners tremble nervously. The enemy freezes, staring eye to eye. Hatred to hatred.
A light breeze blows open the door.
The landowners shudder.
The peasants don't falter.[27]

In the ensuing battle, the central character, a peasant girl named Evdokiia

24 Viktor Shklovski, *Eisenstein* (Moscow: Iskusstvo, 1973), pp. 265-6.
25 The 1926 scenario is published in *Iz istorii kino* VII (1968), pp. 160-82.
26 *Ibid.*, p. 160.
27 *Ibid.*, p. 161.

Ukraintseva,[28] loses her husband, and this later inspires her to work for the formation of a collective to overcome the landowners. The battle culminates with a Cossack charge reminiscent of the Odessa steps sequence in *Potemkin*. In fact, this similarity to *Potemkin* seems to have been conscious, as if Eisenstein intended the film to be a sequel to *Potemkin*, which he had completed only a few months earlier. The land struggle is treated as a manifestation of the same revolutionary ferment as the Black Sea mutiny. This relationship is further illustrated by the fact that Eisenstein had originally written this very scene, an attack on a landowner's mansion, for *1905*, the script from which *Potemkin* evolved.[29] Also, the scene of the demonstration of the cream separator contains a direct reference to *Potemkin*. As the villagers wait to see whether or not the machine will function, their suspense resembles "the time of the battleship 'Potemkin' when the crowd waited for the encounter with the squadron."[30] The success of a cream separator is as significant to the cause of revolution as the rebellion of a naval fleet.

The 1926 version was very specific on technical matters relating to agriculture. Soviet scientists are depicted working to improve breeding techniques by experimenting with flies imported from Texas, of all places, via the "Anikovski Experimental Exchange." As a result of this experimentation at a state farm, startling successes in breeding occur: "Chickens, cows, rams, guinea pigs, horses, pigs, rabbits, cats: they are perfected just as the automobile was perfected."[31] The revolution as depicted in *Potemkin* progressed from maggots to the entire fleet; modernization of agriculture begins with the flies and progresses to include all forms of livestock. The prodigious rate of breeding of the collective bull, Fomka, necessitates that facilities for the calves be found. The old landowner's estate is converted.

> [The Society for] the Preservation of Ancient Monuments has sent a representative. The representative removes the count's memorial wreaths while the peasants bury skeletons from the coffins in a hole: from the sarcophagus they make feeding troughs, from a glass coffin found there they make containers for milk. In the well-lit, large premises of the burial vault the young animals are quartered.[32]

The symbols of death and waste associated with the landowners are converted into utensils for life and productivity by the cooperative.

---

[28] This fictional character is clearly a reference to the important agricultural area of the Ukraine. After shooting had begun on the film, Eisenstein was still searching for a peasant woman who could embody this part and still respond spontaneously before the camera. He found her in Marfa Lapkina, a young woman who worked on a collective farm and had never acted before; see Pera Attasheva, "A Soviet Film Star," *Close-Up*, IV (February, 1929), pp. 48-52. After Marfa was selected for the part, her name was used for the character and the Ukrainian reference was dropped.

[29] *Iz istorii kino*, pp. 160-1; cf. N. I. Kleiman and K. B. Levina, *Bronenosets Potemkin* (Moscow: Iskusstvo, 1969), pp. 33-4. This parallel was brought to my attention by Professor Hill.

[30] *Iz istorii kino*, p. 170.

[31] *Ibid.*, p. 174.

[32] *Ibid.*, p. 176.

While this version shows the Soviets importing flies from Texas, an even more important American import central to the scenario is a Fordson tractor. The cooperative applies to the Soviet government for finances to purchase a Fordson, but the bureaucracy refuses them credit. The members of the cooperative compromise their position to raise funds for the tractor by agreeing to sell shares to the kulaks. Evdokiia reacts to this threat of a concession to the kulaks by insisting that the bureaucracy deliver the tractor, and she is successful.[33] When the tractor finally arrives, the peasants celebrate "Fordzosha" (modernization), and the "Fordson stands like a monument."[34]

If the process outlined in this section of the scenario suggests capitalism, it is because in 1926 N.E.P., with its free market and emphasis on private property, was still in operation. But why would Eisenstein make such a specific reference to Fordson tractors and their maker Henry Ford, the epitome of capitalist ideology? Surprisingly, Henry Ford was a hero to the Soviets in the 1920's. He had done what the Soviets had longed to do by perfecting the techniques of mass production, and he was thought of throughout the U.S.S.R. as a modern revolutionary. More importantly, the Soviets were heavily dependent upon the Ford Motor Company for machine imports. Before industrialization under the First Five-Year Plan, the U.S.S.R. imported nearly all of their trucks and tractors. In 1927 eighty percent of these came from the Ford Motor Company. Of 5,700 tractors in the Ukraine, 5,520 were Fordsons. The name was so magical that the process of mass production was referred to as "Fordizatsia."[35]

The conclusion of this scenario has a dramatic depiction of Soviet prosperity. As a result of modernization, the Soviets go into battle against backwardness: "They go to battle on the front. / FOR THE RENOVATION OF THE EARTH!"[36] Images of war abound in the climax.

> Tractors tear down fences, razing ditches, and the cross-field barriers.
> FOR A COMMUNE!
> They break down windmills; turn dilapidated huts inside out.
> Logs stand up like a fan from the tractor power.
> Individual windmills are smashed into dust.
> Locusts fall back from crop-dusting attacks.
> The war blazes up.
> DARKNESS RETREATS!
> Spiders seek refuge.
> The priests retreat from the atheists.
> The ravens fly away.[37]

This violent imagery of attacks against the symbols of backwardness, from

---

33 *Ibid.*, p. 179.
34 *Ibid.*, p. 180.
35 Allan Nevins and Frank Ernest Hill, *Ford: Expansion and Challenge 1915-1933* (New York: Charles Scribner's Sons, 1957), pp. 604, 673-4.
36 *Iz istorii kino*, p. 181.
37 *Ibid.*, p. 182.

dilapidated houses to priests, again suggests the parallel with the violence and drama of revolution and the link to *Potemkin*. But the destruction is nicely counterpointed by images of productivity which grow out of this conflict.

> Grain grows only like it can in the cinema—in two minutes! And not only grain—young pigs are transformed in only half a minute into one-thousand pound hogs, and a chick into masses of fifteen thousand.[38]

The script concludes on a cheerful note with a shot of Michael Kalinin, ceremonial President of the Soviet Union, smiling and saying, "Eat your fill!"[39] From the opening images of tension and violence, the scenario has progressed to a conclusion of prosperity and goodwill.

The version that Alexandrov and Eisenstein prepared after completing *October* was submitted to Sovkino in April, 1928.[40] Although it has some significant alterations from the 1926 scenario, it is not by any means a completely new approach to the subject. This version is considerably more subdued and less dramatic than the 1926 script, and it is less directly related to *Potemkin*. The allusion to *Potemkin* in the cream separator scene is retained,[41] but there is none of the open conflict of the first script which derived from the action scenes of *Potemkin*. The entire scene of the siege of the landowner's estate was deleted, as well as the later references to the conversion of the landowner's estate for use by the cooperative. Eisenstein apparently no longer felt the need to establish the direct historical link between the Potemkin mutiny and the building of a socialist state. *October* allowed him to render the violence of revolution, which was the logical link between *Potemkin* and *Old and New*. As a result of having made *October*, Eisenstein was free to deal with the question of perfecting socialism without the dramatic clashes of the first version.

The cooperative still relies on imports in the 1928 version. The Texas flies again are instrumental in perfecting breeding techniques.[42] The tractor is still clearly identified as a Fordson, and bureaucratic inertia and kulak machination figure in the problem of obtaining the tractor.[43] Images of the battle for a "Renovated Earth" recur in the coda, but they are much more subdued than in the 1926 script.

> The tractor tears down fences. It razes ditches and destroys the cross-field barriers.
> FOR A COMMUNE!
> They break down the windmills. Tear down old dilapidated cottages.
> Logs stand up like a fan from the tractor power.

---

38 *Ibid.*
39 *Ibid.*
40 The 1928 scenario is reprinted in Eisenstein, *Izbrannye proizvedeniia*, pp. 89-104.
41 *Ibid.*, p. 94.
42 *Ibid.*, p. 95.
43 *Ibid.*, pp. 100-1.

The one-legged mills and the kulak lairs are smashed to bits.
A squadron of machines cultivate the conquered earth.[44]

There is less emphasis on destruction here. Images of war, such as the image of the priests and spiders retreating like withdrawing armies, have been deleted. The new emphasis is on machines conquering the land, but the result is the same, as images of abundance are capped by the same shot of Michael Kalinin offering a toast.[45] Except for a slight tightening of the script, the only major changes from the 1926 scenario were associated with the toning down of images of violence.

The alterations which appear in the 1928 version were made for artistic rather than political reasons, but changes in the third version, which is dated 1929 and based on the final version of the film, suggest that Eisenstein had practical political factors in mind.[46] Not only is the scene of the attack on the landowner's mansion missing from the final version, but many of the topical references have been deleted as well. The scene of the demonstration at the state farm remains, but there is no longer a reference to flies being imported from America.[47] The acquisition of the tractor is considerably different. The central character, now called Marfa, still must cope with bureaucratic inaction, but there is no financial arrangement with the kulaks. Instead, Marfa and a factory worker unite to present the demand for the tractor to the bureaucrats, and when they are finally spurred into action, a Soviet factory produces the tractor. There is no reference to importing a Fordson now.

The deletion of references to Soviet dependence on American science and technology is important. By the time of the final shaping of the film, it was clear that large-scale industrialization would accompany rural collectivization. The decree establishing Machine Tractor Stations, the political bureau which would distribute machines to the villages, was handed down on June 5, 1929.[48] When Eisenstein was performing the final editing on *Old and New* in the summer of 1929, he wisely decided to pay a tribute to Soviet industrialization. But the tribute is undermined; the final version of the film still contains a close-up of the tractor's label, which clearly identifies it as a Fordson. Could this be an oversight, an unconscious admission that the U.S.S.R. still was not industrialized? Or could it be another example of Eisenstein's pixyish sense of humor? It may well be that the director who made a "carnival picture" to fool some snooping economists was offering a good-natured rebellion against the politics of film-making.

Another significant change Eisenstein made was in the conclusion. Perhaps as a result of Stalin's request, the final scenes of abundance were

44 *Ibid.*, pp. 103-4.
45 *Ibid.*, p. 104.
46 The 1929 scenario is translated and reprinted in Lewis Jacobs (ed.), *Film Writing Forms* (New York: Gotham Book Mart, 1934), pp. 25-39, 61.
47 *Ibid.*, p. 32.
48 Nove, p. 182.

omitted. Gone also is the shot of Michael Kalinin offering a toast.[49] After seeing how the winds of Soviet politics could change, Eisenstein must have recognized that too topical a reference could prove to be embarrassing later on. If Trotski could be declared persona non grata, could not Kalinin also?[50] Since Kalinin had risen from a peasant to become President of the Soviet Union, an essentially symbolic post, his function in the script had been to represent the unity of the peasantry with the government. Without his image in the final version, Eisenstein had to devise another coda which accomplished the same end. This was done by the scene of Marfa, now a tractor driver, encountering the former tractor driver who has become a farmer. This was an homage to Chaplin's *A Woman of Paris*, but it was also an image of the unity of purpose under the new Soviet system.

4

Old and New could have been a direct, unambiguous propaganda film, or it could have been an example of the stagnation of the "girl meets tractor" films which characterized many Soviet films. Eisenstein, however, attacked the seemingly mundane subject of farming with all his creative intensity, and he sought to elevate his subject through a complex and dynamic treatment. Ironically, his research into Russian rural life taught him that this so-called mundane subject was very complex indeed. The difficulty lies in drawing all the cultural and historical threads together, and Eisenstein achieved this through a carefully worked out thematic structure. A brief discussion of theme indicates that elements of traditional Russian culture, ancient myths, and tenets of modern Marxism are subtly woven together in the finished film.

Old and New opens with long shots of the most important element in the film, the land. The great Russian plain, "Mother Russia," represents the central myth of Russian civilization, and spiritual attachment to the soil is a unifying force in Russian life. But we are shown agricultural methods which destroy this unity as the land is divided into individual peasant holdings. Division occurs within the family as well, as brothers split their inheritance to the point of sawing their father's house in half. The asymmetrical images of the fences dividing the land and the close-ups of the fences with their criss-crossing wooden posts suggest chaos as well. Within the context of this fragmentation, we are introduced to Marfa, the village woman who is determined to overcome these anachronistic practices. Marfa Lapkina has many of the traditional qualities of the earth mother figure; she is physically strong, and the vitality that she exhibits in her struggles identifies her as a life force. But she soon learns that determination is insufficient without the assistance of modernized methods.

---

49 Jacobs, p. 61.
50 As it happened, Kalinin was never victimized. He remained close enough to Stalin that he was one of the few veteran Bolsheviks to survive the purges; see Bertram Wolfe, *Three Who Made a Revolution: A Biographical History* (New York: Time-Life Books, 1964), II, 121-2.

In response to a drought, villagers form a religious procession to pray for rain, but the scene depicts the inadequacy of spiritualism and ritual in the face of material hardship. The drought, representing death and sterility, and the procession to counter it take on an ambiguously sexual flavor. The procession culminates in a prayer in which the participants display unusual passion. The tempo of the editing increases with the passion of the participants, suggesting a religious orgy. The marchers end their frantic prayer in a state of exhaustion, and their dishevelment lends them the appearance of having joined in some huge debauchery. The drought continues, however, and the frustration of the processioners implies the experience of sex without pleasure, or, more importantly, sex without fertility. The scene contains another interesting ambiguity. The icon of the Madonna and Child is intercut with shots of a lamb suffering from thirst. The lamb image could simply be a comment on the poor condition of Russian livestock, or it could represent a parody of the gullibility of the processioners who follow the dictates of the church like sheep. But the juxtaposition of the icon and the lamb is given added significance by the fact that the lamb is the traditional symbol of Christ. Perhaps the presence of the lamb intimates that the suffering of the peasants may result in a form of redemption. But the attack on mysticism that runs through the scene implies that this redemption must be material, not spiritual.

Many of these religious and erotic elements are further dealt with in the following scene in which the cream separator is introduced to the village. The cream separator is treated with near religious reverence. Eisenstein has stated that the handling of the separator is an allusion to the Holy Grail,[51] the symbol of spiritual perfection. But in *Old and New* the Holy Grail surrogate is functional, a machine which is essential to the production of butter. The theatrical unveiling of the separator, and the fact that it dazzles the peasants, suggests an association with church iconography or art. When the machine is operated, we again see ritual, but, in contrast to the elaborate religious rites of the procession, the ritual here is work. The stylized cranking of the machine handle becomes a substitute for prayer, and the important theme of the replacement of religion by technology emerges. Recurring sexual implications also counter the scene of the religious procession. The prominence of the machine's spout (and Marfa's obvious admiration of it) along with the tempo of the editing give the scene a very erotic tone. Shots of the flow of the cream from the spout are intercut with shots of a fountain, a traditional symbol of the source of life. Thus the sexuality of this scene results in fecundity, and it serves as a foil to the sterility of the scene of the procession. Labor and technology are depicted as life-giving, while spirituality is useless.

The importance of the communal bull, Fomka, reinforces the theme of fertility. Marfa's rather Freudian dream of the bull looming up over a herd

---

[51] Sergei Eisenstein, *Film Form: Essays in Film Theory*, trans. and ed. Jay Leyda (New York: Harcourt, Brace and World, 1949), p. 77.

of cows is an image of this obsession with reproduction, as if Fomka was expected to render a Stakhanovite performance as a breeder. The wedding in which Fomka is mated with a cow is a comic, pagan celebration of life which signals the beginning of the cooperative dairy herd. When Fomka is poisoned by the kulaks, the villagers again revert to paganism as they carry out mysterious rituals in an effort to save him. Eisenstein intercuts the rituals with gloomy shots of skulls which symbolize the inevitability of death and the futility of trying to conquer death through mysticism. Death is conquered through the act of reproduction, however, as Fomka's offspring survive to replenish the herd.

The harvest scene is another example of the synthesis of tradition and modernization. The line of men moving through the field cutting wheat with their scythes recalls the famous harvest scene in *Anna Karenina*, and the harvesters seem to experience the same exhilaration of physical labor as Tolstoi's Levin. But a rivalry develops between two of the harvesters, an enormous man and a smaller, more energetic youth. As they race against one another, their competition becomes increasingly heated and they nearly come to blows. Eisenstein presents this rivalry as a conscious allusion to the ancient David and Goliath legend.[52] Their competition is interrupted when their attention is drawn to a mowing machine which cuts wheat at such a rate that their dispute seems petty and is forgotten. Machinery is a unifying force, and David and Goliath join hands in homage to technology.

The theme of the beauty of technology culminates with the introduction of the tractor to the cooperative. The inertia of bureaucracy is satirized in grotesque images of huge typewriters, pencil sharpeners, and preening secretaries. The ultimate image of bureaucratic sloth is the official signature which is rambling and chaotic. When Marfa and a factory worker confront the bureaucrats and incite them to accelerated action, the sequence is punctuated by the stamp of an official seal, which is an abrupt and precise depiction of administrative action. It also introduces the circle image, which dominates the last scenes of the film. The circle is usually pictured in various close-ups of wheels. This is important, as the wheel, the first great technological invention, contains the implication of movement and progress. It is also significant that the circle is the traditional symbol of unity and perfection. From the chaotic criss-crossing fenceposts of the opening scenes, the imagery of the film has progressed to the symmetry of the circle, suggesting the progression of the peasants toward unity. Since the circle is also a Christian symbol, this reinforces the theme of the supplanting of religion by technology; production becomes the new peasant religion. The role of the tractor as a unifying force is also demonstrated by the fact that, while the horses panic and scatter the village wagons, the tractor is able to pull all of the carts in a long line. The train of carts symbolically unites the village behind the power of the tractor. Finally, the tractor smashes down the fences which have divided the Russian plain. The imagery returns to the

52 Jacobs, p. 34.

original symbol of the film, "Mother Russia," free of barriers and the fundamental element of unity in Russian life.

The integration of tradition and modernism in *Old and New* is achieved in a structure suggestive of a Marxian dialectic. Ancient Slavic culture (thesis) encounters Marxism (antithesis) to create a collective farm (synthesis). The symbol patterns which emerge in the film indicate Eisenstein's fascination with peasant culture and mythology. Although he may not have been the closet Christian that Marie Seton suggests, he was certainly interested in the importance of religion in rural Russia. His intense research in preparation for the film and his interest in anthropological works such as J. G. Frazer's *The Golden Bough*[53] indicate that he was interested in the mythological roots of religious doctrine. Eisenstein saw the religious symbols in *Old and New* as archetypes, and through them he hoped to penetrate to the subconscious of his audience. He and Alexandrov wrote that their film was a call for a "new man"; they were working to develop "the collectivized man and the collectivizing man."[54] By using ancient archetypal elements, Eisenstein sought to make his modernistic, Marxist message more meaningful to his audience.

Eisenstein had made a propaganda film, but his fascination with the ambiguities of his subject and his complex presentation transcended the conventions of propaganda. A cubistic presentation of a cream separator, a subjective depiction of a bull's orgasm, a slapstick satire of bureaucracy, and a light-hearted parody of the American Western film in the scene of the tractor's wagon train are all evidence of an artist who refused to be restricted by his subject matter. Eisenstein seemed to enjoy raising the experiences of farm life to abstractions. He wrote of "emotive structures applied to nonemotive material" in reference to *Old and New*.[55] Hence, a cream separator supplants the Holy Grail as a means to perfection. He has combined elements of the documentary and the fiction film, drama and slapstick with the same subtlety with which he had integrated themes of old and new. This mixing of genres and styles represents the ambitions of an artist who would not comply with the normal expectations of what constitutes a good propaganda film.

How then, was the film received? Critics responded favorably. The review in *Pravda* was enthusiastic; it spoke of "the great mastery, the tremendous emotion, the sweep, and the pulsating tempo of life. . . ."[56] Mordaunt Hall, in *The New York Times*, praised the film as "an enlightening cinematic study."[57] But it is difficult to tell how the Soviet public responded to *Old and New*. It ran for only a week in the Moscow theaters where it opened.[58] Marie Seton reported that a screening of *Old and New* for the

53 Seton, p. 402.
54 *Izvestiia*, December 6, 1928, p. 5.
55 Eisenstein, *Film Form*, p. 77.
56 *Pravda*, October 13, 1929, p. 5.
57 *The New York Times*, May 3, 1930, p. 23.
58 *Izvestiia*, October 7-13, 1929.

Red Army Club at the time of release produced a negative response.[59] If this evidence is indicative of the reaction of the larger Soviet public, it may be because the experimentalism of *Old and New* was disconcerting to its audience. Eisenstein's abstract and episodic film may have seemed out of place in its association with "Collectivization Day" propaganda.[60]

Or more likely, the film was once again victimized by the forces of history. Not long after *Old and New* was released, it became an obsolete depiction of collectivization. Collectivization was undertaken, but it had none of the utopian flavor of Eisenstein's film. Rather than peasants voluntarily joining collective farms after seeing the benefits of Soviet methods, they were forced into collectives by Stalin's rapid and drastic measures. Bolshevik agents sent into the countryside to enforce the policy used harsh punitive measures against those who hesitated to give up their private claims. The peasants then resisted Soviet tactics by slaughtering their own livestock and wrecking property in outbursts of violence reminiscent of ancient peasant and serf rebellions under czarism. Also, Stalin's decision to "eliminate the kulaks as a class" was carried out via the order forbidding kulaks to join collective farms. Their property was confiscated and they were sent to forced labor camps or executed. By the spring of 1930, the turmoil in the countryside had grown so serious that Stalin had to issue a warning against "overzealousness" on the part of those executing collectivization policy. But the resistance continued through the next several years, and the cost in human lives was staggering. Famine, executions, and labor camp conditions took a human toll which, it has been estimated, ran into millions.[61] The harsh reality of collectivization must have made *Old and New* look like a cruel joke for contemporary Soviet citizens.

Eisenstein could not have anticipated the consequences of Stalin's collectivization policies. Eisenstein had sought in *Old and New* to harmonize the dichotomies of Russian life between the Westernizer and the Slavophile, the city and the country, the state and the peasant. To Eisenstein, the collective farm represented the synthesis of the old institution of the peasant commune and the modern methods of Soviet rationalism. But the reaction to forced collectivization demonstrated that the animosities were too deeply imbedded in Russia to be overcome through one film. For Eisenstein, the political complications that he encountered in the making and release of *Old and New* were a foretaste of the difficulties that he and other Soviet film-makers would have to face in the later Stalin years.

1974

---

[59] Seton, p. 115.

[60] Perhaps *Old and New* influenced at least one incident. When the first tractor from the Stalingrad factory was delivered to Moscow in 1930, it was greeted by a musical band, as in the film. The suggestion was even made that the tractor pull a train of farm implements as in *Old and New*; see *Sovetskaia kultura*, November 7, 1973, p. 8.

[61] Nove, pp. 166-80.

The Genesis and Ideology
of *Gabriel over the White House*

Robert L. McConnell

> Yea, while I was speaking in prayer, even the man Gabriel, whom I had seen in the vision at the beginning, being caused to fly swiftly, touched me about the time of the evening oblation.
>
> And he informed me, and talked with me, and said, O Daniel, I am now come forth to give thee skill and understanding.
>
> —*The Book of Daniel*, 9:21,22

1

Few moments in American history have been more bleak than the first days of March, 1933. For more than three years the nation's economic health had been steadily ebbing, taking with it much of the remaining sense of national purpose. The political leadership drifted, with an increasingly paralyzed and frustrated Herbert Hoover in the White House. It was our "winter of despair," that winter of 1932-33, and many Americans seemed too disillusioned to care, much less to revolt.[1] No one seemed to know whom to blame or what to change. Franklin D. Roosevelt was about to take office, but his campaign rhetoric had offered little promise of immediate relief.

In this vacuum there were scattered calls for a strong national leader, but they had the ring of reluctance and wistfulness. *Barron's* magazine, acknowledging the contradiction of proposing a dictatorship in a democracy, mused editorially that

> a genial and lighthearted dictator might be a relief from the pompous futility of such a Congress as we have recently had. . . . So we return repeatedly to the thought that a mild species of dictatorship will help us over the roughest spots in the road ahead.

More graphically, *Barron's* bared its soul:

> Sometimes openly and at other times secretly, we have been longing to see the superman emerge.[2]

[1] William E. Leuchtenberg, *Franklin D. Roosevelt and the New Deal, 1932-1940* (New York: Harper & Row, 1963), ch. 2.

[2] "Semi-Dictator?" *Barron's*, vol. 13, no. 7 (Feb. 13, 1933), p. 12.

Such half-formed dreams, however, were a far cry from advocacy, and hardly anyone was quite prepared for a serious suggestion that such a "superman" could be visualized as President of the United States. An extraordinary motion picture previewed March 1, 1933, in Glendale, California—three days before Roosevelt's inauguration—did just that. *Gabriel over the White House,* an object lesson in narrative form, told the story of a divinely inspired chief executive who simply seizes the power necessary to solve the nation's gravest problems.

The film's title itself was unusual, although familiar to readers of some prestigious American and British magazines and newspapers, who had learned in February that an Englishman had just anonymously published a book by that name. American reviewers of the novel were confused about its intentions and far from unanimous in their reception; some labeled it an obvious satire, while others fretted about the possible consequences of its credibility.

Hollywood trade journals generally took the film seriously, welcoming it as good for business and for the country. *The Hollywood Reporter* declared that *Gabriel over the White House*

> will probably go down in the history of motion pictures as the most sensational piece of film entertainment the world has ever known and, as such, will attract more people to . . . America's theatres than any motion picture of the present age. . . .

Moreover, the paper continued, the film's message

> may put an end to the great problems that confront our nation today by showing them how a President of the United States handled the situation and the marvelous results he attained.[3]

Variety praised its timeliness:

> Wrapping all the world's ills in one bundle and sewering them is going to appeal to the present mental temper of America. At no time in the past 25 years was the U.S. as ready and ripe for a production of this type as right now.[4]

Not all of Hollywood was as happy with the film, least of all the Metro-Goldwyn-Mayer executives responsible for overseeing its production. Among the audience at the preview was Louis B. Mayer, a stalwart Republican and firm supporter of Herbert Hoover. Mayer, who had not seen the film before the preview, was aghast. When it was over, Bosley Crowther writes, Mayer

---

3 " 'Gabriel' a Sensation," *The Hollywood Reporter,* Mar. 2. 1933.
4 Untitled, *Variety,* Mar. 3, 1933.

strode from the theater like an cnrushing thundercloud, grabbed hold of Eddie Mannix, and shouted loud enough for people to hear, "Put that picture in its can, take it back to the studio, and lock it up!"

Mayer, Crowther explained, was reported to have interpreted *Gabriel* as critical of Hoover and Warren Harding and, even worse, as propaganda for the incoming Roosevelt administration.[5]

The film did not stay locked up. Mayer instead shipped it to New York, where it was screened and pondered by Will Hays, president of the Motion Picture Producers and Distributors of America—and a reliable Republican —and MGM president Nicholas M. Schenk. They agreed with Mayer, and back went *Gabriel* to California for alterations. A Hollywood dispatch to the *New York Times* reported that MGM was "gravely concerned" about the film:

A number of film leaders here felt that because of economic and political conditions it was unwise to show a film which might be regarded by the nation at large as subversive and by foreign countries as invidious.[6]

Exactly what changes were made and by whom remains obscure.[7] According to Crowther, Walter Wanger, the MGM supervisor who had originally chosen the story (and who was a Democrat), strongly resisted all suggested script changes. But there were some deletions and reshooting, and it was April (a month later) before distributors finally received prints of the film. It had taken MGM more time to make *Gabriel* presentable than for the original version to be made; the shooting consumed only 18 days, Crowther reports, at a cost of $180,000, with $30,000 more for retakes.[8]

---

[5] Bosley Crowther, *Hollywood Rajah: The Life and Times of Louis B. Mayer* (New York: Rinehart & Winston, 1960), pp. 179-80.

[6] Mordaunt Hall, " 'Gabriel' Film Sent Back to Hollywood," *The New York Times,* Mar. 17, 1933, p. 21, col. 1.

[7] *Ibid.* Mordaunt Hall wrote the following account:

It is reported that in this original form the film depicted Hammond as insulting and very bombastic at Cabinet meetings, that the newspaper correspondents after an interview with Hammond ridiculed the President in the press room; that the relations between Hammond and the girl [his friend and secretary, Pendola Malloy (Karen Morley)] were anything but platonic; that the unemployed army was met by Hammond in Washington and that the President's speech was too bitter; that a crooked politician was appointed Ambassador to the Court of St. James's, instead of to Greece as in the revised film, and that several other incidents were considerably toned down.

The release print obviously retained much of Hammond's aggressiveness with the Cabinet, and the implication is inescapable that he spent at least one night (before his conversion) with Miss Malloy.

[8] Crowther, pp. 178-80. Wanger, Crowther said, had planned for the film to premiere simultaneously in four cities (including Washington and New York) on Inauguration Day.

2

A considerable flurry of publicity accompanied the film's release, but almost buried in the credits—and sometimes wholly omitted—was the name of the man most responsible for its production, William Randolph Hearst. Once Wanger had shaped the story into script form (for which he employed writer Carey Wilson), he had taken it to Hearst. The publisher, according to Crowther, was "delighted with the story. It appealed to his sense of irony."[9] Hearst gave the script to the film branch of his empire, Cosmopolitan Productions, which rushed to put the screenplay on film in collaboration with MGM.

The genesis of *Gabriel over the White House,* however, was not this simple. The novel took form in the mind of Thomas F. Tweed, a political organizer and close adviser to David Lloyd George, former British prime minister (1916-22) and long a major figure in the Liberal Party. Tweed had risen through Liberal ranks, stopping only for service in World War I. Immediately after the war he helped establish the Liberal Summer School, an important movement in British political history and one that included the economic theorist John Maynard Keynes.

Tweed assumed his role as Lloyd George's political counsel in 1926, at a time of steadily dwindling Liberal strength in Parliament. Lloyd George had resigned his party's leadership in 1922, after six years as prime minister, but his most significant achievements were farther in the past. During the first decade of the century the irascible poiltical leader had been, in one historian's words, a "leading architect of Britain's most spectacular social revolution." Lloyd George's "People's Budget" of 1909 was laden with unprecedented social-reform measures, and his national health and unemployment insurance bill of 1911 became a cornerstone of Britain's welfare system.[10]

There is little biographical information about Tweed, but it seems reasonable to conclude that his ideas coincided generally with (and were obviously affected by) those of Lloyd George. There is less doubt about the affinity between Lloyd George and William Randolph Hearst; they were very good friends and frequently met socially when the publisher visited his castle in Wales.[11] How much each influenced the other is conjectural, although many elements of Hearst's editorial platforms (and, for that matter, Roosevelt's New Deal) are discernible in the writings, speeches, and legislative activity of Lloyd George. Their temperaments were markedly similar; one description of Lloyd George's traits would apply almost unqualifiedly to Hearst:

---

9 Crowther, p. 178. As I shall indicate, this was a considerable understatement.

10 Martin Gilbert, "Introduction," in Martin Gilbert, ed., *Lloyd George* (Englewood Cliffs, N.J.: Prentice-Hall, 1968), pp. 13; 5-6.

11 Frances Lloyd George, *The Years That Are Past* (London: Hutchinson, 1967), p. 230. She recalls that "Colonel Tweed" was "fearless in expressing his opinions" to Lloyd George, and "sometimes uncompromising in character," p. 220.

He was . . . an outsider, a nonconformist, a dreamer. Proud of his national traditions, champion of the underdog, enemy of privilege, master of ridicule, lover of music. . . . He strove first to improve the conditions of his compatriots, then to ameliorate international dissensions. He pursued these aims tenaciously, and often with marked success.[12]

Tweed wrote *Gabriel over the White House* while vacationing on a cargo vessel in the Mediterranean in the summer of 1932. In a letter to his American publishers, Farrar and Rinehart, he noted that his vacation had "provided the boredom" necessary to put his ideas on paper. He attributed the theme of the novel partly to chance conversations with fellow passengers and, more specifically, to H. Gordon Selfridge, a prosperous American department store owner in London.[13]

What had apparently intrigued Tweed was a speech which the merchant delivered that June to the American Chamber of Commerce in London. Selfridge said a recent trip to the United States had left him feeling "extreme sorrow over my country's conditions" because "no one is able to step to the bridge and steer safe to port." He then expressed a conviction not uncommon during the booming 1920s—a decade to which, perhaps, Selfridge looked longingly: "In my judgment the country should be managed as a great business controlled by an inspiring, unselfish spirit. . . ." Pessimistic about the future of democracies—whose doom he predicted within two centuries—Selfridge called for the kind of leader who was to emerge vividly in *Gabriel over the White House*: "We don't know enough to govern ourselves. We need a leader to do the thinking while we attend to our own affairs. . . ." A banker had told him, Selfridge said,

that if he were a benevolent dictator he would do three things to help recovery—abolish prohibition, adjourn Congress and impose a sales tax.[14]

Wholeheartedly adopting the concept of benevolent dictatorship, Tweed brought to fictional life an American president whose scope of action surpassed the banker's program.

When Hearst first saw the screenplay based on Tweed's novel,[15] Cosmo-

---

[12] Gilbert, p. 14.

[13] Quoted in Mordaunt Hall, "Gabriel over the White House," *The New York Times*, Apr. 9, 1933, IX, p. 3, col. 1.

[14] "Selfridge Declares Democracy a Failure; Predicts Its End Within 100 or 200 Years," *The New York Times*, June 22, 1932, p. 10, col. 3.

[15] The book was first published in February 1933 as *Gabriel over the White House: A Novel of the Presidency* (New York: Farrar & Rinehart). Another edition, titled *Rinehard: A Melodrama of the Nineteen-Thirties* (London: A. Barker), appeared almost simultaneously. Tweed's only other known novel is *Destiny's Man* (New York: Farrar & Rinehart, 1935), which had been published in 1934 in London by A. Barker under the title *Blind Mouths*. The *British Museum General Catalogue* lists a shorter version of *Gabriel over the White House* (190 pages, versus the original 309) as having been published in 1952 by Kemsley Newspapers.

politan Productions had never produced a film with explicit political or social content. The company, in fact, seems to have existed up to that point primarily as a means for Hearst to insure prominent roles for his very close friend, the actress Marion Davies. Most of Cosmopolitan's films before 1933 had been lighthearted musicals that did not recoup their production costs.[16] But that did not dissuade Hearst from continuing to make them, or from embarking on a new venture in film making. He seems to have been strongly attracted to *Gabriel over the White House*, and with good reason: the dominant ideology of the story coincided closely with some of his most cherished beliefs.

3

One attraction for Hearst the journalist was perhaps the simplicity of the plot. Its structure was a series of episodic treatments of major public issues, with a minor romantic subplot. The film opens with the new president, tall, handsome Judson Hammond, taking the oath of office in 1941. Hammond (Walter Huston) is an amalgam of the small-minded political puppets who had held office at intervals before him; one is reminded most immediately, perhaps, of Warren Harding. Hammond's allegiance to his party (never identified in the film) is made clear at the outset in a brief inauguration-night exchange between the new president and his party cronies, especially campaign manager Jasper Brooks (Arthur Byron):

BROOKS

Did I keep my promise, Jud?

HAMMOND

Well, I'm in the White House . . . and considerably worried . . .

BROOKS

Why?

HAMMOND

. . . when I think of all the promises I made the people to get elected.

BROOKS

You had to make some promises. By the time they realize you're not gonna keep 'em your term'll be over.

---

16 Two of the best known were *When Knighthood Was in Flower* and *Little Old New York*, both made before Hearst moved the company from New York to Hollywood in 1922. Cosmopolitan became first an independent unit of MGM, then of Warner Brothers and later of Twentieth-Century Fox. Crowther briefly traces the history of Cosmopolitan Productions in *Hollywood Rajah*, pp. 122-26. King Vidor, in *A Tree Is a Tree* (New York: Harcourt, Brace, 1952), provides a sketchy insider's account of Hearst's operations in Hollywood. M. R. Werner, a former Cosmopolitan publicist, describes the New York phase of Hearst's film-making enterprise in "Yellow Movies," *The New Yorker*, Sept. 14, 1940, pp. 61-68.

HAMMOND
(to another party man)
Oh, thanks for those unexpected votes from Alabama.

MAN
Wait till you get the bill for them!

The new president is staunchly conservative but even that is overridden by his deliberate avoidance of issues and needs. Unemployment and racketeering are dismissed as "local problems," and the horrors of the depression will somehow disappear when confronted with the invincible American spirit. He confidently tells the press:

> America will weather this depression as she has weathered other depressions—through the spirit of Valley Forge, the spirit of Gettysburg, and the spirit of the Argonne. The American people have risen before, and they will rise again. Gentlemen, remember: our party promises a return to prosperity.

Appointments and other favors are dispensed according to strict political loyalties: campaign manager Brooks becomes the new secretary of state (functioning mainly to keep the party's bit tightly in Hammond's mouth), and another party operative is made ambassador to Greece as a matter of expediency (Hammond to his Cabinet: "That's one way to get rid of him"). John Bronson, leader of a million unemployed men who are marching toward Washington to demand redress, is dismissed as a "dangerous anarchist" and subject to arrest if he approaches the White House.

Director Gregory La Cava skillfully depicts Hammond's obliviousness to suffering and to cries for justice in a scene that is perhaps the film's most cinematically distinguished sequence. As a radio fills the Oval Office with Bronson's plea for the president's help in getting his men to work, Hammond plays gleefully on the floor with his young nephew, apparently hearing nothing. Bronson's accusations are a powerful indictment of the failure of the federal government to provide moral and political leadership in a time of national crisis, and some passages surely caused Louis B. Mayer to wince:

> People of America, this is John Bronson speaking not for myself but for over a million men who are out of work, who cannot earn money to buy food because those responsible for providing work have failed in their obligations.
>
> We ask no more than that which every citizen of the United States should be insured: the right to live, the right to put food in the mouths of our wives and children. . . .
>
> . . . I ask your President now [Hammond is on hands and knees] if he's ever read the Constitution of the United States as it was laid out by those great men that day in Philadelphia long ago—a document which guarantees

the American people the rights of life, liberty, property and the pursuit of happiness. All we ask is to be given those rights.

This country is sound. The right man in the White House can bring us out of despair into prosperity again. We ask him at least to try.[17]

As Hammond leaves the room, his nephew sits at the president's desk, blissfully stuffing marshmallows into his mouth.

Once Hammond's character is established, the film's crucial turning-point occurs. Speeding recklessly along a country road (an analogy to the predepression 1920s?), the president loses control when a tire punctures (the Wall Street crash?) and the car breaks through a fence. For two weeks he apparently hovers near death with a brain concussion (according to his physician), but we learn that in actuality he has been contemplating a vision of the Archangel Gabriel. After a team of doctors solemnly gives up hope, Hammond is shown close-up in bed: there is a far-away trumpet call, a few harp chords, the window curtains ruffle in a slight breeze, and a strong light falls on the bed. Hammond says nothing, but opens his eyes (perhaps a suggestion of reincarnation) and looks upward meaningfully. Thereafter he is a changed man.

At his first Cabinet meeting after recuperation he summarily fires Secretary of State Brooks for defending the possibility of using the army to disperse the unemployed veterans marching on Washington. Later he orders the secretary of war to use the military instead for humanitarian assistance:

HAMMOND
Mr. Secretary, the War Department will supply food, shelter and medical requirements to these men in their camp tonight.

SECRETARY
Mr. President, are you out of your mind?

HAMMOND
In 1918 we forced four million men to accept the hospitality of the government.

SECRETARY
But that was war!

HAMMOND
This is war. The enemy is starvation. As President of these United States my first duty is to the people.

Hammond visits the veterans at a mass outdoor rally in Baltimore, and

---

[17] Here the screenwriter, perhaps at Hearst's behest, adds John Locke's specific protection of "property" to Jefferson's three rights (enumerated of course in the Declaration of Independence, not the Constitution), as the 14th Amendment did add it to the Constitution in 1866.

an opening backward tracking shot (amid the angry shouts of the crowd) tries to establish the audience's identification with the unemployed men. Hammond delivers an emotional and histrionic address with blatantly Lincolnesque rhetoric. In it he not only affirms the obligation of the federal government to directly alleviate the economic distress of the citizenry, but also outlines a broad-scale public-works program that closely resembles the New Deal's Works Progress Administration (created two years after the film) and the Civilian Conservation Corps (passed hurriedly by Congress in March, 1933 at President Roosevelt's suggestion):

It is not fittting for citizens of America to come on weary feet to seek their President. It is rather for their President to seek them out and to bring to them freely the last full measure of protection and help. And so I come to you.

I feel certain the last thing you men want is charity—money for idleness and the demoralization which follows in its wake. . . .

You have been told there is no chance of getting work. But I say there is work, necessary work, waiting to be done. I'm going to make you a proposition. You've been called the army of the unemployed. You're soldiers trained not in the arts of war but in the greater arts of peace—trained not to destroy but to build up, if someone will give you a job.

I propose, therefore, to create an army to be known as the army of construction. You'll be enlisted subject to military discipline. You'll receive army rates of pay. You'll be fed, clothed and housed as we did our wartime army. You'll be put to work, each one of you in your own field, from baking loaves of bread to building great dams, without one dollar of profit accruing to anyone.

Then, as the wheels of industry begin to turn, stimulated by these efforts, you will gradually be retired from this construction army back into private industry as rapidly as industry can absorb you.

Not only oratory is used to invoke Lincoln; a considerable portion of the film's imagery tries to associate Hammond with the Civil War president. It is most noticeable in the effort to portray Hammond as the emancipator of the millions of unemployed. On the eve of his address to Congress he sees a vision of the jobless veterans standing at the White House gates and softly singing the "Battle Hymn of the Republic." The camera tracks slowly toward a bust of Lincoln in the Oval Office.

Congress is largely unimpressed with Hammond's apparent assumption of a divine right to rule, and there are cries for his impeachment just before he enters the chamber. But Hammond, steadfast, minces no words, progressing from homely metaphor to strident threats in a determined effort to impose his will:

A plant cannot be made to grow by watering the top alone and letting the roots go dry. The people of this country are the roots of the nation, and the spirit its trunk and the branches too.

You have spent four billion dollars only to aggravate adversity. I ask for four billion dollars to restore buying power, stimulate purchases, restore prosperity.

You have wasted precious days and weeks and years in futile discussion. We need action—immediate and effective action. . . .

I ask you gentlemen to declare a state of national emergency, and to adjourn this Congress until normal conditions are restored. During this period of adjournment, I shall assume full responsibility for the government.[18]

SENATOR

Mr. President, this is dictatorship!

HAMMOND

Senator Langham, words do not frighten me.

SENATOR

But the United States of America is a democracy. We are not yet ready to give up the government of our past.

HAMMOND

You have given it up. You've turned your backs. You've closed your ears to the appeals of the people. You've been traitorous to the concepts of democracy upon which this government was founded.

I believe in democracy as Washington, Jefferson and Lincoln believed in democracy, and if what I plan to do in the name of the people makes me a dictator, then it is a dictatorship based on Jefferson's definition of democracy —a government for the greatest good of the greatest number.

A VOICE

This Congress refuses to adjourn!

HAMMOND

I think, gentlemen, you forget that I am still the President of these United States, and as commander-in-chief of the Army and Navy it is within the rights of the President to declare the country under martial law!

There is an outraged cry, but the next shot is of a newspaper headline: "CONGRESS ACCEDES TO PRESIDENT'S REQUEST: Adjourns By Overwhelming Vote—Hammond Dictator."

Zealously attacking the country's problems, Hammond fights organized crime with a ruthlessly efficient national police force, urges reorganization of the banking system, and, in a visually dramatic speech to foreign diplomats aboard an American ship in the Atlantic, exhorts America's allies to pay their war debts and to voluntarily disarm. Eventually he arranges an

---

18 This passage might be compared with Franklin Roosevelt's calm remark at the end of his first inaugural address, in which he offered to do much of the work of governing by executive order.

international peace conference which ratifies the "Washington Covenant" on arms control, then dies a martyr to peace. The film closes with a mournful crowd watching the White House flag being lowered to half-staff.

4

There are a number of significant differences between the film's version of *Gabriel over the White House* and the novel. Tweed's prose style is brisk, journalistic, and businesslike, relying heavily on the popular writer's characteristic strategy of explaining events and motivations rather than letting them emerge from the story by themselves. He does provide a more flesh-and-blood Judson Hammond, however. A former Republican from Milwaukee, he is elected governor and senator before winning the presidency under the banner of the National Party, a coalition of conservative factions of old Democrats and Republicans that opposes the Progressive Party, comprising "dissenters, reformers and radicals." The National Party advocates noninvolvement in European affairs and an independent United States.

The unemployed veterans in the book, called "squatters," are less restrained than those in the film. When local authorities refuse to feed them they resort to robbery, and the National Guard is occasionally summoned to protect property. The Gabriel-inspired Hammond does not meet them in Baltimore in the book, but instead outlines his relief programs in a businesslike White House meeting. His sympathy with the veterans is indisputable, however (he was on General Pershing's staff in World War I), and takes unusual form. When Chicago gangsters attack some veterans, Hammond secretly finances a popular Hollywood film that takes the side of the "squatters" and appeals to public sentiment and patriotism. In it Bronson dies wrapped in the flag.

Tweed's president is more politically active and aggressive as well. He packs the U.S. Supreme Court with six additional justices (supposedly to reduce its workload),[19] and labors tirelessly to extend his power, pressing Congress for authority to raise each federal appropriation 20 percent whenever the lawmakers are not in session. To keep state governments in check, he stations federal representatives in each state capital with a hand on the federal purse strings. In case state objections persist, he is to stop all federal funds, and if open rebellion occurs, he is prepared to declare martial law.

Public relations are also more important to the book's Hammond. He establishes a Department of Education which primarily "educates" the public about the rightness of presidential policies; he appeals directly to the public on elaborate nationwide television hookups (going well beyond the scope of Roosevelt's celebrated fireside chats), and bypasses attempts to sabotage the televised addresses by having reprints of his speeches airdropped to the people. Why the novel's Hammond needs to resort to such extraordinary

---

[19] Franklin Roosevelt's proposal to pack the Supreme Court with six additional justices was offered to Congress in 1937.

measures to insure public trust when he is endowed with such official powers is not explained.

Tweed writes repeatedly that his president is generally revered, but
there are some infidels who doubt his sanity. The White House doctor, the
vice-president, and former secretary of state Brooks plot to ease Hammond
out of office and into a sanitarium, but Hammond discovers the ruse and
handles the situation adroitly. Imposing a selective cover-up, he publicly
reveals the names of the civilian plotters while keeping those of the federal
officials secret. "Let the country laugh its head off," he tells an aide.

As in the film, federal police swarm down on gangsters, but their methods
are somewhat more just, if not less efficient—the criminals are at least tried
by judges rather than by the police themselves. More ominous, considering
the real world's political climate in 1933, is Tweed's open admiration for the
elite group of motorcycle-borne, paramilitary marksmen called "Green Jac-
kets" for their uniforms' color. Their only job is to search for contraband
firearms, but they step outside the law when the need arises, raiding gangsters' homes without warrants.

The peace covenant in the novel is signed in London rather than Washington, and Hammond wins the day not by a show of military might but by
eloquence and logic. Encouraged by his triumph, he moves toward further
vistas of power at home, trying to amend the Constitution to allow Congress to convene only at the president's pleasure, and calling for six-year
presidential terms without succession.

Nearing the end of his four years in office, Hammond is opposed for reelection by Jasper Brooks, who has by now been transformed into an out-
right scalawag (he calls Hammond, not implausibly, a megalomaniac).
But Hammond is fired upon while visiting the British embassy by a gangster who had escaped a federal-police ambush. In the confusion, he falls on
his head, and the reformed presidential persona vanishes. Here the book
departs sharply from the film: the "old" Hammond now learns what actions
he has taken in the past four years, and denounces most of them as "acts
of treason." The Covenant of London is "a tragedy for America," and dis-
armament is folly. He also condemns his declaration of national emergency,
his suspension of Congress, the creation of federal police, and the curtail-
ment of states' rights. Refusing to stand for reelection, Hammond prepares
to explain in a television speech to the American people. The Cabinet votes
secretly to prevent his address, and the camera's "on" light is turned off as
he begins to speak. Enraged, he rises, then collapses and dies.

In Hammond's repudiation, the novel closes off the world of fantasy. The
implication is clear that the operation of government will return to normal;
that the inspired Judson Hammond was only a briefly shining light. We
are reminded that such men do not exist in the real world of politics as
ordinary mortals. The film, on the other hand, refuses to disallow flights
of fancy; after his collapse Hammond seems to return briefly to his old self,
but takes nothing back and dies basked in ethereal light and music. His

shining armor is never tarnished by a recognition of his transgressions.

Wanger, Wilson, La Cava, and Hearst shaped the story into a form more directly aligned with the publisher's political and social beliefs than was Tweed's manuscript. The exact nature and extent of Hearst's personal involvement in determining the final version of the film remains unclear, but his role was significant and probably central. Hearst, for example, wrote the entire war-debts speech delivered by Hammond to the diplomats (and a worldwide radio audience), with the U.S. fleet cruising in the background:

> The next war will be a terrible story of the terrible failure of antiquated machinery and antiquated methods and of the horrifying destructiveness of modern agencies of war. . . . Peace and faith are necessary among men, not merely for the welfare of nations but for the very existence of nations. The next war will depopulate the earth. . . .[20]

This may contradict Hearst's previously consistent opposition to the League of Nations, but it fits completely with his personality. Hearst abhorred war, but he equally abhorred any sort of permanent international organization in which the United States could be forced to relinquish sovereignty. President Hammond's approach would avoid these kinds of "entagling alliances" by confronting the fundamental issues head-on and solving them without harmful aftereffects. The "Washington Covenant" conference was dominated by the American government in the film, and, after its close, no residual framework could restrict the United States in world affairs or draw it into wars.

The Hammond administration's war on organized crime is more difficult to reconcile with Hearst's philosophy. He was against crime but never made its eradication a supreme goal of his newspapers. It seems most likely that Cosmopolitan and MGM used the anticrime sequences—and Tweed put them into the novel—as vivid demonstrations of the effectiveness of an American president endowed with such dictatorial powers. There is also the undeniable attraction of the gangster genre for movie audiences of 1933.

The relationship of the chief gangster, Nick Diamond (C. Henry Gordon), to John Bronson is implausible in the film. When Bronson spurns Diamond's suggestion (accompanied by a bribe) that he keep his men in their camps—apparently to distract local police from criminal activities—a machine gun in a passing ambulance cuts down Bronson. But once President Hammond declares war on the racketeers, bootleggers, and kidnapers under a declared national emergency, the hoodlums are doomed. Their brazen defiance in spraying bullets into the White House foyer from a passing black sedan only insures their defeat. This sequence would be ludicrous except by comparison with its epilogue: national police rout the criminals from their hideouts using preposterous little motorized tanks, briskly

---

[20] Crowther reports that Carey Wilson preserved the sheets on which Hearst wrote the speech in longhand (p. 178).

dispense justice at courts-martial ("An eye for an eye, Nick Diamond, a tooth for a tooth, a life for a life," intones the leader of the police force), and execute them by firing squad within sight of the Statue of Liberty.

Hearst's feelings about the unemployed are much better known. The marchers in *Gabriel over the White House* are not specifically identified, but there are many references to their wartime service. They seem obviously meant to suggest the mass of some 15,000 veterans who had marched on Washington in the spring and summer of 1932. The real veterans had not come for general unemployment relief, however; they sought to collect war bonuses they had been promised by law in 1924. The bonuses were not payable until 1945, but the veterans felt that their plight justified their impatience. Hearst agreed with them, and he was incensed when President Hoover, ostensibly acting upon request of the commissioners of the District of Columbia, ordered the War Department to evict the veterans from their makeshift dwellings after a bonus bill failed to pass the Congress in midsummer 1932. Under the command of Army Chief of Staff General Douglas MacArthur, 200 mounted cavalrymen and 300 foot soldiers, escorted by five tanks, drove the veterans and their families away from dilapidated federal buildings downtown. After nightfall the troops routed the remainder of the bonus marchers from Anacostia Flats, outside the city, and burned their tents and huts. There were scores of injuries, but, miraculously, no one was killed (two veterans had been killed in an earlier scuffle with district police).[21]

Furious, Hearst telegraphed the editor of the New York *American*, E. D. Coblentz:

> I do not care if every paper in the United States comments favorably on Hoover's action. I think it was the most outrageous piece of stupidity, if nothing worse, that has ever been perpetrated by the Government. If the idea is to develop Bolshevism in this country, there is no better way of doing it. . . .
>
> Mr. Hoover may explain why he ordered out the forces of government to have the veterans shot down, but no true American with gratitude in his heart for the service of the veterans will feel that such action was wholly justifiable, or that it would have been committed by a Lincoln or a Jefferson, or any of our patriotic Presidents of any party. That is the way I feel about it, and I think our editorials should temperately express that view. . . .[22]

[21] The march and its implications are discussed in two book-length studies: Roger Daniels' *The Bonus March: An Episode of the Great Depression* (Westport, Conn.: Greenwood, 1971), and a much more thorough examination, Donald J. Lisio's *The President and Protest: Hoover, Conspiracy and the Bonus Riot* (Columbia, Mo.: University of Missouri Press, 1974).

[22] Quoted in Mrs. Fremont Older, *William Randolph Hearst, American* (New York: Appleton-Century, 1936), p. 520. Hearst was uninformed on several points. Hoover, it is now clear, ordered MacArthur to use a minimum of force, and no veterans were "shot down" by federal troops. It is also generally agreed that MacArthur exceeded his orders by pursuing the veterans outside the District of Columbia.

Hearst's Washington *Times*, however, received no such telegram, or its editors would not have reacted in print as they did the next day. The *Times'* long lead editorial of July 29, 1932, justified the intervention on the grounds that "radical elements" among the marchers had forced "an open conflict with the regular Army." The use of force was "regrettable," the *Times* concluded, but unavoidable:

> The time always comes when the majority must express itself forcibly to repulse attacks by a predatory minority.

Most other non-Hearst papers expressed equally strong support for Hoover in the days immediately following. But as the 1932 presidential campaign grew hotter, the Bonus March incident was turned against the incumbent by many papers—especially those in the Hearst chain—and Hoover was vilified for his decision almost until his death.[23]

Seen in this light, Cosmopolitan Productions' treatment of the veterans unemployment issue in *Gabriel over the White House* is curious indeed. The film's marchers are fairly well dressed, orderly, and polite. Unlike the real veterans, they do not build embarrassing unsightly hovels. They do not occupy Washington to press their demands, but are stopped in Baltimore by the sheer rhetorical power of President Hammond. Perhaps most important, they are not demanding money, but jobs. It was the immediate payment of the bonus that Hoover fought in 1932, arguing that the federal budget could not tolerate it. The real issue was clear-cut and open to debate. As presented in the film, it is couched in broader, less controversial terms. With a wave of his hand, Hammond easily promises to organize a "construction army" to put them to work and restore prosperity.

5

The most provocative and revealing issue raised by the film is its unapologetic call for a strongly authoritarian president in time of national crisis. Critics of Hearst, from the 1930s to the present, have condemned the elements of fascism in his political thought. In retrospect, his prescriptions do not seem to have constituted fascism of the classic variety—Hearst was a firm believer in free enterprise, and he would not sanction suppression of opposition, whether by censorship or force of arms. But he certainly wanted a strong presidency, and believed he had found a suitable candidate in Franklin Roosevelt, whom he helped nominate in 1932.[24]

---

[23] A conclusion from my unpublished study, "The Bonus March and the American Press," The University of Iowa, April, 1973, based partly on materials at the Herbert Hoover Presidential Library, West Branch, Iowa.

[24] Most historians and biographers credit Hearst with providing the crucial swing votes to Roosevelt at the 1932 Democratic National Convention after Hearst realized that his first choice, Speaker John Nance Garner of Texas, could not win the nomination. See Leuchtenberg, pp. 6-8; W. A. Swanberg, *Citizen Hearst: A Biography of William Randolph Hearst* (New York: Scribner's, 1961), pp. 435-38.

No one has seriously questioned Hearst's steadfast anticommunism, and there is some indication that he saw fascism as the lesser of the two evils and perhaps even as a bulwark against communism.[25] Leftist writers of the 1930s perceived a warmer embrace, however; they cited Hearst's unconcealed admiration for Benito Mussolini, his opposition to the Newspaper Guild and the NRA, his virtual dictatorship of his own empire, and his visit to Adolf Hitler in 1934.[26] Raymond Gram Swing wrote in *Forerunners of American Fascism* that Hearst may have been espousing fascism without being aware of it, and this argument seems persuasive.[27] But when pressed directly, Hearst came down hard against fascism. "Fascism seems to be spreading over here," he wrote one of his editors from Europe. "We have got to keep crazy isms out of our country. . . . Both [fascism and communism] are despotisms and deprive people of the liberties which democracy assures."[28]

If not quite an authentic fascist, Hearst was certainly a dyed-in-the-wool nationalist. He believed devoutly in the traditional American political ethos and rarely overlooked an opportunity to proclaim democracy to be the finest political system devised by man. In the process, he usually contrasted democracy to dictatorship, and his comments in this regard provide a strong contrast with the implicit ideology and imagery of *Gabriel over the White House*. Democracy, Hearst wrote (a decade before the film):

does not mean supplanting the will of the people by the dictatorship of some arrogant class or clique or the despotism of some vainglorious individual. . . .
It does not mean the substitution of imperious divine right for popular constitutional government.[29]

The visitation of Gabriel was, if anything, a sign that Judson Hammond indeed had a divine right to suspend normal constitutional procedure. Only a month after *Gabriel over the White House* opened in April, 1933 in New York, Hearst expressed dismay at the acquiescence of Congress to President Roosevelt, who by then was well into his first hundred days of furious legislative activity:

Constitutional methods are ample to meet any situation. . . .
The only reason for Congress to confer any of its constitutional powers

25 See, for example, Swanberg, p. 446.
26 *Ibid.*, pp. 444-45. Ferdinand Lundberg, in *Imperial Hearst: A Social Biography* (New York: Equinox Cooperative Press, 1936), cited Hearst's provision of two news services to Hitler as evidence that Hearst was allowing Nazi "spying" on the United States, p. 354.
27 Raymond Gram Swing, *Forerunners of American Fascism* (n.p.: Julian Messner, 1935), p. 145.
28 Swanberg, p. 446.
29 Quoted in E. F. Tompkins, ed., *Selections From the Writings and Speeches of William Randolph Hearst* (San Francisco: privately published, 1948), pp. 227-28.

upon the Executive is to give him the opportunity to perform arbitrarily and
perhaps secretly acts which the Congress itself should perform constitutionally
and publicly.[30]

Such dicta, of course, would leave little legal leeway for the sweeping assumption of authority by Judson Hammond, and *The Christian Century*
could not resist pointing out the contradiction in an editorial:

> Gabriel at the White House, according to Mr. Hearst, meant an executive
> with a free hand and a bold tongue. But just at that time a President actually
> did cut himself loose from many of his campaign obligations (including those
> to Mr. Hearst); who did come closer than any of his peacetime predecessors
> to seizing dictatorial powers. . . . We hate to think what might happen to
> Gabriel if Mr. Hearst could get his hands on him now![31]

Unaffected by such criticism, Hearst continued to attack Roosevelt's unprecedented aggregation of presidential power. This was not the first nor
last example of the publisher's lack of consistency—a virtue that he regarded
as irrelevant. Accomplishment, he liked to say, was far more important
than avoiding contradiction:

> I always feel that it is not as important to be consistent as it is to be correct.
> A man who is completely consistent never learns anything. Conditions change,
> and he does not.[32]

Hearst lived up to his maxim, and perhaps the turning point in his gradual
transformation from "radicalism to extreme conservatism"[33] occurred soon
after Roosevelt took office. Hearst interpreted the president's comparative-
ly strenuous activity in international affairs as a repudiation of the candidate's assurance that he would not thrust the nation into "entangling alliances" (a phrase coined by Hearst). Hearst could see in Roosevelt many of
the same dangers he recalled seeing in Woodrow Wilson:

> I recognized that this brilliant, pedantic, inexperienced college professor
> could become a menace to our country. I saw that a combination of events
> . . . plus the man's evident self-hypnosis and the massive grandeur of his of-
> fice . . . could cause Wilson to lead the country into catastrophe.[34]

[30] *Ibid.*, pp. 238-39. From an editorial run in Hearst newspapers May 11, 1933.
[31] "Gabriel Toots Too Soon," *The Christian Century*, vol. 50, no. 19 (May 10,
1933), p. 613. Roosevelt, Crowther reports, liked the film enough to watch it several
times in the White House, p. 180.
[32] Quoted in John K. Winkler, *William Randolph Hearst: A New Appraisal*
(New York: Hastings House, 1955), p. 4.
[33] *Ibid.* Charles Foster Kane, of course, became noticeably less liberal with age
in *Citizen Kane.*
[34] *Ibid.*, p. 188.

Yet Hearst seems to have been blind to these dangers in his fictional president, Judson Hammond.

6

Gabriel over the White House received a mixed reaction from the nation's periodical press. Some journals were aghast at what they perceived the film's message to be, while others were less shocked. But almost every writer recognized the film's historical significance. Even *The Nation,* which vehemently denounced the film for trying to "convert innocent American movie audiences to a policy of fascist dictatorship in this country," conceded that it marked "the first attempt by Hollywood producers to exploit the current popular interest in social and economic ideas. . . . Now for the first time Hollywood openly accepts the depression as a fact."[35] Richard Dana Skinner of *Commonweal* saw another reason for its importance:

> It sets a precedent. It opens up, for good or for evil, a new channel of influencing the mass emotions and judgment of a people. . . . We know now that a most dangerous weapon of propaganda can be forged.[36]

It is curious, and regrettable, that *Gabriel over the White House* has almost been lost in American film history. Lewis Jacobs discusses it more than most historians, but he is disappointingly brief and vague: "This film, in pointing out the advantages of a dictatorship or a similar form of rule, was significant, coming at a time when conditions were critical."[37] Most recent histories analyze it even less, or not at all.[38] Only Andrew Bergman has given the film its due, in *We're in the Money: Depression America and Its Films,* making an effort to place the film in its social and cultural context.[39] *Gabriel* is barely mentioned in most biographies of Hearst, presumably because it came to be an embarrassment during his anti-Roosevelt period.

What seems most remarkable (and worthy of historical mention) today about *Gabriel over the White House* is the naturalness with which an ag-

---

35 "Fascism Over Hollywood," *The Nation,* vol. 136, no. 3538 (Apr. 26, 1933), pp. 482-83.
36 "Gabriel over the White House," *Commonweal,* vol. 18, no. 1 (May 5, 1933), p. 20.
37 *The Rise of the American Film: A Critical History* (New York: Teachers College Press, 1939), p. 516.
38 See, for instance, the absence of treatment in Gerald Mast, *A Short History of the Movies* (Indianapolis: Bobbs Merrill, 1971), in John Baxter, *Hollywood in the Thirties* (New York: Barnes, 1968), and in Robert Sklar, *Movie-Made America: A Social History of American Movies* (New York: Random House, 1975).
39 Bergman's book, begun as a Ph.D. dissertation at the University of Wisconsin and supported by a grant from the American Film Institute, was published by New York University Press in 1971 (and later in paperback by Harper & Row).

gressively dictatorial president assumes almost absolute control over the nation. To accept this premise—and the rest of the film—uncritically requires a considerable exercise of imagination, but the political segments are often credible, especially when considered against the background of the early 1930s. Walter Huston portrays Hammond with skill and conviction. After the conversion, he is a dynamic and charismatic leader even if we reject the suggestions of divine intervention. Hammond's arguments before Congress seem persuasive; it was indisputable in early 1933 that the real Congress indeed had "wasted precious days and weeks and years in futile discussion," as Hammond reminds the fictional legislators. We tend to react sympathetically, perhaps especially in the 1970s, to the observation of his secretary: "If he's mad, it's a divine madness. Look at the chaos and catastrophe the sane men of this world have brought about."

Despite his alarming faults and despite the awesome dangers posed to constitutional law and personal liberty, President Hammond did act, forthrightly and decisively. He seized power, but with an impressive clarity of vision and a disarming openness of purpose. After three years of drifting deeper into despair and paralysis, American audiences must have been heartened by the prospect of a president who would take action. That may account for the film's immediate popularity; it was among the six most popular films in April, 1933, the month it was released.[40]

For Hearst, the film was an unparalleled opportunity to convey his beliefs graphically and dramatically to the public, and with some protective artistic license. His satisfaction in accomplishing that goal surely outweighed his later embarrassment and frustration in watching Franklin Roosevelt do most of the things he had advocated but in ways abhorrent to Hearst's tastes. What Hearst had tried to present in *Gabriel over the White House* was his simple—perhaps simplistic—faith that a well-meaning and clear-thinking president, another Jefferson, Jackson, or Lincoln, could lead the country out of economic and psychological depression. His candidate, to be sure, was a unique individual: a man invincible in strength but righteous in heart, a gentle giant who would pick the country up, pat it reassuringly on the back, and reset it deftly on the path to recovery. Hearst, in *Gabriel*, was not calling for an overhaul of the system or even a reexamination of our goals. Those, to him, were already the best in the world. Only the right kind of leadership was lacking, as he saw it. Install the right man in the White House (or convert him), and the resulting progress, prosperity, and peace would come almost automatically. There was no sadness at the death of Judson Hammond because his mission had been accomplished. Having put us back on the right track, he was no longer needed. The film is Utopian in its assumption that there are inherently good candidates for the presidency, or at least that God will unfailingly send His Archangel to convert them.

---

40 Bergman, p. 118.

While not a cinematic milestone, *Gabriel over the White House* remains a singularly remarkable film, important for what it suggests about the mood of America in the darkest days of the depression, and for what it reveals about William Randolph Hearst, one of the most influential figures in American life throughout most of his career. There is some indication that Tweed might have intended his novel to be a satire,[41] but Hearst, as usual, was dead serious about politics. He did not want audiences to snicker when the invisible presence of Gabriel ruffled the Oval Office curtains, or when trumpet and harp suffused the conversion of Judson Hammond. Although Gregory La Cava, whose most notable films were comedies, managed to include some subtly amusing sequences, *Gabriel's* main messages are undiluted by humor. *Literary Digest* speculated that "perhaps Hollywood has taken a satire [the novel] too seriously,"[42] but there is no reason to suspect that Hearst ever regarded the story as anything except a timely lesson of immense value to the American people.

---

[41] "Flag Waves Smartly O'er 'Gabriel in White House,'" *Newsweek*, vol. 1, no. 8 (Apr. 8, 1933), p. 25.

[42] "A President After Hollywood's Hearst," *Literary Digest*, vol. 115, no. 16 (Apr. 22, 1933), p. 13.

1976

Luis Buñuel and Pierre Louÿs: Two Visions of Obscure Objects

Katherine Singer Kovács

I

Luis Buñuel's most recent assault on bourgeois sensibility is a film with a suggestive and lyrical title, *Cet obscur objet du désir*.[1] At the beginning of the movie, Buñuel informs us that it was "inspired" by Pierre Louÿs's novel *La Femme et le pantin* (*The Woman and the Puppet*).[2] Written in the closing years of the nineteenth century, the novel describes a wealthy Spanish gentleman's frustrating pursuit of an Andalusian girl of sadomasochistic leanings.[3]

Buñuel's film is not merely "inspired" by Louÿs's book, it is remarkably faithful to the novel in terms of plot, character, incident, and dialogue.[4] Buñuel even takes his title from Louÿs's work. At one point in the book the Spanish gentleman tells a friend: "You've heard that I was a woman chaser. It's false. I respected love too much to haunt back alleys, and I almost never possessed a woman whom I did not love passionately. . . . In fact, as I was recently counting up the total number of casual encounters [which I have had], I realized that I had never had a blonde mistress. I have never known those pale objects of desire."[5]

Because so many of Louÿs's ideas and themes reflect certain preoccupations which one has come to associate with Buñuel, it will be helpful to dust off the novel and to examine both its points of comparison with the film as well as the differences. Such an examination will reveal something about the filmmaker's literary preferences, the particular context which influenced his intellectual and artistic formation, as well as the consistency of his themes and techniques, whether found in his surrealist movies of the '20s, in his Mexican melodramas of the '50s, or in his glossy "French" films of the 1970s.

II

Pierre Louÿs was a French novelist and poet who belonged to the generation preceding Buñuel's (1870–1925).[6] In 1894 he first achieved literary renown with *The Songs of Bilitis*, a collection of poems purported to have been written by Bilitis, a Lesbian poetess and friend of Sappho. Although Louÿs claimed that he had merely translated the text, he was in reality its author.

Two years later he published a work in a similar vein, *Aphrodite*, which dealt with life among the courtesans in ancient Alexandria. In this book as in his subsequent publications, Louÿs associated antiquity with estheticism and sensuality; erudition and licentiousness went hand in hand. Louÿs celebrated the beauty of the naked body and the value of physical love; he expressly condemned the hypocrisy and repressiveness of modern life: "Alas! The modern world succumbs under an invasion of ugliness; civilizations move towards the North and enter the fog, the cold, the mud. What darkness! People clothed in black circulate through infected streets."[7]

In choosing Spain as the setting for *La Femme et le pantin,* Louÿs was searching for the modern counterpart of the sunny world of the ancients. Thus the novel continues a tradition established by earlier nineteenth-century writers such as Théophile Gautier, Prosper Merimée, and others who had popularized the Spain of orange trees, guitars, castanets, and dark-haired sensual women—the Spain of Carmen. Of this type of woman Louÿs wrote: "One felt that even though her face was veiled, it was possible to guess her thoughts, for she smiled with her legs and spoke with her torso. Only those women who are not immobilized next to the hearth during the long Northern winters have this grace and this freedom" (p. 20). This is the point of view of one of the protagonists of *La Femme et le pantin,* a young Frenchman who comes to Seville during the Carnival of 1896, seeking sensual pleasures.

This young man, André Stevenol, will serve as the reader's guide to Louÿs's Spain. Throughout the book he delights in noting quaint aspects of Spanish customs and expressions, translating characteristic poems and songs. Thus we the readers come to share his tourist's view of Spain. We also come to share his perceptions of Mateo, the Spaniard who will be the real subject of the story. André describes him as a man of great wealth and considerable education whose appearance and conservative political leanings seem to be typically "Spanish." Like others of his age (40) and class, he has never had to exercise any profession. As he tells André, he has devoted his life to women (p. 64).

The bulk of the novel consists of the story of the central love affair of Mateo's life with a young girl named Concha (Conchita) Perez. By coincidence, the Frenchman is about to have a first rendezvous with this woman on the very day when he meets Mateo. Mateo attempts to discourage André from keeping his appointment, recounting his own frustrating pursuit of Conchita as a warning. This account takes up most of the novel. Thus the omniscient narrator who reported on the thoughts and actions of a French tourist in Seville is replaced by a first person narrator who dominates until almost the end of the novel. This frame narration technique will be used by Buñuel in the film as well.

When Mateo first met Concha three years earlier, she was a provocative and rebellious child of fifteen. They met in the second class car of a train.[8]

When the train arrives, they part company and do not meet until a year has passed when Mateo encounters her working in a cigar factory. On that occasion, she actively encourages Mateo and even informs him that she is a *mozita* (a virgin). With such provocation Mateo decides to accompany Conchita home. She and her mother live in genteel poverty. The mother spends her time in church and Conchita works or sleeps as the mood strikes her. Both in the book and in the film, Mateo begins to visit Concha daily and to bring gifts and money. Conchita is alternately affectionate and reserved. She promises much (Mateo can even watch her dress and undress) but delivers little. One day, Mateo proposes to the indulgent mother that Conchita come and live with him. The mother accepts but Conchita refuses in an angry note: "If you had loved me you would have waited for me. I wanted to give myself to you; you asked to buy me. You will never see me again."[9] Conchita leaves, thus establishing the pattern for their relationship. Each time that they will meet she encourages Mateo, takes his money, flatters and teases him and on some pretext finally disappears.

The third meeting between Mateo and Concha takes place some months later. As the protagonist walks through the streets of Seville, Concha appears and promises to become his mistress in two days time.[10] But at the appointed hour, she appears wearing a corset whose lacing is so intricate that it is impossible to remove. Both in the book and in the film, this final obstacle brings the protagonist to the point of tears: "What I was crying for [he tells André] was my youth, of which this child had just shown me the irreparable collapse. Between twenty-two and thirty-five there are certain humiliations that men avoid. I can't believe that Concha would have treated me that way if I had been ten years younger. That corset, that barrier between love and me, it seemed that henceforth I would see it on all women or at least all women would want to have it before approaching my embrace."[11] This scene inaugurates a period of complete subservience on the part of Mateo. He consents to spending his nights with Concha without touching her.

After a few weeks she again disappears. They renew their acquaintance for a fourth time in a club where Concha works as a flamenco dancer. Each evening she goes upstairs for one half hour to "rest." One night Mateo follows her and discovers that she dances naked for groups of tourists.[12] Upon seeing his beloved clad only in black stockings, Mateo erupts into a rage. His fury is dismissed by Concha as incoherent ravings. In the next instant, softening her tone, she forgives Mateo for his unreasonable actions and graciously accepts his offer of a house and dowry. She promises to surrender to him in that house. But once she is installed there, her first action is to lock Mateo out and to force him to watch as she makes love with another man.

The following morning Conchita goes to Mateo's house to see whether he is still alive: "I thought that you loved me more and that you would have killed yourself during the night'' (p. 225). Concha then confesses that the scene of the night before had been staged for his benefit. In a rage Mateo begins to hit her again and again. The beating inflames her passion. Vowing eternal love, Concha finally surrenders her virginity to the long-suffering Mateo.

Up until this point Louÿs's story is remarkably similar to Buñuel's screen version. Although the denouements differ slightly, their overall effects are the same. In the novel, after Concha and Mateo become lovers, Concha incites Mateo to hit her on numerous occasions, at first for imaginary infidelities and later for real ones (which she likes Mateo to watch). Finally Mateo flees and travels in order to forget her. But he cannot. At the end of the novel, he sends Concha a letter, a letter which André (who has now become Concha's lover) reads: "My Conchita, I forgive you. I can't live without you. Now it's my turn to beg on my knees. I kiss your bare feet'' (p. 254). Thus what had appeared to be the end of Mateo's affair with Concha is revealed to be but a pause in an interminable cycle. The implication (of both the book and the film) is that these two people are drawn together to torture one another and to debase themselves.

In spite of the considerable care which Louÿs takes to describe the customs and sights of Spain, this ''Spanish novel'' ultimately does not have much to do with Spain. The landscape provides nothing more than an exotic backdrop for an elegant ''case study'' of a sadomasochistic relationship. In terms of ideas and sensibility, *La Femme et le pantin* reflects those decadent novels which enjoyed a minor vogue at the end of the nineteenth century, novels in which wealthy, sated heroes such as Huysmans's Des Esseintes searched for new and rare sensations in sexual perversions, drugs, and black magic.[13]

III

There are a number of reasons why Buñuel would be drawn to Louÿs's novel. In many of his films he has dealt with a similar theme—the effects of all-pervasive and frustrated desires. As far back as *L'Age d'or* (1930), Buñuel presented lovers who were unable to fulfill their most vital physical and emotional needs.[14] In countless films he has shown how man's frustrated desires lead to ''distortions'' in one's vision of the world. All objects and places become associated with the beloved person (hence the intimations of fetishism found in so many of his films)[15] and the lines between reality and dreams are often blurred. This is indeed the case with Mateo, whose pursuit of Concha becomes more and more dreamlike. He is forever running without advancing, always touching but never grasping. Conchita is perpetually about to lose her virginity. At times it even seems as if she has, but that mysterious object is forever renewed and renewable. Both the obsessive quality of Mateo's love and the dreamlike aspects of Louÿs's narration probably drew Buñuel to the novel. In it he saw the potential for creating a surrealist adventure of the first order.

In his film Buñuel stresses the unreal quality of Mateo's odyssey in a variety of ways. Both the novel and the film are built upon the principle of chance encounters held in high esteem by the surrealists.[16] Buñuel also maintains the most preposterous elements of Louÿs's plot: the impenetrable corset, the naked flamenco dance, the lovemaking scene between Concha and another man, and the final beating. But while retaining these elements, he changes the context in which they appear. Thus in his film Mateo is transformed into an older Frenchman named Mathieu. The story is updated to modern Paris and Seville, thereby making Concha's spirited defense of her virginity somewhat anachronistic.[17] Buñuel also distances us from the hero and undermines his passion by placing him in ridiculous situations, such as in the scene when the urbane Frenchman throws a pail of water on Conchita in a crowded train station. And finally, Buñuel adds a series of evocative images and sequences to the story, images which focus upon the implications of Mateo's passion.[18]

Buñuel interweaves two groups of unrelated sequences into Mathieu's story. One of them consists of his narration on the train when he tells of the humiliations which he has suffered at the hands of Concha, not to one Frenchman, as Mateo had done, but to a group of French bourgeois men and women.[19] The other is the series of hijackings, explosions, and robberies which occur throughout the film. Thus scenes between Mathieu and Conchita are interrupted by returns to the train car where his audience's reactions are registered. At the same time, terrorist actions punctuate each of the key moments in the love story. Mathieu and Conchita stand between the law-abiding bourgeois witnesses and the terrorist actors: their drama is situated in definite social and political terms.

The passengers on the train serve to underscore Mathieu's allegiance to the values and ideology of the upper classes.[20] Other ways in which Buñuel indicates Mathieu's class affiliations are in those numerous scenes when we watch him eating, enjoying cocktails or after-dinner drinks in posh restaurants and elegant homes, usually in the company of his cousin, who is a judge. All of these ritualized activities not only stress Mathieu's class ties but also place his psychosexual drives in a social context. Buñuel further emphasizes the soical implications of Mathieu's passion by rapid cutting from scenes of great intimacy between Concha and Mathieu to shots of Mathieu narrating those same scenes to the passengers on the train. Occasionally the sounds of the train are heard in scenes between Mathieu and Conchita. In this manner, social rites are juxtaposed with the ultimate personal ritual—sexual intercourse. This juxtaposition is a source of humor throughout the film: at the same time that Mathieu draws his listeners into the story, revealing the most intimate details of his relations with Concha, he manifests concern about maintaining the correct "tenor" for his narration, using polite euphemisms, inquiring whether his audience is bored, etc. In this way he confirms his solidarity with bourgeois mores.

Such concerns are in violent contrast with the debasements and humiliations which he describes. They are also in violent contrast with the attitude taken by Mathieu's listeners. While they too wish to remain proper, they clearly relish the more titillating aspects of his tale and even participate vicariously in the most scabrous scenes. Their complicity is expressed by the expressions on their faces as well as by the frequent cuts from the train to scenes between the lovers. By means of such cuts, Buñuel suggests that in so far as the passengers are observers who relish the most scandalous aspects of Mathieu's account, they are little more than voyeurs for the duration of the tale.

This is only natural, since Mathieu himself reluctantly plays the part of a voyeur in his own story. Several times in the course of the movie, Concha expresses her admiration for Mathieu's eyes.[21] Buñuel repeatedly shows those eyes engaged in voyeuristic activities, looking in on Conchita through glass windows, through gates, over transoms, and in shop windows. Because Concha does not allow the protagonist to possess her, he is reduced to being an impotent gaze, as much a "tourist" as the men who watch her dancing naked. Both Mathieu and his bourgeois audience experience Concha vicariously and incompletely. Because Mathieu must remain at a distance from the object of his desire, his gaze scans the surface without ever making contact with the ultimate reality.[22]

Implicit in the motif of spying eyes is the notion that the obsessive gaze of the looker falsifies and distorts objects.[23] In the movie the role of Conchita is played by two actresses whom Buñuel uses arbitrarily and interchangeably. Although one Concha is French and the other one is Spanish, although they are physically quite different, the two Conchas act the same. They both represent the archetypal bitch goddess whose nationality is only incidental to the fact that she is cruel and capricious.

The use of two Conchas is a brilliant surrealist ploy which disturbs and jars the spectator throughout the movie. The scrutinizing camera registers the face of two women where Mathieu perceives only one. It therefore establishes an ironic distance between spectator and protagonist. This distance allows us to gauge the true nature of Mathieu's passion. By means of the random alternation between the two actresses (they sometimes switch in the middle of a scene), Buñuel suggests that once Mathieu has decided to desire Concha, he no longer perceives her at all. Even Conchita notes, "What you want isn't me." Indeed, what Mathieu wants is not a specific woman, but the obscure object which that woman withholds from him.[24] One is led to speculate that Mathieu's obsession may have as much to do with his fear of aging and impotence as it does with a specific woman.

The use of two actresses therefore causes the spectator to confront the true face of love. It is Buñuel's way of reminding us that it is not an exalted feeling, that it is a product of man's instincts. Love cannot exist without sexuality and violence. Underneath the veneer of such civilized individuals as Mathieu and his fellow travelers, violent sexual forces lie dormant, waiting to be released. Given the right set of circumstances, all-consuming passion can lead to violent excesses which clash with society's notions of decorum and order.

This is the point of view of the surrealist poets, with whom Buñuel worked in Paris in the 1920s. They called this passion *l'amour fou* (crazy love). They saw it as a powerful force which could lead men to violate society's conventions and even their own moral codes.[25] The case of an older man in love with a younger woman dramatically illustrates the power of *l'amour fou* to equalize class differences and to undermine paternalistic authority. As Buñuel has suggested in *Tristana* and in countless other movies, when man abandons himself to *l'amour fou* in this way, he cannot constitute or institute a social body; he will be led to perform antisocial actions in the interests of his passion.[26]

Thus love is a potentially subversive force. Unfortunately, Mathieu is a repressed bourgeois who resists being subverted. He is incapable of taking even that which he so ardently desires. His sexuality remains on the level of voyeurism; his murderous instincts are sublimated into the ridiculous gesture of throwing a pail of water. (To douse his passion?) Mathieu cannot accept the challenge presented by the two Conchas, a challenge which would lead him to break with his bourgeois fellow travelers and to go over to the "other side."

For Conchita is a provocation, an essentially subversive force forever egging Mathieu on to violence. She is as much a representative of terrorism as are the subversive groups which perpetrate political terrorism throughought the film. Every phase of Mathieu's interaction with Concha is preceded or followed by some revolutionary action.[27] As the film progresses, the Spanish girl becomes more directly linked to terrorist assaults. Mathieu's cousin the judge is finally so appalled at the state to which she has reduced Mathieu that he arranges for Concha and her mother to be expelled from France as "undesirable aliens."[28] In the film's final scenes, after Mathieu and Conchita arrive in Paris, the radio announces that, directed by The Revolutionary Army of the Infant Jesus, a number of terrorist organizations including POP, GRIF, RUT, and PRIQUE (sexual acronyms), have undertaken a series of gratuitous attacks designed to provoke a right wing reaction. This apocalyptic announcement is followed by a terrific explosion which obliterates the screen and terminates the film.

Such allusions to revolutionary activity are eminently surrealistic in that they are random stimuli to which the viewer can respond freely. But they are also linked to the emotional turmoil which Mathieu experiences in his dealings with Conchita. It is from Mathieu's point of view that these incidents are perceived, so, to a certain extent, they may be considered as a visual manifestation of the rage and frustration which Concha arouses in the Frenchman.

And yet, Mathieu does not perceive the connections between his own state and the social and political order. His obliviousness represents his own complicity in violence, a complicity shared by his fellow passengers. As the violence and frequency of terrorist assaults escalate, as the world goes to pieces, they display the fastidious manners of the members of a society that will last forever. Comfortably seated in the first-class coach of the train, they condemn Conchita's terrorism and the terrorism practiced by extremist commando groups. Buñuel's point is that they are blind to the coercion implicit in such things as religions, economics, law, marriage, motherhood, and virginity, of which they themselves are the victims.

The final message of Buñuel's latest film is contained in a brown burlap bag tied with a cord that appears throughout the movie. This bag is a surrealist object which is more a leitmotif than a specific symbol.[29] In the second scene of the movie, a workman first appears with the bag slung over his shoulder on the grounds of Mathieu's estate. Later, as Mathieu and Conchita walk outside a restaurant where they have once again met by chance, the same man crosses the screen with the same bag. Still later, as Mathieu and Conchita walk along the Seine, the impeccably-dressed Frenchman picks the bag up from a bench and slings it over his shoulder. Then in Seville, just before encountering Conchita for the third time, Mathieu decides to take a walk. As he leaves his hotel the porter calls out, "Sir, you've forgotten your bag." Mathieu answers, "No, I'll send someone around to get it." And in the final scene of the movie, as the music builds, a woman takes a bloodied dress or nightgown out of the same bag.[30] This recurring element might signify women. For as Mathieu's valet remarks, "Women are just bags of excrement."[31] But its ultimate message remains ambiguous. Like all true surrealist objects, the bag does not denote anything but itself. It is up to the viewer to sort out the particular connotations which it has for him.

And this viewer associates Mathieu's bag with an image from Buñuel's first movie, *Un Chien Andalou.* In one scene the protagonist attempts to make love to an unwilling woman. Just as he is about to rape her, he suddenly backs away and picks up a rope which is tied to a cork, a melon, two priests, and two pianos (stuffed with the putrid carcasses of two dead donkeys). As he strains towards his potential victim pulling the burden behind him, she has a chance to escape. The implication seems to be that the weight of his burden, suggestive of his background and education, keeps him from satisfying his desire.

Perhaps Mathieu's bag impedes his conquest of Conchita in a similar fashion. For although *l'amour fou* has the potential to lead to personal liberation and even to the destruction of society, in *That Obscure Object* it does not result in flames or in social upheavals, just in pails of water and black eyes. At the end of the movie, Mathieu and Conchita seem condemned to a sterile cycle of sadomasochistic interaction unless they are able to transcend certain anachronistic views of men and women, unless they are able to discard antiquated cultural and moral burdens.

One can therefore conclude that *That Obscure Object of Desire* conveys much the same surrealist message which first shocked the world almost fifty years ago. Although the anger and intensity of those early films have been attenuated over the years, Buñuel remains as much a critic of society as he always was. Primarily through the use of two Conchitas and the slapstick scene of a pail of water, he negates the romantic premises of the novel and depicts the decadence of modern life. Faithful to his surrealist mission, he also undermines a certain nostalgic vision of his homeland while gently satirizing the pretensions of the French *haute-bourgeoisie*.

NOTES

1. In French the repetition of the sounds, "ob, ob, du, dé" gives a whimsical quality which is lacking in the English title, *That Obscure Object of Desire*.

2. Louÿs took his title from a work painted by Goya in 1791 or 1792. The protagonist describes it as follows: "Four women in Spanish skirts standing on the grass of a garden hold a shawl by the four corners and as they laugh, they throw a life-sized puppet up into the air." Pierre Louÿs, *La Femme et le pantin: Roman Espagnole* (Paris: Albin Michel, 1959), p. 210. This and all subsequent translations are my own.

3. Despite the relative obscurity both of the novel and of its author, perhaps because of the sensational aspects of the subject, *Le Femme et le pantin* was the source of four screenplays prior to Buñuel's adaptation. In 1920 Geraldine Farrar starred in a silent screen version; in 1929 Conchita Montenegro played the part of the Spanish *femme fatale*, a role which was recreated by Marlene Dietrich in Josef von Sternberg's *The Devil is a Woman* in 1935. Then in the late 1950s Brigitte Bardot was the unlikely choice for the Spanish dancer in a film directed by Julien Duvivier, a film which Buñuel himself was supposed to direct. But when he submitted a scenario to the producer, the latter found it totally unacceptable. Claiming that the scenario had too much of Buñuel and too little of Louÿs, the producer dismissed him from the film. (Reported by J. Francisco Aranda in *Luis Buñuel: Biografía Crítica*, Barcelona: Editorial Lumen, 1969, p. 224).

4. Almost every statement which Concha makes in the film is directly taken from Louÿs's text.

5. Louÿs, *La Femme et le pantin*, pp. 63–64. (I will henceforth place all of the page numbers in the text). It is interesting to note that Buñuel gives an ironic twist to something which Louÿs meant to be a serious commentary on the protagonist's tastes in women. Moreover, the object of desire which Buñuel's protagonist pursues is "obscur" both in the sense of dark-haired and mysterious. By placing the adjective "obscur" before the noun rather than after, the filmmaker emphasizes the mysterious quality of the woman rather than the color of her hair. At the same time, the title has a clear sexual connotation.

6. Louÿs began his literary career as a disciple of an important Parnassian poet, José-Maria de Hérédia, and was later influenced by the Symbolist movement. His friends included André Gide, Henri de Regnier, Paul Valéry, and Oscar Wilde (who dedicated *Salomé* to him).

7. Pierre Louÿs, *Aphrodite: Ancient Manners*, trans. by Willis L. Parker (New York: Dutton, 1932), p. 12.

8. Louÿs's story might have prompted Buñuel to use a train for the telling of Mathieu's story. Mateo comments that he likes traveling on second-class trains rather than first because of the lively company. On the particular occasion when he met Conchita: "I had not been seated for more than 15 minutes and I already knew all about the lives of my neighbors. Certain people make fun of those who reveal themselves so freely. As for me, I always sympathize with the need which simple souls have to cry out their pains in the desert" (pp. 67–68).

9. This note is quoted verbatim in the film.

10. Both in the book and in the film, Concha appears behind the bars of a ground floor window and puts her hair through the bars so that the protagonist may kiss it. In the book when Mateo later returns at the appointed hour, Concha demurs, inquires how long he will love her, and then sends Mateo away. It is on the next occasion that Concha goes to find Mateo wearing the impenetrable corset.

11. This quotation might have suggested to Buñuel the device of using two actresses to play the role of Conchita.

12. "I said naked, she was more than naked. Black stockings as long as a pair of tights came up to the top of her thighs. She was wearing little shoes which clicked on the floor" (Louÿs, p. 186). See David I. Grossvogel, "Buñuel's Obsessed Camera: *Tristana* Dismembered," *Diacritics* (Spring, 1972), p. 55. "One of the forms of a recurrent note in Buñuel that goes back at least as far as the shooting script of *The Golden Age* is a woman clad in black stockings."

13. I am thinking especially of those novels written by J. K. Huysmans prior to his Christian conversion, which would include *À Rebours* (1884), the story of Des Esseintes, and *Là-Bas* (1891), which deals with the legend of Bluebeard and the notion of demonic possession.

14. In one famous scene in that movie, the lovers are in a garden where they attempt to consummate their love. But inexplicable forces hold them apart. As Buñuel noted in the shooting script: "During the shooting the various motions which they make towards each other can be completed, but during the cutting all kisses and caresses must be left unfinished, interrupted at the moment of fulfillment." Luis Buñuel, *L'Age d'or* in *L'Avant-Scène du Cinéma*, 27 & 28 (15 juin–15 juillet, 1963), 42. In a more recent film, *Le Charme discret de la bourgeoisie* (1972), Buñuel builds the action around a similar pattern: guests at an elegant dinner party are never able to complete their meal because of an extraordinary series of unforeseen circumstances.

15. Many critics have remarked on Buñuel's preoccupation with feet and shoes ever since *L'Age d'or* (where the heroine sucks the toes of a statue) to *Journal d'une femme de chambre* to *Tristana* (where the heroine has her leg amputated).

16. As a way of coming into contact with the richness of the unconscious mind, the surrealists rejected notions of causality and favored the cultivation of the fortuitous encounters of seemingly haphazard elements. They felt that chance meetings of objects and people offered a key to deciphering the world. André Breton illustrated this principle in his famous novel entitled *Nadja*. It is interesting to note that the entire structure of *La Femme et le pantin* is based upon the chance encounters of Conchita and Mateo. They meet four times in different cities throughout Spain. In the film, Conchita and Mathieu also meet four times in three different countries.

17. Once before, in *Tristana*, Buñuel updated the setting of the Galdós novel upon which it is based for the express purpose of alluding to the political and social realities of Spain in the late 1920s and early 1930s. See Beth Miller, "La Tristana feminista de Buñuel," *Diálogos*, Núm. 60 (nov.-dic., 1974), 16–20. It is interesting to note that at the same time that Buñuel uses a modern setting, he also stresses those elements of

the myth of Spain found in Louÿs; palm trees, flamenco guitars, Moorish architecture, and church spires appear at regular intervals throughout the film. In evaluating the purpose and impact of such images of Spain, it is important to remember that Buñuel is himslef a Spaniard who is interpreting a view of his country presented by a nineteenth-century Frenchman. And that Frenchman was orchestrating certain literary conceits which he had inherited from a previous generation, images which even then probably did not reflect reality. Buñuel deliberately chooses to present the most hackneyed images which foreigners associate with Spain, and to undermine them by juxtaposing them with scenes of contemporary life. That is to say, he harkens back to another age, an age when gypsies and flamenco dancers really did exist, to show that that age and the values associated with it no longer exist.

18. The first ten or fifteen minutes of the movie consist of scenes of Buñuel's invention. The scenes set in the travel agency, in Mathieu's house, in his car on the way to the train station (when he sees another car explode), and on the train, comprise a sort of prologue to the story in which we are presented with clues and bits of action out of context in a way that we cannot hope to understand. The prologue, then, serves to present a series of images which, while having no direct relation to Louÿs's narration, nevertheless illuminate the emotions, implications and themes which drew Buñuel to Louÿs's book. The tension, drama, and humor of this prologue come from the skillful editing of contrasting scenes, motifs, and concepts. The elegant life style is juxtaposed with revolution, France with Spain, polite social forms with brutal private behavior, rape with slapstick comedy, etc. In this manner throughout the movie, each individual segment derives its meaning from its juxtaposition with often absurdly different elements which alternately reinforce and contradict the words which Mathieu uses to tell his tale. Louÿs's plot is but a pretext for a particular sequence of Buñuelian images. On the primacy of the image in Buñuel's work see Grossvogel, art. cit. p. 55. Also see Theodore A. Sackett, "Creation and Destruction of Personality in *Tristana:* Galdós and Buñuel," *Anales Galdosianos* (abril 1976), 71–90.

19. Buñuel's protagonist is in the company of other French people of his rank and class: a judge, representative of order; a mother and daughter, the bourgeois family; and a dwarf, who is appropriately enough, a psychologist. These individuals, whom Mathieu already vaguely knows, are to be the witnesses and ultimately the judges of the events to follow.

20. Buñuel indicates that Conchita is not of the same social class. She first appears as a maid who waits on Mathieu at lunch. As he tells the passengers, she commits the faux pas of using the water glass for wine. Throughout the film, Buñuel suggests that her role is to administer to the needs of the upper classes as a hat check girl, a dancer, or a sex partner.

21. This detail is absent from the book.

22. That Mathieu's obsessive gaze affords an incomplete view of reality is suggested in those scenes in which he (and we, the spectators) sees things which he does not hear or hears things which he is unable to see. (In a similar manner in *Le Charme discret de la bourgeoisie* airplanes, typewriters and other noises muffle conversations.)

23. A fine dramatization of the same principle is found in Alain Robbe-Grillet's novel *La Jalousie,* where the husband's obsessive jealousy leads to a similar pattern of repeated actions. The word "jalousie" refers both to his emotion and to the venetian blinds through which he peers and which limit his field of vision.

24. In this context the use which Buñuel makes of Louÿs's dialogue takes on special significance. Both Conchas use all of the clichés of romantic discourse. They spout beautiful sentiments about undying love, eternal devotion, etc. At one point

when Concha seems about to surrender to Mathieu she asks: "Will you love me forever? Even when I'm old? If you leave me, I'll die." This is patently absurd, since the twenty-year old Concha will probably still be desirable long after the mid-fiftyish Mathieu has died. By choosing to transcribe Louÿs's dialogue so faithfully, Buñuel underscores the falseness of Concha's words. The use of two actresses to play the one role therefore provides a visual statement of Concha's duplicity.

25. In the final issue of the surrealist publication called *La Révolution Surréaliste*, the editors posed the following questions: "1) How would you judge a man who would go so far as to betray his convictions in order to please the woman he loved? 2) Do you believe in the victory of admirable love over sordid life or of sordid love over admirable life?" See *La Révolution Surréaliste*, no. 12, Dec. 15, 1929.

26. The theme of an older man involved in a sadomasochistic relationship with a younger woman permeates Buñuel's works. As Michael Wood noted: "In 'Viridiana' the woman refuses the man, and he commits suicide. In 'Tristana' she accepts him and they live meanly ever after, she caught in her inescapable hatred for him, he trapped in his neverending desire for her. In 'That Obscure Object' she neither rejects nor accepts him, they seem set up for a life of cruelty and feuding very close to that of 'Tristana.' " "Buñuel's Private Lessons," *The New York Review of Books*, vol. XXV, no. 2 (Feb. 23, 1978), 40.

27. Mathieu himself seems to make this connection as he begins his account of how he met Concha for the first time. It was on the day when his cousin the judge was trying a case involving a group of terrorists, members of The Revolutionary Army of the Infant Jesus. This sparks a long discussion between the two men as to the nature of revolutionary groups, a discussion which is highlighted by the first appearance of Concha.

28. Later in Seville, after being forced to watch Concha make love with another man, Mathieu stops his car because a man is lying on the road. (An image of sexual impotence?) A robber or terrorist steals his car and Mathieu is forced to walk home. On the following morning he hears about a strange virus which is approaching Barcelona. This recalls a scene in *The Discreet Charm of the Bourgeoisie* when the Ambassador from Miranda (also played by Fernando Rey) deplores violence but approves of a "good epidemic" to wipe out a few million people.

29. In addition to Mathieu's bag, there are a number of other "containers" which are indirectly associated with the bag. Even Concha's name, which means "shell," is somehow related to the other "containers" which include boxes, suitcases, hats, and purses.

30. The implication seems to be that the explosion comes from the same bag.

31. It might also signify female genitals.

1979

A Test of American Film Censorship: *Who's Afraid of Virginia Woolf?*

Leonard J. Leff

American film censorship is almost as old as American film itself. Not until the inception of the Production Code Administration and the Legion of Decency, however, was the content of motion pictures effectively controlled. Offsprings of the Motion Picture Association of America (MPAA) and the Catholic Church, these regulatory agencies influenced the language, tone, and themes of American cinema from the mid-1930s to the mid-1950s. Complaints against them were voiced privately and publicly: under the Production Code, Walter Wanger said in 1939, "it was—and is—almost impossible to face and deal with the modern world."[1] Yet rather than individual complaints, social and artistic forces within a changing society at last challenged these two groups. *The Moon Is Blue* (1953), *On the Waterfront* (1954), and *The Man With The Golden Arm* (1956) were early tests. Beginning in 1960, others came in the wake of wider distribution of European films.

By 1964 the stress was internal as well as external. *The Pawnbroker* revealed this compounded pressure: the Legion's "Condemned" rating sparked a public controversy among vocal Catholic intellectuals and the Production Code Administration's decision to deny a Code Seal was overturned by its own Review Board. Neither organization could long survive intact. Within two years the Legion had recognized its deficiencies and effected a major reform; in turn, as the Legion had done thirty years before, it directly influenced the Production Code Administration. Yet what specifically occurred during this crucial period from 1964 to 1966 has remained obscure. For various reasons the Production Code Administration (PCA) and, to a lesser extent, the Legion have not fully disclosed the details of their relationship with individual Hollywood films of this or any era. In his otherwise well-documented book on censorship, Richard S. Randall occasionally resorts to conjecture because "the PCA has never made public its decisions or their rationalizations. Information that has become public . . . has usually been supplied by dissatisfied film proprietors."[2]

For research on this paper, however, both the PCA and the Legion opened their files to the author.[3] As primary evidence now demonstrates, one film played a pivotal role in defining the philosophy, structure, and operation of these agencies following their evaluation of *The Pawnbroker*. The watershed that demonstrated the Legion's new commitment to mature works and forced the industry to abandon the Code was the most expensive non-spectacle film of its time, Warner Brothers' *Who's Afraid of Virginia Woolf?* With the appropriately brash "screw you," Martha and George not only ushered in Nick and Honey but dispatched a whole era of film censorship.

On 5 March 1964, the *New York Times* announced that Warner Brothers had purchased Edward Albee's *Virginia Woolf* for $500,000.[4] Because of its explicit language, if not its theme, many assumed that the play could not be adapted for film. Yet the PCA—which sensed its potential as a film property—began a file on *Virginia Woolf* only two days after it opened: on 15 October 1962 an MPAA executive circulated among his colleagues some Broadway reviewers' reactions to the play's language.[5] Six months later Jack Warner, who had apparently recognized the play's commercial possibilities and thus optioned it, sent the PCA a copy of the text for its review and comment. The PCA responded promptly: the text was unacceptable. In a brief letter, PCA director Geoffrey M. Shurlock advised Warner that to earn a Code Seal he must "remove all the profanity and the very blunt sexual dialogue." Shurlock acknowledged that such action "would considerably reduce the play's impact" but concluded that "under the circumstances" the PCA could render no other judgment (20 March 1963). Five days later, Walter MacEwen and Steve Trilling, two Warner Brothers executives, met with Shurlock to discuss the objectionable material. In the detailed letter (26 March 1963) that resulted from their meeting, Shurlock listed eighty-three page references to hundreds of objectionable words, phrases, and actions.

Upon Warner Brothers' purchase of the play, Richard Barr, who had produced *Virginia Woolf* for the stage, said that he had "no knowledge of any contractual stipulations . . . regarding changes in content or dialogue."[6] Barr's comment seems deliberately ambiguous: it could mean that Albee forbade changes (thus enhancing the film's commercial prospects but not its reception at the PCA) or that Albee permitted them either with or without his involvement. Whatever its meaning, Warner Brothers initially sought Albee's participation. On 29 March 1963, Steve Trilling wrote to Albee's agent that Warners could film *Virginia Woolf* and observe the Code. The necessary changes included, among other things, the elimination of over twenty "goddamns," seven "bastards," five "sons-of-a-bitch," and assorted anatomical phrases such as "right ball," "monkey nipples," and "ass." The studio was confident that "Albee is sufficiently inventive and creative to substitute potent and pungent dialogue that could prove highly effective, even though possibly reducing somewhat the 'shock' impact of this highly regarded play." Almost as an aside, Trilling concluded by mentioning an alternative: they could take the Art Theatre route without a

Code Seal, but "this would certainly reduce the commercial potential."[7]

Meanwhile, limited pre-production activities continued. In November 1963, Ernest Lehman was sent a script "to see whether [he] thought it was possible movie material" (ELC, 2). According to Lehman, Abe Lastfogel (both Lehman's and Albee's agent) subsequently arranged a meeting between Albee, Lehman, and Warner that solidified the actual sale. Lehman was named screenwriter and, later, producer. Since the sale price and the selection of key artists (over which Albee had no control) would give some approximation of the film's projected budget, speculation immediately centered on the choice of a director. A Warner Brothers spokesman told the *New York Times* that Fred Zinnemann would direct. Both the *Hollywood Reporter* (in a front page story) and the *Los Angeles Times* confirmed Zinnemann's selection.[8] According to Lehman, however, Zinnemann was "never even discussed" (ELC, 26). Zinnemann's involvement would have connoted a substantial budget, and at this point, because of the film's controversial nature and certain battle over a Code Seal, Warner Brothers seemed unready to make such a financial commitment.

As late as midsummer 1964 the studio was still seriously considering alternative distribution channels. "The Art Theatre route," though, had given way to the "theatrofilm," which was not regulated by the PCA. Richard Lederer, Warner Brothers' vice-president in charge of advertising and publicity, had alerted the PCA to this possibility; accordingly, PCA executive Michael Linden suggested that the Administration consider its response to an alternative release pattern for *Virginia Woolf*.[9] As a "theatrofilm," *Virginia Woolf* would have been handled like Warner Brothers' then-forthcoming *Hamlet* with Richard Burton. This production continued the studio's experimentation with a kinescope-like process called Electronovision. On 30 June and 1 July 1964, Electronovision, in which Burton was a stockholder, brought seven cameras into a Broadway theater to film two performances of *Hamlet*. Cut primarily during production, the "negative" was ready a few days later. Jack Warner must have then observed what reviewer Bosley Crowther noted when the film opened: "the photography is fuzzy, especially in the long shots; the lighting is poor and distractingly uneven, the recording of the voices allows for . . . annoying vibration or echo."[10] Based on the poor cinematic quality of *Hamlet*, Warner probably decided that Electronovision was too risky for a $500,000 property. His decision proved wise. Though its budget for filming, promotion, and distribution was just over $1 million, *Hamlet* returned only $3 million from its four exhibitions in 971 theaters.[11] By fall 1964, it was clear even to the public that *Virginia Woolf* was going to be not a "theatrofilm" but a Hollywood blockbuster.

In September 1964, the *Hollywood Reporter* told Patricia Neal and Henry Fonda to "go on hoping," but that Jack Warner wanted Elizabeth Taylor and Jack Lemmon to star (8 September 1964, p. 4) and John Frankenheimer to direct (17 September 1964, p. 4; ELC, 26). Towards the end of the year, negotiations with Taylor, Richard Burton, and Mike Nichols, the film's director, had begun. Sandy Dennis tested in February 1965, and by spring the major artists had all been signed, Lehman had finished a working screenplay, and filming was set to start in mid-August. During that six-month period, Warner Brothers had vacillated about how to handle Albee's language. In early screenplay drafts, Lehman tried such substitutions as "Make the Hostess"/"Hop the Hostess" (ELC, 1), "For cry sake!" (ELC, 3), and (for "Jesus Christ") "oh my God" (ELC, 16). Lehman recognized their limitations, and in the third draft (14 March 1965), he restored most of the original dialogue. When Jack Warner read this script, he still was not committed to film an unexpurgated *Virginia Woolf*. Most of his marginalia supported the compliment he gave Lehman near the end of the script: "Best writing/reading in years" (p. 149). But throughout, he either circled references or dog-eared pages that he obviously wanted Lehman to review: words like "sons of bitches," "goddamn," "bastard," "stud," and "chastity belt" as well as phrases like "with your melons bobbling" and "mount her like a gd dog" (ELC, 6). With "theatrofilm" rejected and thus the PCA still to be considered, Warner remained undecided about the language. His decision was finally made for him by the director, Mike Nichols.

The whimper that Dustin Hoffman uses in *The Graduate* originated with Nichols. "I was told that I used to do that in meetings with Jack Warner," Nichols told an interviewer. "Somebody said, 'When Mr. Warner is telling his jokes, you must stop whimpering.' "[12] Nichols could afford to whimper. Hand-selected by the Burtons to direct, he was paid handsomely (the budget for "Direction and Supervision" was over \$350,000, his fee \$250,000 [ELC, 19]). Though he was young and inexperienced, his Broadway reputation—as well as Hollywood's shifting ideology—gave him virtually total artistic control. He worked on the screenplay with Lehman for eight weeks during spring 1965, and together, with Warner's approval, they permanently restored most of Albee's dialogue. The filming itself, on a closed set, was relatively uncomplicated and, though finally thirty-six days behind schedule, not grossly overbudget by Hollywood standards.[13] Rudi Fehr, head of editing at Warners in 1965, said that Nichols was "the domineering force on the picture": what he wanted, Warner gave him. The reverse did not hold true; Warner wanted "protection" footage for the stronger language, but he was afraid to alienate Nichols by pressing for it. According to Fehr, Nichols filmed no alternative scenes.[14]

Midway through production, Warner Brothers sent the PCA the *Virginia Woolf* shooting script. Though MPAA Acting President Ralph Hetzel and Jack Warner had apparently conferred about the script shortly after the film went into production, few differences existed between the text the PCA read in March 1963 and the script it received in October 1965. As Shurlock wrote Warner on 9 October 1965, "We note that [the script] still contains a good

Who's Afraid of Virginia Woolf?
(U.S., 1966, Mike Nichols) Production photo

deal of the profanity, the blunt sexual references, and the coarse and sometimes vulgar language which we noted in the original playscript when we first
commented on it.'' Interestingly, Warner Brothers, the PCA, and even the
public knew that the language was in not only the script but also the film. On
9 October 1965, a *Saturday Evening Post* feature article reported that the
filming left ''the play's salty dialogue . . . virtually intact.''[15] Later, Shurlock was chastised for not having taken a firmer stand about the filming; yet
he told Warner clearly, if not firmly, that the script remained ''unapprovable
under Code requirements'' (ELC, 23). The way had now been cleared for the
final confrontation between *Virginia Woolf* and its regulatory agencies.

Throughout late spring 1966 *Virginia Woolf,* which had been filmed in
secrecy, lay finished in the studio's vault; Warner had denied access to the
press, exhibitors, and even high-ranking studio personnel.[16] Though the
studio and the PCA did not communicate between the time the script was
rejected in October 1965 and the film was submitted, the PCA finally saw
Virginia Woolf on 2 May 1966. The following day Shurlock telephoned
Warner that the picture was unacceptable. According to the *New York
Times,* the West Coast PCA denied the film a Code Seal because the studio

had refused to make certain cuts.[17] Shurlock, however, urged Warner to appeal the PCA's decision "in the hope that [the Review] Board would see fit to give this picture an exemption."[18] On 3 June 1966, Warner appealed. If he lost, he had two alternatives: he could cut the film or resign from the MPAA. Cutting the film, practically impossible without "protection" footage, would have subjected Warner Brothers to "a good deal of criticism for 'knuckling under to the blue-noses' " in mutilating its " 'class' offering."[19] Ironically, the other alternative would have subjected the MPAA to "a good deal of criticism."

To release *Virginia Woolf* unchanged, Warner would have had to resign from the Motion Picture Association because all members agreed to exhibit only approved films. (Unlike other MPAA members, Warner Brothers had no non-MPAA "art" subsidiary that could have released the film.) Although United Artists had withdrawn in 1956 over *The Man With The Golden Arm,* Warner Brothers' withdrawal in 1966 would have disadvantaged the MPAA. The MPAA's loss would have exceeded the studio's: the absence of a Code Seal on *Virginia Woolf* would have had little effect on box office[20] but would have revealed the MPAA's deficiencies in dealing with mature films. Periodically in motion picture history, state and municipal forces have exploited Hollywood's inefficient self-regulation; again in the 1960s public officials threatened to do what the industry could not. A Warner Brothers retreat from the MPAA would undoubtedly have been used against Hollywood. A few film executives believed that a studio's restricting admission to adults would allow the MPAA to award a Seal to *Virginia Woolf* and similar films,[21] but the MPAA was not ready to trade its Code for classification, a likely alternative that had only limited industry support.

Meanwhile on 24 May 1966 the Advertising Code Administration of the MPAA approved *Virginia Woolf* promotional materials conditional upon the PCA Review Board's favorable action on the film itself. The ACA formally required two changes: with an orange crayon, it indicated on a one-sheet how far Warner Brothers should raise Elizabeth Taylor's dress to eliminate her "excessive exposure," and it deleted from a one-minute radio spot George's line, "Shove it." Though it made no comment, it must have noted with considerable interest the prominent announcement in the ads: No admission of anyone "under the age of 18 unless accompanied by his parent." In its front page story on 26 May 1966 the *Hollywood Reporter* best summed up the significance of Warner's unexpected action: "In an unprecedented move that literally forces the movie industry into classification of films, something strongly opposed in the past, Jack L. Warner . . . yesterday announced he would insist on an 'Adults Only' policy for the presentation of 'Who's Afraid of Virginia Woolf?' by including a clause in all contracts with exhibitors."[22]

Throughout his presidency of the MPAA (1945–63), Eric Johnston had led

Who's Afraid of Virginia Woolf?
(U.S., 1966, Mike Nichols) Publicity still

the association's strong opposition to film classification. Johnston believed that it was not viable; it would simply inspire dozens of legislators to enact hundreds of laws that differed from state to state and thus bring chaos to the industry. To most studio executives, classification also meant reduced box office revenue. The interim Hetzel administration (1963–66) was no more sanguine about classification. With Warners' *Virginia Woolf* policy, however, classification had become a reality. The MPAA puzzled over the implications. In Dallas, "adults" were sixteen and older, an MPAA internal memo noted; should, then, "Warner's include in the contract an exemption for kids younger than the company age limit in those areas already covered by a more liberal governmental censorship law? Or should Dallas and other censorship cities (or states) amend their laws to ban kids under 16, 'or an age determined by a distributor, whichever is higher?' "[23] Though the tone of the memo was whimsical, Warner Brothers' action, Jack Valenti, new head of MPAA, told the press, had "effected broad discussion of film classification possibilities, now under study."[24] Since the advent of adult films, the

American Catholic hierarchy had urged the MPAA to develop a policy of self-censorship based upon voluntary classification; *Virginia Woolf* gave the Church the opportunity to reiterate its point.

Both from inside and outside his organization, Jack Warner had been cautioned about the effect of the play's text on the Legion of Decency. "It might be well to obtain Catholic technical advice," Shurlock wrote Warner on 26 March 1963, "in order to avoid anything offensive regarding the Latin prayers in [George's Dies Irae]." The characters' blasphemy concerned Rudi Fehr, Warner's head of editing. Shortly before filming began, Fehr read a screenplay peppered with the word "goddamn"; "the Legion of Decency will object to its use," he predicted to Walter MacEwen. "I have the same concern in regards to the use of the name 'Jesus.' It is not approved when used lightly" (4 August 1965; ELC, 19). Warner, however, apparently gambled that the integrity of the property—and, significantly, the absence of nudity—would carry *Virginia Woolf* through the Legion.[25] After the picture was finished, he grew very anxious about this risk, but Richard Lederer reassured him: "Don't worry; the film's artistic."[26] Their reading of the Legion proved accurate.

The Legion's liberalization began in 1957 with Pius XII's "Remarkable Inventions" encyclical. In the following years, the pledge became more positive, the number of categories for film classification increased, and the organization became more sympathetic to adult films. On the Legion's thirtieth birthday (1964), an *America* editorial praised the organization's broad-minded purpose: not to censor, but to give "an intelligent and discriminating moral guide to moviegoers"; the Legion does not, the U.S. Bishops' media committee said, discourage work for "mature viewers."[27] Eighteen months later the American Bishops changed the name of the Legion to the National Catholic Office for Motion Pictures (NCOMP) as a fitting climax of "the broad transformation that has taken place in the functions and services of the Legion during its eight-year period of renewal."[28] Illustrating this new perspective, Richard S. Randall shows that from 1964 to 1966, the percentage of films restricted decreased, "probably a fundamental reflection of the Office's new liberalism."[29]

Why, then, in spring 1966 should Warner have become so anxious? For two reasons. First, a "Condemned" rating would have hurt *Virginia Woolf* financially.[30] Second, though in philosophy the Legion was liberal, in practice—as Warner certainly knew—it often acted conservatively. The guiding principles of the Legion group that actually rated films predated not only the "moral guide" of 1964 but the "Remarkable Inventions" of 1957. This screening body was the International Federation of Catholic Alumnae. IFCA applied to films "*traditional* standards of morality upon which the sanctification of the individual, the sacredness of the home and ethical foundation of civilization necessarily depend."[31] Characterized by one NCOMP executive as "little old ladies in tennis shoes," these middle-aged women took their task seriously, if inflexibly. Their "new liberalism" was questionable: they "Condemned" the major work for "mature viewers" in 1964, *The Pawnbroker*. To the Alumnae, fleeting shots of a black woman's breast proved inflammatory; could they, Warner might have pondered, condone the bobbling melons of *Virginia Woolf*? Fortunately for the studio, after 1965 IFCA no longer screened films alone.

NCOMP knew that, given its principles and history, IFCA was unlikely to offer "positive backing to films of superior artistic and spiritual value."[32] But because of the women's long, faithful service, NCOMP could not simply dismiss them. In 1965 its solution was to dilute their strength. To the ranks of IFCA it added "Consultants": film teachers and scholars, business people, writers. The ratio of the Consultants to IFCA was 3:1. William Mooring, a new addition and a conservative, resigned early. Forced out by a majority of liberals, he urged NCOMP to return to a policy of "realistic guidance" and to drop "its emphasis upon ideological, ofttimes antireligious drama as superior 'art' for mature sophisticated people."[33] Mooring notwithstanding, the newly constituted screening board was conservative on some points. It still discouraged nudity; furthermore, it engaged in prior restraint. In his 1965 review of Legion modifications, Msgr. Thomas Little frankly admitted that "in the last two years 34 films, of which 20 were major American productions, would have been released with scenes employing nudity had not the producers realized that they would then have been condemned."[34] The Legion's action on *Virginia Woolf* indicated that its friendly persuasion continued in 1966 and the Consultants' era.

Two days after Warner Brothers announced its "Adults Only" policy for *Virginia Woolf*, *Variety* reported that the studio's decision to classify its film was the result of a " 'recommendation' from National Catholic Office for Motion Pictures."[35] Father Patrick Sullivan, Msgr. Little's associate, later confirmed that the Legion was directly instrumental in Warner Brothers' admittance policy.[36] The determining factor was not NCOMP's evolving "new liberalism"; it was the screening body's recent addition of Consultants who apparently felt that, properly restricted, *Virginia Woolf* could be approved for certain Catholic filmgoers. IFCA disagreed. The voting distribution shows that even with Warner Brothers' concession, IFCA acting alone would have "Condemned" *Virginia Woolf*:

	CONSULTANTS			IFCA	
A-II	1	7%	A-II	—	0 %
A-III	7	10%	A-III	2	11 %
A-IV	40	61%	A-IV	3	15.5%
B	11	17%	B	3	15.5%
C	7	10%	C	11	58 %

Acting together, however unwillingly, the new screening board awarded *Virginia Woolf* an A-IV.[37] On 9 June 1966, one day before the PCA Review Board met to reconsider the film, NCOMP announced its decision.

Like NCOMP's, the MPAA's dilemma was clear: "How do we preserve our obligation to the society in which we live," Valenti asked, "and at the same time widen creative dimensions?"[38] In its rating of *Virginia Woolf*, confidently predicted by the trade press over a week before its public announcement, NCOMP had answered the PCA's question. More important, by "recommending" that Warner Brothers voluntarily restrict its film, NCOMP had vigorously endorsed the classification system that the MPAA had long opposed. Neither course open to the MPAA was attractive to it: if it exempted *Virginia Woolf* from Code restrictions, it involuntarily supported classification; if it denied Warner Brothers' appeal, it demonstrated its weakness in dealing with a film that even NCOMP had found artistic and thus acceptable for its clientele. To complicate matters further, *Virginia Woolf*—as the Review Board knew and was again reminded at the hearing—was not just a movie but a $7.5 million investment, "near a high for a non-spec[tacle] studio film."[39]

The Review Board met in Warner Brothers' New York screening room at 10:00 a.m., 10 June 1966. Following the film's exhibition and a luncheon, the Board reconvened in a private suite at the St. Regis. The "Notes" preserved by the PCA were subsequently reviewed and, at some points, silently altered by participants in the discussion; though only this amended, formal version now exists, it gives a sufficient idea of the content, if not the tone of the discussion and, more important, a clear indication of the voting.[40] After Valenti opened the meeting, Shurlock summarized the PCA's previous communication with Warner Brothers, including his recommendation that the studio appeal his decision. Both the Legion and *Life* had recognized the film's merit, Shurlock said; the PCA must also find a way to recognize quality "in making exemptions on our own and approving a picture without having to call this entire Board into session" (p. 3).

Speaking for Jack Warner, Richard Lederer highlighted the serious, artistic purpose of the film, the voluntary classification, and the studio's general responsibility to its public. He also noted that Warner "has a lot of money invested in [*Virginia Woolf*]" (p. 3). Valenti then rehearsed his own "lonely soul-searching" and subsequently recommended an exemption for the film. He gave five reasons:

1) Virginia Woolf was "a superior picture";
2) Warner Brothers' classification assured the MPAA that the picture would be shown only to mature audiences;
3) "In the interests of the industry," Warner Brothers had honored the MPAA's request to delete two words ("screw you" and "frigging");[41]
4) Exemption would apply only to *Virginia Woolf*, not films of lesser quality;
5) NCOMP gave the film an A-IV rating (pp. 4–6).

The objections to Valenti's recommendation came from Sherrill Corwin, representing 15,000 theater owners, and Spyros Skouras, former head of Twentieth Century-Fox. The former maintained that exhibitors had success-fully handled mature films in the past with no mandatory "adults-only" clause inserted in the contract: "We feel we can police our theatres for pictures that need policing" (p. 8). He feared what Eric Johnston and the MPAA had always feared: classification. But he must have realized that classification was inevitable. Moments before, Valenti had said, almost ominously, that he knew little about classification, yet "speaking con-fidentially, I intend to know more" (p. 4). Skouras objected on moral grounds. He praised the film's artistry but sought to remove "God damn," "son of a bitch," and "Hump the Hostess" from its soundtrack. Their retention, he argued, would not only make Code enforcement impossible but injure society. During the voting that followed, all endorsed exemption ex-cept the studio head. Valenti then spoke directly to him. The new MPAA president explained that, according to Warner Brothers, the film's text was unalterable without some reshooting, but in the future the Association was "going to be stronger and tougher . . . to get scripts, dialog, etc., before a picture is completed and before a lot of money is invested" (p. 10). Skouras blamed Shurlock and Warner: Shurlock should have communicated more often with the studio, Warner should have made "replacement scenes for the ones that the Code Authority was bound to oppose." As a result of their joint negligence, the studio head concluded, the floodgates were open (p. 11).

In the press release that announced the Board's decision to grant *Virginia Woolf* a Code Seal, Valenti noted that *Virginia Woolf* had been granted an exemption because of its quality and the studio's classification; he empha-sized that the exemption applied only to "a specific important film." But the Code itself was obviously under fire. Ten days later in Hollywood, Valenti spoke to three hundred studio executives, directors, and performers about the "adoption of a 'revised Code,' actually a new Production Code."[42] When it appeared three months later, *Newsweek* greeted this streamlined Code disparagingly: the "new code, like the old, is a glittering diadem of hypocrisy."[43] Ultimately, it served as a temporary resource to be used until the industry could accept classification. Codes had obviously outlived their viability. Martin Quigley, Jr., whose father had coauthored the original Pro-duction Code, said in a caustic *Motion Picture Herald* editorial that "it is pointless to consider whether the Code expired when the decision was made to film *Virginia Woolf* without regard to the Code, or when the decision was made by the Review Board to grant the picture an 'exemption' from the Code." The film was of "high quality" and "great cost": both triumphed over its "torrent of blasphemy, profanity and obscenity."[44] Quigley's title said it all: the Code was dead.

Virginia Woolf, as Valenti must have known, had indeed opened the floodgates. Motion picture classification was implemented within two years of the première of *Virginia Woolf*,[45] and films became increasingly more outspoken in theme, content, and language. But *Virginia Woolf* was not an intentionally political weapon. Warner did not make the film to effect a decisive change in the way the MPAA mediated between the industry and its public. Albee's play was a good commercial property, the price of Mike Nichols was the preservation of its text, and with or without a Seal the film would have been distributed. However much it advocated film classification, NCOMP did not force Warner Brothers to restrict *Virginia Woolf* in order to bring about a comparable practice industry wide. In all likelihood, the Consultants sought assurance that a film "morally unobjectionable for adults, with reservations" (A-IV) would be seen only by adults; with Warner Brothers' concession, NCOMP could more easily defend an unpopular rating against its critics.

Finally, after three years with an "acting president," the MPAA was being led by events; implicit in Shurlock's urging the Board to discover a way to recognize quality was a plea for leadership. Valenti offered it. He promised "new ideas, new objectives, new programs."[46] One member of the MPAA staff found his leaderhip "inspiring": Valenti "used words like 'loyalty' and 'energy' and 'vigor'—words, said the staffer, 'that all of us needed to hear.' "[47] Valenti quickly grasped the ineffectiveness of the Code and the futility of trying to preserve it. He spoke with Warner for three hours about the language of *Virginia Woolf* and concluded that "it seemed wrong that grown men should be sitting around discussing such matters."[48] NCOMP had allowed Valenti to assume a leadership position both morally and politically opportune. His Washington experience, the "historical inevitability" of *Virginia Woolf* irrespective of the Board's decision, and the obvious need for strong leadership at the head of the MPAA earned him the support of his Board.

No one had conspired to kill the Code, no one was capable of saving it. Warner Brothers' commitment to film *Virginia Woolf* largely as written, internal changes at the National Catholic Office for Motion Pictures, a concentrated fiscal, social, and political pressure on the Production Code Administration—these cohered at one moment in history to change the face of American film censorship.

NOTES

[1]Paul W. Facey, *The Legion of Decency: A Sociological Analysis of the Emergence and Development of a Social Pressure Group,* Diss. Fordham 1945 (New York: Arno Press, 1974), p. 179.

[2]Richard S. Randall, *Censorship of the Movies: The Social and Political Control of a Mass Medium* (Madison: University of Wisconsin Press, 1968), p. 202.

[3]The author wishes to thank the Motion Picture Association of America; the Division for Film and Broadcasting, U. S. Catholic Conference; Ernest Lehman; and the

Hoblitzelle Theatre Arts Library, Humanities Research Center, The University of Texas at Austin, for their gracious assistance during the research phase of this paper.

[4]"Movie Rights to 'Virginia Woolf' Sold to Warners for $500,000," *New York Times,* 5 March 1964, Sec. 1, p. 37, col. 2.

[5]Unless otherwise indicated, references to the Motion Picture Association of America (MPAA) and the Production Code Administration (PCA) are taken from materials in unnumbered file folders pertinent to *Virginia Woolf* at the MPAA, New York City.

[6]"Movie Rights to 'Virginia Woolf' Sold to Warners for $500,000," p. 37, col. 2.

[7]A copy of Trilling's letter is located in Box 19, The Ernest Lehman Collection, Hoblitzelle Theatre Arts Library, Humanities Research Center, The University of Texas at Austin. The Lehman Collection contains twenty-six boxes of uncatalogued materials pertinent to *Virginia Woolf.* All further reference to the Collection will appear in the text. "(ELC, 19)," for example, means that information is drawn from the Ernest Lehman Collection, Box 19.

[8]"Movie Rights to 'Virginia Woolf' Sold to Warners for $500,000," *New York Times,* p. 37, col. 2; the Ernest Lehman Collection contains the *Hollywood Reporter* (7 April 1964) and *Los Angeles Times* (n.d.) stories (ELC, 22).

[9]PCA internal Memorandum, to Ralph Hetzel (MPAA Acting President) from Michael Linden, 1 July 1964.

[10]"The Screen: Stage 'Hamlet' With Richard Burton," rev. of *Hamlet,* by William Shakespeare, *New York Times,* 24 September 1964, Sec. 1, p. 46, col. 2.

[11]Information on the Electronovision *Hamlet* was gleaned from the following articles in the *New York Times:* A. H. Weiler, "Broadway 'Hamlet' to Be Filmed For Short Run in 1,000 Houses," 27 June 1964, Sec. 1, p. 14, col. 1; Sam Zolotow, "Stage's 'Hamlet' Becomes a Film," 3 July 1964, Sec. 1, p. 13, col. 1; Peter Bart, "Filmed 'Hamlet' Gets Costly Push," 19 September 1964, Sec. 1, p. 19, col. 4; "Broadway 'Hamlet' Grosses $3 Million in Movie Houses," 30 September 1964, Sec. 1, p. 34, col. 7.

[12]Joseph Gelmis, *The Film Director as Superstar* (Garden City, N.Y.: Doubleday, 1970), p. 291.

[13]The $7.5 million negative cost resulted in part from the principals' six- and seven-figure salaries combined with the four-week schedule slippage. According to a proposed contract (15 January 1965; ELC, 19), Elizabeth Taylor was entitled to $100,00 for each week the film was overschedule; both she and Burton "voluntarily settled for a sizeable reduction, reportedly so as not to penalize director Mike Nichols in his film debut" ("Four Actor 'Woolf' Cost $7,500,000;Liz-Dick Gesture to Mike Nichols," *Variety,* 4 May 1966, p. 215, col. 5).

[14]Telephone interview with Rudi Fehr, 22 June 1979.

[15]C. Robert Jennings, "All for the love of Mike," *Saturday Evening Post,* 9 October 1965, p. 86.

[16]"Hold 'Virginia Woolf' From Tradeshowing Until Eve of Preem," *Variety,* 18 May 1966, p. 4, col. 4.

[17]Vincent Canby, "Valenti Is Facing First Film Crisis," *New York Times,* 28 May 1966, Sec. 1, p. 12, col. 6.

[18]"Notes of Meeting of Production Code Review Board on Friday, June 10, 1966 . . . ,"

[19]"MPAA Nixes Its Seal for 'Woolf'"; Puts WB, Sans 'Art' Subsidiary, In Possibly Awkward Position," *Variety,* 8 June 1966, p. 4, col. 2.

[20]"MPAA Nixes Its Seal for 'Woolf'. . . ," p. 4, col. 2.

[21]In 1965 Adolph Zukor, an executive emeritus in the film industry, called for an MPAA president who could stop "censorship classification threats," but Zukor also advocated that admission to certain motion pictures be restricted to persons over

sixteen (A. D. Murphy, "Overseas Biz, Morals at Home Make Vital MPAA Front Man—Says Zukor," *Variety*, 13 January 1965, p. 3, col. 5).

[22]Clipfile, Academy of Motion Pictures Arts and Sciences. Previous films "recommended for adults only" included *Lolita, Elmer Gantry*, and *Darling* (which the Legion designated the best adult film of 1965); rather than "recommend," Warner Brothers' contract with exhibitors mandated "adults only" and further specified that children be admitted only with their *parents*.

[23]PCA internal Memorandum, to Ralph Hetzel from Tim Clagett, 3 June 1966.

[24]"Valenti and Nizer Handle Selves Expertly in First Hollywood Press Row," *Variety*, 22 June 1966, p. 3, col. 1.

[25]In the 1960s, a Legion condemnation could generate publicity not altogether harmful to a film's promotional campaign, but Warner had a work of high quality. Negative publicity could have adversely affected the reaction of the Review Board and the public.

[26]Telephone interview with Richard Lederer, 22 June 1979.

[27]"Legion of Decency," Editorial, *America*, 9 May 1964, pp. 624–25. Since 1963, the classification categories have been as follows: A-I, morally unobjectionable for general patronage; A-II, morally unobjectionable for adults and adolescents; A-III, morally unobjectionable for adults; A-IV, morally unobjectionable for adults, with reservations; B, morally objectionable in part for all; C, condemned.

[28]Editor's foreward to Msgr. Thomas F. Little, "The Modern Legion and Its Modern Outlook," *America*, 11 December 1965, p. 744.

[29]Randall, p. 198.

[30]"MPAA Nixes Its Seal for 'Woolf' . . . ," p. 4, col. 2.

[31]Harold C. Gardiner, S. J., *Catholic Viewpoint on Censorship* (Garden City, N.Y.: n.p., 1958), p. 99, as quoted in Randall, pp. 187–88.

[32]Little, p. 746. In the eight years following the encyclical, the Legion cited forty films for their notable value, Little said; but (as will be demonstrated) IFCA's standards regarding the depiction of alternative modes of expression, physical and verbal, were more conservative than those of the Legion generally.

[33]*Motion Picture Daily*, 1 September 1965, p. 1; as quoted in Randall, p. 191.

[34]Little, p. 746.

[35]"Catholic Office's A-4 Rating to 'Woolf'; Industry's Own Seal Still Not Bestowed," *Variety*, 1 June 1966, p. 7, col. 1.

[36]Many Catholics protested NCOMP's action on *Virginia Woolf* (see n. 37); Father Sullivan wrote to one of the organization's critics that "this office was directly instrumental in having Warner Brothers restrict patronage of the film . . ." A copy of this letter dated 28 June 1966 is preserved in NCOMP files. Unless otherwise indicated, references to NCOMP are taken from materials in unnumbered file folders pertinent to *Virginia Woolf* at NCOMP, New York.

[37]A "Legion of Decency Inter-office Memo" (25 May 1966) contains this distribution. A total of 89 persons voted (the total given elsewhere is 91, but the distribution accounts for only 89); five persons were undecided about a specific category. Of 67 Consultants, 33 were clergy; of those, 64% voted for "A-IV," 3% for "C." 34 Consultants were laity; of those, 55% voted for "A-IV," 15% for "C." NCOMP files on the *Virginia Woolf* rating contain two folders of correspondence, much of it critical of the rating, the screening body, or the Office leadership. Most of the mail was generated by a *Life* article entitled "A surprising Liz in a film shocker" (10 June 1966, pp. 87–98). Prominent in the piece was a production still of Martha's "scorching, sexual frug with Nick" (p. 88) and samples of the film's "earthy, uninhibited dialogue" (p. 92). The article, which also included a photograph of Msgr. Little and Father Sullivan, explained how NCOMP had arrived at its rating. Writing to *Life* (15 June 1966), Little protested that the article's concentration on a "relatively brief

sequence" gave the impression that *Virginia Woolf* was "an obscene exercise." Such coverage was unfair to both the film and NCOMP. But what undoubtedly irritated the Office's critics most was seeing a provocative Martha/Liz and a drunken George/Dick pictured in the same article as Little and Sullivan. Little's final comment to *Life* touched on this sensitive area: NCOMP bases "its evaluation only on the film itself and not upon the personal lives of anyone associated with the production." (*Life* deleted the portions cited above when it published two paragraphs from the letter on 1 July 1966, p. 21.)

[38]"Notes . . . , " p. 14.

[39]"Four Actor "Woolf" Cost $7,500,000," p. 1, col. 5.

[40]Unless otherwise indicated the account of the meeting is taken from this set of "Notes . . ." (see n. 18); page numbers are given in parentheses following specific references.

[41]*Variety* later reported these changes, though it named neither word. "There has been some puzzlement about why these changes were thought necessary, since those who might be offended by strong language are hardly likely to be mollified by only two small deletions" ("Two Phrases Cut From Soundtrack Of 'Who's Afraid of Virg. Woolf?' " 13 July 1966, p. 1, col. 1).

[42]Vincent Canby, "Public Not Afraid of Big Bad 'Woolf,' " *New York Times*, 25 June 1966, Sec. 1, p. 21, col. 1.

[43]"Hollywood: Three-and-a-half Square," *Newsweek*, 30 October 1966, p. 22.

[44]"The Code is Dead," 6 July 1966; Clipfile, Academy of Motion Picture Arts and Sciences.

[45]Two Supreme Court decisions, each announced on 22 April 1968, hastened the industry's adoption of a classification system. *Interstate Circuit v. Dallas*, the more important one, implied that local and state censorship boards could operate unchallenged by constitutional tests. In an attempt to prevent a proliferation of such boards, the industry established a national classification system (Stephen Farber, *The Movie Rating Game* [Washington, D.C.: Public Affairs Press, 1972], p. 14).

[46]Ronald Gold, "Ex-LBJ Aide's Film Vision," *Variety*, 1 June 1966, p. 52, col. 4.

[47]"Valenti Meets Manhattan Press," *Variety*, 25 May 1966, p. 18, cols. 2–3.

[48]Valenti, *The Movie Rating System: How It Began, Its Purpose, How It Works, The Public Reaction* (New York and Washington, D.C.: Motion Picture Association of America, n.d.), p. 2.

1980

THEORY AND CRITICISM

CINEMA
JOURNAL

Dennis L. White

The Poetics
of Horror

William Blum

The Cinema
of Cruelty

SPRING 1971

Volume X, No. 2

The Poetics of Horror:
More Than Meets the Eye

Dennis L. White

The concepts commonly associated with and used to describe the horror film may not be enough to explain horror or how films produce it. This is not just to say that horror films are more than the sum of their parts—that can be said of any good film and most bad ones—but that what makes a good film, no matter what its genre, is something which cannot be entirely accounted for by its parts or elements; it is something within the identities of the pieces from which the film is constructed and within the nature of the ways in which they are combined.

Since horror films are usually considered B-movies and are seldom the product of prestige studios, it is particularly easy to think of them as entertainments, as examples of a certain director's, producer's, or actor's skills, or as souvenirs from film history. As a result their analysis is apt to be unusually superficial and specious, and limited almost exclusively to a summation of their plot or a listing of their credits. The possibility that a horror film may be, or may have to be, a work of art, although one of the stock reflections of film criticism, tends to go unexplained and undeveloped.

The linking of horror and art, in fact, goes back to Greek tragedy. The word "horror" itself is found in Aristotle's *Poetics:* "fear and pity may be aroused by spectacular means; but they may also result from the inner structure of a piece . . . even without the aid of the eye, he who hears the tale told will thrill with horror and melt to pity at what takes place." Shots of Gothic manors lit by lightning, of shadows glimpsed under doors, or of a hand gliding along a banister are examples of the "spectacular means" of horror; they are the kinds of devices that have been used so often that they have come to define the genre of the horror film. Free of the broader context of the films of which they are a part or of our memory of similar images in other films, however, such shots may not necessarily produce fear and dread; what is essential to horror may be something else. Films such as Bava's *Nightmare Castle* and Kenton's *House of Frankenstein* that are nothing more than a stringing together of every horror cliché from dark castles and mad scientists to the return of the dead to terrorize the living provoke only laughter, while a film such as Frankenheimer's *The Manchurian Candidate* that has none of the traditional surface characteristics and gimmicks of the horror film, or Hitchcock's *Psycho*, with its obvious elements of humor, become something profoundly hideous and shocking.

If a film has anything to do with the supernatural, cults, monsters, mad scientists, graveyards, old castles, or uncharted islands it is classified as a work of horror while films not dealing with such particulars are apt to be classified as something else. Any genre whose assumed characteristics are so superficial is easy to affect and easy to abuse—from carelessness, from overconfidence, from a film-maker's inability to bridge the gap between what he wants to say and do, and what he thinks he wants to say and actually knows how to do. The test of a film must be the film itself, not the blanket of terms used to explain or describe it. When judged in terms of its acting, photography, or direction, or in terms of the relevance, significance, or contemporary nature of its content, the horror film is probably no better and is often a great deal worse than the ordinary western, melodrama, or comedy. Such traditional concepts may not touch what is the real essence of some films. Likewise, a film is not a horror film only when it contains certain elements common to the genre; the number of these elements is no measure of horror or of quality.

A film succeeds if it can provoke emotion; the more meaningful the emotion the better the film; one emotion a film can produce is that of horror. The outward appearance of horror films may not even indicate the right direction for their production or their criticism to take. By ignoring the emotions associated with horror such an approach could just as easily point in the wrong direction. It is hard enough to find words and syntax that begin to represent our reactions and our opinions about a film, but it is even harder to express the beliefs and the logic that lead to that opinion or are responsible for that reaction. A critic's attempt to simply describe a film, for example, is apt to be just as much a rationalization for the underlying, but unstated, assumptions he brings to bear in his analysis of films generally as it is a communication of what he actually saw or heard in the film in question. To suggest anything more than an unembellished positive or negative response may require an argument that implies more than a critic intends to imply or more than he actually knows. Unfortunately the more elegantly the criticism is written the more reasonable it appears and the more persuasive and potentially misleading it is apt to be.

Moreover, like any work of art a horror film, when successful, generates some of its power by its confounding of analysis. The existence of often seen films such as Weine's *Cabinet of Dr. Caligari*, Murnau's *Nosferatu*, Julian's *Phantom of the Opera*, Whale's *Frankenstein*, or Browning's *Dracu-*

la can make analysis even more difficult. That these films are better distributed than others may imply something about their quality when in fact it proves nothing. On the other hand, seldom seen films such as Ingram's *The Magician*, Curtiz's *Mystery of the Wax Museum*, or Weine's *Hands of Orlac* can also confuse the issue by becoming the justification for elitist attitudes on the part of critics and film buffs. When those on the outside of the I've-seen-it clique finally have a chance to see the film for themselves they are apt to be more interested in it as a ticket into the cognoscenti than a chance to see it for what it is or is not. As a result a film, no matter what its merits or lack of them, may have no trouble in maintaining a reputation or in establishing one.

In a field such as the horror film, in which the same story may be filmed again and again, this attitude can distort our historical and aesthetic perspective to such a degree that it may be difficult for film-makers setting out to remake a classic to either learn from its mistakes or duplicate its successes; even more difficult is the creation of a work of horror independent of the subjects and patterns of the genre's established classics. *The Cabinet of Dr. Caligari*, for instance, may have had an influence on the German films of the twenties, but it seems also to be a case of a popular and acclaimed film having little serious influence on films generally. The appearance of its characters and the style of its sets show up in an incomplete sort of way in subsequent films, but duplicating these elements alone may not even suggest what gives *Caligari* its power. What is essential to *Caligari* is not even recaptured by its maker, as Weine's ludicrous *Genuine* testifies.

WHAT IS PRIMARY?

Any film-maker must turn a concept or script into a series of images and sounds that expresses the essence, as well as the surface, of the source. To make a successful horror film a film-maker must decide what is primary to the production of horror, and if the characteristics found in existing horror films are the best or the only way to achieve it. Why, for example, is a film such as *Psycho* generally labeled a work of horror and not a detective or murder thriller? Anyone who has seen *Psycho* would agree that it inspires fear and dread and therefore deserves to be called a horror film. Its success in spite of its de-emphasis of many of the elements common to the horror film is an indication that the essence of horror results from other more subtle elements in its make-up. From the first shots our attention is on Marion, played by Janet Leigh, and her frustrated love affair. Throughout her stealing of the money and her attempt to reach her lover the camera stays either on her or on the envelope containing the cash. The detailing of her behavior and of her handling the envelope center our interest on her state of mind, resulting in a sense of security and inevitability in our following of her life that is shattered by her murder; yet the killing, surprisingly, does not alter the inertia of the film. One story does not stop and another begin; Marion is more than a way of leading us to Norman Bates. Instead we see Norman only as the detective sent to recover the money, Marion's lover, or her sister see him in their search for her. The rainy night, the hint of something odd about Norman and his mother, the Gothic house on the seldom traveled road—these similarities to other horror films are there, but they are not obtrusive or fitted into the plot to give a superficial illusion of horror. They are used because of the qualities they actually possess, the indications they actually make, and because they are the most practical narrative devices.

Ulmer's *The Black Cat,* on the other hand, openly uses what amount to horror clichés, but uses them to set up a contrast for some departures from tradition that are to follow. It begins with a young couple's midnight journey through a strange country, adds a mysterious and menacing stranger, and ends up stranding the three of them in the middle of a fierce storm. But instead of a dark castle, the film reverses the cliche and has their refuge be a spotless modernistic estate; the storm clears to reveal a beautiful spring day; the stranger becomes the couple's protector; and instead of the usual stark high contrast photography we get the soft patterns of grey usually associated with Sternberg. *The Black Cat* in comparison to *Psycho* is not a complex or profound work, but it does achieve horror. Its success in spite of plot or technique further suggests that it is something else in the film to which we respond.

If the majority of films achieve anything it is only the selling of the illusion that they are a phenomenon of our times, that they tell us something we have not been told before, or that they are the latest, and therefore the best, examples of film as art. When such reasons are tempting enough we can fool ourselves into seeing what we have been led to expect even if it is not there in the film at all. Unfortunately, if we can respond to what is not there we may fail to respond to what is. *The Kremlin Letter* is an example; its horror, and as a result, its quality, is overlooked. The fact that it stars Bibi Anderssen, Richard Boone, Patrick O'Neal, George Sanders, Max Von Sydow, and Orson Welles, and that it is written and directed by John Huston have not made it a critical or popular success. Being on the surface a spy film, it doesn't quite meet the standards of the masses of the art house audience; not being pure-Bond or pure thriller it doesn't quite meet the entertainment demands of more general audiences. *The Kremlin Letter*'s box office failure is an indication of how judgments based on acting, direction, technique, story, or social relevance are arbitrary, inadequate, and misleading.

It is unfortunate that few people will be motivated to see *The Kremlin Letter* and that few critics have been able to describe it as what it is, because besides being a good film, it is essentially a work of horror. It treats the complexities of its plot as an artistic problem the solving of which gives each line of dialogue, each shot, and each cut more concentrated meaning. Instead of simplifying the plot, the director chose to stylize the film's technique and point of view. In lieu of the usual unities of time, place, or theme, the film unifies itself by establishing an ever-building momentum in the sequence and pacing of its episodes. When not seen as a composition of these episodes in time the film looks as if it were just a conglomeration of sex, sadism, and torture. But in context such elements are neither blatant nor obtrusive. We do not see a series of sensationalist scenes passing before us but experience the feeling of being trapped in a world of perversion, violence, and death. Seeing only this threatening world, but not the usual characters and trappings we have come to expect from horror films, *The Kremlin Letter* is more than most are willing to take. It is not a study of espionage, nor of the politics that thrive on and perpetuate it. These things are there but only as a pretext for the film itself. It is the film's design, the way its elements are combined in time, that makes *The Kremlin Letter* horrible, yet satisfying and beautiful. However, this perfection of form is hard to accept for most people since they are neither accustomed nor willing to see something as beautiful when its primary purpose is to capture ugliness, evil and misery.

THE STRUCTURE OF HORROR: UNCONTROLLABLE CAUSATION

The murder mystery, the black comedy, the Chandler-Hammett variety of detective film, and the spy film are obvious examples of films that employ much the same methods and devices as does the horror film. It is the form these films give their content, however, that determines if they contain elements of horror, or whether, in the case of films such as *Psycho* or *The Kremlin Letter,* they become exclusively works of horror. The suggestion of mysteries and secrets or of evil doings in an old house can be a beginning, but by itself such a suggestion cannot provoke horror. A murder or detective story such as Leni's *The Cat and the Canary,* West's *The Bat Whispers,* or Brahm's *The Lodger* is structured with an end other than horror in mind. Some scenes may achieve horror, and some characters dramatically experience horror, but for these films conventional clues and a logical explanation, at least an explanation plausible in hindsight, are usually crucial, and are of necessity their makers' first concern.

A horror film, on the other hand, is not just a sequence of certain events: it is the unity of a certain kind of action. It must be more than just the unity of a life, such as that of a mad doctor; of an act, such as his crimes or experiments; of a place, such as the castle where he conducts his experiments; or of a period defined by the prejudices of his colleagues or of the society that drives the doctor to misuse his discovery. Likewise, perfect characterizations, plots with no loose ends, the perfect rendering of atmosphere, elegant camera work or editing may offer the possibility of evoking horror, but by themselves are secondary to its creation. It does no good if a film has no faults in these areas if at its core it has no cardinal virtue. *Psycho* and Seigel's *Invasion of the Body Snatchers* in fact use would-be flaws as means of achieving horror. It does not subtract from *Invasion of the Body Snatchers* that the girl's personality is destroyed and replaced before our eyes whereas all the preceding victims had had their bodies replaced as well. We see that this variation does not destroy the film's believability or quality; it adds to its horror. Neither does it subtract from *Psycho* that Janet Leigh, the supposed star, is killed in the first third of the film; in the long run the fact that the film goes on without her teaches a great deal about what and what not to be concerned with in a film.

No matter how many or how few shots compose a work, each shot and each instant of each shot must communicate the motivations and relationships of the whole of which they are part. Shots may be taken from fresh camera set-ups that force on us specific points of view, or within a single shot a traveling camera, shifting lighting, moving actors, or changing sound or content of some kind may be used to emphasize distinct actions or elements within a more general action. In a successful film each shot must contribute to the integrity, the character of the larger composition that holds the shots together. I am not implying that each shot in a horror film must show us a severed limb or a vampire stalking a victim, but that a pervading sense of horror, like a pervading sense of suspense, comedy, or drama, is a fundamental way of providing the causation in terms of which the elements of a film, like the events of its plot, are unfolded. Similarly I do not intend to imply that each shot must maintain the integrity of a single such force. Hitchcock's most suspenseful films such as *The 39 Steps* or *North by Northwest* are highly comic; the comedy of Preston Sturges' *Sullivan's Travels* or *The Miracle at Morgan's Creek* depends on suspense; Whale's *The Bride of Frankenstein* and *The Invisible Man,* or Freund's *Mad Love,* in addition to being works of horror, employ comedy and suspense as well; *Dracula,* Schoedsack's *The Most Dangerous Game* or Frankenheimer's *Seconds* are highly dramatic.

Horror, like drama, comedy, or suspense need not be an obvious component in a film's composition to be the major factor behind that composition. In the case of *Psycho* or films not usually classified as works of horror, such as *The Kremlin Letter* or Huston's *A Walk with Love and Death,* Gance's *J'Accuse* or Fleischer's *The Boston Strangler* the element of horror is subtle and comes from the peculiarities of the progression of the narrative. No one in *The Kremlin Letter*, for example, is ever in control of his life or environment. No one is ever sure that his allies or enemies are what they seem to be; evil geniuses plot everyone's fate and force people to give up the lives they have chosen and to be separated from those they love. Like pawns people move from one insecure situation to another. Very soon we, too, feel isolated and defenseless. Such films are best described and, therefore, best criticized as works of horror because of the continual revelation of random, but at the same time, inevitable forces asserting themselves within their events and characterizations. Their lack of comprehensible causation is clearly intentional.

The Psychological Base: Fear of Powerlessness

The two most popular subjects in films of all types are probably love and death, and ironically they are often linked. The horror film is particularly fond of violent death and bizarre love. Because we all fear death and try to protect ourselves from it, even the most clinical presentation of a murder is apt to interest us. But the arousing of our fear of death by itself is not enough to produce horror; horror requires a certain kind of manipulation of that fear. The murder sequences in *Psycho*, for example, do not represent the high point of the film's plot or the high water marks of its direction. The film is a composition in time; its purpose is much more than to establish a framework for these scenes. *Psycho* is not shot and edited to match these highly stylized sequences. They are startling, but not out of place, because they are part of the total composition and are linked in a network of causes and effects with each part of the film. If a film is to frighten us it must use elements that are genuinely frightening: in the case of *Psycho*, not just an old dark house, but the madness of a man like Norman who lives in that house—not just murder, but the kind of death from which there is no protection, no warning, and no escape.

The fact that audiences tolerate, even seek out and enjoy, a film designed to horrify them, can tell us a great deal about what it is in these films that makes them inspire fear or dread. Conversely these films can tell something about those who enjoy them, and, by induction, about people in general. Beneath the castles, creatures, and the supernatural elements of successful horror films are less obvious, but equally prevalent themes. Like the forces behind a dream, these themes appeal to and as a result gain power from basic psychological forces. An aesthetic of horror is almost a materialization of psychology—not just an abnormal psychology, but a psychology of all of man's behavior and experiences. To analyze horror films is to examine them in terms of the causes and effects, the links, that exist between them and the world that surrounds them, between mechanisms within them and mechanisms within us.

Generally the force at work in a horror film might be defined as the triggering of our basic fear of the unknown, our fear of being unable to deal with our environment. The most obvious embodiments of this fear are monsters and nightmarish situations beyond our comprehension and control. But there is no reason to assume that horror must deal with the supernatural. It is not necessary to go beyond conventional situations or beyond science in the usual sense to find ingredients for horror. Although the preponderance of supernatural themes in horror films and the fact that it is traditional to associate horror only with the supernatural does indicate the richness of such a source, we must be careful not to neglect other possible sources or to ignore films that have employed other subjects and circumstances to produce horror. Equally effective as a situation beyond reason and explanation is that in which the protagonist understands the dynamics at work and can predict what is going to happen to him as a result but still can do nothing to change his fate, as in *Seconds* or *The Kremlin Letter*. Characteristic of horror is a continual loss of means of escape until there is no safety and no hope of safety. The fear of the panicked man in the opening scene of Tourneur's *The Curse of the Demon*, for example, is easily transmitted to us even though we have as yet no justification for sharing his fears. It takes an unforeseeable discovery or accident, in the case of *The Invasion of the Body Snatchers* to effect the outcome in such intimidating circumstances. Unforeseeable elements in a situation thought to be under control can also embody horror. The tightrope walker in Browning's *Freaks* thinks she has successfully hidden her crime from the freaks, and Dr. Moreau in Kenton's *The Island of Lost Souls* thinks he has his island and his creations hidden from the world and under his power. But a combination of insight and accident proves them wrong and in the process produces horror for them and for us.

Art has always shown that the destructive forces of man's life are as much a part of his personality as they are of the world in which he lives. Almost unintentionally any horror film is apt to dramatize this abstraction through a kind of counterpoint. For example, there are two kinds of men contrasted in *The Black Cat*, two states of mind in *Psycho*, in the case of Murnau's *Faust* or Mamoulian's *Dr. Jekyll and Mr. Hyde* one personality divided between two bodies, and in *Dracula* or *The Island of Lost Souls* two kinds of beings—men and those less than men. In each case there are two forces at odds with one another that through their conflict define one another. Horror films tend to dismiss the possibility of making simple moral judgments on their content or characterizations, the result being that they are left with the more general but also more profound themes of guilt and responsibility, and of life and death. Even the most simple-minded horror film, as if by accident, asks the same questions as do the greatest works of art. The fact that many of us find horror films so intriguing may indicate that they also provide an answer of sorts.

In films such as *Faust* and *Seconds* the fear of powerlessness is so all embracing that it even subordinates that of death, forcing us to recognize that it is more than just our biological lives we are trying to protect. A creature such as King Kong or a man such as Zaroff in *The Most Dangerous Game* can be frightening, but not as horrifying as the threat of something seen, but not comprehended, as are the phenomena in *The Invasion of the Body Snatchers, Dracula,* or Tourneur's *I Walked with a Zombie* or the power of the organization in *Seconds* or of the espionage network in *The Manchurian Candidate.* The physical possession of someone else's body in *The Black Cat, Psycho,* and *The Most Dangerous Game* symbolizes this fear; in *Mad Love* such possession is represented by a wax statue, in *I Walked with a Zombie* by a voodoo doll, in *The Island of Lost Souls* or Franju's *The Horror Chamber of Dr. Faustus* it is symbolized by mutilation. The dread of not possessing one's self is so recognizable that in a film such as Dreyer's *Day of Wrath* it needs no physical manifestations at all, only its suggestion through dialogue. These possibilities express every man's concern for his physical and psychological safety and individuality. When we see this integrity violated it is a threat to our ego's ability to protect itself because it dramatizes the failure of another ego to preserve itself.

THREATS OF ANIMALIZATION, FEAR OF THE ID

The horror film offers the possibility of carrying to its most effective extreme an element common to many genres of film: it is the same process at work in an individual's de-humanization as in Losey's *The Servant* and his *Accident,* in a family's drift to barbarism as in Visconti's *The Damned,* in a symbolic society's fall from civilization as in Hitchcock's *Lifeboat* or Brook's *Lord of the Flies.* In the horror film, however, the process becomes one of animalization. It results in ape men and werewolves, of people turning into something more primitive than man, or in *Island of Lost Souls* and Schaffner's *Planet of the Apes,* animals becoming more than animals.

The problem of making the distinction between an animal and a perverted member of our own species is generally solved in one of two ways. The first involves having a man change from a conventional well-socialized being to a beast as the result of some spell as in *The Cat People,* a drug as in *Dr. Jekyll and Mr. Hyde,* or disease (be it physical or mental) as in Dreyer's *Vampyr, Nosferatu,* or *Dracula.* In their normal lives these people are capable of resisting the destructive impulses to which they freely submit in their other form. The second solution is to emphasize the sexuality of the beasts, the most common pattern being a human woman threatened by an animalistic male. Monsters are usually male with such exceptions as the girl in *The Cat People* who becomes the animal personification of the ferocious female; their threat is sexual. In *Nosferatu* and *Dracula* the vampire's threat is more of seduction than of death; in *Jekyll and Hyde,* Hyde is physically ape-like and abnormally sexual; in *Frankenstein* the villagers seem to fear not so much a murderer as a child molester. The horror producing element in such occurrences is the simultaneous presence of both a desire to gratify and the fear of losing control of the *id*—a fear that the *id* will become one's whole personality.

A more subtle, but in its way even more disturbing variation of this fear is that of being under someone else's power, of losing control over not just the *id* but the entire self. Often in films this fear is part sexual, but it is more than just the desire for sex, it is the conscious or unconscious perversion of sexual or romantic attraction. In the world of *Day of Wrath,* for example, sexuality and love are unknowns and as such are to be feared; the misinterpreted forces of sexuality become as threatening as any creature or monster and are defined as witchcraft. When a man feels a sexual attraction as did the old husband for his young wife he accounts for it in terms not of something within him, but of something beyond his control, something for which he need accept no responsibility, in short as his coming under someone else's power.

God-mania is also a common element in the horror film. Zaroff in *The Most Dangerous Game,* Moreau in *Island of Lost Souls,* and Dr. Pretorius in *Bride of Frankenstein* are the most obvious examples, because they state their desire to play God. The theme is just as prevalent, however, in *The Magician, The Cabinet of Dr. Caligari, The Invisible Man,* Fisher's *The Man Who Could Cheat Death,* or in the actions of the mother in *The Manchurian Candidate* or the old man in *Seconds.* Of course, there is nothing horrifying in the desire for power. It is only when someone is accused of being mad with power and the desire for undreamed of freedoms, of sinning against nature, or of dealing with forces beyond the reach of man that such themes become material for horror. The issue then becomes one of loyalty or resistance to a set of beliefs; it becomes a matter of faith. We are usually so socialized that we are not aware of the viewpoint or the orientation by which we live. We tend to be insulated from criticism of our assumptions and prejudices and blind to the potential validity of others' assumptions. As a result a direct attack on something such as our society's political or religious beliefs is apt to be ineffective. The horror film, however, can dramatize the frailty and arbitrariness of such assumptions in its characters and institutions, and can let us see our assumptions in a more critical way than is comfortable. In a film such as *Bride of Frankenstein* the result is humorous; the film's personalities are nothing more than a lumping together of ludicrous prejudices. In a film such as *Island of Lost Souls*, on the other hand, the result is true horror. When the beasts' society crumbles it carries its laws and beliefs to their logical conclusion releasing a sort of mass animalization.

The orientation of the society of *Day of Wrath* is so enclosed and self-perpetuating that the destructiveness of its assumptions becomes visible only through its distortion of sex. The satirical metaphor of Victorian sex codes of *Nosferatu, Dracula,* or *Island of Lost Souls* represent similar sexual world views. Misinterpretations of sex, however, can also be shown through a single man's perverted point of view. In *The Black Cat* Karloff's character preserving the bodies of his dead wives and marrying his daughter is a shocking but at the same time intriguing breach of conventional taboos. Whereas he builds his own isolated world to hide his madness, Dr. Gogol in *Mad Love* constructs a socially acceptable facade that both disguises and satisfies his fixation with the mutilated—he becomes a plastic surgeon and habitué of a theater specializing, like him, in the sadistic and physically grotesque. Norman Bates in *Psycho,* on the other hand, builds an interior wall to hide one half of his personality from the other. The frustrations behind the actions of his two selves become apparent because they parallel the frustrations of Marion and her lover. Marion's stealing of the money springs from the healthy and normal desire to be able to marry and be independent of her family. Next to her crime, however, are Norman's murders that are a perverted and abnormal working out of the same sexual drives and conflicts that motivate Marion. He wants sex, but he is afraid of it. In lieu of it he kills and gains both a sexual release and an excuse for abstinence. In short, all that is represented by Norman's life and all that is represented by Marion's are paralleled as well as contrasted. Such counterpoint is characteristic of the way that horror films inadvertently define what is supposedly madness and what is not.

FEARS OF REJECTION AND PERFECTION

Perhaps the least obvious fear to be found in horror films, but also the most encompassing, is that of being cut off from others, of being rejected by those around one. Like the fear of death which centers attention on things which could destroy life, the fear of alienation draws our attention to those things in us and around us by which we define ourselves as living human beings. As compelling as any scene in film is the sequence in *Invasion of the Body Snatchers* in which the girl's personality changes before our eyes and those of her lover, in fact changes during their kiss. In a similar scene in *Vampyr* one sister already infected by the vampire must be restrained from attacking her sister. In both cases within a single shot all that is meant by trust and love is shattered. The projection of this fear of estrangement is also effective. The young couples in *The Black Cat* and in *The Most Dangerous Game* are cut off from the society they know and can deal with; they are forced into a strange world without knowing the rules of that world. Until they learn them they are under the power of forces they do not understand. In a film such as *Day of Wrath* it is the fact that one person does understand more than his peers that isolates him, or in the case of *Invasion of the Body Snatchers* and *The Cat People* compels him to go to a psychiatrist. For knowing more than the conventional viewpoint allowed by their society someone is declared mad or, in *Day of Wrath*, a witch. Just seeing such mechanisms at work is enough to provoke horror. The threat is always there that even knowing the rules or carrying the correct assumptions is no guarantee of understanding or of being a part of the world into which you are born. The monster in *Bride of Frankenstein* and the doctor in *The Invisible Man* are rejected by their worlds because they personify the unknown. They gain our sympathy because of this rejection and cease to be a threat; the bloated villagers, the shrieking women, and the police in their ignorance become the monsters. That such people can threaten those who deviate from their codes of behavior forces us to recognize that similar threats can be made on us.

The fears in horror films rise from sociological as well as psychological themes. Count Dracula's power over the villagers or Dr. Moreau's authority over his creatures is, for example, the result of social stratification. The villains of horror get away with their crimes because they are, like Dracula or Baron Frankenstein, aristocrats and as such are unquestioningly obeyed; because they have achieved a respected status as professors or scientists like Jekyll or Gogol in *Mad Love;* or because they are rich like Moreau and can buy the complicity they need and employ men rejected by the respectable world. In contrast the scientist in *The Invisible Man* fails not in his experiments, but in his plan to capitalize on them because he cannot establish authority over the convention-bound man. Characteristic of horror is the theme of unrestricted freedoms for the few and too many covert regulations for the many. In *Invasion of the Body Snatchers* the fear is specifically that of a perfectly regulated society, perfect in the sense that its members are free of disruptive individuality and each is inescapably locked in his sociological niche.

No matter how bizarre or twisted the world of a film, it still must co-exist with our memory of the larger world. The problem in *Psycho,* for example, is to create the appearance of a friendly, healthy, although troubled young man while at the same time showing in his actions the menacing base beneath the appearance; it is the same problem as that in *The Manchurian Candidate* and in *Seconds,* and the reverse of that in *The Black Cat* where the hint of a friend must exist beneath Bela Lugosi's menacing surface. Because of the potential contrasts between a character's appearance and his actions, or because of the abrupt changes possible in his behavior through time, the horror film builds a degree of unpredictability into its view of human personality and, as a result, nullifies the usual clues and indicators we use in judging what to expect of people. We are constantly reminded that there is a potential for evil in some; we are constantly warned that we can never protect ourselves from evil in us or in someone close to us. The fact that horror films are not bound by convention to dwell on the good in men only emphasizes this fear.

It is in films employing a simple plot, few characters, and a limited range of themes and techniques that it is easiest for a film-maker to construct parallels, references, and a structure that fully utilizes all the elements possible in the work's conception. This can result in a kind of perfection, but it is the perfection of a design and not a composition; *I Walked with a Zombie,* Balcon's production of *Dead of Night, Island of Lost Souls,* and *The Black Cat* are works of this kind.

CHAOS OF THE WORLD AND OF DREAMS

When a more complex conception with more elements to interrelate achieves perfection the result can be levels of meaning not possible in the simpler work. It is the adding of profound statement to perfect design that makes such films as Dreyer's *Vampyr* or his *Day of Wrath, Freaks, Jekyll and Hyde, Invasion of the Body Snatchers, Psycho, The Manchurian Candidate,* or *The Kremlin Letter* such achievements. The best horror films create something that stands for the chaos of the world. *Mad Love, Psycho,* and *Bride of Frankenstein* create parallel worlds of confusion in their characters' minds; *Vampyr, Island of Lost Souls,* and *Day of Wrath* create societies that can stand as microcosms for that confusion. Films such as *The Manchurian Candidate* or *Invasion of the Body Snatchers* do both. They may present a simplified view of the world but they never take the world for granted.

A successful horror film forces us to suspend our reliance on the conventional frame of reference of normal life; we are forced to function on its terms. We do not have to believe that people can turn into panthers as in *The Cat People,* into birds as in *Freaks* or wolves as in *Dracula.* We only have to give up for a time facts we bring into the theater with us, and accept that some of the film's characters believe that such occurrences are facts. If the film's propositions do not refute each other and are not dependent on each other in such a way that if we reject one we must also reject those that follow from it then the horror of a film can expand to include every element and every scene. *Mad Love, Bride of Frankenstein,*

Island of Lost Souls, and *Vampyr* are perfect examples of an entire film becoming expressive. Like the musical the horror film is under no pressure to conform to the conventions of film or of daily life. It is free to translate everything from psychoanalytic theory to the whimsical intuitions of its maker into the forms of film, to become an objective presentation of subjective human experiences. In this sense films such as *Mad Love* and *Bride of Frankenstein* are the extreme examples not only of their genre, but of film in general. Each contains so many elements at odds with each other that they effectively cancel one another out to reveal something of what lies beneath. Their mixture of comedy and tragedy, reality and fantasy, captures something of the chaos of the world and some of the ways men go about giving that chaos the illusion of order. These films show that normal society, and normal people and their lives, are not as rational as they seem and that abnormal people like Gogol in *Mad Love* or Norman in *Psycho* are not as irrational or their acts as unintelligible as they seem.

Horror films come in black and white and in color; they can be highly stylized as is *Caligari* or pseudo-documentary as is Watkins' *War Game;* they are made by both good and bad film-makers. There seem to be no particular camera angles or movements, editing techniques, acting styles, make-up methods, or set designs common to all horror films or essential to the production of horror. However, there is a technique, as distinct from theme, that is found to some degree in all works of horror. It can result from the way a writer describes a shot or a cut, from the way a camera man frames a shot or lights a scene, from the way an editor assembles that scene or from the way the sound mixer manipulates its sound, or it can result from the way a director places and moves his actors and props. We all dream and as a result can see elements or scenes in films as having the quality of a dream, of psychological aberrations or hallucinations. The horror of Polanski's *Repulsion,* for example, does not come just from the theme of the girl's fear of sex. Instead it results from film's ability to make her real life and her fantasy life look and sound the same, and to manipulate the physical appearance of both to capture her increasing isolation and madness by literally making the ceilings increasingly nearer, the corridors longer, the rooms larger, the lighting darker, and the sounds more distant.

In Preston Sturges' comedy *Unfaithfully Yours,* there is a dream sequence for the length of which the film becomes a work of horror. An orchestra conductor suspects his wife of adultery, and while conducting a concert visualizes a grotesque plan to kill her and blame her death on the suspected lover. He dreams of making a phonograph record of what sounds like his wife's screams calling her lover's name, of killing his wife, placing the record player in the room with her corpse, and inviting the boyfriend to wait for her in the next room. When the record comes on the fake screams attract the innocent man into the adjoining room where he is confronted with the woman, her throat cut, yet apparently naming him as her murderer. Horror depends on the linking or superimposition of events, objects, or sounds that may have no conscious or logical meaning, but contain a subconscious, irrational association. The horror of the dream-sequence in *Unfaithfully Yours* comes from the contrast of the film's images and sounds, and the ability of that contrast to communicate the incongruency of the boyfriend's knowing the woman is dead, but hoping she is alive, coupled with the husband's simultaneous desire to see her dead, yet also alive. If this scene had not been handled as a fantasy, if it had been identified as a dream only when over, its potential for comedy within the context of the film would have been lost.

As the dream can express what a character would not normally express consciously, the aberration elements of the dream can become confused with normal life, providing a character with a way of doing what he wants to do while denying that he has done it or desired to do it. The husband's aberration in *Day of Wrath* that his wife is a witch, for example, lets him avoid the responsibility of his lust. In *Mad Love* Gogol's belief that the statue, like Pygmalion's, has come alive is the illusion he constructs to deal with the pressures of a world he cannot overcome. The murderer's belief in Florey's *Beast with Five Fingers* that the severed hand has come alive is his way of hiding from himself that he, not the hand, is the killer. Each of these men have suppressed forces within themselves and transferred the threat to objects or to other people; for them a dream has become reality. Each film shows their insanity by distorting the world in terms of their point of view. Horror depends on sensing, but not knowing, what to believe or who is or is not mad. Seeing the brain-washed soldier killing his wife in *The Manchurian Candidate*, Perry kill the family in Richard Brooks' *In Cold Blood*, or the plumber skillfully and randomly kill in Fleischer's *The Boston Strangler* is a threat to us because we see the vulnerability of victims and the inevitability of the crimes in light of the killers' twisted yet sympathetic personalities.

Films may also harness the dream's potential for communicating abnormal mental processes, not by incorporating a dream sequence or by a character's experiencing dream-like aberrations, but by the film itself becoming like a dream or in the case of horror films a nightmare, such as Hitchcock's *Vertigo* or *Marnie*, or *Dead of Night*. The effects of confusion, misinterpretation, or prejudice are often a concern in films, and are of necessity always a theme in horror films. The dreams of the hypnotized soldiers in *The Manchurian Candidate*, for example, provide a way to project elements of their personalities as well as their plight. Each soldier sees in his dreams the conference at which the extent of their suggestibility is demonstrated to Russian and Chinese officials; but each remembers the conference in a jumbled way, sometimes as it was, sometimes as the garden club meeting they were told it was, but more often as a jumbled merging of the two. For example, the voices of the officials come out of the mouths of the lady members of the garden club. At other times the lady lecturing about begonias is seen before portraits of Stalin and Lenin; one black soldier sees the odd sounding ladies as Negroes. In *Marnie* a childhood dream blends with the present. A shot begins at night in a shabby room with a hand tapping on the outside of a window, then pans to show Marnie sleeping during the day in her expensively furnished room.

In *Dead of Night* sets, characters, and dialogue from the film's half a dozen independent episodes merge into a progressively more complex and horrifying finale that ends by repeating the film's beginning like a *deja vu* experience. Characteristic of these examples is that that they fall into a recognizable whole only when they depict a murder, repressed in the case of *Marnie*, committed under suggestion as in *The Manchurian Candidate*, or not yet committed, but foreshadowed, as in *Dead of Night*. Many films not usually thought of as works of horror can be described and analyzed in terms of their dream-like qualities, Bunuel's *El*, Bergman's *The Silence* or *Fellini-Satyricon* to suggest a few. In each of these films there is the chance and sometimes the inevitability that the dream will become a nightmare, and that like the characters in the film we will be trapped in that nightmare. The degeneration of the beggars' banquet in Bunuel's *Viridiana*, Juliet's worsening neurosis in Fellini's *Juliet of the Spirits*, or the interrogations in Bergman's *Shame* or Welles' *The Trial* are in their essence scenes of horror that taint the entire film of which they are a part.

EXTENSIONS OF EVERYDAY FEARS

Horror should not be considered an exotic emotion, but rather one based on the common fears of everyday life. Like the fears expressed and resolved through dreams, the fears found in horror often take exotic and barely recognizable forms so that they will not be unbearably threatening while being resolved. Films such as *The Kremlin Letter* and *The Boston Strangler* however, do not disguise their horror-producing elements. They do not create a safe emotional distance for the viewer, and as a result, are often seen as depraved, repulsive, and unrealistic even though they thematically parallel the popular horror films of the past. *The Boston Strang'er*, for ex-ample, explores the consequences of the fear of death, fear of powerlessness, fear of alienation and fear of mutilation; it dramatizes man's ability to see threatening forces in himself as evil in others; it finds the extreme examp'e of a man who has lost control of himself, and who is both overpowered by his society and in revolt against it; and it is a good example of film's ability to capture the confusion of reality, memory, and dream. The only way to reveal the forces at work in, and the implications of the events and techniques in such films as *The Boston Strangler, A Walk with Love and Death,* or *Seconds* is through the use of horror. As a critical tool, horror should not be restricted to films employing the same devices, plots or actors as the classics of the genre. Anyone not willing to apply the concepts of horror to all films that employ the themes and forces of horror has little chance of appraising the total value of many, perhaps most, works.

Seconds is one of the most realistic horror films; it is set in the recognizable present and deals with the problems of contemporary American society as experienced by a central character bound, defined, and frustrated by the conventions, ambitions, and standards of our times. Through surgery, falsified documents, and relocation he is offered a second life, a chance to be free of the restrictions with which he has lived so long. His change of perspective, however, besides letting him recognize the assumptions and prejudices that make up his personality, lets him see that the organization that sold him his new life has assumed the same role in that life that the pressures and institutions of society took in his old life. First society, and then the organization that has replaced it, become like monsters. Society and the omniscient organization know all about him and can control the most subtle details of his behavior. In contrast he knows nothing about their workings and is powerless to influence any of their decisions concerning him. One by one the indicators he has used to judge people, situations, and emotions are shown to be useless, leaving him helpless to deal with the most mundane events. Out of the ordinary events of life—meeting a girl, having a cocktail party, talking to an old friend—comes horror. He is told to adjust to his new surroundings and to find a personality to match his new appearance. But there is no way to justify the assumptions of his society or to determine his position within it. Instead of gaining a new personality he loses confidence in his old. His ego is confronted with the most horrifying realization possible—that it is nothing. The arbitrariness, efficiency, and inevitability of his death emphasizes his impotence and unimportance in the world around him.

The horror of impotence in the face of overwhelming authority expressed traditionally through figures such as Caligari, Moreau, or the sorcerer in *The Magician* is no more and no less powerful than this fear expressed more realistically by the Inquisition-like threat of *Day of Wrath*, the computer in Sargent's *Colossus*, the feudal system in Mizoguchi's *Sansho, the Bailiff,* or the organization in *Seconds*. The fears of modern life are essentially the same as fears found throughout human history and art; if they differ it is only in form, as the threat of mass annihilation from plague differs from that of nuclear war. More realistic, more contemporary horror films can do everything the traditional horror films do, and achieve something more. They can help people deal with such fears, can help both those who make the films and those who experience them to face and, as a result, see more clearly not only the nature of the fears brought on by contemporary society but the nature of that society itself.

Names, release dates, and directors of the films mentioned in the text:
Accident, 1967, Joseph Losey. *The Bat Whispers*, 1931, Roland West. *The Beast with Five Fingers*, 1947, Robert Florey. *The Black Cat*, 1934, Edgar G. Ulmer. *The Boston Strangler*, 1967, Richard Fleischer. *The Bride of Frankenstein*, 1935, James Whale.
The Cabinet of Dr. Caligari (Kabinett Des Dr. Caligari, Das), 1920, Robert Weine. *The Cat and the Canary*, 1927, Paul Leni. *The Cat People*, 1942, Jacques Tourneur. *Colossus (The Forbin Project)*, 1970, Joseph Sargent. *Curse of the Demon (Night of the Demon)*, 1958, Jacques Tourneur.
The Damned, 1969, Luchino Visconti. *Day of Wrath*, 1943, Carl Dreyer. *Dead of Night*, 1945, Cavalcanti, Charles Crichton, Basil Deardon, and Robert Hamer. *Dr. Jekyll and Mr. Hyde*, 1932, Rouben Mamoulian. *Dracula*, 1931, Tod Browning.
El, 1952, Luis Buñuel. *Faust*, 1926, F. W. Murnau. *Fellini-Satyricon*, 1970, Federico Fellini. *Frankenstein*, 1931, James Whale. *Freaks*, 1932, Tod Browning. *Genuine*, 1920, Robert Weine.
The Hands of Orlac (Orlacs Haende), 1925, Robert Weine. *The Horror Chamber of Dr. Faustus (Yeux Sans Visage)*, 1960, Georges Franju. *House of Frankenstein*, 1944, Erle C. Kenton. *I Walked with a Zombie*, 1943, Jacques Tourneur. *In Cold Blood*, 1967, Richard Brooks. *Invasion of the Body Snatchers*, 1956, Donald Siegel. *The Invisible Man*, 1933, James Whale. *Island of Lost Souls*, 1933, Erle C. Kenton.
J'Accuse, 1938, Abel Gance. *Juliet of the Spirits*, 1965, Federico Fellini. *The Kremlin Letter*, 1970, John Huston. *Lifeboat*, 1943, Alfred Hitchcock. *The Lodger*, 1944, John Brahm.
Lord of the Flies, 1962, Peter Brook. *Mad Love*, 1935, Karl Freund. *The Magician*, 1926, Rex Ingram. *The Man Who Could Cheat Death*, 1959, Terrance Fisher. *The Manchurian Candidate*, 1962, John Frankenheimer. *Marnie*, 1964, Alfred Hitchcock. *The Miracle of Morgan's Creek*, 1944, Preston Sturges. *The Most Dangerous Game*, 1932, Irving Pichel and Ernst B. Schoedsack. *Mystery of the Wax Museum*, 1933, Michael Curtiz.
Nightmare Castle, 1966, Mario Bava. *North by Northwest*, 1959, Alfred Hitchcock. *Nosferatu, Eine Symphonie Des Grauens*, 1922, F. W. Murnau. *The Phantom of the Opera*, 1925, Rupert Julian. *Planet of the Apes*, 1968, Franklin Schaffner. *Psycho*, 1960, Alfred Hitchcock.
Repulsion, 1965, Roman Polanski. *Sansho the Bailiff (Sansho Dayu)*, 1954, Kenji Mizoguchi. *Seconds*, 1966, John Frankenheimer. *The Servant*, 1964, Joseph Losey. *Shame*, 1968, Ingmar Bergman. *The Silence*, 1963, Ingmar Bergman. *Sullivan's Travels*, 1941, Preston Sturges.
The Thirty-Nine Steps, 1935, Alfred Hitchcock. *The Trial*, 1963, Orson Welles. *Unfaithfully Yours*, 1947, Preston Sturges. *Vampyr*, 1932, Carl Dreyer. *Vertigo*, 1958, Alfred Hitchcock. *Viridiana*, 1961, Luis Buñuel. *A Walk with Love and Death*, 1969, John Huston. *The War Game*, 1967, Peter Watkins.

1971

Some Structural Approaches to Cinema: A Survey of Models

David A. Cook

1

The theory of an art form usually evolves at some distance from its inception, and this has surely been the case with cinema. As Roland Barthes has recently put it, "Born technologically, sometimes even esthetically, the film is yet to be born theoretically."[1] But today this latter birth is not long in coming. The small arena where the proponents of Eisensteinian montage once did battle with those of Bazinian composition in depth has enlarged within the last decade to include other forces—the vidistic analysis of Sol Worth and Calvin Pryluck in the United States, the auteur-structuralism of Peter Wollen and his colleagues at the British Society for Education in Film and Television, and the cinesemiotics of Christian Metz, Umberto Eco, and Pier Paolo Pasolini on the continent.

All these new theoretical approaches represent in some measure the application of Saussurian linguistic analysis to the syntactical structure of film. While none has to date achieved the systematic comprehension of filmic structure toward which they strive, all have been suggestive of radically broader theoretical horizons for the cinema than had been dreamt of in the first seventy years of the medium's existence. The ultimate purpose of this study is to examine the impact of these emergent linguistic and structural methodologies on the still embryonic domain of film theory. But first, as always, we must begin in the past.

To paraphrase Frederic Jameson's recent comment on human thought,[2] the history of cinema is the history of its models. Nothing comes into being without precedent and nothing can be practiced without a paradigm. The models for the practice of cinema should therefore be closely observed. From the beginning there have been two distinctive tendencies in cinema—the documentary or naturalistic, historically represented by the films of Lumières *fréres*, and the fictive or expressive, represented by the films of Georges Méliès. The formal model for the first was the reality continuum

---

[1] Roland Barthes, "The Third Meaning," trans. Richard Howard, *Artforum*, 11 (January, 1973), p. 50.

[2] Frederic Jameson, *The Prison-House of Language: A Critical Account of Structuralism and Russian Formalism* (Princeton: Princeton University Press, 1972), p. v: "The history of thought is the history of its models."

itself; for the second, the telescoped reality continuum of the legitimate stage.

For the Lumières, who were businessmen and inventors, cinema, like photography, was the act of choosing a meaningful or entertaining subject like *L'Arrivé d'un train en gare* (1895) and then recording it in the most precise, invariable, and unqualified manner. Their camera was an inert machine whose sole function was to reproduce whatever lay before it, and their films were *actualités*—unmediated glimpses of empirical reality reduced by a single dimension. For Méliès, the magician and illusionist, cinema was the arrangement of dramatic scenes linearly on a filmstrip, and his films—quintessentially *Le Voyage dans la Lune* (1902)—are fantastic narratives which proceed in the manner of nineteenth-century plays. The camera is stationary, like a theater-goer in his seat; the actors move across the "proscenium" of the image frame from left to right and right to left, never backward or forward; and no action or sequence of actions is terminated in the film before it normally would be on the stage. In its infancy, then, the cinema was dominated and to some extent retarded by the notion that film must be made to obey the conventions of other and quite dissimilar media—i.e., empirical reality as found and as represented on the stage.

But, whereas the raw material of what I have called the documentary tendency was always some unmitigated reality which the cinema subserved by recording, the raw material of the fictive tendency was the filmstrip itself which, it was later determined, could be manipulated and ordered according to whatever conventions or paradigms its practitioners could discover, whether theatrical, novelistic, or indeed linguistic. The history of the opposition between these two contradictory impulses—on the one hand, to reproduce reality mechanically (thus infallibly), and on the other, to *create* it aesthetically—is the history of the cinema and the history of its theory, such as it stands. The great debate which has raged for the past two decades between the adherents of Bazin's "ontological realism" and those of Eisenstein's montage theory has this opposition squarely at its center.

Historically and intellectually, Eisenstein precedes Bazin in his realization that the truly cinematic lies in some combination of the documentary and the expressive. With several of his colleagues at the State Film School in Moscow, and especially Lev Kuleshov, Eisenstein grasped the semiological paradox which resides in the dual nature of the cinematic sign —that it signifies both its own object and the relationship of the object to all others within a given sequence. This was the burden of Kuleshov's famous experiment in editing reported by Pudovkin in which shots of a completely neutral face were intercut with shots of various highly motivated objects (a dead woman in a coffin, a child playing with a teddy bear, a bowl of soup). When the filmstrips were shown to randomly selected audiences, the response was invariably that the face had accurately portrayed the emotion appropriate to the intercut object. Kuleshov concluded from these results that the shot or cinematic sign has two values, that which it possesses in itself as a photographic image and that which it acquires through its relationship with the other shots around it.[3]

Kuleshov and Eisenstein by identifying both elements of the cinematic sign theoretically promised their fusion. In his own silent films, Eisenstein literally attempted to synthesize the documentary and the expressive by fictionalizing historical events and filming them in a highly stylized manner which nevertheless offered the illusion of a documentary surface. In his theoretical writings, however, no matter how variously elaborated or refined, Eisenstein finally returned to the second principle of the shot demonstrated by Kuleshov and practiced in rudimentary form by Méliès—that meaning in cinema is a function of the filmstrip and arises from the linear arrangement of its parts. Ultimately for Eisenstein, cinematic "speech" was what occurred in the interstices between frames when they collided. As his theoretical writings proliferated, the content of these frames became increasingly important to him, but his basic assumption about the nature of cinematic signification remained unchanged.[4]

André Bazin represents the other side of the semiological coin. He puts all his faith in the cinematic sign as a photographic representation of reality because, as he writes in "The Ontology of the Photographic Image":

> The photographic image is the object itself, the object freed from the conditions of time and space that govern it. No matter how fuzzy, distorted, or discolored, no matter how lacking in documentary value the image may be,

---

[3] Forty years later the French structuralists, after de Saussure and Lévi-Strauss, would insist that the meaning of all individual elements in any given structure—social, psychological, linguistic—arises out of *and only out of* the relations of the elements to one another and their mutual interdependence (Michael Lane, *Introduction to Structuralism* [New York: Basic Books, 1970], p. 35). As Ronald Levaco has recently remarked in the pages of *Screen* (Winter, 1971/72), Kuleshov was our first legitimate film semiologist. Under the influence of Russian Formalism (like structuralism, a lineal descendant of Saussurian linguistics), especially the influence of literary theorist and poet Viktor Shklovsky, Kuleshov sought to create "a taxonomy of cinematic expression" (p. 107) through a wide-ranging series of experiments and theoretical writings.

[4] Eisenstein's late obsessions with symbolism, synaesthesia, and "monistic ensemble" so excellently discussed by Peter Wollen (*Signs and Meaning in the Cinema* [Bloomington: Indiana University Press, 1969], pp. 57-65) do, of course, represent a gradual turning away from the dialectic toward the organic. Furthermore, Eisenstein's exclusive affirmation of relationality was always more theoretical than practical. One has merely to glance at a few stills from any of his films, early or late, to see how fully he appreciated the compositional and photographic value of the individual frame. His protégés, however, went much farther toward denying the representational value of the cinematic sign than Eisenstein himself. Slavko Vorkapich's comment is typical: "[Film] is a problem of composing visually, but in time. Individual shots may be incomplete, as individual musical tones are incomplete in themselves, but they must be 'Just right and go well together' with other shots, as tones must with other tones, to make complete and esthetically satisfying units. Beautiful photography is only surface embellishment, while *cinematography* is the gathering of visual-dynamic-meaningful elements, which creative cutting combines into living entities" ("Toward True Cinema," *Film: A Montage of Theories*, ed. Richard Dyer MacCann [New York: Dutton, 1966], p. 176).

it shares, by virtue of the very process of its becoming, the being of the model of which it is the reproduction; it *is* the model.[5]

Bazin is so taken with this aspect of the sign that he founds a theory of film history upon it. He begins by maintaining that the cinema was born out of man's ageless aspiration toward a total representation (or "re-presentation") of reality, "a recreation of the world in its own image,"[6] which suddenly became a viable proposition in the mid-nineteenth century with the invention of photography. From this point, Bazin goes on to argue that each and every technological advance made by the cinema since its inception—the addition of sound, color, deep focus, and wide-angle photography —serves to bring it closer to its original impulse, the desire to achieve an unmediated vision of reality freed from the constraints of time and space. But Bazin is trapped in the very paradox he seeks to confute. As with Eisenstein, his pursuit of one level of cinematic meaning to the exclusion of the other finally predicates and then validates the other.

Essentially, what Bazin fails to recognize is that every innovation which brings the cinema closer to complete mimesis requires increased artifice to manipulate in the filming process itself. The *event filmed* (the real object) moves farther from nature as on the screen the *filmed event* (photographic image) moves closer, because the more closely the image approximates reality in terms of sound, color, width, and depth, the more sophisticated the technical manipulation and preparation required to present it so. Thus *Citizen Kane,* Bazin's *locus classicus* of "ontological realism," with its elaborate sound montage and painstakingly articulated composition in depth, is a far more contrived film than *Potemkin;* and certainly the elephantine proportions of any film shot today in color, stereophonic sound, and cinemascope make *October* look austere by comparison.

Bazin is on safer ground when he affirms the sign's value as a representation of reality for metaphysical rather than aesthetic reasons. Composition in depth and the sequence shot (long take), both of which bring "the spectator into a relationship with the image closer to that which he enjoys with reality,"[7] are more democratic than the Soviets' analytical montage because they allow the spectator some degree of perceptual and dramatic choice within the frame. Charles Barr, one of Bazin's most original and articulate spokesmen, writes that Eisenstein's montage is essentially agit-prop (or, as Eisenstein himself called it, "agit-guignol")—a kind of political pornography which manipulates the spectator's associations while giving him the illusion of choice.[8] It compels him to participate in the film but allows him no freedom in the process. Furthermore, because a high percentage of their frames are close-ups and because the spectator has little chance

---

5 *What Is Cinema,* (Berkeley: University of California Press, 1967), p. 14.
6 "The Myth of Total Cinema," *What Is Cinema,* p. 21.
7 "The Evolution of the Language of Cinema," *What Is Cinema,* p. 35.
8 Charles Barr, "Cinemascope: Before and After," *Film Quarterly,* 16, No. 4 (1961), pp. 15-17.

to focus on the back- and middle-ground during the rapid succession of images, montage sequences have no true depth of field.

What Bazin and Barr advocate, on the other hand, is the literal *in*-volvement of the spectator through composition in width (either by lateral camera movement or a wide-screen process) and depth and the sequence shot. According to Barr, these techniques both eliminate the necessity for analytical montage, since they increase the number of objects or events which can be emphasized simultaneously without cutting, and eliminate its "danger," since objects cannot be radically divorced from their context in deep focus images. For Bazin and his followers, then—however elaborately they might state their case—cinematic meaning arises from the disposition of the reality photographed, whatever its nature, and the truly cinematic is that which least distorts its "re-presentation" on film. Siegfried Kracauer, of course, arrives at very nearly the same position from a rather different path in his *Theory of Film* (New York: Oxford University Press, 1965), arguing that the only legitimate purpose of cinema is the photographic "redemption" of the real.

Where does this leave us? For Eisenstein, the act of cinematic signification occurs on the printed filmstrip; for Bazin, the act of cinematic signification has occurred in real time and real space before the negative stock leaves the camera for the dark room. Two contradictory models, two contradictory aesthetics—total representation versus total illusion. The two most influential and respected theorists of the medium have scarcely advanced us beyond Lumière and Méliès. To make that advance requires a shift from diachronic to synchronic thinking, so that the categories understood to be mutually exclusive by Eisenstein and Bazin can be re-thought in their simultaneous co-existence with each other and with the cinematic sign. The overlapping methodologies of Saussurian linguistics, semiology, and structuralism provide a pathway for us here; and we must begin to walk on it if we are not to be stranded forever between a train arriving at a station and a trip to the moon.

2

The path begins with Ferdinand de Saussure, the Swiss linguist who is credited with having discovered the dual nature of language and founding the discipline of structural linguistics in his posthumously published *Cours de linguistique générale* (1916). Language, he wrote, "is comparable to a sheet of paper: thought is the recto and sound the verso; one cannot cut the recto without at the same time cutting the verso; and the same is true in language, one can neither isolate sound from thought nor thought from sound."[9] In the previous century, linguistics had largely been a matter of philology and semantics, but Saussure's radically new articulation focused attention upon the nature of the linguistic sign itself, which he briefly de-

---

9 Ferdinand de Saussure, *Cours de linguistique générale* (Paris: Payot, 1922, second edition), trans. by author, p. 157.

scribed as follows "The linguistic sign unites, not a thing and a name, but a concept [signified] and an acoustic image [signifier]."[10] Furthermore, the linguistic sign is competely arbitrary in that its meaning is determined by social-convention rather than by any naturally inhering relationship between signifier and signified.

Whereas the practice of historical philology had been local and contingent, taking as its object individual changes in language, Saussure insisted on the fact, as Frederic Jameson puts it, "that language as a total system is complete at every moment, no matter what happens to have been altered in it a moment before."[11] Thus, to follow Jameson a step farther, language is "a series of complete systems succeeding each other in time . . . with all the possibilities of meaning implicit in its every moment" (Jameson, p. 6). The units which comprise these systems are literally insubstantial. Instead of *substances* which can be named, classified, and described according to the methods of historical philology, language is composed of *values* and *relationships* which are, additionally, in a constant state of flux. This way of perceiving the structure of language, Saussure called the "synchronic" in contradistinction to the older, historical mode of the "diachronic" (borrowing both terms from the science of geology). According to Saussure, the relationships within a synchronic system are simultaneous, interdependent, and *entirely independent of history*.

Within the synchrony of language Saussure found a single fundamental opposition, that between the *langue* and the *parole*. The *langue* is "the ensemble of linguistic possibilities or potentialities at any given moment," i.e., the language as institution, whereas the *parole* is "the individual and partial actualization of some of those potentialities," i.e., the individual act of speech (Jameson, p. 22). Saussure conceived of the relationship between these elements in terms of a "circuit of discourse," or a relationship between two speakers. As Frederic Jameson explains, Saussure "separates the *parole* of the speaker from the *langue* of the person who understands him, for whom *parole* is the active, *langue* the passive dimension of speech, for whom indeed . . . *langue* is not so much the power to speak as it is the power to understand speech" (Jameson, p. 26). In the end, however, only the study of the *langue* is scientifically feasible. Study of the *parole* is always complicated by the presence of "local accent, mispronunciation, personal style," but study of the *langue* is objective and concrete: it can be investigated by "testing the limits and forms of any native speaker's understanding," according to the model established by the circuit of discourse. Finally, to study these phenomena, Saussure proposed a general science of "semiology" (from the Greek *semeion*, "sign") which would have as its ob-

---

10 Ibid., p. 98.
11 Frederic Jameson, *The Prison-House of Language* (Princeton: Princeton University Press, 1972), pp. 5-6. Hereafter cited parenthetically. I am indebted to this excellent study for much of my information on Saussurian linguistics. It is an essential text for anyone wishing to undertake semiological or structural analysis of film.

ject "the life of signs within society" and of which linguistics would be a single, if important, branch.[12]

At this point, it is possible to apply the Saussurian model to cinema. It seems likely that a true semiology of film will be a semiology of the cinematic *langue*[13] and that the cinematic *parole*, the individual filmic utterance and its nature, will remain the province of evaluative critics and aestheticians. If we cannot arrive at a semiology of the films of Welles or Renoir or Eisenstein or Méliès, we may be able to arrive at a semiology of film, for we are dealing with the general nature of the cinematic sign and the system of signification within which it has its activity. We must not be concerned with semantic analysis, for this would require a continual movement outside the sign system toward the thing symbolized. Finally, we should have no recourse to those other sign systems with which cinema is so frequently and disastrously confused—especially literature and theater—because they have semiological structures radically opposed to that of film. Like music, film can communicate only in the continuous present of performance, and so its system of signification is necessarily synchronic. Indeed, the experience of cinematic speech, like the experience of language, is wholly insubstantial. The fleeting and quite literally illusory images which are cinematic signs appear and vanish before our eyes like objects in a dream. They are ephemeral and evanescent, forever emerging, forever dissolving away; and they finally cannot signify as *cinematic* signs independently of their relationship with all the other signs in the localized system which is a particular film.

The principle of relationality adumbrated here is perhaps Saussure's most important. As Jameson articulates it, the principle states that

> it is not so much the individual word or sentence that "stands for" or "reflects" the individual object or event in the real word, but rather that the entire system of signs, the entire field of the *langue*, lies parallel to reality itself; that it is the totality of systematic language, in other words, which is analogous to whatever organized structures exist in the world of reality, and that our understanding proceeds from one whole or Gestalt to the other, rather than on a one-to-one basis (pp. 32-33).

Similarly, it may be true that individual cinematic signs (photographic images) or sign sequences (montages) do not finally signify because they "stand for" or "reflect" some object or event in the real world through me-

---

12 Saussure, quoted from *Signs and Meaning in the Cinema,* p. 116.

13 Christian Metz's contention that cinema is a *"langage sans langue"* is well met by this comment of Geoffrey Nowell-Smith in "Cinema and Structuralism" (*Twentieth Century Studies,* No. 3, May 1970): "If . . . one replaces the articulation *langue/parole* with one that we can call *écriture/légende,* where the *légende* (thing to be read) represents the individual written text and the *écriture* (writing) represents the general system of rules for cinematic expression, then many of the problems raised by the apparent non-existence of *la langue* disappear" (p. 138).

chanically reproductive means. They may signify, rather, because the whole system of cinematic signs—the cinematic *langue*—is analogous to the organized structures of reality itself, including the structure of the human psyche. Thus, cinematically as linguistically, our understanding would proceed not on a one-to-one basis from one signifier-signified relationship to another but rather from one whole to the other. It is quite possible, then, that we understand cinematic speech and can infer its structure because it is analogous to the other basic structures through which all our perceptions, thoughts, and experiences are mediated.

With this statement we arrive at one of the major premises of structuralist thought as it has proceeded from Saussure to Lévi-Strauss, Chomsky, and Piaget—namely, to quote from Michael Lane, "there is in man an innate, genetically transmitted and determined mechanism that acts as a structuring force," which, moreover, is "so designed as to limit the possible range of ways of structuring."[14] Adopting the Saussurian linguistic model, structuralism regards all patterns of human social behavior, including the "human sciences," as codes with the fundamental characteristics of language; and the search for the "deep" structure of these codes (to borrow Chomsky's term) and the laws which govern them is the primary impulse of the method. In a very real sense, the ultimate goal of structuralism is to discover the deep structure of all conscious and unconscious human thought.

The most influential exponent of modern structuralism (and, after Saussure, its founder) is the French anthropologist Claude Lévi-Strauss, whose analyses of South American Indian myths between 1955 and the present have been credited with establishing the structuralist methodology. Lévi-Strauss begins with the assumption that all social life is systematically structured and that social structures are the product of a genetically determined reason (or *esprit*) accessible to us "only through the systems that it forms" (Lane, p. 31)—whether they be mythic, familial, linguistic, aesthetic, or cultural. Since these structures are innate and unconscious, the members of a society are not aware of them, but only of their concrete manifestations[15] (just as the native speaker of a language requires no knowledge of its structure in order to speak it). Chief among these concrete manifestations are a society's myths, which Lévi-Strauss sees as a means of dealing symbolically with unresolved problems submerged in its own deep structure which are otherwise inaccessible. Mythical thought, or *pensée sauvage*, then, is a kind of "primitive philosophizing which is not yet aware of itself" (Jameson, p. 119).

Charles W. Eckert puts this nicely in a recent article in *Film Comment* when he writes that for Lévi-Strauss the essential nature of myth is

---

[14] Michael Lane, "Introduction to Structuralism," *Structuralism: A Reader* (London: Jonathan Cape, 1969), ed. Michael Lane, p. 15. Hereafter cited parenthetically. This is another essential text for the English reader who would come to terms with structuralism.

[15] Ibid., p. 32.

an obsessive, repetitive conceptualizing of a dilemma or contradiction, the meaning of which is hidden from the narrator [and, initially, from the structural analyst] who rather compulsively tells and retells versions of the myth. . . . If its content were not hidden from the narrators, they would have no reason to obsessively reshape it, retell it, and accord it such significance in their lives.[16]

In the same article Eckert goes on to suggest how structuralist methodology might be applied to the study of film. Among other things, he points out the essential communality of film production, the taxonomic schematization of objects within genre films, and the opacity of a given film's meaning for creators and consumers alike, and concludes that "the cinema, after sensationalist and arty beginnings, took over the communal myth-making functions of a variety of dramatic, literary and oral forms—and all but supplanted them" (p. 51). It seems to me entirely possible that films have become the central myths of modern Western culture. The German psychologist Hugo Mauerhofer, for example, has shown how the experience of filmviewing—the "cinema situation"—resembles a collective ritual trance in which "the unconscious [communicates] with the consciousness to a higher degree than in the normal state"[17]; and the art historian and film writer Lawrence Alloway has recently produced a book demonstrating that the thematic oppositions of popular American films symbolize the unarticulated dilemmas of the society at a given point in time.[18] If any or all of these findings are correct, film should prove highly susceptible to structural analysis.

One of Lévi-Strauss's major reasons for choosing myths as the objective data by which to analyze the innate structure of a particular society is that they are free from individual authorship; and the same is true for an overwhelming number of films, as even some of the most thoroughgoing *auteuristes* have been compelled to realize. Indeed, in Peter Wollen's lexicon, the term *auteur* itself has come to mean something very like "deep structure"—not a creative human intelligence but a configuration of themes, motifs, and gestures which recur throughout the corpus of a given director's work. As Wollen puts it, "What the *auteur* theory does is to take a group of films—the work of a single director—and analyze their structure" (*Signs and Meaning*, p. 104). Thus, ironically, far from exalting the act of individual creation in cinema, auteurism has begun to posit the withering

---

16 Charles W. Eckert, "The English Cine-Structuralists," *Film Comment*, 9, No. 3 (May-June, 1973), p. 49. Hereafter cited parenthetically.

17 Hugo Mauerhofer, "Psychology of Film Experience," in *Film: A Montage of Theories*, pp. 229-235. Harvard physiologist Andrew Weil has also recently argued that the experience of film-watching constitutes a mild state of trance not unlike that experienced under the influence of hypnosis and such drugs as marijuana (*The Natural Mind: A New Way of Looking at Drugs and the Higher Consciousness* [Boston: Houghton Mifflin, 1972]).

18 Lawrence Alloway, *Violent America: The Movies 1946-1964* (New York: The Museum of Modern Art, 1971).

away of the personal auteur and his replacement with a structural model hypostatized from his films. This procedure is as semiologically precise as it is anti-humanistic (all the methodologies discussed here, of course, are profoundly so in their assumptions, if not in their results) because, again, it seems that the sole province of cinesemiotics must be the cinematic *langue* and not the *parole* of individual directors. This is why auteur-structuralists like Wollen and Alloway ultimately prefer to deal with the popular genre film, for the more rigidly conventionalized and programmatic a film, the less the opportunity for personal stylistic mediation by the film maker (*parole*), and thus the more closely will the organization or semiological system of the film approximate the *langue* by which the mass audience codes it.[19]

But if the notion of communal origin is valuable to a comprehension of the cinematic *langue*, another important principle of Lévi-Strauss gives difficulty when applied to film. This is the idea that all the relationships within a structure are ultimately reducible to a series of binary oppositions. As Michael Lane writes:

> The structuralist method . . . is a means whereby social reality may be expressed as binary oppositions, each element, whether it be an event in a myth, an item of behaviour or the naming and classification of natural phenomena, being given its value in society by its relative position in a matrix of oppositions, their mediations and resolutions (p. 32).

On a technical level, the principle of binary opposition is extremely close to Eisenstein's view of montage as a successive collision of opposites which drives a film forward like the explosions in an internal combustion engine. In fact, montage theory, Saussurian linguistics, and structuralism are all intimately related by way of Russian Formalism.

At the level of theme, however, the search for binary oppositions within a specific film or set of films can be astonishingly unrevealing (as I believe Peter Wollen's analysis of Hawks and Ford in *Signs and Meaning* has demonstrated)[20] since it reduces very complex thematic statements to what Sam Rhodie has called "computer-like binary systems."[21] Yet, as Geoffrey Nowell-Smith points out, this is not the fault of structuralism as such "but of the particular structural grid being applied."[22] Indeed, we should be prepared to consider the possibility that no single model or paradigm can

---

19 Wollen and Alloway would probably not agree with this blanket description of their much varied activities, but I believe it to be an accurate statement of their procedure.

20 This is not to fault Wollen's *critical* perceptions, which are generally quite brilliant. It is rather to suggest that the search for binary thematic structuration is in itself not particularly illuminating of either film or director.

21 Sam Rhodie, "Signs and Meaning in the Cinema," *New Left Review*, 55 (May-June, 1969), p. 69.

22 Geoffrey Nowell-Smith, "Cinema and Structuralism," *Twentieth Century Studies*, No. 3 (May, 1970), p. 134.

ever fully comprehend a medium of communication as complex, an art form as rich, as cinema. And in appropriating the new methodologies of semiology and structuralism, we should beware of the snares of dogmatism and mutual exclusivity associated with the older theoretical approaches discussed in Part I. There is no reason why we should not take the most valuable aspects of each and use them to form multiple analytic perspectives, just as there is no reason why we should force a choice between Lumière and Méliès, Eisenstein and Bazin. In fact, if we do not adopt multiple perspectives on the cinema, *if we do not approach it synchronically,* we shall end in the sectarian fanaticism which has all but engulfed literary studies in the United States today.

3

The final linguistically oriented approach to cinema examined here comes to us by way of communications and information theory. Its chief proponent is Sol Worth of the Annenberg School of Communications, University of Pennsylvania, who for the past decade has been working toward the construction of a semiotics of film on strictly empirical grounds.[23] Worth calls his study of cinematic speech "vidistics" and states its twin goals to be 1) "the determination and codification of visual 'language' elements as used in sequence by the film-maker," and 2) "the determination of [the] laws of 'language' by which a viewer infers meaning from cognitive representations and interactions of the elements and their sequence."[24] He finds five parameters along which the structural elements of cinematic speech can be defined: an *image* in *motion* / over *time* in *space* with *sequence.* As in Eisenstein, the basic image unit is the shot, or *videme,* which Worth defines as "any photographic image event that . . . is accepted by viewers as something that represents the world" (p. 133). There are two varieties of videme: the *cademe,* or camera shot, which depicts one continuous photographic image event from one frame to infinity; and the *edeme,* or editing shot, which is formed by cutting a cademe apart and eliminating the unwanted or unusable segments. This latter is the basic element of film language, from which all coding and decoding begins.

The other parameters are defined by Worth as follows. *Motion* is either internal (movement of objects *within* the frame) or external (movement of the frame itself through camera movement or zooming). *Space* is determined by the size and position of objects in relation to the spatial bounds of the frame, while *time* is either internal and real as a function of the videme, or external and illusory as a function of the sequencing of edemes (mon-

---

23 Calvin Pryluck has also been working on the scientific analysis of filmic communication as a symbol system. His most important articles are "Toward a Psycholinguistics of Cinema" (with Richard E. Snow), *A-V Communications Review,* 15, No. 1 (Spring, 1967), and "Structural Analysis of Motion Pictures as a Symbol System," *A-V Communications Review,* 16, No. 4 (Winter, 1968).

24 Sol Worth, "Cognitive Aspects of Sequence in Visual Communication," *A-V Communications Review,* 16, No. 2 (Summer, 1968), pp. 132-133.

tage). *Sequence* is defined as "a deliberately employed series used for the purpose of giving *meaning rather than order* to more than one image event and having the property of conveying *meaning through* the sequence itself as well as through the elements in the sequence" (p. 138). Cinematic signification, then, is a function of the sequencing of edemes, and it seems that we have not come far from Eisenstein after all. In fact, Worth regards montage theory as "a special theory of cognitive interaction" and has conducted experiments in editing similar to Kuleshov's.

It is in the linguistic application that Worth differs from his predecessors. Seeking to answer the question, is there "anything in [a sequence of image events] . . . that allows or helps a viewer to infer meaning from them, *regardless* of the semantic content attached to each of the elements by itself" (p. 137), Worth borrows the first premise of structural linguistic analysis as articulated by Noam Chomsky in his *Syntactic Structures* (The Hague: Mouton, 1965):

> The fundamental aim in the linguistic analysis of a language L is to separate the *grammatical* sequences which are the sentences of L from the *ungrammatical* sequences which are not sentences of L and to study the structure of the grammatical sequences. The grammar of L will thus be a device that generates all of the grammatical sequences (p. 13).

The only way to test the adequacy of the grammar proposed for L, according to Chomsky, is "to determine whether or not the sequences that it generates are actually grammatical, i.e., *acceptable to a native speaker*" (Chomsky, p. 13, my italics). In other words, to discover the grammar of a language is first to discover its *anti*-grammar, i.e., those sequences which regularly refuse to mean, as verified by a native speaker[25]; and Worth proposes this very procedure for the analysis of cinematic speech. If, through a series of controlled experiments, we could discover the anti-grammar of the cinema—i.e., the types of sequences, tropes, and arrangements of edemes *which render semantic inference impossible* for an audience of experienced film-goers—we could then construct the grammar of the cinema which would "generate" the rules governing all cinematic speech. In other words, if we could discover the ungrammatical parameters of the cinema through empirical means, we could begin to construct its grammar by analogy and inverse corollary. (We might, of course, only discover a set of conventions, as Christian Metz and others have recently suggested.) Worth has already begun to gather such data and has apparently succeeded in generating several "laws" of cinematic speech,[26] but his ultimate goal, like Chomsky's, is much more profound.

---

[25] As previously mentioned, the native speaker—unless he is the analyst himself—will not normally be aware of the grammar, or structure, of his speech; and yet, as in Lévi-Strauss's analysis of myth, the speaker's *speaking* is the only empirical proof that a grammar or structure exists at all.

[26] For example, through a series of experiments conducted at the Annenberg School of Communications, Worth has discovered that in the absence of semantic content

One of Chomsky's chief contributions to the field of structural linguistics has been the notion that the native speaker's sense of grammar is genetically inherited rather than culturally acquired, and, further, that this faculty of "innate grammaticality" is one of the deep structures of human thought. Worth similarly believes that the very nearly universal *apprehension* of the structure of film language (as opposed to *comprehension,* because structures are innate and unconscious to those who participate in them) may depend upon "a deep structure of innate responses in the brain, governing our coding habits for film and being responsible for the grammar of film."[27]

The results of Worth's widely known experiment (conducted with the anthropologist John Adair and discussed at length in the authors' *Through Navajo Eyes* [Bloomington: Indiana University Press, 1972]), in which six bilingual Navajo Indians who had never seen a film were taught to photograph and edit in 16mm silent film, argues strongly for an innate, cross-cultural capacity for cinematic perception within the human psyche. The Navajo film makers—who were given no instruction whatever in cinematic conventions, only in cinematic technology—grasped the notion of sequence implicitly, and their "grammatical errors," like the errors of children learning to speak, were the result of having intuited the "rules" of structure but not their exceptions (exceptions, of course, are "learned" or culturally acquired). That is, wherever their films appeared "ungrammatical" to the analysts, it was determined that the Navajos had actually substituted "grammatical" structures for exceptions which they hadn't yet learned. This finding may lead us toward an understanding of how and why film communicates across cultural boundaries to broad portions of the human race. It might also aid toward the discovery through empirical means of what I have called film's anti-grammar, those points at which for a large number of "native speakers" cinematic meaning breaks down.

4

The semiological and structuralist approaches to the cinema examined in this essay are ultimately concerned to comprehend film as a process of cognition and communication, not as an art form. Or, more broadly, they are not concerned with art itself but with why there can be art. Cinema is a unique nonverbal language which necessarily fragments reality (as even Bazin admits) and confutes familiar modes of apprehension and yet one which, almost from the outset, has been understood by vast numbers of people wholly unprepared in a practical sense to receive it. How and why do cinematic signs acquire meaning? How and why are mass audiences all

---

"*sequence will be more critical in determining the meaning in pairs of highly similar elements than in pairs of dissimilar elements*" (*op. cit.,* p. 141). If this is true, it has far-reaching implications for Eisenstein's "dialectical" montage.

27 Sol Worth, "The Development of a Semiotic of Film," *Semiotica,* 1, No. 3 (1969), p. 317.

over the world able to "read" them? Until recently, we have never really tried to answer these questions—questions which must, after all, be prior to all considerations of aesthetics. Certain evaluative critics argue that we already know *too much* about the mechanism of cinema and not nearly enough about what constitutes good cinema. But before we can establish what is cinematically "good" in a classical sense, we must first establish what is "cinematic," and this almost fifty years of film theory have failed to do. Unless we are prepared to accept the proposition that film is a phenomenon which can be experienced but not understood, we will have to strike out on new theoretical paths or, at the very least, render the old ones more accessible and complete.

I am the first to admit that the methodologies examined here are profoundly anti-humanistic in their assumptions: French structuralist Michel Foucault, for example, boldly proclaims the "Disappearance of Man" from a universe whose systems of exchange can get along without him (*The Order of Things*, Tavistock, 1970). But perhaps an overload of humanism is precisely what has kept us from coming to terms with the filmic process thus far. We have tried to make of cinema, by turns, theater, novel, music, a written language, a graphic art, reality itself—everything, in fact, but what it *is* before it can be anything else: a visual language based on perceptual and cognitive illusions created by machines and, to confuse matters further, a language whose signs are simultaneously referential and reflexive. If semiology, structuralism, and vidistics can help us comprehend this quintessentially modern paradox of a mechanized art form which always means on two levels at once, then we had better let them. We live in a world in which the language of film has become more familiar, but much less understood, than the terms of human speech. It is possible, even likely, that media reality has become more persuasively real for large portions of the human race than reality itself. As humanists—and I believe that the vast majority of people working in film studies today can lay claim to this title —we may wish things were otherwise, but we cannot fail to acknowledge the pervasiveness and importance of the phenomenon. If we persist in our ignorance of the process of cinematic signification by retreating into the ivory tower of aesthetics, film will soon find itself in the situation of literature—a situation in which a handful of elite specialists dictates the orthodox canon for the benefit of other elite specialists while humanity at large grows increasingly ignorant of the operations of its native speech.

1975

The Showgirl and the Wolf

Jane Gaines

Off duty, Tyrone Power, an American pilot enlisted in the British RAF, commandeers a reserved table up front and close to the show at the Regency House, all the better to "get a load of" Betty Grable's singing and dancing. The classic construction of the sequence that follows in *Yank in the R.A.F.* (Twentieth Century-Fox, 1941) is an alternation of shots of Grable in the show with shots of male onlookers either applauding or otherwise indicating "enjoyment" by nodding or smiling. The four reaction shots of Power within the sequence catch him: a) fixing his tie as he looks; b) moving his eyes up and down as though "taking her in," all the while chewing gum; c) sighing heavily and waving at her while she waves at the audience in the song "Hi Ya Love"; and d) applauding loudly long after the audience has stopped. This is the scene in which Power exhibits the most active enthusiasm in response to Grable, otherwise two-timing her, standing her up, and bungling their engagement. Her show is also the vehicle for sharing her with two openly admiring, avidly pursuing, RAF officers in Power's flight squadron. *Yank in the R.A.F.* contains two Regency House night club spectacles featuring Grable, nuggets which were expanded into her seven Technicolor song and dance hits made during World War II.

As the spectacle of the showgirl and the active spectator seems to be the central convention on which these pictures were based, I am interested in beginning the larger project of connecting the features to the war effort with an itemization of the conventionalized cultural units and an examination of the way they are cinematically arranged in the spectacle within the film. The persistent popularity of the spectator-views-showgirl indicates wide-spread agreement between movie-going public and filmmaking personnel as to how she should play to her all-male audience. This cultural agreement is the basis of the theory of codes I will use. I am considering the collaboration between representation and a special public which was required to produce female forms that lubricated historical imperatives. Specifically, how did the "wolf" spectator and the girl playing to him expediently serve the version of the attraction of male to female held in the U.S. Armed Forces during World War II?

In the position of advertising features by satirically shredding them up, the theatrical cartoon in the anarchic "Tex Avery School" tradition pokes at ideas that are hidden in the "life-like" folds of the feature. The cartoon promises to yield much to semiological analysis because, first of all, the iconography doesn't have to be "separated out" from the photographic layer of signification.[1] Secondly, cartoon comedy uses the motivated sign. ("Springing body" is signified by a cartoon character's body metamorphosed into a literal spring, a typical Wyle E. Coyote gag.) This is why systematic meanings peel off the images so easily, the simple indication of which is humorous meaning. One of Avery's trademarks is his play with the resemblance of sign to referent. If it's "raining cats and dogs," animals drop out of the sky. Similarly, the Hollywood "wolf-about-town" is a virtual animal in a tuxedo. Among the animators who were the original "Termite Terrace" unit at Warner Brothers, there has also developed a distinct style of play with cinematic forms which has been described as a kind of self-reflexivity.[2] Their cartoons imitate and exaggerate live-action formal and generic conventions and relentlessly repeat, variegate, cross-pollinate and inbreed the same signs. This is the exegesis of the wolf-"goes ape"-over-showgirl situation which Avery began with *Little Red Riding Hood* made at Warner Brothers in 1937. He returned to the wolf and the showgirl after moving to MGM in 1942, using them in six cartoons, ending with *Little Rural Red Riding Hood* in 1949.[3] Because these cartoons are so highly formulized, the structure of an underlying semantic system protrudes enough to glimpse how it may be working.

Cartoon situations and iconography are based on the most universally known, highly conventionalized and overworked material and as such function as what Roland Barthes calls mythic speech. Caricature as much as symbol has a special susceptibility to mythic signification. "Myth," he says, "prefers to work with poor, incomplete images, where the meaning is already relieved of its fat, and ready for signification. . . ."[4] Thus it is possible for the highly-charged publicity image of Jane Russell's breasts, censored in *The Outlaw*, to be represented so expressively by two dots within two circles written in the sky above San Francisco. So the sketchiness of the showgirl cartoon body is only the tip of the iceberg of cultural information and depends on myth to "fill it out," semiotically speaking. What audiences in 1942 were well-versed in visually was the décolletage of the chorus girl's costume, Mata Hari's heavy-lidded eyes, Betty Grable's flawless legs and poodle dog bangs and the new Technicolor vision of the fiery redhead. Avery's showgirl is a composite of essential popular elements, useful to us because with its obvious references it indicates that a representation is separable into iconographic parts (which will be dealt with later as signs). This makes it possible to argue that cultural icons are constructed to stand for a particular version of social relations, against the idea that they correspond with "reality."

*Swing Shift
Cinderella,* Tex
Avery, 1945

To begin with, the showgirl, animated in all the Avery cartoons by Preston Blair who made the hippos dance in *Fantasia,* is always graphically the same. Although she is either the story-book Red Riding Hood, Cinderella (*Swing Shift Cinderella,* 1945), or Little Eva (*Uncle Tom's Cabaña,* 1947), she performs the same physical rotations on stage. She is a summation of the cultural opposition of license and control, the vacillation between which is sexual teasing. What is graphically thrust upward—her hair, lips, breasts, and hips—must come down. Like Betty Boop, she stands tip-toe in tiny high heels and is drawn with a disproportionately large head and two exact circles cut out at the top of her scant swimsuit. The product of mixing over-sized with the under-sized as seen in both Betty Boop and Red Hot Riding Hood is the child-woman which has come to have erotic connotations.

The child-woman is so much a part of the cultural woodwork that we think of it as "just the way people are," whereas it works as a concept uniting two incompatible terms, seeming to explain an inexplicable phenomenon—how a grown woman could still be a child.[5] Richard Dyer in *The Stars* has suggested that star images perform a social function by uniting the contradictory expectations we have of women and, consequently, serving two demands. Marilyn Monroe, for example, is both sexy and innocent, which is impossible given a strict social definition of the terms. However, her image "magically" reconciles the contradiction between sexuality and innocence.[6] Other cultural hybrids, such as the "sex kitten" also help to combine innocence with sexuality. Likewise, the puerile is fused with the sexually ripe by combining fairly tale character and stripper in the red hot cartoon body.

With the cartoon showgirl, it is more possible to locate how the "innocent" connotation is actually added to the image as a graphic ingredient, whereas with an actress such as Monroe, "innocence," considered as her own natural quality, illusively evades visual analysis. "Innocence" is not signified by storybook plot alone in the *Red-Hot Riding Hood* cartoon. The corpulent graphic style of cartooning also signifies a quality of being "for children." The style is essentially derived from the Walt Disney studio method of drawing cuddly creatures which Disney animators carried over into the way they sketched the human form. Although Snow White's movements were rotoscoped, giving her form some relationship to an actual female body, she was still graphically "fattened" in the same style as Bambi and Dumbo. Red Hot Riding Hood, like Snow White, carries the "cute" connotation signified by the Disney style, marked by jointless, puffy arms and legs and based on a "rounded" skeletal structure. The connotation is further built up by association with darling little animals. Although *how* the original Warner Brothers animators "borrowed" from Walt Disney is another story, it is significant that they continued to draw their most irreverent characters à la Disney.[7] The pairing of the Snow White body with the Big Bad Wolf from *The Three Little Pigs* (1933) is a reflexive moment in the development of an American erotic aesthetic that accommodates a cultural taste for sexuality served with innocence. Artists who found the market for pornographic cartooning have also played profitably with the incongruity between cartoon form and adult subject matter.

Audience familiarity with the showgirl type explains in part why her role is sketchy and her performance repetitive in both this cartoon and in the wartime live-action features. This sketchiness is a test of the existence of a stereotype. Another way of studying the stereotype, putting aside the issue of how a type often misrepresents a social group, is as a sign that has become so widely circulated that it appears to be widely agreed upon. However, it is not so much that the offending type is agreed upon as that it is *comprehended* by culture members. Considering the stereotype as sign (in this case, /showgirl/ is the sign), it is possible to see that it has become a kind of shorthand for a popularly held version of womanhood.[8] In the same way that the gangster in the lounging robe in the movies has come to stand for a range of ideas about decadence and corruption, /showgirl/ is a kind of stand-in for a whole set of ideas about sexuality.[9] The Red Hot show-girl, seen as a synthesis of the bodies of Mae West, Rita Hayworth and Betty Grable (among others), is a version of biology as destiny for women, an offshoot of which is, for the stars, "Their bodies made them." The showgirl type stands for a social presupposition that women are decoration (to be looked at) and that the body parts that mark them as different from men determine their lot in life.

How the representation works ideologically is related to the way it has come to be incorporated into the non-verbal sign system of social types within the culture (considered as like verbal language in its systematization and adherence to rules internalized by culture members). As Pam Cook explains the star as sign in her response to Dyer's book, "Stereotypes function in language as part of a process of repetition by which ideological meaning accumulates and solidifies so that we experience it as 'natural,' unchanging and essential."[10] My interest in the showgirl caricature is the possibility it presents for grasping how signification is built over time and how in its approximation of the female form the caricature repeatedly uses the same shapes, emphasizing only selected body parts. Because it is a construction and not a replication, one cannot say of the caricature that it has the attributes of an actress who really exists outside a film. Neither can it be said of it that the camera captured the woman the way she really was. The beauty of the photographic image of woman for the uses of ideology is this: that which is thought of as "natural" (woman's place in society is determined by her body, i.e., biological reproductive function) is represented by the traces of the "natural" body of a "real" woman captured on celluloid. The pin-up photo constitutes "proof" that women are the physical opposite of men, although male and female humans are physiologically alike in more ways than they are different. The caricature signifying "woman" by means of those signs which are endemic to womankind (bare legs, round hips, breasts) signifying "sexuality" by means of /female body/ can be seen as responding directly to social suppositions. Just as caricatures of blacks feature exaggeratedly large lips, the showgirl cartoon features swivelling hips, reiterating that the explanation for the position of blacks and women is located in physiology. What is thought to be more determining and irreversible than physiology?

The showgirl and the wolf cartoons are significant here because in fooling with the convention, they hypothesized a reversal of the convention. What would happen if sexuality were not represented exclusively by the body of the woman? What if, instead, it backfired onto the body of the male spectator? In shifting the action to the spectator, the cartoon also pushes the essentially static showgirl to the point that she becomes superfluous, the extreme extension of the convention of the "show-stopper."[11] With the situation reversed as it is here, with the action centered on the wolf in the audience, the "show" becomes the sexual arousal in response to the showgirl. The basic situation, "milked" over and over in the six Avery cartoons, follows this formula: The wolf has the first couple of minutes to establish that he is a lecher. Then the showgirl gets the spotlight and does her minimal dance and song. (In two of the cartoons, she sings, "Oh, Wolfy, Oh, Wolfy.") The sight of her electrifies the wolf's body—turns it into a mechanism "gone haywire." This is the real attraction of the cartoon. In the first, *Red-Hot Riding Hood*, the sight gags include a machine that whistles, claps and stomps, wolf's body stiffening up horizontally like an arrow, and wolf clobbering himself on the head with a mallet. Always thwarted in every cartoon, he never "gets the girl."

In the context of moviegoing, the cartoon works as a primer somewhat like the "lurid" poster outside the theatre, only more so. If it contains savage, ruthless graphics, it is a preview of the action which isn't expected until two-thirds of the way into the big picture. Avery's wolf and the showgirl is a distillation of the static moment: nevertheless the big scene (the spectacle) when the audience gets its first look at "the girl." By convention, the protagonist also sees "the girl" first within the context of the spectacle where she is the center of visual attraction for other men. The narrative development then concerns how to get her out of the limelight and either possess her for herself or keep her from performing for her own stage career or for a rival. (This is the plot of Betty Grable's *Coney Island*, 1943.) The cartoon defines the terms of male versus female, stripped of romantic interlude or complicating, diverting enigma.

Further considered as popular entertainment during World War II, the wolf and the showgirl repeat both the way things are in society and the "way it's gotta be" in the Army. Theatrical cartoons were as much a part of the war campaign as training films. Every month, features and shorts, along with 4 million books and 10 million magazines, were shipped to the front by Special Services Division of the Armed Forces.[12] From 1942 to 1944, 30,000 short subjects and 25,000 features and newsreels were made available to the government for shipping overseas, compliments of the Hollywood studios.[13] Special Services provided 16 mm projectors and audio-visual mechanics so the boys could have Saturday night movies like back home.[14] In the Navy when they were safe in port, movies were projected outside up on deck after dark. Under way, they were projected below deck.

The troops in active duty were the audience for whom Avery and his team at MGM were making pictures in 1942. During the time he made *Red-Hot Riding Hood* he was also drawing training films for the U.S. Army Air Corps. They created Bertie the Bomber, a plane with eyelashes and red lips and who dragged her bottom to demonstrate the danger of overloading the fuselage.[15] It was a sergeant helping them on the Army training films who singled out *Red-Hot Riding Hood* at a screening for the producer. This led to a wholesale order of prints for Armed Forces use. Avery tells the story of the Colonel who wanted to be sure the Army was sent an uncensored version:

> We had it rather rough on the reaction of the wolf, you know, steam coming out from under his collar and getting too worked up, so we had to trim and juggle and cut back. It got back to Washington to some Colonel or whatnot that the censor had cut out quite a bit on us. Finally, Louis B. Mayer got a telegram from the Colonel saying that he wanted an uncut version of a *Red-Hot Riding Hood* cartoon for his personnel overseas. The studio dug around and I don't know how many prints they gave him but, man, it went over great overseas.[16]

The wolf stiffening up at the sight of the girl served the ideological purposes of the Army in wartime. First of all, it was essential for morale that men be assured of their virility. Remember that it is a basic cultural premise that aggressiveness, the mark of a fighter, corresponds with a "healthy" taste for the *opposite* sex. The Army was well aware of the danger of sexual identity crises to their ranks. The massive psychological study of the World War II soldier anticipated and found a connection between enlisted men going AWOL and fear of latent homosexuality.[17] In one way, the wolf and the showgirl spectacle flattered males with an appetite for women, celebrating the theory of the magnetic, irrepressible attraction of opposites. In another way, simultaneously, it snatched the pleasure out of the soldiers' mouths, undercutting the ritual by breaking down and toying with the sacred components: looking, arousal, aggression.

First, I will deal with the cartoon spectacle pared to its basic connotative components—looking, arousal, then aggression—returning later to its subversive potential. The popular use of "voyeurism" in American speech indicates there is probably a corresponding wide-ranging belief that "looking" is somehow connected with "sexual arousal." Since the late 1930's psychoanalytic terms have been in common use.[18] Separated from science, they are now part of popular knowledge. Although the popular usage of "voyeurism" (along with "inferiority complex," "fetish," "fixation," and "inhibition" among others) has lost its connection with the psychoanalytic theory behind it, it still retains the connotation "scientific." The "scientific" connotation is significant because it places sexual looking in the ideological category of those things in life that are just the way they are. I am dealing here with Freud only as a set of social meanings which have become cemented into both verbal language and cultural iconography, although the extensive integration of psychoanalytic concepts into daily speech suggests that these concepts are now in a position to anticipate and form behavior as well as describe it. It would not be possible for the showgirl and the wolf caricature to use the signs signifying "sexuality" so effectively if it were not for the audience's social knowledge of Freud. In *The Shooting of Dan McGoo* (1945), the wolf's disembodied eyes, at first sight of the girl, burn holes in the menu, then whip up to her on stage and rove over her body. In *Wild and Wolfy* (1945) they turn into pool balls and bounce off the table, and in *Swing Shift Cinderella* (1945) they pop out on springs. One look at the "babe's" picture and the rural wolf's eyes swell to the size of pontoons (*Little Rural Red Riding Hood*, 1949). From the usage of /eyes/ here, it would seem to a culture member who would be familiar with the characterization of male sex organs as swelling, springing, dropping, burning and stiffening that /eyes/ equal sex organs in the cartoons. /Eyes/ are relatively unmotivated signs signifying "male sexual arousal" and depend for this meaning on a learned analogy between looking and the sex act. (We do not know that looking is connected with sexuality in all cultures or even for all humans and therefore cannot say that looking is "by nature" a preface to arousal.) The Freudian concept of voyeuristic drive works as a code organizing the signification of /eyes/.

*Little Rural Red
Riding Hood*, Tex
Avery, 1949

Semiotics is used here to help demonstrate that cultural units mean not because of natural equivalence but because of conventionalization. As elaborated by Umberto Eco, ". . . even where we presume a vital spontaneity to exist, it is really swallowed by culture, convention, system, code, and therefore, by extension, ideology. Semiology gets to work here with its own tools, translating nature into society and culture."[19] Eco's concept of *code-changing* can explain how the culturally competent viewer makes the connection between /eyes/ and /sex organs/ thus comprehending the cartoon humor intended. The theory is that if two signs, in this case the iconic /eyes/ and /sex organs/ both share the same connotative marker, they are semiotically interchangeable. As both signs share the connotation "arousal," theoretically they can be exchanged.[20]

On closer examination of the relationship between /eyes/ and "sexual arousal," one sees that /eyes/ are not associated with "arousal" by biological function in the same way as /sex organs/ and "arousal" are related. As the participation of the eyes is not a physiological requirement in sexual intercourse, the connection between eyes and "arousal" has to have been made in some way other than the "logic" of biology. What has happened historically, following Eco's theory of social communication, is that by means of *rhetorical code-switching*, the sign /eyes/ has acquired a new connotation, "sexual arousal." Eco has argued that *rhetorical code-switching* is always an ideological operation and that the newly acquired connotation is a false connotation. In a sense, the theory can explain how the falsehood of one generation can become the logic of the next at the level of language. *Rhetorical code-switching* has two semiotic prerequisites: first, the signs being exchanged need to be *overcoded* (conventionalized), and second, the change of connotation requires the *help* of an accepted social premise. In this case popular Freudian psychology provides the premise, explaining that the male "gets turned on" (aroused) when he sees parts of the female body. Thus /looking/ can stand in for /sexual desire/. It may appear here that I am arguing against the science of psychology which has established that humans (both male and female) are prone to seek out scopophilic objects of desire even as children. Freud's theory, however, has found its way into mainstream culture and become part of general social knowledge in the way I have just described using a theory of codes as cultural consensus. What was once nonsense (eyes=arousal) to the lay person has become "natural" by repeated use and popular acclaim—certainly at the level of the theatrical cartoon.

In the movies, the Freudian premise has been romanticized and colloquialized into "One look (at her) and that was it." The idea of

"One look and that was it" operates along with the premise "attraction of opposites" to establish the female as motivator and the male as aggressor. Further, the cartoon's exaggeration of cinematic cross-cutting and use of "mechanism" iconography convey a sense that the male/wolf's sexual response is automatic. Avery's "imitation" reaction shots of the wolf (to the girl) are jarring in close-up, exaggeratedly calling attention to the editing convention. In addition, the shot-reaction-shot configuration suggests the popularized stimulus-response explanation of sexual behavior according to which the sight of the female corresponds with the bell and the male erection with the dog's salivation.[21] The clapping and stomping machine that becomes an extension of the wolf's body and the way his tongue spools out onto the floor, signify that his responses are out of his control.

The soldier spectator in 1943 may not have known about mechanisms in a scientific sense, but the cartoon would corroborate what he thought about his own "healthy, normal" drive, which, he would be convinced, required a sexual motivator or stimulus. Army psychology depended on the food analogy to explain to the men what was happening to their bodies during wartime. The manual *Psychology for the Fighting Man* deals with it in the chapter "Food and Sex as Military Problems." As one of the "two great desires of the flesh," sex, it says, is much like hunger and can be confused with it.[22] It is the healthy, strong, aggressive appetite image of male sexuality that is celebrated by the wolf seated at the empty night club table, clawing the tablecloth at the sight of the showgirl. Iconographically, the wolf is much more tricky to "read" than the showgirl. At the same time that he validates healthy, heterosexual lechery, and the behavior of men who are "all in the same army," he is after all a wolf, and victim of his own erotic "reflexes." The derivation of the World War II "wolf" exemplifies how meaning fluctuates historically and demonstrates that it is not ever self-evidently contained within a representation. The original use of "wolf," earliest cited around 1917, was for the male homosexual who was particularly aggressive. Its use spread to the dangerous ladies' man in the 1930's. By World War II, "wolf" was a more complimentary term for a man who was successful with ladies, but it could be used negatively to refer to the guys back home ravaging the women. Less commonly, if a woman was too loose she was a "wolfess."[23] There is also some "natural" motivation in the use of /wolf/ to signify "male spectator"—hairiness contributes to this, for instance, although the resemblance between man and animal might not have become standard usage if it hadn't been for Charles Darwin.[24] Indication of how close sign is to referent here is the censor's ruling that the wolf couldn't touch the girl because of the implication of "bestiality."[25] It may be that the theory of the origin of the species makes anthropomorphic cartoon characters comprehensible in a society in which this theory is common currency. The cultural idea that man descends from animal and the historically specific wolf-about-town both contribute to the signification of the "wolf" spectator in the cartoon.

Another source of the iconography is the Hollywood night club scene, one of the spectacle's favorite milieus. (Another favorite, the savage Western bar, is the scene of *The Shooting of Dan McGoo* and *Wild and Wolfy*.) Instead of lighting a casual cigarette, the wolf lights his nose, a reference to the meaning-laden movie gesture of the distracted spectator "sizing up" the woman performer from his table as he simultaneously lights up and takes a long drag. The gesture of nonchalant observation takes on meaning in the context of movie convention which has established that "enjoyment" of the cigarette signifies "enjoyment" of the show and by historical analogy, since she is "the show," "enjoyment" of the woman. The culturally competent viewer would make these connections by the process of *code-changing*. Since /woman/ and /cigarette/ both carry the connotative "enjoyment," they can be exchanged as signs. Thus the reader can receive the message that the male on screen would like to do to her what he does to his cigarette.

Still another social premise serves to exonerate the male for his behavior, shifting the responsibility to the female. The fact that they are human woman and animal wolf, different species, carries the mistaken idea that male and female are *not* the same species, romanticized as *vive la différence*. An overly aggressive male is a "beast" to the woman, but since "You bring out the beast in me, *she* gets the blame if he is extremely ravenous. "You bring out the beast in me" works the other way if he wants to romanticize his virility quotient by giving her a credit. Thus it was possible for a soldier to say of the World War II pin-up that "She gives us a good idea of what we're fighting for," evoking something outside of themselves to rationalize and elevate their "beastly" deeds, their destructive aggression, their extreme territoriality.

The value of a theory of codes based on cultural consensus for feminist theory is that it makes it possible to deal with meaning as historically changing social belief. To understand that female iconography has been assigned connotations of looking and sexual stimulation out of historical necessity is a step toward demystifying signification. If meaning is not inherent in cultural objects and gestures, it is "man-made," and can be remade. To say that the spectacle of woman has come to mean the looking of her sexual opposite and his consequent arousal is not, however, the same as saying that the spectacle of woman is based on voyeuristic drive, or that the cinematic situation replicates the position of the psychoanalytic subject in the formation of language. I am speaking strictly about usage.

The connection between looking and the female form, the consequent male arousal and his fighting aggressiveness is the system that drives the narrative to *Yank in the R.A.F.* Grable is in the position of "love object" for three flyers who fight several large-scale air battles within the film. They share the spectacle of her as they share the heat of battle. Their appetite for her insures their fitness for combat as their aggressive performance in battle establishes their romantic right to possess (marry) her. Most interesting in the film is the visual analogy between the Regency House stage show and the cinematically constructed air battles. Reaction shots catch the men's faces lit up from exploding bombs in the same way they are lit from the "glitter" of Grable's all-girl show. Tyrone Power's wildly enthusiastic reactions to her dance number are matched by his fierce relish for dropping cartons of leaflets and bombs on Germany. There are two types of scenes in which rowdiness and risk come into play—the spectacle and the battle. Wide searchlights intersecting across a black sky are styled to match theatre floodlights, and officer Roger Pillby, fatally attracted to the searchlights, goes down with his plane, as he gasps that this must explain his passion for nightlife. It's a running gag in the film that Pillby never meets Betty Grable in person but haunts her show, waiting around for an introduction. Is Pillby's suicide a self-inflicted punishment for his desire to look at Grable?

Taking a clue from the wolf and the showgirl, the film spectacle acts out the entire popularized account of human sexuality including guilt and castration. Sadistically, the wolf hits himself over the head with a mallet, lights up his nose, removes it and puts it out as he would a cigar. Self-inflicted punishment, which might be worked out within the narrative of an entire feature (as in the case of *Yank in the R.A.F.*) is intensified in the cartoon parody. The intensification and graphic distortion of the spectacle iconography, action, generic convention, and cinematic technique make the cartoon potentially subversive.

At the same time that the cartoon validates the meaning of the horny wolf salivating at the spectacle (celebration of the difference between male and female "species" that gives the male such a rise) it subverts by revealing how ludicrous all this aggressive commotion has become. The wolf's gyrations signifying male sexual arousal and consequent castration dare to "speak" about the bizarre cultural usage of this originally arbitrary pairing of terms: /eyeballs/ and /male sexual organs/, which further explains the hybrid "eyeballing." The demolition of the spectacle suited the patriarchial version of male-female relations equally as well as its celebration, particularly during wartime when, under pressure, the cross purposes of this version came into focus.

Analogous to the way the star image reconciles contradictions in social expectations and types of women, the satire on the spectacle united irreconcilable differences in the demands on the enlisted man. First, as I have already demonstrated, virility was defined in terms of response to the showgirl stylization of the female body carrying the required connotations of childlike innocence and sexual ferocity. At the same time that a man's virility had to be assured, the Army was also in danger of losing him to the VD epidemic. It was vital that every man learn how ". . . prostitutes can contribute to the defeat of an army," the psychology manual states.[26] The Army could not afford to let every man prove his potency in terms of real women. "Autoeroticism" was officially all right, provided it didn't become "habit-forming." Army position on rape depended on whether the victims were "our girls" or the enemy's. Magazines and movies answered the need of a situation in which *desire* was imperative because *pleasure* had to be restricted. The cartoon wolf is an essay on desire without pleasure.

As imperative as winning the war was the maintenance of a social order based on opposite sex mating and monogamy. In the psychology manual it is put to the soldier in terms of substitutions. Sex is a craving that will crop up regularly as does appetite for food. In wartime, when it is impossible to find the proper sexual outlets, the soldier must find substitute satisfactions. Among the acceptable substitutes listed are letters from home, pictures, band concerts, ball games, religion, mass singing, and vaudeville shows. Although he must find substitutes, "Strictly speaking, there are no real substitutes for sexual satisfaction . . . . For love there is no substitute."[27] Speaking of substitution is a way of displacing or transforming continence, the practice of which was preferred by both the society requiring that he marry the girl back home and the Army requiring that he only be a healthy, husky ascetic fighter.[28] The romantic ideal that there is no substitute for real sexual satisfaction (i.e., love) really served the purpose of continence. Abstience, however, does not lend itself to a gala group celebration as do other signs of maleness. The showgirl and the wolf would be most useful to the Army here in that it resolved the opposite expectations that the soldier be both continent and virile. Its subversive message is that the substitute for sexual satisfaction is an unsatisfactory situation,

the search for which is futile, and the guys who go after it just get more
frustrated. Simultaneously, the idea of looking at the girl confirmed his
maleness, along with everybody else's, and insured his fighting spirit.

Notes

1. See Bill Nichols's introduction to "Meep Meep," Richard Thompson's analysis of
Chuck Jones's animation in Nichols, ed., *Movies and Methods* (Berkeley: University of California Press, 1976), p. 127. Nichols says that Thompson has
opened up the territory for semiological analysis of the cinema. "Even more than
gangsters and westerns, cartoons develop an iconography of their own that is not
an overlay on the neutral representation but is the representation."
2. Dana Polan discusses formal self-reflexivity using Chuck Jones's *Duck Amuck* in
"Brecht and the Politics of Self-Reflexive Cinema," *Jump Cut*, No. 17, April,
1978.
3. Joe Adamson, *Tex Avery: King of Cartoons*, (New York: Popular Library, 1975).
4. Roland Barthes, *Mythologies*, Annette Lavers, trans. (New York: Hill and Wang,
1972), p. 127.
5. Richard Dyer, *The Dumb Blonde Stereotype*, (London: British Film Institute Educational Advisory Service, 1979), p. 55.
6. Richard Dyer, *The Stars* (London: British Film Institute, 1979), p. 30.
7. See Mike Barrier, interview with Frank Tashlin, in *Frank Tashlin*, eds. Claire
Johnston and Paul Willemen (Edinburgh Film Festival, 1973), p. 47. According
to Tashlin, all of the animation they were doing at Warner Brothers when they
"invented" Bugs Bunny came from Disney. Even Bugs himself came out of *The
Tortoise and the Hare*.
8. I am using a graphic convention to differentiate the non-verbal signs from words
(verbal signs). /Showgirl/ thus from here on refers to the iconographic representation itself which also corresponds with the verbal form—showgirl.
9. See Charles Eckert's discussion of the gangster in "The Anatomy of a Proletarian
Film: Warner's *Marked Woman*," *Film Quarterly*, 27, No. 2 (Winter 1973–74),
pp. 10–24.
10. Pam Cook, "Star Signs," *Screen*, 20, Nos. 3/4 (Winter 79/80), p. 83.
11. Richard Dyer, "Resistance through Charisma: Rita Hayworth and *Gilda*" in
Women in Film Noir, ed. E. Ann Kaplan (London: British Film Institute, 1978),
p. 97.
12. John Lafflin, *Americans in Battle* (New York: Crown Publishers, 1973), p. 134.
13. Editors of *Look*, *Movie Lot to Beachhead* (New York & Garden City: Doubleday,
Doran and Co., 1945), p. 104.
14. *Variety*, September 23, 1942, p. 55.
15. Adamson, *op. cit.*, p. 182.
16. Joe Adamson, "You Couldn't Get Chaplin in a Milk Bottle," interview with Tex
Avery, *Take One*, January-February, 1970, p. 11.
17. Robert K. Merton and Paul F. Lazarsfeld, eds., *Continuities in Social Research*,
Studies in the Scope and Method of "The American Soldier" (Glencoe: The
Free Press, 1950), p. 35.
18. Stuart Berg Flexner, *I Hear America Talking* (New York: Van Nostrand
Rheinhard & Co., 1976), p. 156.
19. Umberto Eco, "Artioulations of the Cinematic Code" in Bill Nichols, ed., *Movies
and Methods* (Berkeley: University of California Press, 1976), p. 599.
20. Umberto Eco, *A Theory of Semiotics* (Bloomington: Indiana University Press,
1976).

21. Note that in the popularized version of classical conditioning, the meat stage required in the conditioning has dropped out.
22. National Research Council, *Psychology for the Fighting Man* (Washington: The Infantry Journal, 1945), p. 334.
23. Harold Wentworth and Stuart Berg Flexner, *Dictionary of American Slang* (New York: Thomas Crowell, 1960).
24. There is always some motivation in every sign, according to Roland Barthes. "Motivation is unavoidable. It is none the less very fragmentary. To start with, it is not 'natural'; it is history which supplies its analogies to the form," *op. cit.*, pp. 126 and 127.
25. Adamson, *Tex Avery: King of Cartoons*, p. 182.
26. *Psychology for the Fighting Man*, p. 335.
27. *Ibid*, p. 341.
28. Harry Benjamin, "Morals Versus Morale in Wartime" in Victor Robinson, ed., *Morals in Wartime (New York: Publishers Foundation, 1943), p. 177.*

1980

The Contributors

CHARLES F. ALTMAN was an assistant professor of French at the University of Iowa in Iowa City when he wrote his bibliographic study of American film history for volume 16, number 2, Spring 1977; he is now associate professor of French and comparative literature at Iowa. Recently he was also appointed director of the Inter-University Center for Film Studies in Paris, where he has also taught cinema at the University of Paris.

J. L. ANDERSON, coauthor of *The Japanese Film: Art and Industry* (New York: Grove Press, 1960), was professor of film in the College of Fine Arts at the University of Ohio in Athens when his article on Japanese *jidai-geki* appeared in volume 12, number 2, Spring 1973. He is now manager for operations, WGBH Educational Foundation, Boston.

DAVID A. COOK was assistant professor of English at Emory University in Atlanta, Georgia, when he wrote "Some Structural Approaches to Cinema," which appeared in volume 14, number 3, Spring 1975. His research was supported by a grant from the National Endowment for the Humanities. He is now an associate professor and author of *A History of Narrative Film* (New York: W. W. Norton, 1981).

PHILIP DYNIA was assistant professor of political science at Loyola University, New Orleans, when his comparison of Alfred Hitchcock and Thomas Hobbes was published in volume 15, number 2, Spring 1976. He is now an associate professor there and teaches a course in politics and film.

JANE GAINES, a Ph.D. candidate at Northwestern University in Evanston, Illinois, when her article on sexuality in World War II Hollywood cartoons appeared (volume 20, number 1, Fall 1980), has most recently taught at Slippery Rock State College, Pennsylvania.

DOUGLAS GOMERY's study of motion picture exhibition practices of the 1920s appeared in volume 18, number 2, Spring 1979. He has taught at the University of Wisconsin, Madison, the University of Wisconsin, Milwaukee, and Northwestern University, Evanston. Currently he is associate professor in the department of communication arts at the University of Maryland, College Park.

STEVEN P. HILL, associate professor of Slavic languages and literatures at the University of Illinois in Urbana, has written many articles about Russian and East European film and theater history for such magazines as *Film Culture*, *Film Quarterly*, and *Modern Drama*. His analysis of film production data in the Soviet Union was published in volume 11, number 2, Spring 1972.

VANCE KEPLEY, JR., was an undergraduate at the University of Illinois in Urbana when he wrote a paper on the history of Eisenstein's *Old and New*, which won the Student Award for Scholarly Writing of the Society for Cinema Studies and was published in volume 14, number 1, Fall 1974. Having completed a Ph.D.

in film studies at the University of Wisconsin, Madison, he has since taught at the University of Delaware, Newark, and at the University of Wisconsin.

WALTER F. KORTE, JR., was a Ph.D. candidate at Northwestern in Evanston and a Fulbright fellow at the University of Milan when he embarked on his study of Luchino Visconti. When his article appeared in *Cinema Journal* (volume 11, number 1, Fall 1971), he was assistant professor of English at the University of Virginia in Charlottesville, where he is now associate professor of drama and director of film studies.

KATHERINE SINGER KOVÁCS's analysis and criticism of Buñuel's *That Obscure Object of Desire* appeared in volume 19, number 1, Fall 1979. She teaches in the department of Spanish at the University of Southern California in Los Angeles.

LEONARD J. LEFF was teaching film history and aesthetics in the department of English, Oklahoma State University in Oklahoma City, at the time he undertook his investigation into the censorship history of *Who's Afraid of Virginia Woolf?* (volume 19, number 2, Spring 1980).

ROBERT L. MC CONNELL was a Ph.D. candidate in American studies at the University of Iowa in Iowa City when he wrote his seminar paper on *Gabriel over the White House*. It appeared in somewhat expanded form in volume 15, number 2, Spring 1976, and in his completed dissertation. He is now an editorial writer for the *Des Moines Register and Tribune*.

RUSSELL MERRITT, whose Harvard dissertation analyzed the impact of D. W. Griffith's Biograph films on American culture, was assistant professor of film in the communication arts department at the University of Wisconsin in Madison when his article on *The Birth of a Nation* was published in *Cinema Journal*, volume 12, number 1, Fall 1972. He is now an associate professor there and was recently a fellow at the Institute for Research in the Humanities.

HOWARD RIEDER's M.A. thesis at the University of Southern California (Los Angeles) department of cinema (1961), *The Development of the Satire of Mr. Magoo*, was based on tape-recorded interviews. The present edited extract was in *Cinema Journal*, volume 8, number 2, Spring 1969. He is director of advertising and public relations at Revell Corporation in Los Angeles.

PHILIP G. ROSEN was a graduate student in American studies at the University of Kansas in Lawrence when he wrote his paper on Chaplin's political views; it was published in volume 9, number 1, Fall 1969. More recently he has completed a Ph.D. in film at the University of Iowa, Iowa City, and taught at the University of Wisconsin, Milwaukee, the University of Illinois, Urbana, and Columbia University, New York.

JOHN SCHULTHEISS expanded a seminar paper at the University of Southern California, Los Angeles, for publication in volume 11, number 1, Fall 1971, as "The 'Eastern' Writer in Hollywood." Since 1973, when he received his Ph.D. from USC, he has become an associate professor in the radio-television-film department at California State University, Northridge.

JANET STAIGER was a graduate student in film at the University of Wisconsin, Madison, when her study of Thomas Ince was published in volume 18, number 2, Spring 1979. She was coeditor of the Purdue University (Lafayette, Indiana) *Film Studies Annual* in 1976 and 1977.

DENNIS L. WHITE's analysis of the horror film began as an undergraduate paper at the University of California, Los Angeles; it was published in expanded form in volume 10, number 2, Spring 1971. He has since completed his M.A. degree in film at UCLA and was most recently a free-lance writer in Los Angeles.

Outstanding Studies of Film and Filmmaking

THE AMERICAN ANIMATED CARTOON
  A Critical Anthology
  edited by Danny Peary and Gerald Peary
  $10.95 paperback   ISBN: 0-525-47639-3

THE AMERICAN CINEMA
  Directors and Directions
  by Andrew Sarris
  $5.50 paperback   ISBN: 0-525-47227-4

FILM: A MONTAGE OF THEORIES
  by Richard Dyer MacCann
  $6.25 paperback   ISBN: 0-525-47181-2

Available at bookstores or from E. P. Dutton. To order from Dutton, list titles and ISBN numbers. Send a check or money order for the retail price plus appropriate sales tax and 10% for postage and handling to Dept. CW, E.P. Dutton, 2 Park Avenue, New York, NY 10016. New York residents must add sales tax. Allow up to six weeks for delivery.